# ACROSS THE SEAS

## AUSTRALIA'S RESPONSE TO REFUGEES

### A HISTORY

### KLAUS NEUMANN

Black Inc.

Published by Black Inc.,
an imprint of Schwartz Publishing Pty Ltd
37–39 Langridge Street
Collingwood Vic 3066 Australia
enquiries@blackincbooks.com
www.blackincbooks.com

The National Library of Australia Cataloguing-in-Publication entry:

    Neumann, Klaus, 1958– author.
    Across the seas: Australia's response to refugees: a history / Klaus Neumann.
    1st edition.
    9781863957359 (paperback)
    9781925203080 (ebook)
    Refugees—Australia—History. Immigrants—Australia—History.
    Australia—Emigration and immigration—History.
    362.870994

Cover and text design by Peter Long
Cover image:
    Vic O'Connor
    *Flight – Illustration for Herz Bergner's novel 'Between Sky and Sea'* c. 1944
    Oil on canvas on composition board
    56.6 cm x 51.5 cm
    National Gallery of Victoria, Melbourne
    The Joseph Brown Collection. Presented through the NGV Foundation by
    Dr Joseph Brown AO, OBE, Honorary Life Benefactor, 2005
    Reproduced with permission from the Bridget McDonnell Gallery.

# CONTENTS

*In memory of Hank Nelson*

T his is a riveting book, vast in scope and timely. Taking into account recent United Nations estimates of the numbers of internally and externally displaced people and asylum seekers worldwide, there are currently 50 million refugees. This is how it stands in April 2015, as the book goes to press.

The figures fluctuate. The estimates require constant adjustment. But judging by the expansion of conflicts in many parts of the world, the numbers may well rise. In the not-too-distant future we may also see populations from low-lying islands, coastlines and river deltas displaced by the impact of climate change. The challenge of how to respond to this chronic crisis is urgent and immediate, and will remain so well into the future.

In Australia the public debates over refugee policy are intense and vigorously contested. Many claims and assertions are made about past responses to refugees as being better or worse than contemporary responses, or as being better or worse when compared to those of other countries.

Given the amount of attention focused on the issue, it is surprising to learn that there has been only one comprehensive account of Australia's immigration history, and that *Across the Seas* is the first full-length monograph about Australia's response to asylum seekers and refugees since Federation: this, as Neumann says, in a country with a history that is marked by two key themes, Indigenous dispossession and immigration.

It takes time to explore what happened in the past. It demands the hard slog of research – wading through archives, parliamentary records, newspaper files, departmental statements, the proceedings of policy debates within parties, the records of lobby groups and successive governments – in order to see what was actually said and done, and who said it and did it. Neumann places himself in the eye of the storm in order to sift through the evidence, and synthesises it into an accessible narrative. It is a mammoth undertaking. The result is a far-reaching chronological account written with clarity and insight.

The chronicle begins with Federation in 1901 and ends with the federal election campaign of 1977. By this time, says Neumann, the public responses to refugees that we are now so accustomed to had been fully formed. His account thereby sheds much light on the present. It allows the reader to discern both the parallels with the past and the uniqueness of contemporary policies.

Neumann employs both the wide-angle lens and the close-up. We should never lose sight of the individual refugee, and the tales of the countless men, women and children who have chosen to make perilous journeys, risking all on a gamble for freedom. This is encapsulated in a seminal incident that took place beyond the timeframe of Neumann's book, but which can be better understood because of it.

When the Norwegian freighter the *Tampa* was anchored off Christmas Island in mid-2001 with 438 rescued asylum seekers on board, the Prime Minister ordered that the boat be boarded by Australian special forces, the SAS. As David Marr and Marian Wilkinson write in their book Dark Victory:

> Once the SAS was on board, Canberra would decree that anything to do with the *Tampa* involved 'operational security' and declare a 'no-fly' zone around the ship. No one on board was to be allowed ashore and civilians on the island – especially doctors, lawyers and journalists – were not to be allowed out to the ship. No cameraman would get close enough to the *Tampa* to put a human face on this story. The icon of the scandal was to be a red-hulled ship on a blue sea, photographed through heat haze by a very long lens.

In other words, we saw no individual faces. We heard no specific voices. We did not know, for instance, that the Hazaras, the major group among the rescued, had fled the horrors of the Taliban. Instead, we received images of a horde of people crammed on the deck of a steel freighter. A horde inspires fear and misunderstanding.

Neumann does not lose sight of the individual. His account is studded with anecdotes, stories and significant case histories. It is humanist in orientation and empathetic to the plight of refugees, but most concerned with documentation. To read it is to be informed and better armed to take on the challenge.

Thus, we see, for instance, that while some advocates may believe that today's hostile community and government attitudes towards refugees is unprecedented, there were in fact, Neumann points out, 'proportionately at least as many virulent xenophobes' among those who responded to refugee challenges in the past.

This applies equally to the late 1930s and 1947, as evidenced in the negative responses to the potential arrival of pre- and post-Holocaust Jewish refugees, and to 1977, as can be seen in some of the responses to the challenges posed by the Indochinese refugees who made up the first wave of 'boat people'. In contrast, both in the past as in the present, there were many advocates who campaigned tirelessly for refugees. Neumann's account brings to light the efforts of many unsung champions of refugee rights whose foresight and compassion have fallen below the radar.

The book is studded with unexpected facts, gems of information and statements that betray the prejudices of particular times. We learn, for instance, that Thomas Hugh Garrett, the assistant secretary of the Department of the Interior, after visiting Europe on the eve of war to investigate the selection of suitable 'alien immigrants' for resettlement, asserted, in a letter to his departmental secretary, that Polish Jews 'are the poorest specimens outside blackfellows that I have seen'. Yes, dear reader, this is what he wrote.

We learn that the first 'boat people' were, arguably, the eight West Papuans who landed on Moa Island in the Torres Strait on 16 February

1969, after a harrowing month-long journey by raft, in flight from the Indonesian occupation of West Irian. We learn that until the 1970s, with the arrival of Indochinese refugees, government policy was predominantly based on pragmatic rather than humanitarian concerns. Neumann contends that it was not until 1977 that a government defended its approach to refugee policy by drawing on the language of humanitarianism and by invoking Australia's international legal obligations.

We learn of the succession of refugee crises that continue to erupt unexpectedly. Each challenge is directly connected to international events: the fall of Saigon in 1975, the 1973 CIA-backed coup against the Allende government of Chile, the relentless civil war in Lebanon and the brutal division of Cyprus in 1974, to mention just a few. Each crisis demanded a response. Each generated debate and challenged the conscience of the public.

We see also how the measure of the suitability of specific ethnic groups has changed over time. Neumann sheds light on what La Trobe academic Gwenda Tavan has called, in her book of that name, 'the long, slow death of White Australia'. We see the pragmatic reasons for the shift, the interplay between an urgent need for new sources of immigrants to make up for severe post-war labour shortages, public opinion, international pressures and the rise of the newly independent nations of Asia and the Pacific.

While Australia may have officially abandoned the White Australia policy by the 1970s, the debates over the suitability of particular groups for resettlement have never ceased. In 1947 the first source for immigrants remained the British Isles. 'Non-White' immigrants included not only Chinese and Japanese, but also Jews and southern Europeans. As these groups became accepted as part of White Australia, other groups were placed beyond the boundaries of acceptability.

It is a great irony that in recent years, as Neumann points out, Lebanese and Vietnamese Australians could demonstrate their belonging to White Australia 'not least by joining the chorus that demanded the exclusion of Hazara, Iranian and Tamil "boat people"'.

To turn the spotlight back on the present: in 2015, at the time of writing, asylum seekers who have in recent years sought protection in Australia are incarcerated both in onshore and offshore detention centres. Many others remain in limbo out in the community on various types of temporary visas. The centres on Nauru and Manus Island are hellholes, the inmates' agony compounded by isolation. Out of sight, out of mind is the name of the game. Journalists are not permitted. Information is hard to come by. Disturbing claims of sexual abuse, beatings, self-harm and attempted suicides are denied, but proven true on the rare occasions when independent investigators are allowed access.

As Neumann reiterates in his conclusion, 'there is nothing self-evident or natural about Australia's current response to asylum seekers and refugees'. He hopes instead to have encouraged the reader 'to imagine alternative futures', which 'take into account Australia's capacity to assist people in need of a new home, its responsibility as a regional power, its legal obligations as a member of the international community, and, most importantly, the precarious circumstances of the men, women and children who are seeking Australia's protection'.

As one of the first readers of *Across the Seas*, I will take up the challenge. The word 'imagination' stems from the word 'image'. An act of imagination is an act of seeing, and I have seen alternative futures at work.

Take, for instance, Melbourne, the great cosmopolitan city in which this book is being published. In this sprawling metropolis the impact of past policy is made visible. We witness the creativity and energy of the diverse and varied communities that have made their way to our shores and been allowed to settle, whatever the reason. We see the impact of the many cultures whose migration stories Neumann has documented. We see, for instance, how within just a few years the local Hazara community has helped transform the city of Dandenong into a thriving metropolis.

I end with one last example of the future in action, encapsulated in the tale of a notebook. The notebook is blue, the spine reinforced with tape. The covers are fraying at the edges. The pages list every person assisted by the Asylum Seeker Resource Centre since June 2001, the month it opened. The notebook is full. It contains 7579 names. Pick any name at random and Kon Karapanagiotidis, the CEO and founder of the centre, knows the story. A second notebook is filling. Fourteen years after the centre opened, the number of those it has helped is now over 10,000.

The centre, which began as a shopfront, is now a massive undertaking. To see the daily presence of hundreds of asylum seekers, volunteers and supporters, and to observe the empowering programs and expanding facilities, is to see an alternative future at work. The centre is a haven, a bridge between past and present, and a model of what is possible when Australian citizens reach out to the latest arrivals.

Name number 1259 in the notebook is Amal Basry. She was one of forty-five survivors of a capsized fishing boat that became known as the SIEV X. Three hundred and fifty-three asylum seekers drowned when the boat sank en route to Christmas Island on 19 October 2001. Amal was rescued after clinging to a corpse for over twenty hours.

She told the tale of the sinking many times to many audiences, including one of over two thousand people at a Melbourne town hall. She would get out of her sick bed to tell it. She was condemned to bear witness. Her happiest moment came when she learnt she had received her permanent residency. 'I am a free woman in a free country,' she repeated over and again.

In a cruel irony, Amal died of cancer in 2006. Her tale is a reminder of the courage it takes to risk the seas in search of a life free from oppression. It enjoins us to search for safer alternatives. *Across the Seas* shows us what has happened in the past, so that as we move forward we are armed with the facts and aware of the continuities and the departures, and of some of the many options we can draw upon. It helps us imagine a more compassionate future.

*Arnold Zable*
*Writer, novelist and human rights activist*
*April 2015*

History allows us to see the present in a new light. It high-lights the particularities of the status quo and suggests affinities between what was and what is. I hope that this history of Australia's response to refugees and asylum seekers makes the present appear unfamiliar, both by drawing attention to how Australia's approach was radically different in previous times *and* by identifying continuities and parallels.

The resettlement of refugees from camps in Thailand or Kenya in the twenty-first century, for example, has very little in common with the resettlement of so-called DPs (displaced persons) from camps in Germany sixty-five years ago. The latter were expected to be healthy and fit, and to be in full-time employment within weeks of their arrival in Australia. They were supposed to leave behind their experiences of suffering, and their allegiances to their native countries. By contrast, those resettled today as part of Australia's humanitarian intake are often thought of as patients who require long-term care before they can become fully functioning members of society. It would therefore be wrong to regard today's refugee policy as a seamless continuation of policies inaugurated in the late 1940s.

In the late 1940s, the government distinguished between those admitted as settlers largely according to two criteria: whether they were British or non-British ('alien'), and whether or not they arrived per assisted passage. Then, Australia did not have a refugee policy; refugees, such as Polish or Estonian DPs, were resettled as alien immigrants whose passage had been paid for by the International Refugee

Organization (IRO), which in turn received a comparatively small contribution per settler from the Australian government. Once a DP had landed in Australia, it did not matter whether or not she had been a refugee in her previous life. The government did not have an asylum seeker policy either – simply because at that time, the occasional ship jumper or stowaway aside, refugees did not seek Australia's protection after having landed on its shores. In the twenty-first century, Australia has an elaborate policy that guides its response to refugees who are selected offshore and resettled in Australia. Seemingly unrelated to the government's refugee policy, an asylum seeker policy determines Australia's response to people who claim asylum or refugee status after arriving in Australia or in Australian territorial waters.

Yet while this is a history of a discontinuous past, it is equally one that draws attention to congruities between the past and the present. The refrain about the unprecedented challenges supposedly posed by 'boat people' in recent years is a good example. Concerns about 'economic refugees', 'queue jumpers' and people-smuggling syndicates are not unique to the twenty-first century. Politicians and bureaucrats voiced them also during the Indochinese refugee crisis of the late 1970s. The policy of 'turning back the boats' – which John Howard's government devised after the arrival of the *Tampa*, and which was dusted off nine years later by the then leader of the opposition, Tony Abbott – bears some similarities with a policy that prime minister Gough Whitlam put in place in 1975, and with policies that Labor leaders Bob Hawke and Bill Hayden toyed with a couple of years later.

Sometimes the past seems to be a foreign country and eerily familiar at the same time. 'Is there an Australian federal leader prepared to risk the national and international outcry by sending out the Navy physically to turn back the fleet of small boats?' asked the journalist Bruce Wilson in a *Courier-Mail* opinion piece in 1977. 'And what if the Vietnamese say no? Does HMAS Ardent, the fast patrol boat now working in the Arafura Sea, turn its guns on them?'[1] He meant these to be rhetorical questions; he would have been astonished if told that, a generation later, politicians would think the risk small and anyway worth taking, and that in 2001 an Australian prime minister would order special operations commandoes to board a Norwegian ship which had rescued asylum seekers in the Indian Ocean.[2] Wilson's article continues:

> I should not like to be the Australian politician or diplomat trying to explain to Australians and the world, how, on the one hand, we saw it necessary to help anti-communist Vietnamese fight a civil war, while on the other we refuse to accept anti-communist Vietnamese as refugees from those same countries.[3]

Does an Australia that sent its armed forces to help fight the Taliban in Afghanistan need to explain why it refuses to accommodate those seeking its protection after fleeing the Taliban?

The success of my undertaking relies on my ability to confound expectations. That I can realistically hope to surprise readers says a lot about how refugee and asylum seeker issues have been discussed in recent years. Australian debates about forced migration have been remarkably parochial. There have been few references to the problem's global dimensions, and scant attempts to draw on the experience of other countries. References to historical precedents have been similarly rare. In recent years, commentators and policy-makers alike have often appeared to be talking and acting in a bubble, removed from what is happening in other parts of the world and oblivious to the genealogies of phenomena.

Politicians, journalists, academics, refugee advocates and other contributors to debates about refugees and asylum seekers could be excused for disregarding a historical perspective when discussing Australian policies, because there aren't many insightful and readily available historical analyses for them to draw on. Most general histories of Australia only mention refugee policies in passing, if at all.[4] Biographers of political actors who played a major role in Australia's response to refugees and asylum seekers tend to skim over that role, or omit it altogether.[5] The scarcity of books, films, websites and other accessible historical scholarship about the history of asylum seeker and refugee policy is part of a wider problem: the comparative lack of interest in histories of Australia as a nation of immigrants – by historians, by policy-makers and by the general public.

A visitor to this country who browsed the shelves of local bookstores to get a sense of the dominant themes in Australian history would have to assume that the makeup and identity of Australia have been shaped by its participation in a series of major armed conflicts, beginning with the First World War. Arguably, the number of military history books reflects a popular interest rather than the relevance of the topic. And while a visit to a bookstore might allow our visitor to correctly recognise the importance of the relationship between Australia's Indigenous peoples and settlers, she would fail to understand that Australia's history is marked by *two* key themes: Indigenous dispossession and immigration. Australia is an immigrant nation as well as a settler nation. Thus far, there has been only one monograph, Eric Richards' *Destination Australia*, that tries to provide a comprehensive account of Australia's immigration history.[6]

When it comes to contextualising the response to refugees and asylum seekers, Australia is no exception. There have been comparatively few attempts elsewhere to understand refugee movements, the experience of displacement and refugee policies historically, leading the British historian Peter Gatrell to lament 'the general absence of refugees in historical scholarship'.[7] Gatrell himself, however, is an exception to the rule, as is his British colleague Tony Kushner, who blames historians' lack of attention to refugee issues on their focus on national frameworks and continuity, rather than on temporariness.[8]

This book has not been written in an attempt to fill a gap, however, because often such gaps merely indicate that particular topics are irrelevant or uninteresting. I am convinced that the response to refugees and asylum seekers is a key issue in Australian history, that it allows us to understand broader developments in the national story, and that an informed historical perspective is sorely needed if we are to come to grips with one of the twenty-first century's most controversial and seemingly intractable ethical, political and social issues, in Australia and elsewhere. I also believe the episodes discussed in this book are fascinating in themselves. All this I hope to be able to demonstrate over the next five chapters.

Not only is it necessary to contextualise responses to refugees and asylum seekers historically, it is also important not to lose sight of broader international contexts. In this book, therefore, I try to situate Australian developments in the context of refugee movements outside Australia and the events that gave rise to them. I also attempt to put Australian policies into perspective by referring to those of comparable countries, such as New Zealand and Canada.

*

Who are the refugees and asylum seekers this book discusses? Most Australians would associate either of four images with the term 'refugee': somebody who has to seek refuge abroad because he is a political opponent of the regime in his home country; somebody who has to flee on account of being a member of a persecuted religious or ethnic minority; the resident of a crowded refugee camp somewhere in the developing world; or a passenger on a fishing boat that has been intercepted by the Australian navy.

The first image describes many of the refugees of the nineteenth century; they included, for example, democrats or nationalists who fled authoritarian regimes in Central, Eastern and South-eastern Europe to the United Kingdom, France or the United States. Only a small proportion of the world's displaced people – who currently number more than 50 million – still fit the image of the political refugee. Australia has traditionally not been a preferred destination for political refugees, because most of them perceive it to be too remote. Political refugees have often wanted to be close to the country they have fled, so that they might still influence events there; it is therefore not surprising that Australia's most prominent political refugees in recent years have been the West Papuans who arrived in Australia by boat in 2006.

The second image is most commonly associated with Jews who escaped, or tried to escape, Nazi Germany, but also, more recently, with members of the Hazara ethnic minority. The latter have been fleeing Afghanistan because they have been persecuted, or they fear persecution, at the hands of the Taliban, most of whom, like the majority of Afghanis, are ethnic Pashtun.

Australians are familiar with the third image – of refugees in camps – because it regularly appears on their television screens. While refugees of the first category are often portrayed as heroes, those of the second and third categories tend to be depicted as victims. At least for those who conform to the second image, the reason why they have been displaced appears to be obvious. Pictures of rows of tents or other makeshift shelters, or of 'boat people' being disembarked at the Christmas Island jetty, however, say little about the causes of their displacement, which might include natural disasters, famines, armed conflicts or persecution. Many Australians also expect 'genuine' refugees to be evidently traumatised, to be obviously in fear for their lives and to have no worldly possessions other than the clothes they wear; often it is assumed that only refugees who exhibit such markers of suffering are deserving of compassion.

The second, third and fourth images adequately represent many of those admitted to Australia as refugees, but there are others whose situations defy the stereotypes. They include, for example, Lebanese who escaped the civil war in the 1970s to Syria or Cyprus (and moved from there to Australia), Polish sailors who jumped ship in Australian ports in the 1950s and 1960s, and Eastern European Jews who migrated to Australia in the first three decades of the twentieth century. Sometimes referred to as 'quasi refugees' by Australian policy-makers, they too feature in this book. There are also many people who are categorised as refugees (whether by the United Nations High Commissioner for Refugees [UNHCR] or by the Australian authorities) but who do not fit the stereotype of ragged individuals whose bodies bear the marks of suffering.

Even with the benefit of hindsight, it is often almost impossible to draw a line between refugees and other migrants, between those leaving their homes for political reasons and those who were attracted by the lure of a new home. Furthermore, retrospective assessments may differ from those made at the time. Polish or Russian Jews who arrived in Australia in the 1920s may have been thought of as ordinary immigrants then, but would now be considered refugees. The same could be said of some Italian immigrants in the late 1920s and some Greek immigrants in the late 1960s: they were ostensibly embracing economic opportunities, but the former may have in fact been political opponents of Benito Mussolini's fascist regime, whereas the latter could have been fleeing the repressive dictatorship of the Greek junta. Conversely, with the benefit of hindsight, some of the Lebanese, Chileans and Vietnamese arriving in the second half of the 1970s identified as refugees at the time and were often admitted as such, but may have been motivated to leave not so much by persecution as by the prospect of material advancement in Australia.

It is not my aim to neatly distinguish between refugees and other migrants. I am interested, however, in how others have tried to make that distinction in the past. The question of who has and who has not been considered a refugee is one of the key issues explored in this book. According to Article 1 of the 1951 United Nations Convention Relating to the Status of Refugees, a refugee is a person who, 'owing to well-founded fear of being persecuted for reasons of race, religion, nationality, membership of a particular social group or political opinion, is outside the country of his nationality and is unable or, owing to such fear, is unwilling to avail himself of the protection of that country'.[9] This definition has been used by the Australian government to determine whether or not an asylum seeker is eligible for a protection visa. However, long after 1951, the government repeatedly also referred to refugees in a much broader sense, and devised policies for the admission of refugees that made no reference to the Convention's criteria. At the same time, government officials have sometimes openly or implicitly questioned the credentials of people recognised as refugees. For example, in a book he wrote in 1976 about the Australian administration of the Territory of Papua and New Guinea, Paul Hasluck, minister for territories from 1951 to 1963, referred to the West Papuans who were permitted to remain in the Territory (because they were believed to be facing persecution in Indonesian-controlled West Irian) as 'refugees' in quotation marks.[10]

In this book I also write about people who were forced to leave their home countries before the Refugee Convention was drafted, regardless of whether or not they themselves identified as refugees – rather than as, for example, émigrés, fugitives or expellees – at the time, as well as those who fled persecution but did not seek to be recognised as refugees or were prevented from seeking such recognition. In fact, the people I write about variously described themselves as refugees, exiles or immigrants; often, these self-identifications do not match the labels put on them by others.

While I use the term 'refugees' in this book in a very broad sense, I have excluded two groups who are sometimes identified as such. In the following, I am not concerned with Indigenous Australians who were forced from their land, nor with people who became displaced within Australia due to military conflict or natural disasters, as happened to the residents of Darwin following the Japanese bombing of their town in March 1942, and then once more after the devastation wrought by Cyclone Tracy in December 1974, even though in both instances the term 'refugees' may also characterise their experience.

By 'asylum seekers' I mean people who seek to be granted *protection* as refugees (under the terms of the 1951 Convention) and those who seek *political asylum*. As a legal concept, political asylum is far older than the protection afforded to people who have been recognised as refugees. Whereas the latter emerged in the twentieth century, the former was known to the ancient Greeks. The word 'asylum' is derived from the Greek *asylon*, which denotes the absence of *sylon* (robbery; theft; pillage), and refers to a sacred site from which people or objects must not be removed. Thus, anybody who fled to such a place was safe from those pursuing her. The ancient Greeks extended this concept by applying it to non-citizens seeking protection from the clutches of their home state.[11] Similar practices can be found in other societies.[12]

The term 'refugee status' is now used to denote whether somebody seeking asylum is a bona fide refugee and thereby ceases to be an asylum seeker. However, other than in a preamble, the 1951 Convention and its 1967 Protocol do not actually mention 'asylum' or 'asylum seekers'. The 1948 Universal Declaration of Human Rights does.[13] Its Article 14(1) says: 'Everyone has the right to seek and to enjoy in other countries asylum from persecution.' Later in this book, I say more about Australia's role in the drafting of the Universal Declaration and the 1951 Convention, and about the different genealogies and trajectories of these texts.

Most of the refugees and asylum seekers I write about were resettled in, or fled to, Australia. Others were trying to seek refuge in Australia but failed to do so. Some were admitted on a temporary basis, in the understanding that they would return to their countries of origin once it was safe to do so. I also discuss government responses to people who entered the country on temporary visas – for example, in order to study – and attempted to extend their stay or remain in Australia permanently because of changed political circumstances in their country of origin.

'One refugee, even a crowd of refugees, if you like, pushing their children and possessions in wheelbarrows in front of them – this we understand. But millions of these, hunted like game from country to country . . . here our minds stop dead; instead of producing images, they merely play back the statistics presented to them.' So said Fredrik Stang, chairman of the Nobel Committee, in a speech in 1922 when awarding the Nobel Peace Prize to the then High Commissioner for

Refugees, Fridtjof Nansen. Stang also thought that his contemporaries would be unable to appreciate the work of international humanitarian organisations: 'a program whose aim is to rescue a continent's millions from misery and death – this presents proportions so immense and involves such a myriad of jumbled details that we give up and allow our minds to rest.'[14]

Stang identifies some of the dilemmas the writer of a text dealing with refugees faces, whether in the 1920s or in the 2010s. Readers are likely to be overwhelmed by the dimensions and complexity of the refugee issue, and it is therefore necessary to also write about 'one refugee'. Some individual asylum seekers and refugees – including, among others, a German-Jewish journalist, a Ukrainian stewardess, three Portuguese sailors and a West Papuan diplomat – therefore feature prominently over the next five chapters.

However, this is a book not so much about refugees and asylum seekers as about Australian responses to them. I am particularly interested in government policies and practices, and here one might easily confront the reader with 'a myriad of jumbled details'. But policies are not abstract constructs – they are made by women and men, and by the groups, parties and organisations they form. Moreover, as a historian, I am fond of telling stories, and such stories require protagonists whose actions we can applaud, criticise or puzzle over. Thus, my account also discusses the contributions of key political actors, such as immigration ministers Arthur Calwell, Alexander R. ('Alick') Downer, Al Grassby and Michael MacKellar.

In order to understand how federal ministers and senior public servants arrived at particular decisions, it is often necessary to explore the views of other contributors to the public debate: politicians, newspaper editors and church leaders among them. It is important to gauge public sentiment. And it is essential to be aware of the fact that refugees and asylum seekers have not only been the subject of policies and public debates; they have also shaped these policies and debates – by turning up uninvited on Australia's doorstep, by articulating their interests or offering their explanations for why they sought refuge in Australia, and as citizens who are contributing to a national conversation.

*

Over the following chapters, I provide a more or less chronological account of Australia's responses to refugees and asylum seekers from Federation until 1977. I tell many discrete episodes; some overlap, and others can only be understood by reference to earlier events. While I hope to have covered all major developments, I do not pretend to have been able to write about Australia's response to every single group of refugees or asylum seekers; like any history, my account is partial in that it is informed by the availability of sources and by the fascination a particular archive of material holds for me.

My selection of past episodes is also guided by a political concern: I understand this book to be an intervention in *current* debates about refugee and asylum seeker policy, and so I privilege past events that allow me to achieve what the German playwright Bertolt Brecht called the *Verfremdungseffekt* – that is, an effect that makes the present appear odd and strange.

The five chapters cover particular periods in Australian history. In my view, each of these periods was distinct on account of the pre-dominant government and public approach to refugees and asylum seekers.

The first chapter covers Australian history from Federation in 1901 until just before the beginning of the Pacific War in 1941, and thus government responses under the country's first twelve prime ministers, from Edmund Barton (1901–1903) to Arthur Fadden (1941). During this period, Australia had neither a refugee policy nor an asylum policy, and explicitly or implicitly tried to limit the immigration of refugees.

The second chapter covers the Labor governments of the 1940s, under prime ministers John Curtin (1941–1945), Frank Forde (1945) and Ben Chifley (1945–1949). During this time, Australia embarked on a mass immigration program, which initially relied on shipping provided by the International Refugee Organization.

Robert Menzies, who had been prime minister during the early phases of the Second World War (1939–1941), had a second, much longer stint as prime minister from 1949 until 1966, and the policies of his government, which saw a continuation and diversification of Labor's immigration program, are the subject of Chapter 3. Several high-profile asylum seekers feature prominently in this period of Australian history, which is also significant on account of two policies developed by the government in relation to people claiming political asylum in Australia and in the Australian territory of Papua and New Guinea, respectively.

The fact that I have decided to discuss the approaches of conservative prime ministers Harold Holt (1966–1967), John McEwen (1967–1968), John Gorton (1968–1971) and William McMahon (1971–1972) together with those of Labor prime minister Gough Whitlam (1972–1975) may surprise some readers; however, in Chapter 4 I argue that – one significant exception aside – Whitlam's response to refugees and asylum seekers did not depart significantly from that of McMahon, his Liberal predecessor. The fifth chapter details and analyses the policies of the first and second Fraser governments (1975–1977).

My account ends with the 1977 federal election campaign. There are a number of reasons for this. One is pragmatic: I wanted to provide a reasonably detailed history, which paid attention also to some less well known but no less relevant episodes. A book also covering the period from 1978 would have been too unwieldy. Perhaps more importantly, though, in this book I am particularly interested in deploying narratives of the past to unsettle ideas about the present. I believe this is easier to do when writing about events that most of my readers would remember only vaguely, if at all. Finally, it makes good sense to end this book in 1977. By the end of that year, the public response to refugees that we are now accustomed to had been fully formed. Ideas about 'queue jumpers', but also about refugees who need special assistance when settling in Australia, first appeared in 1976 and 1977. It was in 1977 that the government made a first attempt at developing a comprehensive refugee policy. Also in 1977, the arrival of 'boat people' prompted unprecedented public anxieties, which, when viewed from today's perspective, appear all too familiar.

This book is a history, but it is also an extended commentary on Australia's response to refugees and asylum seekers in the early twenty-first century. Thus I hope the following five chapters and the conclusion provide a much-needed critical history, *and* offer an engagement with present-day policies, practices and attitudes that is informed by detailed historical analysis.

1
─────

UNDESIRABLES

T
he men who gathered in Melbourne's Exhibition Building on
9 May 1901 to constitute Australia's first federal parliament
were not interested in refugee issues. Three-quarters of a century would pass before a comprehensive refugee policy was announced
in parliament, and almost a hundred years before refugee and asylum
seeker issues were regularly at the top of the lawmakers' agenda. Australia's first parliamentarians were preoccupied with immigration
matters, but they were not so much trying to issue a welcome to prospective immigrants, including refugees, as to exclude migrants on the
basis of their race, both by preventing non-Europeans from entering
Australia and by legislating for the deportation of thousands of long-
term residents who were of the 'wrong' skin colour.[1]

On 12 December 1901 the federal parliament passed the Pacific
Island Labourers Bill, which eventually resulted in the deportation of
about 7500 Melanesians who had been brought to Australia as inden-
tured labourers to work on the Queensland sugarcane fields. The same
day saw the passage of the Immigration Restriction Bill, which was
designed to ensure that only Europeans would migrate to Australia; it
became the legal cornerstone of the so-called White Australia policy.
The Chinese were its main target, and the principal object of the parliamentarians' anxiety, but the legislation did not explicitly exclude
them or any other ethnically or racially defined migrants (as the Labor
Party had wanted it to do). Because of reservations expressed by the
British government, which was concerned about offending Japanese
and Indians, the Act provided a means to exclude racially undesirable

migrants indirectly: through the application of an 'education test' (soon called the dictation test), whereby anybody – including Europeans – arriving in Australia could be declared a prohibited immigrant if they were unable to correctly write a fifty-word text in English or any other European language, as dictated by a customs officer. At the same time, the legislation provided penalties for the masters or owners of ships that brought passengers to Australia who were then declared prohibited immigrants. Consequently, the number of non-Europeans who were refused entry after failing the dictation test was low.

Australia's immigration restriction legislation was soon to comprise more than the two laws designed to exclude Pacific Islanders and Chinese. Its overall purpose has always been to allow the government to 'decide who comes to this country and the circumstances in which they come', as the then prime minister, John Howard, famously put it during the 2001 federal election campaign.[2]

When the Australian colonies federated in 1901, Australia had a population of about 3.8 million. Approximately a quarter had been born overseas. Aboriginal and Torres Strait Islander people comprised about 3 per cent of the population, and Asians and Pacific Islanders less than 2 per cent. Culturally and ethnically, Australia's population was more homogenous than that of the motherland, Britain.[3] The residents of the new nation were overwhelmingly from the British Isles, either by birth or by descent, and British subjects. Australian citizenship was still forty-seven years away. As a result of the immigration restrictions imposed in 1901, over the next four decades Australia became even more homogenous racially: between 1901 and 1947, its Chinese-born population, which constituted the largest non-Indigenous non-European minority, shrank from 29,900 to 6400.

\*

In recent years, some Australian refugee advocates have suggested that all non-Indigenous Australians are 'boat people' or their descendants,

and that contemporary Australia is indeed founded upon a tradition
of boat arrivals, thereby implying that the Vietnamese 'boat people'
of the late 1970s and the Iranian and Tamil asylum seekers trying to
reach Australia by boat in more recent years have much in common
with the convicts transported to the Australian colonies between 1788
and 1868.[4] Such a suggestion can easily mislead, because it assumes
that eighteenth- and nineteenth-century transportation was a form
of persecution akin to that suffered by people fleeing their homelands
in the twentieth and twenty-first centuries. The comparison would be
more convincing if it were applied only to the Irish political prisoners
among the convicts. Most of them were United Irishmen, exiled to
Australia after the failed anti-British rebellion of 1798.[5] However, their
numbers were only in the hundreds; at most, they comprised just 0.5
per cent of the approximately 160,000 convicts transported to the Australian colonies.

The Australian colonies never formally invited refugees to settle,
but usually they did not turn away people who came to Australia because
they had been persecuted in their homelands. These people included
German Lutherans who were persecuted because they refused to join
the united Protestant church created by King Friedrich Wilhelm III of
Prussia. In 1838 the first four ships carrying more than 500 German
Lutheran émigrés from Prussia arrived in South Australia. German
Lutherans continued to migrate to Australia after the Prussian authorities stopped persecuting the so-called Old Lutherans when Friedrich
Wilhelm III died in 1840; in fact, by the 1860s, even in South Australia
only a small minority of German settlers could claim to have been refugees from Prussia.[6]

Prior to Federation, the Australian colonies also admitted a few
prominent exiles, but most stayed only for short periods of time. In 1837
the former Chilean president Ramón Freire was banished to Australia;
after a few months he moved on to Tahiti, before returning to South
America in 1839.[7] In the 1870s and early 1880s a handful of French exiles
stayed for brief periods of time in Sydney; they had been among some

4000 political prisoners transported to the French penal colony of New Caledonia after the defeat of the Paris Commune in 1871. In 1874, for example, six deportees escaped from New Caledonia to Sydney, where they were feted during their short stay.[8] Others came to Australia after they were pardoned or amnestied.

These French exiles included Juliette Rastoul, who, together with her two children, had been deported from New Caledonia in 1874 for assisting in the escape of political prisoners. In 1875 she published a letter in the Melbourne *Argus* in which she defended her right to 'busy herself with politics' because, in her view, a political cause had been the reason for her exile.[9] In 1880 she married the artist Lucien Henry, a communard who had been exiled to New Caledonia and arrived in Sydney in 1879 after he was amnestied.[10] He returned to France in 1891; his estranged wife, who, according to the historian John Docker, became 'a well-known figure in Sydney intellectual circles', remained in Australia and died in Sydney in 1898.[11]

While Australians now included the descendants of the German Lutherans who had fled Prussia in the late 1830s and the odd émigré from Europe, Australia was barely touched by the major population movements of the late nineteenth century. By the turn of the twentieth century Europe had experienced several refugee crises comparable with those of more recent times. They affected countries in Eastern and South-eastern Europe, in particular. Tartars, whose ancestors had come to Eastern Europe with Ghengis Khan in the thirteenth century, were forced out of the Crimea in the aftermath of the Crimean War (1853–1856) and ended up in Anatolia, Romania and other parts of the Ottoman Empire.

Then, many displaced people, if they crossed national borders at all, fled to neighbouring countries – as they still do in the early twenty-first century. Thus, in the late nineteenth century Christians living in Bosnia, which was then part of the Ottoman Empire, sought refuge in adjacent Croatia, which belonged to the Austro-Hungarian Empire, and Bulgarian refugees settled in neighbouring Greece.

Foremost among refugee movements in the late nineteenth and early twentieth centuries was the exodus of Jews from the Tsarist empire and, to a lesser extent, from Romania and Galicia. Between 1881 and the outbreak of the First World War, 2.5 million Jews, almost half of Eastern Europe's Jewish population, emigrated as a result of persecution or extreme poverty or both.[12] In the nineteenth century, Jews who fled Tsarist Russia (after the assassination of Alexander II had triggered pogroms throughout the Pale of Settlement in the Russian Empire's western provinces) were the only refugees who were explicitly unwelcome in the Australian colonies. Initially, many Australians were sympathetic towards the plight of Jews in the Tsarist empire. However, in 1891 the publication of a rumour that a German Jewish philanthropist, Baron Maurice von Hirsch, wanted to settle half a million Russian Jews in Australia prompted a racist scare campaign, particularly in New South Wales and Victoria, which persisted even after news of the Baron's settlement scheme had proven to be incorrect.[13]

Both before and after 1901, most Jewish refugees from Tsarist Russia settled in France, Germany, the Austro-Hungarian Empire, the United Kingdom or the United States. Some had come to Australia before Federation, and some more came after 1901. They included Judah Waten, who was born in 1911 in Odessa to a Romanian father and a Belarusian mother, and who, together with his parents, arrived in Australia via Palestine in 1914.[14] Waten became a prominent communist activist (albeit one who was twice expelled from the Communist Party of Australia) and an acclaimed writer of fiction. 'Facts are the new literature,' Waten proclaimed in a manifesto published in 1933. 'The proletarian writer . . . will create a new form based on facts.'[15] The 'facts' of particular interest to Waten were autobiographical: much of his writing was informed by his experience of growing up as a refugee immigrant in 1920s Australia. His novel *Distant Land*, for example, tells the story of Joshua and Shoshana Kuperschmidt, a Jewish couple from Poland who migrate to Australia in 1925.[16] His most famous book, *Alien Son*, first published in 1952, is a collection of stories which capture the immigrant experience in the early twentieth century. For many of Waten's protagonists the new surroundings are 'bewildering'; the advice provided by one narrator's father to a friend – 'don't live in two worlds! . . . It's no good' – seems impractical, at least for the first generation of refugee immigrants.[17]

Another early-twentieth-century refugee family from Eastern Europe was that of Moses Cass, a locksmith by trade, who arrived in Perth in January 1906.[18] He was born in 1859 in Białystock, which today is a Polish city near the border between Poland and Belarus, but in the early twentieth century was part of the Russian empire and had a predominantly Jewish population. In late 1977 Moses Cass's grandson, Henry Moses ('Moss') Cass, became the Labor Party's spokesperson for immigration, and was later (incorrectly) credited with pioneering the image of an orderly queue for immigration to Australia, one that asylum seekers arriving by boat were disregarding. He recalled his parents telling him that:

> the Cossacks had entered the part of the town where they were and . . . that's when my grandmother looked out the door, noticed some Cossacks coming down the road and they suddenly stopped and knelt down and raised their rifles, she looked and saw her son coming around the corner, and they fired and they were near her so she just had to shut the door. They didn't know what had happened to him for three days or so. Fortunately he'd seen the soldiers and he'd ducked round the corner and scrambled into a Jewish shop where they were pulling down the shutter because they heard the noise and so the grandmother said, 'We're getting out.' And within a year they were in Perth.[19]

The Cass family left Białystock just in time. A few months after their arrival in Western Australia, dozens of people died in a pogrom in their former home town.

Not all Jewish immigrants from Eastern Europe were refugees.[20] And not all refugees from Tsarist Russia were Jewish. After the revolution of 1905, a few Russian political refugees also reached Australia via the Far East.[21] At the time, many of the Russian émigrés settled in Brisbane, their principal port of disembarkation. One of the most prominent Russian exiles was Fedor Andreyevich 'Artem' Sergeyev, a Bolshevik who had been imprisoned after the 1905 uprising, then exiled to Siberia; from there he made his way to Australia via China in 1911. In Queensland he became a prominent trade union activist, before returning to Russia after the February Revolution of 1917, where he played a major role in the October Revolution and its aftermath.[22] Almost a century later he would be immortalised by the Australian writer Tom Keneally in the novel *The People's Train* (although its protagonist is called Samsurov).[23]

Artem Sergeyev and the Cass and Waten families immigrated at a time when Australia admitted non-British migrants indiscriminately – provided, of course, they were European. Immigration controls were lax. One Russian Jew, who arrived by ship in Brisbane from the Far East in 1913, recalled that a customs officer was demanding to see immigrants' passports, whereupon one of the passengers, 'an ex-soldier of the Russian Imperial Army who had "resigned" rather in a hurry, displayed a coloured theatre programme'; this satisfied the official, who apparently could not make sense of the Russian text.[24] Then, passports were only sometimes required to enter Australia, and if they were, they were of little use to identify their bearers, as they did not contain photographs or descriptions of physical markers.[25] This was often known to prospective immigrants.

A newspaper article published in Russia in 1913, for example, included the following information: 'On arrival [in Australia] no one asks about any money and does not take any duty . . . no one needs any documents'. It advised would-be migrants that they could enter Australia under a different name, which was relevant for those who considered Australia a country of exile and wanted to evade surveillance by the authorities of their home countries.[26] Such perfunctory immigration controls were not peculiar to Australia.

Unlike in the twenty-first century, European migrants – including refugees – generally experienced few problems leaving or entering countries. Their countries of birth did not try to prevent them leaving, nor did potential countries of refuge close their borders to them. Borders were not secured by walls, barbed-wire fences or patrol boats, and crossing them did not usually require permits. Countries of immigration did not set quotas (although some, such as Australia and New Zealand, had race-based immigration restrictions). In the years immediately preceding the First World War, about a million Europeans migrated to the United States every year; they included people attracted by economic opportunities or escaping persecution, and it is now almost impossible to either quantify the number of refugees or to neatly distinguish them from other migrants arriving at New York's famed Ellis Island.[27] It was not until 1924 that the US authorities required visas and photographs of all immigrants, and introduced permanent immigration restrictions for Europeans.[28]

Far fewer displaced people migrated to Australia than to North America, not least because the passage from Europe to Australia was comparatively expensive. The government made no concessions specifically to prospective immigrants who were forced out of their own countries. In 1916 the Brisbane Hebrew Congregation, which had enquired whether Australia would resettle Polish and Russian Jewish refugees, was told that no special provisions would be made for them, and that prospective Jewish immigrants would simply have to meet the normal criteria for non-British migrants.[29] In subsequent years this became the government's standard reply to similar enquiries concerning other groups of refugees. Although the response suggests that the immigration authorities were neither privileging applications from refugees nor discriminating against them, refugees tended to be under-represented among those migrating to Australia. That was also because many non-refugee immigrants were assisted in coming to Australia – by federal or state governments, and sometimes also by prospective employers or their countries of origin. As intercontinental travel was then far more expensive than it is today, subsidised fares and settlement assistance upon arrival were often essential for migrants who wanted to make the long journey from Europe to Australia. Before 1947, there were no government schemes that provided assisted passages specifically to migrants who could be regarded as refugees.

In some instances, Australia appeared to disadvantage applicants who had been forced out of their home countries. In these cases, however, the reason was not that the prospective immigrants were refugees but that they belonged to a national, ethnic or religious group that was considered undesirable. In 1921 the Australian high commission in London conveyed an enquiry from the British government: would Australia accept any of the 40,000 'Anti-Bolshevik Jews from Russia' and Jews from Ukraine ('fugitives from an indescribable anarchy and carnage') who had recently fled to Poland, because the Polish government had decided to close its borders to Jewish refugees and expel those already in the country unless they could demonstrate that they could be resettled elsewhere within five months?[30] In a file note, Albert Robert Peters, a senior officer in the Department of Home and Territories, reminded the department's acting head: 'In regard to Russian refugees at Constantinople (probably a superior class to the Russian Jews referred to in the cablegram) it was decided not to give any encouragement to their coming to Australia.'[31] Accordingly, the Department of Home and Territories advised the Prime Minister's Department to inform the Australian high commission that Jewish refugees would not be admitted.[32] Australia's high commissioner, however, was provided with a more diplomatic answer to the British government's enquiry. 'Immediate requirements of Commonwealth being met by immigration ex-service men whose passages paid by British Government, in addition to large number of British immigrants which are being nominated by relatives and friends here,' the Prime Minister's Department cabled the high commissioner in London. 'Immigration of refugee Jews would involve exclusion of some of these British emigrants. Commonwealth Government therefore regrets inability to co-operate.'[33]

Over the following years there were further requests to admit East-ern European Jews, and again they were declined with reference to the prospective immigrants' 'type'. Thus, in 1925, in response to informa-tion that Polish Jews might try to migrate to Australia, the Department of Home and Territories advised the Australian representative in London:

> As the information available in this Department bears out the opinion expressed by the [British] Passport Control Officer [in Warsaw] that the Polish Jew is not a good type of immigrant, the Minister is desirous that the migration of these people to Australia should be discouraged as far as it may be in the power of the Brit-ish Passport Officers in Poland discreetly to do so.[34]

Directives similar to that given in 1925 by home and territories min-ister George Pearce have been issued throughout Australian history. The Australian government has always been concerned, however, to disguise discriminatory policies and practices lest they attract unfa-vourable international attention. It has also preferred to leave prospective immigrants in the dark about the criteria that see some of them accepted and others rejected. Yet attempts to be 'discreet' about the immigration authorities' selection criteria and about Australia's preference for par-ticular groups of migrants were not always successful. Prospective immigrants often understood how to present their cases in order to maximise their chances of being accepted, and it was the immigration officers who were left in the dark about how applicants were able to manipulate the system to their advantage.

*

On account of its scale and its long-lasting consequences, the exodus of Eastern European Jews was the most significant refugee movement between the late nineteenth century and the beginning of the Second

World War. But there were other major population transfers in the first three decades of the twentieth century. The First World War led to the displacement of millions of people. Almost a million Germans fled westwards when the Tsarist army invaded Prussia; 1.5 million Belgians fled to the Netherlands, France or Britain when Germany invaded and occupied their country in August 1914; hundreds of thousands fled Austrian Galicia and Bukovina when these regions were occupied by Russia; possibly as many as 7 million people were displaced in the Russian empire after the tide of war turned in Austria and Germany's favour in 1915.[35]

Most of those who became displaced between 1914 and 1918 were able to return home after the war ended. There were important exceptions, however. Hundreds of thousands of Armenians who had survived ethnic cleansing and were forced out of Turkey from April 1915 became permanently displaced. The same fate befell more than a million so-called White Russians, who were associated with the losing side in the Russian civil war and went into exile between the October Revolution of 1917 and the introduction of emigration controls by the Soviet government in 1922. Most settled in northern China or in Central and Western Europe. In the early 1920s, in Berlin alone there were some 360,000 Russian emigrés, comprising about 10 per cent of the population of Germany's capital.[36] The war between Greece and Turkey (1919–1922) resulted in an enforced exchange of populations, with more than a million Greeks being driven out of Asia Minor and resettled in Greece, and some 400,000 ethnic Turkish refugees from Greece resettled in Turkey.[37]

Significant population movements had occurred before the early twentieth century. In the nineteenth century millions had migrated to the United States, and many – for example, the hundreds of thousands of Irish escaping the Great Famine in the mid-nineteenth century – had been driven from their homelands rather than attracted by the opportunities available in the 'new world'. From the early twentieth century onwards, the governments and nationals of potential host states increasingly perceived refugees as a potential threat – to their material wealth, to their individual and national security, and to the cohesion of a supposedly homogenous and distinct (for example, 'Australian' or 'French') nation-state. Paradoxically, while the number of refugees increased, they were seen as an aberration, and the state that was entitled to (and that expected to be able to) regulate access to its territory became the norm. Now this norm appears self-evident, if not natural;[38] by now it is difficult to imagine that only a hundred years ago immigration controls were lax and sometimes non-existent, and that the imaginary threats posed by refugees have only increased as border controls have become more sophisticated.

What distinguished forced migration in the twentieth century from that in previous times was the fact that those compelled to leave their homes were often unwelcome where they sought refuge, and sometimes unable to leave because no other country would admit them. Unlike in earlier periods, from the early twentieth century onwards migrants were usually expected to have identity documents, and often obliged to obtain a visa or similar permit before entering a country other than their own.[39] That meant that those who most needed to flee often did not become refugees; thus, Stalinism and Nazi Germany's persecution of Jews resulted in millions of deaths rather than millions of refugees.[40]

In 1919, in the wake of the First World War, forty-four countries joined to set up the League of Nations, an intergovernmental organisation that was intended to prevent a recurrence of international armed conflict. Australia was among its founding members. Two years later the League appointed Fridtjof Nansen, the famous Norwegian polar explorer, as its first high commissioner for refugees.[41] Earlier, he had organised the repatriation of prisoners of war on behalf of the League, and then coordinated the provision of famine relief to the Soviet Union. Initially, Nansen and his office were tasked only with finding a solution to the problem of Russian refugees, but soon they were given responsibility for others, including Armenians and Assyrians. However, Nansen had only limited financial resources at his disposal – he began with a budget of £5500 for 1921/22 – and was not expected to use his organi-sation to provide long-term humanitarian relief on a large scale.[42] Private voluntary organisations were essential sources of funding and material assistance, but often their impact was limited because they lacked the clout of governments or international organisations.[43]

The main contributions of Nansen and his Geneva-based office were the creation of an internationally recognised identity card for stateless people – the so-called Nansen passport – and the inauguration of an international legal framework for the protection of displaced people.[44] Initially, that framework focused on the recognition of refugees as mem-bers of specific groups, such as Armenians or Assyrians, rather than on their protection needs and entitlements due to individual circumstances.[45]

While Nansen and his office were able to secure the legal recogni-tion of refugees in countries of asylum, they were less successful in persuading prospective host countries to admit people who had fled their homelands or who were desperate to do so. As the UNHCR would later do, Nansen identified three durable solutions for refugees: repa-triation, resettlement and local integration. Initially, when trying to address the problem of Russian refugees, he favoured repatriation, only to realise (as several high commissioners for refugees would do after the establishment of the UNHCR) that this was potentially the most controversial option because of well-founded suspicions that refugees were being returned to their countries of origin without safeguards guaranteeing their protection.[46]

Australia contributed financially to the League's efforts and ratified its 1922 and 1924 arrangements relating to Russian and Armenian refu-gees, but did not participate in any of the ten intergovernmental conferences held between 1921 and February 1938 to discuss refugee issues.[47] Nor did the Australian government formally recognise that refugees occupied a special category of migrants: that they had particular needs, and their lives often depended on the relaxation of immigration controls.

*

The work of Nansen had no impact on Australia's immigration policies. Nevertheless, during the first three decades of the twentieth century, some White Russians and Eastern European Jews did migrate to Australia. Between 1920 and 1940 Australia recorded a net migration gain of 2148 Russians.[48] And despite Australia's reluctance to admit Jews from Poland, the 1920s saw the arrival of about 2000 Eastern European Jews, most of whom settled in Victoria.[49] These were very small numbers, however, in relation both to Australia's population and to the overall number of White Russian and Jewish refugees. This was not just because Australia did not encourage refugee immigration, but also because only a small minority of Russian exiles and Jewish refugees considered Australia a viable destination. It was very far from Europe, fares were prohibitively expensive, and, most importantly, Australia had no sizeable established communities of migrants from Eastern Europe. For Eastern European Jews, Australia became an option mainly after the 1921 *Emergency Quota Act* and the 1924 *Johnson-Reed Act* introduced a quota system for immigration to the United States, which nevertheless remained the most desirable destination for many refugees throughout the twentieth century.

The Wall Street crash of October 1929 triggered the onset of what became known in Australia as the Great Depression. Unemployment skyrocketed, with more than half a million people, or close to 30 per cent of the workforce, out of a job in 1931–1932.[50] Australia experienced a net loss of migrants. From 1931 the government suspended its assisted passage scheme for British migrants. By restricting the issuing of landing permits (the precursors of today's visas) and by varying the amount of landing money required of migrants, the government also controlled the level of non-British ('alien') immigration.

The appointment of Adolf Hitler as Germany's chancellor on 30 January 1933 had no immediate impact in Australia, because most of those driven out of Germany in 1933 and 1934 – who included a large proportion of the country's artistic and intellectual elites – sought refuge in neighbouring countries. In 1934, however, the Australian government became embroiled in an affair involving a high-profile exile from Nazi Germany. Prague-born Egon Erwin Kisch was a left-wing journalist and travel writer in Weimar Germany. In February 1933 he was arrested in Berlin and then deported to his native Czechoslovakia. In 1934 the Movement against War and Fascism invited Kisch to speak at a congress in Melbourne, which coincided with celebrations for the city's centenary. In early November of that year Kisch arrived in Fremantle aboard the *Strathaird*, but was not allowed to land on account of his close associations with communist organisations. When the *Strathaird* docked at Port Melbourne, Kisch defied the order to remain on board and jumped more than five metres off the quarterdeck onto Station Pier, breaking a leg in the process. He was taken back on board and the ship continued its journey to Sydney.

In the federal parliament, attorney-general Robert Menzies defended the government's refusal to let Kisch land. His argument was similar to that used by later government ministers who suggested that asylum seekers arriving by boat should be prevented from entering Australia, irrespective of Australia's legal obligations. 'We have, as an independent country, a perfect right to indicate whether an alien shall or shall not be admitted within these shores,' Menzies said.[51] His colleague, the Nationalist trade minister Thomas Walter White, reminded parliament that in excluding Kisch, the government was merely acting in the spirit of the country's immigration restriction legislation: 'This Parliament has passed an act for the purpose of keeping out of Australia persons of criminal or diseased type, and others with revolutionary ideas.'[52]

Kisch's supporters took his case to the High Court, where Justice Herbert Vere ('Doc') Evatt, who seven years later would become attorney-general in a Labor government, ordered the authorities to let Kisch land.[53] The government of Joseph Lyons then used the *Immigration Restriction Act* to exclude Kisch. Kisch was set a dictation test in order to declare him a prohibited immigrant. As he was known to be fluent in many European languages, he was tested in Scottish Gaelic; predictably, he failed.

His supporters successfully challenged the government's action in court once more, this time on the grounds that the Scottish-born police officer who had administered the test did not actually speak Gaelic himself. To avoid further embarrassment, the government eventually struck a deal with Kisch, which obliged him to leave Australia by March 1935. In return, the legal proceedings against him were stopped and he received a £450 compensation payment.[54]

*

It took more than ten years for Australia's economic performance to return to the level of 1928. Yet from 1935 some industries experienced labour shortages. As the economy slowly recovered in the mid-1930s, immigration resumed. British migrants again had access to an assisted passage scheme, and for non-British migrants sponsored by family or friends the landing fee was lowered from £500 to £50.

Among those who migrated to Australia in the mid-1930s were refugees from Nazi Germany. They included a German travel writer and journalist, Walter Stölting (who changed his name to Stolting after his arrival in Australia). In August 1933 he lost his job as a radio broadcaster with Berliner Rundfunk, left Germany, and landed in Melbourne three years later. This was not the first time he had been to Australia; in 1927 he had visited for nine months to research a travel book, which was published in 1930 as *Australien: Das Land von morgen* ('Australia: The Country of Tomorrow'), the most informative and readable German-language account of Australia written in the first half of the twentieth century.[55]

Even before becoming a refugee, Stölting had led a colourful and peripatetic life. He was born in the small town of Bentheim, in the north-west of Germany, but grew up in Berlin, where his father, Richard Stölting, was a district court judge. His mother, Rosemarie Stölting (née Mamroth), was Jewish, but Walter was brought up in his father's Protestant faith. When he was fifteen his parents divorced. Walter remained with his father. In early 1915 he volunteered to fight for *Kaiser* and fatherland, and joined a signals corps as a wireless operator. He deserted in the war's final stages, became involved in the formation of a soldiers' soviet in Brussels at the war's end, and was eventually taken prisoner by the Belgians. After his release he worked in a variety of jobs, including as a publicist for Dornier, the company that built the Zeppelin. He visited Argentina in 1926 (and later wrote two books about that country), before venturing to Australia the following year. In the early 1930s he joined the government-owned Berliner Rundfunk.[56]

Politically, Stölting belonged to the left. For about two years he was a card-carrying Social Democrat, but he left the party in 1932 because, unlike the party leadership, he believed that the threat of Nazism could only be countered by an alliance of Social Democrats and communists. But when he lost his job as a broadcaster at the end of August 1933, it was on account of his Jewish ancestry rather than his politics. In October of that year, unable to see a future for himself in Germany, he left for Paris, where he remained for six months. From France he moved to Barcelona, and then to Denmark. In February 1935 he travelled to Colombia, where he worked as an airport superintendent for the Colombian-German airline Sociedad Colombo-Alemena de Transportes Aereos (Scadta). He returned to Europe at the end of 1935 after also losing that job on account of being Jewish; he initially stayed with his mother, who by then was living in Spain, and then went to Italy.

From Colombia Stölting had applied for an Australian landing permit. He did not tell the immigration authorities that his circumstances had changed dramatically since his last visit to Australia, and that he had in fact become a refugee; instead, he pretended that he wanted to produce a sequel to his earlier book: 'Now, after a two years trip through Spain, France, Denmark and Columbia [sic], I would like to return to Australia if your permission could be granted for which I kindly might ask you, and I intend to go first another time to the interior parts.'[57] When his application was approved, he departed Italy for Melbourne, where he arrived aboard the *Viminale* on 10 April 1936.

Even three years after the beginning of Nazi rule, Stolting was still an exception; the majority of German refugees were biding their time in Europe, in the hope that they would soon be able to return home. Before 1938, most Jews remained in Germany, either because they had nowhere else to go or because they were expecting the Nazi regime to be a temporary phenomenon. Many of those who had fled the country were socialists and communists who were either not Jewish or who, like Stolting, did not identify with the Jewish faith.

Australia was not a sought-after destination; the Australian immigration authorities were untroubled by the small number of German refugees applying for admission, and willing to accommodate those eager to move to Australia. Stolting, for example, was granted a landing permit even though he seems not to have had the stipulated landing money. When it became obvious that he was not headed to central Australia and that he was no longer working as a travel writer or journalist, the Department of the Interior simply accepted that he had come to Australia to stay.

*

In 1937 the Royal Institute of International Affairs in London commissioned a retired British politician and administrator, Sir John Hope Simpson, to undertake a survey of the global refugee problem. In the course of collecting information for this study, the Institute wrote to the Australian government to enquire about its approach to refugees. The Department of the Interior responded in December 1937. It explained that Australia did not distinguish between refugees and other prospective alien immigrants, and that all non-British nationals had to be in possession of a landing permit when entering Australia. The advice implied that Australia would admit an unlimited number of refugees, provided they met Australia's normal immigration requirements. However, the department also advised the Royal Institute that 'mass immigration of any class of aliens is not viewed with favour', and that it was wary of the 'inherent difficulty of complete assimilation of people of Jewish race, who always retain their identity as Jews'.[58]

Within a few months, both the refugee situation in Europe and the Australian approach to refugees had changed. In March 1938 the German Reich annexed Austria, whose population largely welcomed this so-called *Anschluss*. The persecution of Jews intensified. By May, Australia House in London was receiving 300 applications each week from Germans and Austrians who wanted to emigrate.[59]

Being the minister for the interior at the time, the Country Party's John McEwen was responsible for immigration matters. Unlike his party leader, Archie Cameron, who was an anti-Semite, and his successor as minister for the interior, Hattil Spencer ('Harry') Foll, McEwen was sympathetic towards the plight of Jewish refugees.[60] Yet he was also anxious to impose an upper limit on the number of refugees admitted to Australia. In May he told Cabinet that if the immigration authorities let in everybody who was in possession of the £200 landing money required then of non-British applicants, they would have issued 20,000 permits to Jewish migrants by the end of the year. On 9 June Cabinet imposed a monthly quota of 300 landing permits for Jews, with a preference for those of German or Austrian nationality.

In June 1938 Nazi Germany's control did not yet extend beyond the borders of Germany and Austria (although that was soon to change, with the annexation of the Sudetenland in October 1938, and much of the remainder of what used to be Czechoslovakia in March 1939). But Germany was not the only country that tried to expel its Jewish residents. Romania and Hungary were ruled by governments whose leaders often shared the anti-Semitism of the Nazis. In the second half of the 1930s Poland experienced a growing tide of anti-Semitic violence. In March 1938 its government introduced a law whereby the citizenship of Poles who had been living outside Poland for more than five years was automatically cancelled. That law was to have a devastating effect on Polish Jews living in Austria and Germany, who were suddenly no longer wanted by their country of residence or their country of birth.[61]

In July 1938 Hope Simpson published a preliminary report that drew on the results of his survey. He recognised that refugees posed a problem because of the introduction of immigration controls; their existence was 'a symptom of the disappearance of economic and political liberalism'.[62] Nevertheless, he concluded that the refugee problem was manageable because of its 'relatively small proportions'.[63] He estimated that there were probably some 600,000 refugees worldwide, about half of them from the Soviet Union, and another 25 per cent from Germany.

The sense of urgency that pervades the report, and which had prompted Hope Simpson to release an early version of it, was informed not so much by an existing problem as by the 'imminent danger of new refugee movements':[64] of Republicans from Spain, of Jews from Germany and Austria, and, most importantly, of Jews from countries in Eastern Europe. In Hope Simpson's view, the solution to the emerging problems in Eastern Europe did not lie in large-scale international resettlement schemes; rather, the international community needed to influence governments to revoke their anti-Semitic policies and eliminate anti-Semitic propaganda. He had little hope that the situation in Germany and Austria was reversible in the foreseeable future, but was anxious for the response to that situation to be considered exceptional.[65]

The early publication of Hope Simpson's report was also designed to inform a concerted international response to the refugee crisis. A couple of weeks after the *Anschluss*, President Theodore Delano Roosevelt of the United States had invited governments from around the world to attend a conference to discuss such a response. His ambitions were modest. According to a letter received by the Australian government, 'no country would be expected or asked to receive a greater number of emigrants than is permitted by its existing legislation'.[66] Australia accepted the invitation, not least to avoid criticism for shunning it.[67] In July, delegations representing thirty-two countries gathered in the French spa town of Évian-les-Bains, on the shores of Lake Geneva. Australia was represented by the trade minister, White – not because the issues discussed during the conference were of particular interest to him or relevant to his portfolio, but because he happened to be in Europe at the time.

One of the advocates of an Australian involvement in international efforts to address the issue of refugees was Australia's high commissioner in London, the former prime minister Stanley Bruce. Like Hope Simpson, Bruce was concerned to ensure, however, that attempts to solve the predicament of German and Austrian refugees not encourage governments in Eastern Europe – most importantly, in Poland – to expel their Jewish populations.[68]

It would be a mistake to consider the pre-war refugee policies of governments in Western Europe, the Americas and Australasia only through the lens of the Holocaust; leaders such as Roosevelt, Britain's Neville Chamberlain and Australia's Joseph Lyons did not – and, in fairness, probably could not – anticipate the genocide perpetrated by Nazi Germany. Instead, they had reason to be worried that the exodus of German and Austrian Jews – which was, after all, numerically less significant than that of White Russians from the Soviet Union in the early 1920s – would soon be dwarfed by an exodus from Poland, whose Jewish population was about six times larger than Germany's.

The Évian conference was a dismal failure. According to the historian Michael Marrus, most delegations 'seemed to be addressing their home constituencies rather than the pathetic representatives of refugee organizations and persecuted Jews who, uninvited, hung about the conference'.[69] Several delegates emphasised that their countries had generously accepted significant numbers of refugees in the past, but that for economic or other reasons they were unable to do so now. The Swiss delegate, for example, claimed that the 'Swiss people have always been moved by the suffering of others', but also said that his government did not accept refugees unless they were simply in transit.[70]

The Australian delegate saw no need to invoke the traditional generosity of his fellow Australians in the way post-war Australian representatives would routinely do when defending their restrictive or harsh refugee and asylum seeker policies. White merely assured the assembled delegates that Australia was already doing its fair share. The irony of his proud declaration that Australia was doing as much as everybody else must have escaped him. After all, the conference had been called because the response of all countries was woefully inadequate; an effort that was 'comparable with that of any other country', as White put it, was therefore obviously insufficient. White explained why his government had decided not to do more:

> [I]t will be appreciated that in a young country man power from the source from which most of its citizens have sprung is preferred, while undue privileges cannot be given to one particular class of non-British subjects without injustice to others. It will no doubt be appreciated also that, as we have no real racial problem, we are not desirous of importing one by encouraging any scheme of large-scale foreign migration.[71]

Other delegations were similarly reluctant to commit their governments to welcoming refugees from Nazi Germany. The New Zealand delegate, Cyril Burdekin, promised that his government would consider individual applications, but cautioned that New Zealand would not accept 'any large number of refugees', and that applicants found to be acceptable would not necessarily be granted a permit. He also pointed out that applicants likely to become a charge on public funds would not be accepted, and that an applicant was more likely to become a charge on the government's purse 'if he is not allowed to bring from his country of origin more than an insignificant proportion of his possessions'.[72] Of course, this put German and Austrian refugees, who were generally prevented from bringing any possessions with them, in a very difficult position.

The Canadian representative said that 'the continuance of serious unemployment and of economic uncertainty and disturbance' meant that Canada was unable to accept a considerable number of immigrants.[73]

Even the delegate of France, which had accommodated a comparatively large number of refugees and, until a few months earlier, had been more accepting of them than other countries, announced that his country had 'reached, if not passed, the extreme point of saturation'.[74]

The only tangible outcome of the conference was the establishment of the London-based Inter-Governmental Committee for Refugees, but this committee had few resources – Australia contributed £415 to its £10,000 budget[75] – and no teeth; it turned out to be as ineffective as the Évian conference. Ironically, the disappointment of refugee advocates was matched by that of the German government, which had been hoping that other countries would be willing to accommodate Germany's Jewish population to solve the 'Jewish question', and which kept emphasising to those classified as Jewish under the Nuremberg racial laws that emigration was their only option. However, those meeting at Évian were mindful not just of the refugee problem created by Nazi Germany; a member of the Australian delegation noted that 'there was the fear that if the Conference should by any chance show any very great readiness to accept Refugees, Poland and Roumania would feel encouraged to get rid of the several millions of Jews within their borders, and might start repressive measures to achieve that end'.[76]

By August 1938 the number of weekly applications received by Australia House from German and Austrian refugees had risen to 500. In a single week that year the Australian Jewish Welfare Society (AJWS) received 1700 letters from Jews beseeching it to help secure them landing permits.[77] In their desperation, some prospective immigrants wrote directly to the Australian prime minister. 'I, Your Excellency's petitioner, am 14 years old and have finished the 4th class of a grammar-school with best results,' Alfred Andermann, a Viennese high school student, wrote in a letter addressed to Joseph Lyons.

Here I have no possibility, neither to learn a trade, or to study on. My 45 years old father Arthur Andermann who is diplomed insurance-mathematician and electrical engineer, and who is also well versed in the production of marmalade, juice of fruit, jam and ice, has here no possibility to earn his living . . . We are all healthy and strong and will make it to our study to be useful to the country in working industrious and loyal.[78]

There is no trace in the files of the Department of the Interior to suggest that the Andermanns' application was successful and that they made it to Australia. However, they do not appear either in a database of Austrian Holocaust victims, and there are references to the naturalisation of an Arthur Andermann (born in 1893) and an Alfred Andermann (born in 1924) in the United Kingdom in 1947 and 1948, respectively.[79] Thus, it is reasonable to assume they survived. Many of those appealing to be admitted to Australia did not.

*

On 9 and 10 November 1938, Nazi storm-troopers, sometimes aided by ordinary citizens, burned down more than a hundred synagogues in Germany and Austria in a nationwide and orchestrated pogrom. They took thousands of Jewish men to concentration camps, partly in order to increase the pressure on them and their families to leave the country. In Australia, news of the pogrom strengthened the position of organisations that had been arguing for a liberalisation of the country's immigration policy.[80] In fact, support for the admission of Jewish refugees now came from an unexpected quarter: on 18 November the New South Wales Trades and Labour Council, which had traditionally opposed immigration, passed a resolution asking the government to accept Jewish refugees and, if necessary, to support them financially.[81]

From London, Stanley Bruce told the government on 21 November that 'strong feeling is rapidly developing' that an unprecedented international effort was required to deal with Jewish refugees from Germany, and that Australia might find itself in an 'embarrassing situation' if it did not make a statement regarding its approach.[82] He was not so much guided by humanitarian considerations as by concerns about Australia's reputation, particularly in the United States and the United Kingdom. He suggested that Australia announce the establishment of a quota of 30,000 refugees over three years.

Cabinet agreed to Bruce's proposal in principle but halved the figure. On 1 December McEwen announced the new policy (which had been approved by Cabinet the previous day) in parliament. He said that Australia would admit up to 15,000 refugees from Europe over three years, with permits granted in accordance with Australia's white alien immigration policy. 'The Government feels that, if a solution of this problem is to be found, countries must be prepared to receive a proportion of those to be expatriated, in relation to the capacity of the countries to assimilate them,' he explained.[83] This was a long way from White's statement at Évian.

But McEwen's announcement came with two important provisos. The first was that refugee policy was not to trump Australia's broader immigration policy:

> Although the refugee problem is one quite apart from the general question of immigration, in that it deals with the specific question of the amelioration of the conditions of oppressed people, at the same time it is essential that it should be considered in relation to the general question of immigration so far as the Commonwealth is concerned.[84]

The second proviso was that the specific circumstances of applicants were not to be taken into account: 'Desperate as is the need of many of those unfortunate people, it is not the intention of the Government to issue permits for entry influenced by the necessity of individual cases.'[85]

There was some grumbling among McEwen's colleagues and in the press, but in federal parliament the new policy had bipartisan support, although it was obvious that the government and the opposition agreed to the admission of refugees for different reasons; in response to the minister's announcement, opposition leader John Curtin declared: 'Australia is a place where lovers of liberty should be welcome.'[86] While McEwen made Australia's quota public, he did not provide any detail about its likely composition; most importantly, he did not reveal that the government had also agreed to limit the number of Jewish immigrants accepted under the quota to 4000 per year, and that it had decided that the quota 'may be exceeded in admitting approved Aryans'.[87]

Bruce was disappointed about the government's decision to halve the numbers suggested by him, but thought 15,000 was a 'respectable' figure.[88] The announcement received a positive response in London, as Bruce had intended. The *Times* referred to a 'characteristically generous contribution' and opined in an editorial that '[t]he Commonwealth Government have certainly done their full share'. According to the paper, '[a] great part of their wide territory is uninhabitable; their chief cities are crowded, and the majority of the immigrants are unlikely to be acquainted with agriculture or stock-raising'.[89] In a similar vein, the *Observer* wrote that the decision was a 'striking illustration of how noble compassion can circle the globe'.[90]

Outside Australia, the announcement of a quota encouraged those who were lobbying their own governments for a liberalisation of entry restrictions; for example, the Australian decision put pressure on the Canadian government to follow suit.[91] At home, the announcement also appeased those who had lobbied for a more generous policy.

Both in Australia and overseas the announcement was read as an indication that Australia was doing more than what at Évian it had considered its fair share, and was now making a significant contribution to alleviating the refugee crisis caused by Nazi Germany's racial policies. Observers did not draw attention to the policy's double-edged nature, which allowed for the admission of 15,000 refugees but also effectively restricted the number of refugees entering Australia by setting an upper limit on the number of applications that would be approved from people identified as refugees, irrespective of how many of them met all of Australia's criteria.

After the war, the newly formed immigration department established that 1556 refugees had arrived in 1938, and 5080 the following year.[92] These figures underestimate Australia's intake of refugees, because the government statistics only captured the number of migrants entering Australia who were identified as refugees. Given that the chances of applicants being issued with landing permits were greater if they managed to hide their precarious circumstances, there were probably scores of people from Central Europe who entered Australia disguised as 'ordinary' migrants. Others ostensibly arrived as tourists.[93] Taking into account the overall migrant arrivals from Germany, Austria, Czechoslovakia and Poland between 1933 and 1939, I have estimated the number of refugees admitted by Australia in the 1930s to be closer to 10,000.[94] That number is significant when compared to Australia's intake of non-British migrants in the aftermath of the Great Depression, but small when considered in the context of the size of the refugee problem in Europe.

In comparison with other countries, Australia was not particularly miserly; in fact, it was a little more generous than others. New Zealand, whose population at the time was slightly less than a quarter of Australia's, admitted only about 1100 refugees from Europe.[95] The Canadian government only let in refugees with farming credentials, which excluded almost all Jewish refugees from Germany and Austria; between 1933 and 1945, Canada admitted fewer than 5000 Jewish refugees.[96] In September 1939 Switzerland, whose population was about two-thirds of that of Australia, only harboured 7000 to 8000 refugees, even though it shared borders with two refugee-producing countries, Italy and Germany.[97]

Australia was reluctant to admit *Jewish* refugees, and opposed to the immigration of Jewish refugees from countries other than Austria and Germany. In that, too, it was not alone; in fact, Australia's reservations towards Jewish refugees were mild in comparison to those of Canada. According to the historian Paul Bartrop, Canada's policy was partly shaped by an 'antisemitic Director of Immigration, a disinterested Minister [and] an indifferent Prime Minister with anti-Jewish leanings'.[98]

It is often assumed that a government's refugee policy comprises two elements: its approach towards the alleviation of refugee crises by providing financial or material assistance (for example, by funding emergency relief administered by the Red Cross), and its approach towards the resettlement of refugees. It is easy to lose sight of another option governments might have: namely, to tackle refugee problems at their source. Thus, in recent years the Australian government, which has tried to deter Tamils from attempting to seek asylum in Australia and has collaborated with the Sri Lankan government to prevent prospective asylum seekers from leaving Sri Lanka by boat, could have instead focused its efforts on persuading the government in Colombo to afford ethnic Tamils the same rights, privileges and recognition that are enjoyed by ethnic Singhalese. Yet successive Australian governments have often appeared to condone human rights violations in Sri Lanka, perhaps in the interest of maintaining a friendly relationship with their Sri Lankan counterparts.[99]

Australia's response to the German refugee crisis might also be evaluated in light of its approach to the government responsible for the exodus. Particularly after the pogroms of November 1938, the Australian government received many letters from individuals and organisations demanding that something be done to make Nazi Germany desist from persecuting Jews; the government's standard reply was that 'the Commonwealth Government considers that no good purpose would be served were a formal protest to be made to the German Government in connection with the treatment of Jews in Germany'.[100] In that respect, too, the Australian government was in good company; other governments were also most reluctant to respond in ways that could be seen as interference in the internal affairs of a sovereign nation.

The suggestion that such interference might be necessary, however, was widely discussed. In December 1935 Fridtjof Nansen's successor as high commissioner for refugees, the American James G. McDonald, resigned from his position, having become increasingly frustrated by the constraints within which he had to operate. He used a carefully crafted letter of resignation (work on which had apparently begun months earlier) to demand that the root causes of the forced displacement of Jews from Germany be addressed.[101]

The Australian government's approach ought to be seen also in the context of the overall Australian response to the European refugee crisis. Refugees had their lobbyists, but these did not wield much influence and represented only a small minority of Australians. As the Hungarian refugee Emery Barcs (who migrated to Australia in 1939 after the introduction of anti-Semitic racial laws in his native Hungary) observed, the anti-refugee sentiment was pervasive, even though Australians displayed 'little overt hostility' towards refugees.[102] The newspapers – with one notable exception, the *Sydney Morning Herald* – were largely unenthusiastic about the admittance of refugees.

Some key professional organisations were opposed either to letting European refugees in or to letting them use their qualifications and skills. The Musicians' Union of Australia (MUA), for example, opposed the admission of refugees outright. Their secretary conceded that Australia might benefit from the immigration of a select number of orchestral musicians, but declared that his union only approved of musicians from Britain. In a recent book, Kay Dreyfus has told the story of the Weintraubs Syncopators, who became famous as the on-stage band in the 1930 von Sternberg film *The Blue Angel*, and who arrived in Australia in 1937. All bar one were Jewish, and were therefore not able to return to Germany, where most of them had grown up. According to Dreyfus, the MUA fought a long and bitter battle to prevent the Weintraubs from securing employment in Australia, or even becoming permanent residents.[103]

The Australian Dental Association, on the other hand, did not object to the immigration of European refugees, but required German and Austrian dentists to enrol in the third year of a four-year dentistry degree. A spokesman for the association justified this measure by saying that he had been 'amazed at the low standard of dentistry required in Germany'.[104] One of Vienna's leading dental surgeons, who practised his profession without registration, commented dryly: 'I have neither the time nor the money to attend their silly school, which is 50 years behind the times, anyway.'[105]

Self-interest drove some Australians to welcome the arrival of refugees. In January 1939 the general secretary of the United Graziers' Association of Queensland wrote to the government 'to ascertain what percentage of female domestics would be amongst these refugees and whether any would be available for country districts in Queensland to serve in the capacity of domestic servants'.[106] Such exceptions aside, the general public and the press were overwhelmingly not in favour of the admission of sizeable numbers of refugees, particularly if they were Jewish.[107] Frequently, the papers reported xenophobic or anti-Semitic views without dismissing them as inappropriate.

Some political leaders, when complaining about the admission of Jewish refugees, employed the same kind of language that German Nazis used. For example, in 1939 Frank Clarke, then president of the Victorian Legislative Council and a former state government minister, referred to Jewish refugees as 'weedy East Europeans' and 'slinking, ratfaced men under five feet in height'.[108] Still, public sentiment before the outbreak of the war never resembled anti-alien hysteria; most Australians simply did not care.

In 1938 the government had tried to impose limits on the number of Jewish refugees arriving in Australia by the same ship. In April it had allocated 500 places for Jewish immigrants to the AJWS, 'with the proviso that no more than 20 sponsored cases arrive on any one ship'.[109] Also that year, the government advised German travel agents not to accept more than twenty bookings per ship from refugees, but it knew it could not enforce this policy.

The attempt to restrict numbers was motivated not so much by the government's unwillingness to accommodate refugees as by the expectation that mass arrivals would prompt a public backlash: 'When large numbers arrive by boat . . . Press immediately gives prominence to the fact and strong representations for curtailment of issue of permits are made,' the Prime Minister's Department advised the office of the Australian high commissioner in London in November 1938. 'It would be in the interests of the Associations connected with the refugees that they do everything possible to prevent large numbers arriving by one boat.'[110]

As the number of refugees issued with landing permits increased in 1938, it was obvious that passenger ships arriving from Europe would often carry far more than twenty people fleeing Germany and Austria. A ship with a particularly large contingent of refugees on board was the mail liner *Strathmore*, which docked in Fremantle on 16 May 1939. The Perth *Daily Mail* noted that the ship brought '320 aliens', many of them 'fleeing refugees', to Australia, and singled out three of them on account of their skills or fame.[111] Other papers were more specific, providing information about the number of Jews among the aliens.[112] In a later edition, the *Daily Mail* published a feature article about Nazi policy and fashion in Germany, which drew on information provided by one of the refugee passengers.[113] In other newspaper articles, individual refugees were featured among other, British or Australian, passengers.[114]

The overwhelmingly positive response gave way to a more ambivalent attitude when, a few days after the ship's arrival, eight of the *Strathmore*'s Australian passengers wrote an open letter in which they complained about the refugees on board the ship. They claimed their encounters during the voyage had made them revise their 'sympathetically-inclined views towards European refugees'. According to the letter, the refugee passengers were able 'to spend extravagantly upon luxuries for themselves', which was inconsistent 'with their poverty-pleading appeals', most of them had no intention of 'becoming Australians at heart', and they were 'definitely not the type of citizen Australia requires'.[115] The letter was reported without comment in several newspapers, but the response to these allegations varied. They prompted at least one letter to the editor whose author, another Australian *Strathmore* passenger, refuted them,[116] and the Sydney *Sun*, rather than reporting them, published a detailed and sympathetic article about one of the refugees on board the *Strathmore*, who expressed his joy at having arrived in Australia.[117]

It is important, however, to keep the overall response to the ship's arrival in perspective. The allegations neither triggered nor accompanied a broader debate about the admission of European refugees to Australia. Compared to the controversies prompted by the arrival of Jewish refugees in 1946 and 1947, and of 'boat people' in the late 1970s, in 2001 and between 2008 and 2013, public discussions about the arrival of European refugees in the late 1930s were remarkably low-key.

*

In the first half of 1939, the flight of Jews from Germany and Austria was not the only significant refugee problem in Europe. It was not even the biggest. Between Hitler's appointment as German chancellor in January 1933 and the beginning of the Second World War in September 1939, just over 200,000 Jews fled Germany. In the first two months of 1939 between 350,000 and 500,000 refugees crossed the Spanish–French border.[118] Their flight was triggered by the fall of Catalonia in January 1939.

About half of the Spanish nationals among them were repatriated to Spain that same year; others remained in France or moved on to other countries, particularly in the Americas. In France, refugees from Spain were even less welcome than Jews from Germany. Many were interned in camps, and often lived under appalling conditions; some later favourably compared their time in German concentration camps with that spent in French internment camps. While the popular front government of Léon Blum had welcomed Spanish refugees who had crossed into France in the early phases of the civil war, the government of Édouard Daladier sought to establish amicable relations with Franco and tried to rid itself of his political opponents. The only country that warmly welcomed Spanish Republican refugees after 1939 was Mexico, which admitted between 15,000 and 20,000 of them and offered them Mexican citizenship.

After the fall of France in 1940, many Spanish refugees ended up in German concentration camps. As Spanish prime minister José Luis

Rodríguez Zapatero said in a moving ceremony in 2005 at the site of the former Mauthausen concentration camp, in Austria, where approximately three-quarters of the 8000 Spanish Republicans imprisoned there did not survive, the Spanish exiles 'suffered twice'.[119]

The plight of the Spanish refugees in France attracted attention also in Australia, although, as the historian Robert Mason has observed, the majority of Australians were 'studiously uninformed and apathetic' about what was happening in faraway Spain.[120] A small minority, however, formed groups and committees, such as the Spanish Relief Committee or the New South Wales Council for Relief of Spanish Distress, to assist the Spaniards. They lobbied the government to provide funds for relief operations in France and to admit Spanish refugees to Australia. In April 1938 Nellie Quinlan, the secretary of the International Peace Campaign in Sydney and a well-known communist, wrote to Prime Minister Lyons, advising him that if the government agreed to admit Spanish refugees, her organisation and others stood ready to look after them.[121] Not all those advocating on behalf of Spanish refugees were in favour of their admission to Australia, however. The Spanish Relief Committee's Adelaide branch, for example, warned of the dangers of immigration and recommended that only 'a few of the most urgent cases' be admitted.[122]

In 1938 the government had committed £3000 for humanitarian relief in France, on the understanding that the aid would be 'truly international in character' and that it would benefit both sides in the war.[123] The following year the government was prepared neither to provide further funds nor to resettle Spaniards in Australia. On 22 June 1939 Cabinet decided that no action should be taken to encourage Spanish refugees to migrate to Australia. As far as Robert Menzies, who had become prime minister after Lyons's death in April 1939, was concerned, refugees had no reason not to return to Spain; he told the leader of the opposition, John Curtin, that there was no evidence to suggest that those who returned would 'suffer punishment except for proved criminal offences'.[124] Earlier, Albert Robert Peters of the Department of the Interior had advised his minister: 'It is not unlikely that many of the Spanish refugees are Communists and precautions are desirable against admitting any who are likely to be political extremists.'[125]

On the face of it, the government's decision not to make special provisions for the admission of Spanish refugees but to treat applications from Spaniards for landing permits in accordance with the normal immigration requirements (which at the time included £200 landing money, unless the migrant was sponsored) seemed to allow for the immigration of any Spanish refugees who could afford the passage to Australia and the landing money. But as had happened in relation to Russian Jews some twenty years earlier, and as would happen time and again after the Second World War, Cabinet's ruling effectively meant that Australia excluded people desperate to be admitted. Not everybody who met the formal requirements was granted a landing permit; it was at the discretion of the Australian officials whether or not to approve an application. The immigration statistics suggest that Spanish refugees did not rate highly as prospective immigrants; in 1939 a mere twenty-four Spanish nationals were admitted to Australia.[126]

Eastern European Jews were considered at least as undesirable as Republicans from Spain. The prejudices held by senior bureaucrats in Canberra came to the fore in a report written in 1939 by Thomas Hugh Garrett, the assistant secretary of the Department of the Interior, who had visited Europe to investigate the selection of alien immigrants.[127] Upon his return, he told the secretary of his department – in a letter marked 'personal' – that Polish Jews 'are the poorest specimens outside blackfellows that I have seen'.[128] His views were apparently shared by migration officials attached to the British embassy in Warsaw, who did not consider Polish Jews suitable for emigration to the dominions.[129]

The quota set by Cabinet in November 1938 did not cover Jewish refugees from Poland unless they were stateless;[130] nevertheless, they featured prominently in Garrett's report – as did Jews from Hungary, Slovakia and Romania – because he thought that it made little sense to make a categorical distinction between refugees from Nazi Germany and Jews from Eastern Europe. '[T]heir desire to emigrate to Australia is not for the reason that the attractions of Australia are such that they wish to be admitted in order to improve their economic conditions,' Garrett noted under the heading 'Non-Refugees'. 'They are apprehensive that political changes in the various countries in which they are resident may render their continued living there intolerable. Although they are not in fact refugees, they may be regarded for practical purposes as coming within that category.'[131] As far as Australia's immigration authorities were concerned, however, being refugees did not entitle Polish, Hungarian, Slovakian and Romanian Jews to any concessions; admission to Australia was, to use the words of historian Paul Bartrop, a matter of 'quality control' based on assumptions about racial characteristics, rather than being guided by applicants' relative needs.[132]

Garrett was also critical of prospective Jewish immigrants from Austria, who were 'not as a good a type' as those he had encountered in Germany.[133] The British passport control officer in Vienna explained to Garrett that this was due to the fact that most Jews in Austria were in fact from Poland, Hungary or Romania, and that 'the further east one went, the poorer was the type of Jew'.[134] Given that Garrett completed his report shortly before the outbreak of the Second World War, it had little impact on the selection of immigrants admitted under Australia's refugee quota. But the fact that his choice of words did not raise any concerns at the time suggests that his views were widely shared.

Of those who in the late 1930s were in search of refuge, Spanish Republicans and Polish Jews were at one end of the spectrum; the Australian government considered them undesirable settlers either because of their politics or because of their culture and faith. At the other end were non-Jewish Germans and Austrians, and so-called non-Aryan Christians. The Society of Friends (the Quakers) and prominent individuals – such as the Anglican coadjutor bishop of Sydney, Venn Pilcher, and the anthropologist Camilla Wedgwood – championed the cause of the latter.[135]

In March 1939 the Society of Friends presented sixteen 'non Aryan Christian refugee lads' to the Australian immigration authorities at London's Australia House. The immigration official reporting about the group to Canberra was suitably impressed; in his opinion, 'the lads interviewed [were] superior physically and mentally to the type of British boy offering at the present time'. The fact that they were refugees – presumably, most of them had come to England as part of the *Kindertransport*,[136] the rescue effort that brought some 10,000 Jewish children and teenagers, most of them from Germany and Austria, to Britain between December 1938 and May 1940 – was irrelevant; what mattered was that they spoke English and seemed to be able and willing to work on farms. Four of the sixteen were excluded on medical grounds (one because he was flat-footed); the immigration officer in charge of their selection commented that there were 'many alien migrants offering, and we can afford to pick and choose, thus ensuring that only the best are issued with permits'. The other twelve, ranging in ages from sixteen to twenty-two, were accepted; Harry Foll, as minister for the interior, decreed that for members of this particular group, the required landing money be reduced to £5.[137]

Australia approved the immigration of other small groups of unaccompanied minors from Europe. As early as 1937, a Melbourne-based Polish Jewish Relief Fund had lobbied for the admission of up to twenty Jewish boys from Poland. Although the Department of the Interior was initially against the proposal, citing the usual arguments about the supposedly inferior class of people from which the children would be chosen, in June 1938 Cabinet gave its approval. It stipulated that the children had to be between fourteen and sixteen years of age and needed to be sponsored, but waived the landing money requirement. In late 1938 and early 1939 the education arm of JEAS, the Central Jewish Emigration Agency in Poland, selected twenty children, half of whom were from the small border town of Zbąszyń (Zbonszyn), where thousands of Polish Jews deported from Germany in October 1938 were being confined. The children arrived in Australia in May 1939.[138]

The Australian Jewish Welfare Society also successfully lobbied the government to sponsor the immigration of refugee children: twenty German and Austrian Jewish boys and young men aged between fifteen and nineteen arrived in Melbourne in May 1939; eighteen boys and two girls of the same age group, who had been trained at the Groß Breesen agricultural training farm in Silesia, landed in July 1939; and seventeen German Jewish children aged between seven and twelve arrived that same month.[139] Few of these children had any prior links to Australia. The older children were looked after by guardians identified through the AJWS and the Polish Relief Fund, while the younger ones were accommodated at the Larino children's home, an old mansion in the Melbourne suburb of Balwyn, which the AJWS had acquired.

The Australian government had initially stipulated that all these Jewish child migrants had to be orphans, but those selected were in a similar position as children and teenagers who came to Britain through the *Kindertransport* scheme: usually they had parents who had to remain behind. While several of the German and Austrian parents survived the Holocaust and were reunited with their children, of the children in the Polish group, only one had a parent who survived.[140]

Non-Jewish Social Democrats from Czechoslovakia's Sudetenland region comprised another group of desirable prospective immigrants. These were ethnic Germans who had fled to the non-occupied part of Czechoslovakia after the German annexation of the Sudetenland in October 1938. Harry Twyford, the lord mayor of London, had launched an appeal to provide material assistance to refugees in Czechoslovakia,[141] and he lobbied the British and Australian governments to accommodate as many of them as possible. His appeal had been so successful that he was able to offer to pay the required £200 landing money on behalf of successful applicants.[142] Another champion of the non-Jewish Sudeten refugees was Edward Cavendish, the 10th Duke of Devonshire, whose voice carried weight in Canberra if only because he also happened to be the under-secretary of state for dominion affairs, and thus responsible for the British government's relations with Australia. Both he and Twyford had been lobbied by Wenzel Jaksch, the leader of the German Social Democrats in Czechoslovakia, who had found asylum in Britain after the Munich Agreement of September 1938.

The government in Canberra was receptive to these overtures. Once again, it was principally concerned about the politics, 'race' and employability of prospective immigrants. An Australian diplomat in London was assured by one of his contacts in the British government that they were not communists but 'a good solid lot, bricklayers, etc.'; another contact offered to look through the list of applicants to ensure that Australia would only admit Sudeten Germans who were neither Jewish nor communists.[143] The government approved the admission of no more than 500 non-Jewish ethnic German refugees from Czechoslovakia, who were to be counted among the up to 15,000 refugees Australia was prepared to accommodate.[144]

The extant government files do not reveal how many non-Jewish Germans from Czechoslovakia actually arrived in Australia in 1939; it is unlikely that more than a handful of the 500 places offered by Australia were filled. The Australian government was not alone in its preference for Sudeten Germans; the Canadian government, too, was enthusiastic about the prospect of attracting non-Jewish refugees, and was even willing to accept Sudeten Germans as a group rather than on individual visas.[145]

*

Refugees had a far better chance of being admitted if they were sponsored by relatives or friends in Australia. Frequently, refugees lodged sponsorship forms almost as soon as they landed. As the majority of refugees from Nazi Germany arrived in the twelve months before the outbreak of the war, however, there was often not enough time to successfully sponsor relatives.[146] Thus, many refugees who made it to Australia in 1938 and 1939 left loved ones behind who perished in the

Holocaust. In later years the survivors often blamed themselves for not having done more to secure visas for their families.

Walter Stolting sponsored three applicants. Very soon after his arrival he successfully nominated his mother, who arrived in Melbourne in 1937. Then he tried to sponsor a friend, the actor Erich Kuttner, who had migrated to Italy but was threatened with deportation as the Mussolini regime began clamping down on exiles from Nazi Germany. Initially, that second application was unsuccessful, but Stolting was able to enlist the help of an Australian friend, the Labor member of federal parliament Edward James ('Jack') Holloway, and Kuttner arrived in 1939. As would happen time and again in the case of individual refugees – in the 1930s, in the 1970s and in more recent years – the support of a federal politician, irrespective of whether he belonged to the government, swayed the responsible minister to make a ruling in the refugee's favour.

The last person to be sponsored by Stolting was his son. In 1929 Stolting had married a fellow journalist. She was not Jewish, did not share her husband's political views and divorced him in 1934, after he had left the country. Their only child, Klaus Peter, remained with her. In 1938 she asked her ex-husband to take their son. She may have feared for his safety, because his paternal grandmother was Jewish, and he was thus classified as a *Mischling zweiten Grades* (part-Jewish on account of one Jewish grandparent).

Klaus Peter arrived in Sydney in July 1939, having travelled as an unaccompanied minor by plane. His arrival attracted the attention of journalists and was reported in newspapers across the country; none of the articles, however, referred to Klaus Peter or his father as a refugee.[147] A photo published in the *Sydney Morning Herald* shows him at Kingsford Smith Airport in Sydney, wearing *Lederhosen* and looking unperturbed by the nine-day flight and his arrival in a country whose language he did not speak.[148]

Refugees arriving from Europe could not expect any financial or material help from the government. They relied on relatives and friends, and on non-government organisations. The Quakers provided assistance to non-Jewish refugees and so-called non-Aryan Christians. The most important organisation was the Australian Jewish Welfare Society, which by 1938 had fourteen full-time employees in Sydney alone, who were supported by 200 volunteers.[149] According to Paul Cullen (the son of one of the society's founders and himself once its president), 'The last thing the Welfare Society wanted was that the government should ever have to pay one penny for Jewish migration for fear of a possible backlash against the Jews.'[150]

That statement reflected the mixed feelings within the Jewish community about the arrivals from Europe. While the Jewish community provided generous assistance to newcomers, many of its members feared that a dramatic increase in the number of Jews in Australia would lead to a rise in anti-Semitism.[151] Isaac Herbert Boas, the Victorian AJWS president from 1936 to 1948, who regarded himself as a Jew for two hours on a Saturday morning and as an Australian for the remainder of the week, told an interviewer in April 1938, shortly after the *Anschluss*, that Australia's Jews were 'opposed to anything in the nature of mass migration from Austria'.[152]

In May 1939 the *Sydney Morning Herald* reported that AJWS staff had met ships arriving from Europe and handed cards to Jewish immigrants that urged them to adapt quickly to Australian culture, not to congregate in the cities, and to learn English (with the help of classes provided by the society). 'Above all, do not speak German in the streets and in the trams,' the text advised. 'Modulate your voices . . . Remember that the welfare of the old-established Jewish communities in Australia as well as of every migrant depends on your behaviour.'[153] The AJWS was concerned to direct refugee arrivals away from suburbs such as Bondi and Kings Cross in Sydney,[154] presumably because it feared that greater visibility of Jews would lead to anti-Semitism.

The government, too, tried to keep a close watch on the geographical distribution of the newly arrived refugees. In April 1939 an official of the Department of the Interior noted in a memorandum that a postman in North Bondi had found every single resident in a block of eighteen flats in North Bondi to be a recently arrived Jewish refugee, and suggested that 'the Chief Electoral Officer might be requested to obtain reports from the Commonwealth Electoral Officers of the respective States in order to ascertain if there is any noticeable tendency on the part of Jewish refugees to form colonies.'[155]

\*

The Évian conference had demonstrated that neither Germany's European neighbours nor the traditional countries of immigration (such as the United States, Canada, Argentina and Australia) were willing to accommodate a sufficiently large number of refugees to solve the humanitarian crisis of the late 1930s, and that the British government was opposed to the large-scale migration of Jews to Palestine. This reluctance gave rise to numerous proposals to resettle Jews in Africa, the Caribbean or South-East Asia. Suggested sites included the Philippines, Borneo, Haiti, British Guiana and the Congo.

Most of these ideas were little more than thought bubbles. The only proposal that seemed to have some prospect of being realised, if only because it kept reappearing, concerned the French colony of Madagascar.[156] This large island off the east coast of Africa had first been mooted as a potential site for European Jews in the late nineteenth century. It was put forward again in the mid-1930s by the Polish government. The idea was revived once more by the German government in the late 1930s and early 1940s, and favourably discussed at various times in France, the United States and Britain. In fact, the British government explored the possibility of resettling Jews in Madagascar as late as 1946, because at the time it was still anxious to curtail Jewish migration to Palestine.[157]

From the vantage point of some of those living in the cities along Australia's south-eastern seaboard, large parts of northern Australia were unpopulated. 'I was instructed to inform you that we oppose to [sic] the Policy of the Federal Government, in regard to the Jewish people, and all other oppressed Nationalities,' the secretary of the Labor Party's Newcastle district told Prime Minister Lyons in October 1938. 'It was also resolved that the question of the Northern Territory being handed over to the Jews to form a colony be considered, as we believe that they would prove a great asset to Australia.'[158] Non-Australians could be forgiven for expressing similar sentiments. From a European perspective, much of Australia was as remote as the Congo, Borneo or Guiana; much like the locations in Africa, Asia or the Americas that were proposed for a Jewish colony from the late nineteenth century, large parts of the Australian continent were also considered underused. It is therefore not surprising that Australia was considered a potential destination for a Jewish resettlement scheme.

In the early twentieth century, Israel Zangwill's Jewish Territorialist Organization (ITO) explored the possibility of purchasing large areas of land to establish Jewish colonies.[159] The ITO and its supporters in Australia considered sites in the Northern Territory, the south-west of Western Australia and along the Murray River near Mildura. In 1910, for example, Zangwill asked the West Australian premier, Newton Moore, to 'mark out for us a little country which will become a land of refuge for the Jews',[160] and which was large enough to accommodate 1 million Jews from Russia. However, neither the states nor the Commonwealth welcomed suggestions that envisaged large-scale group settlements with a high degree of political autonomy, and the ITO's plans foundered.

In 1938 Zangwill's plans were resurrected by the ITO's successor, the Freeland League for Jewish Territorial Colonization, which identified the East Kimberley region of north-western Australia as the most suitable site for the resettlement of European Jews; it proposed the resettlement of 50,000 refugees on 7 million acres that were for sale at the time.[161]

In 1939 the Freeland League's Isaac Steinberg travelled to Australia to convince the government and the public of the merits of the scheme. After the October Revolution, Steinberg had been a member of Lenin's first government, but resigned in protest against the Treaty of Brest-Litovsk between the Bolshevik state and imperial Germany. He went into exile in Germany, and from there fled to England when the Nazis came to power. In Australia, Steinberg proved an effective lobbyist: he gained the support of influential church leaders, of the West Australian government and of the Australasian Council of Trade Unions (ACTU).[162] He was not able to win over the leaders of Australia's Jewish community, who were opposed to the immigration of a large number of Jews either because they feared the emergence of anti-Semitism or because they were committed Zionists. Most importantly, he failed to gain the backing of the Australian government. In 1941 the Menzies Cabinet deferred a decision on Steinberg's proposal, without setting a date for its reconsideration.[163]

*

In the late 1930s the Commonwealth Investigation Branch (CIB), the intelligence organisations of the military and the special branches of the various state police forces began compiling lists of residents who were believed to pose a security risk in case war broke out. During the First World War, Australia had interned thousands of German-born residents.[164] According to the 'war book' drawn up by the Department of Defence in 1939, in the event of a new war the number of residents interned was to be 'restricted to the narrowest limits consistent with public safety and public sentiment'.[165] Following this policy, in September 1939 only a small minority of German nationals were interned. They included prominent members of the German Nazi Party and other Germans who had repeatedly voiced sympathies for Hitler's Germany. Among the internees were Germans who had arrived in Australia as refugees.[166] Whether or not somebody had *fled* to Australia was of no consequence for his or her status; as soon as war was declared, all nationals of Germany – including Austrians who had become Germans as a result of the 1938 *Anschluss* – automatically became 'enemy aliens'.

Walter Stolting had been on the radar of Australia's intelligence organisations since landing in Melbourne in 1936. Soon after his arrival, he drew additional attention to himself when he sought contact with the CIB, presumably hoping that the intelligence agency would be interested in the services of a committed anti-fascist with an extensive knowledge of European affairs. The CIB's suspicions about Stolting appeared to be confirmed by events involving Melbourne's Jewish community. In April 1939 unidentified persons smashed the windows of a Jewish library in Carlton and assaulted a Jewish lawyer and his wife.[167] There had been similar incidents in Melbourne in previous weeks. Hooligans, rather than anti-Semites, were widely thought to be responsible.

Stolting disagreed. He approached Jewish community leaders and suggested to them that the 'hooliganism' could well be the work of Nazis trying to stir up anti-Semitic sentiments. He recommended that, if the police were unable to protect Jewish property, Melbourne's Jews should form vigilante groups. Being law-abiding citizens, the Jewish leaders contacted by Stolting reported him to the authorities. Stolting's concern for the safety of Jewish institutions was genuine but the Melbourne CIB clearly thought otherwise. The fact that he was a refugee and the author of a series of articles for the Adelaide *Advertiser* that demonstrated his anti-fascist credentials counted for little.

Refugees could not understand why they were classified as 'enemy aliens'. Was Australia's enemy not also their enemy? 'Isn't it stupid: in Hungary I would be shot as an enemy of the actual regime and here I am put in the camp because I am Hungarian,' Emery Barcs, who was interned in 1941, complained to his wife.[168]

Refugees also protested bitterly about being prevented from assisting in the war effort. In November 1940 the Migrants' Consultative Council of the AJWS wrote to interior minister Foll to assure him that 'every Jew, whatever country he may come from, and wherever in the world he may live, will do everything in his power to help the British Empire in its heroic fight to save civilization and freedom by defeating Nazi Germany'.[169] 'I could serve you as an operator or teacher in wireless Telegraphy, as a expert photographer, as a journalist, or as a translator,' Walter Stolting said in a letter to the Australian Army's Intelligence Section in September 1939. 'Do understand, please, that my disaffection with, or rather against, the Hitler Government is at least as intense as yours.'[170]

But for many Australians, including policy-makers and members of the security services, there was no discernible difference between Germans who had been driven out of Germany and Germans who were loyal supporters of the Nazi regime. According to the Security Service in Sydney, 'a person born and bred in Germany, of German parents, will never be anything but a German at heart'; in the event of an invasion, 'such a person would unhesitatingly resume his German obedience'.[171] In parliament, Archie Cameron suggested that the term 'friendly alien' was a contradiction in terms. He also did not respect the motivations of aliens who wanted to side with Australia against their country of birth:

> [W]hen my country is engaged in a life and death struggle with Germany and Italy any man of German or Italian birth is an enemy alien. If he is friendly to this country, then he must be a traitor to his own, and I do not think it is our part to encourage treason.[172]

Stolting was among the first enemy aliens to be interned. Four days after Germany's invasion of Poland, which triggered the Second World War, and only a few weeks after his son's arrival in Australia, he was arrested, and was forced to leave his son in the care of friends in Adelaide. Like many others among that first group of internees, Stolting was released in December 1939. By then, the initial alarm had given way to a false sense of quiet, because within five weeks of the declaration of war, Germany, aided by the Soviet Union, had defeated Poland; apart from a naval battle involving Germany and Britain in the South Atlantic, the hostilities between Germany and the Western Allies seemed to be over before they had properly begun. This so-called phoney war ended with Germany's invasion of Denmark and Norway in April 1940, which was followed by its invasion of Belgium, the Netherlands and France in May. Suddenly, Britain was directly threatened, which prompted heightened public anxieties about the loyalty of German nationals living in Britain and in Australia.

Stolting was re-interned in June 1940. This time, he was one of many Austrian and German refugees arrested and locked up. Some had been reported by neighbours or work colleagues for allegedly having engaged in suspicious activities or for supposedly having made pro-German statements. For some of the anonymous letter-writers, being – or even looking like – a German was sufficient reason to report a neighbour. 'Looking for spies?' read a note referring to a former member of the Weintraubs Syncopators, which was received by Military Intelligence in Sydney in May 1942. 'Have a look at Mr. Graf (the name speaks for itself) and see if you can see a German officer in mufti looking at you.'[173]

After May 1940, even slight suspicions were usually sufficient if the enemy alien in question was male, of military age and a recent arrival. Contact with a German consulate (which supposedly disproved claims of refugee status) was also grounds for internment. Refugees who still had close relatives in Germany were considered particular risks because the security services thought that the Nazi authorities would be able to recruit them by exerting pressure on their relatives.

There was no loud public outcry against the internment of refugees; historian Konrad Kwiet observed that even the Jewish establishment's attitude towards internees was marked by 'ignorance and reserve'.[174] Yet in November 1940 the government granted enemy aliens the right to apply for leave to appeal against their internment. Four so-called aliens tribunals dealt with these applications. Their recommendations were not binding; in cases in which a tribunal's verdict conflicted with the army's advice, it fell to the minister for the army to make a decision.[175] Also, the onus of proof lay with the applicant, rather than with the security agencies.

Because the government did not reveal the reasons for someone's internment, it was difficult for internees to successfully convince the tribunal they were loyal to Australia or would cause no harm if released. In June 1941 Stolting appeared before Aliens Tribunal No. 4 in Melbourne. The tribunal recommended that he not be released; its three members did not consider him a Nazi but believed he got into fights easily. They also thought, based on his performance in front of the tribunal, that he was prone to emotional outbursts, and that Australians would be seriously troubled by such behaviour if he were released into the community.[176] Neither he nor his lawyer were told of these reasons; in fact, Stolting initially thought that a particularly damning piece of evidence against him was the fact that he owned a coat with buttons imprinted with the image of an eagle, which the security agencies had mistaken for a Nazi emblem.[177]

By the end of 1941 most of the refugees interned in mid-1940 had been released because the suspicions against them had proven groundless. Stolting, however, remained interned. When arguing the case for his continued detention before the aliens tribunal in 1941, the representative of the minister for the army had pointed out that Stolting was 'a man skilled in wireless telegraphy and photography, and if that skill were to be utilised against the Commonwealth, it could be a very serious matter'.[178] The fact that, two years earlier, he had offered to assist the war effort by sharing his knowledge of telegraphy mattered little.

In fact, like other long-term internees, Stolting attracted negative attention on account of his sharp mind. In 1943 a military intelligence officer attached to one of the internment camps considered Stolting 'probably the cleverest in the compound'.[179] Possibly the same officer wrote a year later about Stolting's 'Character & Behaviour': 'An extremely clever & brainy man, is well educated, being able to speak several languages.'[180] Many of the long-term anti-Nazi internees were fluent speakers of German, English and at least one other European language. In the Australia of the 1930s and early 1940s, polyglots were an exception and tended to be viewed with suspicion. The Australian security services were also routinely suspicious of Germans who identified as refugees but who were not Jewish – or who, like Stolting, were Jewish in terms of the Nuremberg Laws but did not identify as Jewish. The assumption that the latter somehow had less reason to leave Germany is evidence of the high level of ignorance in the Australian intelligence community about the conditions in Nazi Germany.

Such ignorance was also on display during Stolting's aliens tribunal proceedings. There, a military intelligence officer who represented the Crown in numerous aliens tribunal hearings seemed to believe that the Nazi Party was a successor organisation of the German Social Democratic Party: 'Is it not a fact that Hitler took over the German Labour Party and called it the National Labour Party? . . . I suggest that the Social Democratic Party was known as the National Labour Party until the advent of the Nazis,' he ventured at Stolting's 1941 hearing.[181] Another member of the security services, apparently only dimly aware of German history, wrote about Stolting in 1943: '*Although* he fought for Germany as a volunteer in Great War I, he claims that his history since then has been that of a Social Democrat and anti-Nazi.'[182]

*

The outbreak of the Second World War made it very difficult for European refugees to reach Australia. Germans and Austrians became enemy aliens, even if they were Jewish, and were therefore not welcome as immigrants. More than 2000 European refugees nevertheless ended up in Australia after September 1939 – not because they were refugees but because they were German or Italian nationals who had been interned by the British and sent to Australia to be accommodated in internment camps. (Initially, these were referred to as 'concentration camps' in Australian phone directories.)[183]

Much like its Australian counterpart, the British government had shied away from mass internments at the beginning of the war.[184] German and Austrian nationals automatically became enemy aliens, but usually that only meant that they had to register with the local police. The United Kingdom and France had declared war on Germany when it invaded Poland on 1 September 1939, but neither the British nor the French came to Poland's military assistance, and initially the war had little impact on the United Kingdom.

In the wake of the evacuation of British expeditionary forces at Dunkirk and the threat of a German invasion of the British Isles, and Italy's declaration of war on France and Britain on 10 June 1940, the British government revised its earlier internment policy. Because it could not cope with the large number of enemy aliens detained in May and June 1940, Britain asked Canada and Australia to accommodate some of these internees, and on 10 July 1940 the *Dunera* left Liverpool for Australia with 2542 internees on board.[185] More than 2000 of them had come to Britain as refugees; most were German or Austrian Jews. The *Dunera* reached Australia on 3 September, and most of the internees were transferred to a hastily erected camp in Hay, 750 kilometres west of Sydney.

From 1940, the government also interned children and teenagers. Most of them were only interned to allow them to remain with their parents. A few of the local internees, however, had come to Australia by themselves as teenagers. Gerd ('Gerald') Engel, who had arrived in Australia in September 1939 as a fifteen-year-old, was interned for six weeks in 1942.[186] He later remembered other internees of a similar age 'who really went quite beserk and who had to eventually finish up in psychiatric institutions'.[187]

The *Dunera* internees also included unaccompanied minors.[188] One was Walter Kaufmann. In 1938, when he was fourteen, his parents had sent him to safety in the United Kingdom as part of the *Kindertransport*. In 1940 he was arrested and then sent to Australia. Like many others, Kaufmann experienced the journey on the *Dunera* as hellish, but remembered his first encounter with Australia fondly, because the soldier guards on the train that took the internees to the Hay internment camp recognised that they were refugees and said they could not understand why they were being locked up.[189] In August 1941 Kaufmann appealed to the Australian authorities to be released, pointing out that friends of his parents, who owned a farm in the Southern Highlands of New South Wales, had offered him employment.[190] He remained interned for another seven months, spending the last two months picking fruit near Shepparton.[191]

Britain also interned Germans and Italians in its colonies in Southeast Asia, and transferred 267 internees to Australia using a converted luxury liner, the *Queen Mary*, which sailed from Singapore on 18 September 1940 and arrived in Sydney one week later.[192] The *Queen Mary* internees also included women and children, the youngest being only one month old. Again, most were refugees from Nazi Germany.

The Australian government readily agreed to house refugees interned by the British in the Straits Settlement and in the United Kingdom. However, it firmly declined to accommodate another contingent of internees, although most of them too were Jewish refugees from Central Europe. For many Jews fleeing Germany and Poland, the most obvious destination was Palestine, which since 1920 had been a British-mandated territory. In the 1930s more than 200,000 Jews migrated to Palestine. The influx of Jewish settlers was considered largely to have caused the Arab revolt of 1936–1939; in order to protect Arab interests, the British restricted Jewish immigration. Jewish refugees resorted to entering Palestine illegally. In November 1940 Australia's high commissioner in London reported that large numbers of Jews were trying to reach Palestine in 'unseaworthy vessels', which kept coming despite the fact that the captains and crew of these ships were sentenced to long terms of imprisonment.[193]

In order to discourage Jews from entering Palestine without permits, the British decided to prevent illegal arrivals from landing and deported more than 3000 of them to the British colony of Mauritius.[194] The British government then sounded out the Australian high commissioner to find out whether Australia would agree to accommodate another 3500 illegal Jewish immigrants in internment camps for the duration of the war, provided that Britain covered all expenses and ensured the internees would be repatriated after the war. The Menzies government commended the British for trying to restrict Jewish immigration to Palestine but declined the request.[195] The following year Australia did accept hundreds of internees from Palestine – but nearly all of them were Templars, members of a German religious sect who had settled in Palestine in the nineteenth century.[196]

\*

The *Dunera* and *Queen Mary* internees aside, only a trickle of European refugees reached Australia in the first two years of the war. Barring exceptional circumstances, after 3 September 1939, when Great Britain declared war on Germany, the Australian government did not admit German nationals, regardless of whether or not they were refugees, unless they had commenced their journeys before the beginning of the war.

The government did agree to accommodate a small number of non-German refugees from Europe. However, its approval did not necessarily result in the arrival of refugees. Thus, in December 1940 the British Foreign Office approached Australia's high commissioner with a request to admit 180 Polish boys who had fled to Romania. The high commissioner learned that:

> Most of these boys are Scouts and Roman Catholics, less than 10 per cent being Jews. Age 14 to 18. Nearly all belong to Polish intellectual class which is singled out for prosecution [sic] by Germans. British Minister at Bucharest reports that boys are of good stamp and will be in serious danger if left where they are.

The British proposed that the boys be 'given agricultural training' during the war and then offered the option of settling in Australia. The Australians were assured that the Polish government in exile would bear all associated costs.[197] In late January 1941 the Menzies government approved the idea, after receiving offers from the New Settlers' League and from Catholic and Jewish organisations to look after the boys.[198] However, the approval came too late. In mid-February the British government broke off relations with Romania's *conducător*, General Ion Antonescu. Later, the Australians learned that the British embassy, before it was closed, had issued visas to only twenty of the boys, and that none had been able, or were likely to be able, to leave Romania.[199]

*

France and Great Britain – and, by extension, Australia – had entered the war because they had signed a pact with Poland, which had been invaded by Germany on 1 September 1939. During the German campaign against Poland, they remained largely on the sidelines, but when France and Norway came under attack in 1940 tens of thousands of Poles, fighting under Polish command, came to their aid. After the fall of France, at least 20,000 Polish soldiers retreated to England, where they regrouped. In the course of the Second World War, Polish forces loyal to the Polish government in exile fought alongside the Allies in a range of military campaigns. The Australian government was therefore not adverse to suggestions to harbour Polish refugees, provided that the numbers were small, they did not include men who could join the fight against Germany, and the government did not have to foot the bill for their accommodation in Australia.

In early 1941 the Australian legation in Tokyo was invited to join discussions involving British and Canadian diplomats about the evacuation of Polish refugees from Japan. More than 4000 refugees, most of them from Poland and nearly all of them Jewish, had reached Japan after crossing the Soviet Union overland. Many had been among some 15,000 refugees who had fled Poland in 1939 for Lithuania. There, a Japanese diplomat, Chiune Sugihara, freely issued transit visas for Japan.[200] He did so in defiance of an order from the government in Tokyo, and knowing that refugees who had only a transit visa were likely to be stuck in Japan; the only places that then still accepted refugees without a visa were the Dutch colonies of Surinam and Curaçao.

In April 1941 the Australian Cabinet approved of the admission of sixty-six Poles and their dependants from Japan for the duration of the war, provided that they were 'of good character and personality' and 'in sound health', and that 'each is possessed of or will be supplied with adequate means'. Cabinet was not enthusiastic about the admission of these refugees; its members qualified their approval by saying that 'we are not desirous of giving effect to the decision if it can be avoided'.[201] The government acted upon the recommendation of Sir John Latham, a former attorney-general and external affairs minister, and since 1935 chief justice of the High Court. In 1940 Latham was appointed Australia's first minister to Japan, while still continuing to serve as chief justice. Latham argued for the admission of a limited number of refugees 'as a practical demonstration of both appreciation and sympathy'.[202]

In August 1941 eighty-three Polish refugees arrived on the *Kasima Maru* in Sydney. When they disembarked they were joined by Hersz Rozenberg, who had boarded the ship in Kobe as a stowaway. Like the regular passengers, he was allowed to land and to remain in Australia.[203] Unlike the refugees who had arrived directly from Europe in 1938 and 1939, the Poles were told that they would only be 'admitted for the duration of the war'.[204] This was the first time that Australia admitted refugees on a strictly temporary basis. The fact that their admittance was only meant to be for the duration of the war was conveniently forgotten after 1945, however, both by the refugees themselves and by the Australian government.

Not all Jewish refugees stranded in Japan in 1941 were able to leave at the time; after the beginning of the Pacific War, those who had not been resettled by Western countries were deported to Shanghai. As the next chapter will reveal in more detail, some were admitted to Australia after the war.

*

This chapter has traced the beginnings of Australia's response to refugees. In the period before the First World War, the immigration
authorities were strict in their application of the White Australia policy,
but they barely screened European arrivals. European refugees – including Russian Jews and political opponents of the Tsar – were able to enter
Australia with ease. Once Australian immigration officials demanded
to see passports and landing permits, it became far more difficult for
refugees to enter Australia uninvited. Thus, between 1918 and 1941 –
a handful of stowaways (such as Hersz Rozenberg) and deserters
aside – Australia was not confronted with spontaneous arrivals.[205]

In the first four decades after Federation, Australia's approach was
designed largely to limit the number of refugees entering the country.
The government was particularly concerned to restrict the immigration of Jews and of people aligned to parties of the far left. Nobody was
invited to settle in Australia *because* she was a refugee. Thousands of
refugees, including Jews, were nevertheless admitted, but they comprised only a tiny proportion of refugees worldwide.

The government welcomed some refugees more so than others. Non-
Europeans were generally barred from migrating to Australia. Until
1939, Germans and Austrians were preferred over other Europeans.
Gentiles were preferred over Jews. And occasionally the government
identified groups of refugees who were considered particularly suitable
immigrants: teenage boys, for example, and non-Jewish Sudeten Germans. But schemes to facilitate the immigration of such groups tended
to fail. And in no case was the government's enthusiasm linked to the
fact that the prospective immigrants were *compelled* to leave their home
country.

The public was neither particularly hostile nor particularly sympathetic to the resettlement of refugees in Australia; the majority was
simply apathetic. When refugee issues surfaced in public discussions,
Australians overwhelmingly argued against the mass immigration of
Jewish refugees, irrespective of the suffering they had endured or were
likely to face. In monocultural Australia, Eastern European Jews, in

particular, were often considered to be too different (and, in the eyes of the immigration authorities, to be an 'inferior type'), but the same could be said about other groups of European immigrants in the early twentieth century, such as Greeks or southern Italians.

Until 1941, refugees did not play a role in the Australian government's overall population policy. That was to change, as the next chapter will show. As non-British refugees began to be courted as migrants, the government abandoned its hands-off approach and tried to convince a sceptical public that some refugees would make ideal 'New Australians'.

# WARTIME REFUGEES
# AND NEW AUSTRALIANS

The First World War had been accompanied by refugee crises of an unprecedented magnitude, with millions having been forced to leave their homes. Forced migration became an even bigger problem two decades later, when the Second World War and the war between Japan and China once again precipitated the displacement of civilian populations on a massive scale.

In China, up to 95 million people were uprooted following the Japanese invasion in 1937. A single disastrous decision by the Chinese military leadership in 1938 – to breach the dykes of the Yellow River in the hope that the flooding would arrest the Japanese advance – led to the drowning of at least 300,000 people and the displacement of millions.[1] As brilliantly captured in Irène Némirovsky's unfinished novel *Suite Francaise*,[2] which is set in France in 1940, millions of people became displaced in Europe as they tried to stay ahead of the German invaders. Towards the end of the war, millions of Germans fled westwards to escape retribution at the hands of the Red Army.

From the vantage point of today, the wars between 1937 and 1945 seemed to have triggered two enormous refugee crises, one in Asia and one in Europe. There were, however, numerous discrete incidents of mass displacement, many of which are barely remembered outside the countries affected at the time. Who recalls now that, after Finland's defeat in the so-called Winter War of 1939–1940, and the subsequent incorporation of the Karelian Isthmus into the Soviet Union, some 415,000 ethnic Finns fled to Finland, thereby boosting its population by more than 10 per cent?[3]

In October 1941 two independent members of parliament switched their support from the Country Party's Arthur Fadden, who had succeeded Menzies as prime minister in August that year, to Labor's John Curtin: nine years after the defeat of James Scullin, the Australian Labor Party was once again able to form government. Initially at least, Curtin's policies affecting refugees differed little from those pursued under Menzies and Fadden. However, exactly two months after he was sworn in as prime minister, Curtin faced a new and unprecedented challenge when the Pacific War broke out.

Until Japanese planes bombed Pearl Harbor, Australia had been only peripherally affected by the refugee movements caused by the Second World War. Even after 7 December 1941 and the beginning of the war with Japan, Australia had to cope only with comparatively small numbers of war refugees. While the figures are small in comparison to the overall number of people displaced by the wars in Europe, Asia and the Pacific, however, they were large in the Australian context – not so much in relation to Australia's overall population of 7 million, but because Australia had never before had to deal with an *unplanned* influx of refugees. Between 1941 and 1945 Australia accommodated some 15,000 refugees who had fled, or been evacuated from, South-east Asia and the Pacific Islands ahead of the advancing Japanese, or who became stranded in Australia because they could not return to their home countries in South-East Asia. The latter included the Malay, Indonesian or Chinese crews of Dutch ships that were in Australia when the war with Japan broke out.

Most of those who came to Australia because they were uprooted by the Pacific War were Europeans who had lived in the Dutch East Indies or Papua New Guinea. Among the refugees and evacuees were some 6000 Asians. Their number included a few dozen Javanese and Chinese men, women and children who had been living in Sumatra and had been at sea on their way to Java when the Japanese occupied the Indonesian archipelago. They were accommodated at a Methodist church hall in Port Melbourne.[4] Also among these refugees was

33-year-old Annie Maas Jacob from the Celebes, her husband, Samuel, and their seven children, who were evacuated on HMAS *Warrnambool* from the island of Aru near Ambon to Darwin in September 1942, and then taken to Melbourne.

The arrival of thousands of Asians displaced by the war marked the first time in the history of federated Australia that a sizeable number of non-Europeans were allowed to enter the country. Some other non-Europeans were also admitted to Australia for extended periods during the Pacific War, irrespective of the White Australia policy. From early 1942 the United States stationed large numbers of military personnel in Australia, or sent them there on R&R leave; they included African Americans, Asian Americans, Filipinos and others who would not normally have been admitted. And in 1943 the Netherlands East Indies authorities evacuated more than 500 Indonesian political prisoners from Tenah Merah, in West New Guinea, to Australia. Most were initially interned in Cowra, New South Wales, but later released, some after only a few months in internment.[5]

*

Meanwhile, the government had to decide what to do about the refugees who were already in Australia and who were (or once had been) nationals of a country with which Australia was at war. When the Labor government came into office in October 1941, many 'enemy aliens' were still interned. They included the majority of those sent to Australia on the *Dunera* and on the *Queen Mary*, and hundreds of Australian residents who, much like Walter Stolting, had been interned because they were suspected of being loyal to Germany or Italy rather than Australia, or because their release was considered likely to 'cause disaffection'.[6]

For the first four years of the war the Australian authorities did not distinguish between refugees and other enemy aliens. This was despite developments in Germany which meant that those considered

'Germans' in Australia were not necessarily recognised as German citizens in Germany. Since July 1933 a law had allowed the German authorities to denaturalise citizens either on the grounds that they had acquired their citizenship after 1918 or because they had agitated against the Hitler regime from abroad,[7] and after the 1935 Nuremberg Laws, Jewish Germans no longer had the same citizenship rights as non-Jewish Germans. In October 1941 a regulation issued by the German government summarily deprived all Jewish Germans who had their permanent residence abroad at the time of their German citizenship.[8] This regulation affected thousands of refugees in Australia. It made little difference to the Australian authorities, however, who merely changed the wording of the definition of 'enemy aliens' in the National Security Regulations to account for people who were stateless but had previously been nationals of a country at war with Australia.

The *Dunera* internees were the responsibility of the British government. In Britain the internment of German and Austrian nationals who were evidently refugees was far more controversial than in Australia.[9] In November 1940 Penguin Books published François Lafitte's *The Internment of Aliens*, a scathing and detailed criticism of the British government's internment policy, with a print run of 50,000 copies.[10]

In 1941 the British Home Office sent Major Julian Layton to Australia to arrange for the repatriation of any *Dunera* internees who were prepared to serve in the Pioneer Corps. Almost half of all *Dunera* internees took up the offer, with the first 139 internees leaving for England on 2 June 1941. They would not have made the decision to return to the United Kingdom lightly; ships travelling between Australia and Europe risked being attacked by German submarines, and indeed forty-seven internees lost their lives on the return voyage.[11] The pioneer corps was not an option for everybody; Walter Kaufmann, for instance, was considered ineligible as both his parents were then still living in Germany. (Later, both were murdered in Auschwitz.) Layton arranged for other *Dunera* internees to go to the Americas or to Palestine. Beginning in 1941, most of those remaining in Australia were released to allow them to contribute to the war effort. But at the end of 1943 almost 500 were still interned.[12]

In 1943 the attorney-general, Doc Evatt, set up the Aliens Classification and Advisory Committee, and appointed his Labor colleague Arthur Calwell to chair it. Calwell was of Irish Catholic ancestry, and strongly identified both as a Catholic and as an Irish Australian. He had been elected as the Member for Melbourne in 1940, and appointed minister for information three years later. Calwell disagreed with Archie Cameron's essentialist view that somebody born a German would always remain a German; he later observed that it was both absurd and unjust to treat refugees from Nazi Germany as enemy aliens.[13] Calwell's position was supported by the other members of the committee, which recommended in its first interim report to distinguish between 'enemy aliens' and 'refugee aliens'.

Evatt backed the committee's recommendations, even though the security services were strongly opposed to them. Four years after Australia first interned refugees from Nazi Germany, enemy aliens were able to apply to be reclassified. Their applications were vetted by the security service. Walter Stolting applied on 17 November 1943. Asked to provide the names of Australians who could vouch for his bona fides, Stolting put together an impressive list of referees. Among others, they included labour minister Holloway, the editor of the Adelaide *Advertiser*, Clive Kelly, prominent literary figures Nellie and Vance Palmer, and Brian Fitzpatrick of the Council for Civil Liberties, which supported Stolting and other interned refugees and had lobbied the government to acknowledge that they were on Australia's side.[14] Stolting's application was approved on 10 December 1943, but his new status did not earn him a release from internment. He remained locked up in the Loveday internment camp in South Australia until March 1944.

Many of those released from internment were drafted into one of thirty-nine employment companies, eleven of which were wholly or in part comprised of aliens. Most of the *Dunera* internees who had elected or been compelled to remain in Australia, including Walter Kaufmann,

joined the 8th Employment Company.[15] Although the physical work –
for example, loading and unloading ships and trains – was taxing, many
of the refugees cherished the opportunity to contribute to Australia's
war effort.[16] But often they were also disappointed that they had not
been allowed to join the fighting forces.[17]

*

In 1942 evidence of the genocide of Europe's Jewry mounted. On 17
December the Allies released a joint statement condemning the mass
murder of Jews and calling for the punishment of the perpetrators. In
the United States and Britain the media's attention to Nazi Germany's
attempts to exterminate the Jewish people led to calls to rescue Europe's
Jews. In the United States, Jewish organisations took out full-page newspaper advertisements to put pressure on the government. A mass rally
in New York's Madison Square Garden, attended by more than 20,000
people (with another 75,000 reportedly having been turned away),
adopted a resolution that called on the Allied governments to approach
Nazi Germany through neutral intermediaries to ask it to release all
Jews and allow them to emigrate. The resolution also proposed the
establishment of sanctuaries to accommodate any Jews who were rescued.[18] Not least to placate public opinion, in April 1943 British and US
officials met on the Caribbean island of Bermuda for a conference to
discuss refugee issues, but little came of it.

There were no similar demonstrations in Australia, but in March
1943 the Anglican, Presbyterian and Methodist churches wrote to Prime
Minister Curtin to suggest that the government reconsider the Freeland
League's proposal for a Jewish settlement in the Kimberleys. By then the
government had become convinced of the need to increase Australia's
population for strategic reasons, and Steinberg tried to draw a firm link
between his scheme and the imperative for mass immigration. 'Australia's post-war plans . . . all will demand first and foremost – people, people
and people,' he told Curtin in September 1943. 'The Kimberley project

appeared, thus, to public opinion as one of the reasonable ways of contributing to Australia's need for population and economic development.'[19]
The government remained unconvinced: having deferred a decision in
1941, three years later it made up its mind and decided against Steinberg's proposal.

This decision was informed by the findings of an interdepartmental committee, which rejected the idea of a 'settlement by a group of any
one single type of alien immigrant' because it feared the development
of a 'new political entity which would inevitably be non-Australian in
outlook'.[20] Concerns about the emergence of non-British ethnic enclaves
were to influence immigration policy until at least the late 1970s. Steinberg, however, did not give up easily. He continued to lobby the
Australian government, but in 1945 and 1946 both Frank Forde, during his one-week stint as prime minister after the death of Curtin, and
Ben Chifley rejected his ideas.[21]

Emboldened by Australia's post-war mass immigration schemes,
Steinberg made a last attempt to convince the government in 1950.[22]
Cabinet once more discussed his proposal, and once more declined it.
By 1950 the Freeland League's scheme appeared to be an anachronism:
economic development focused on the cities rather than on remote areas
of Australia, and the establishment of a colony of Jewish immigrants
ran counter to the ideal of assimilation – 'of one Australian family of
peoples, devoid of foreign communities', as Steinberg was told by the
prime minister's office.[23]

*

In 1925 the Queensland government had appointed a Royal Commission to report on the settlement of alien migrants in North Queensland.
It resulted in a controversial report (named after its author, Thomas
Arthur Ferry), which recommended that the government restrict the
admission of migrants from southern Italy, Malta and Greece because
they were supposedly racially inferior.[24] Before the Second World War,

this remained the only example of an Australian state or federal government being sufficiently concerned about a particular migrant group to commission an independent inquiry.

That should not come as a surprise; after all, in the first four decades after Federation, the overwhelming majority of immigrants were from the British Isles and had few problems integrating in a population in which more than nine out of ten people were of Anglo-Celtic descent. Italians, particularly in the North Queensland cane-growing areas, were one exception. German-speaking refugees arriving in the late 1930s were the second significant group of recent immigrants who were not from either the United Kingdom or Ireland.

In the 1940s the Sydney anthropologist Caroline Kelly produced several reports commissioned by federal government agencies about the settlement of non-British migrants, including Jewish refugees from Nazi Germany.[25] Unlike in 1925, this time the results of the government-sponsored investigation were not primarily prompted by public opposition to a particular group of immigrants, and its findings were not made public. In fact, its purpose seemed to be at least as much to gauge the potential for recruiting more migrants in continental Europe as it was to address issues faced by a particular group of immigrants.

Kelly's views were significant not least because, until the early 1950s, hers was the only research done in Australia on the settlement of refugees and other non-British migrants. The reports produced by her were the first in a long line of government-funded studies into the settlement of refugee migrants. Unlike many researchers undertaking similar projects in more recent years, however, Kelly assumed that she needed to understand both how migrants were – or were not – making a life for themselves in their new country, and how other Australians were responding to them. Some of the prejudices she encountered during her fieldwork seemed almost generic. 'Whoever heard of refugees with thousands of pounds?' asked one Australian informant when surveyed by Kelly in the early 1940s. 'It's anomalous. These people are not refugees in the real sense of the term – only the smart Alecs who know when to move on.'[26]

Kelly's study followed attempts by writers of fiction to make sense of the experience of recent non-British migrants, including refugees. In 1939 Pinchas Goldhar, who had arrived in Australia from Poland in 1926, published a collection of short stories in Yiddish, *Dertseylungen fun Oystralye* ('Stories from Australia'); two years later another acclaimed writer of Yiddish fiction, Herz Bergner, a native of Galicia who had migrated to Australia in 1938, followed with *Dos naye hoyz* ('The New House'), which, like Goldhar's book, depicted the lives of non-British Jewish immigrants in Australia.[27]

\*

After the arrival of the refugees aboard the *Kasima Maru* from Japan in August 1941, Australia agreed to accept three more small groups of Polish refugees. But very few of them were able to make their way to Australia. All were among the hundreds of thousands of Polish nationals who had fled to the Soviet Union after Germany's occupation of western Poland, or had been deported from eastern Poland by the Soviets following the partition of Poland in September 1939.[28] Of the latter, many ended up in forced labour camps; others were banished to remote areas of Siberia. While the Australian government was willing to authorise the admission of some of these Poles with the proviso that the Polish government in exile would sponsor them, it required the cooperation of the Soviet authorities in tracing people, and then in providing them with the necessary exit permits. After its annexation of eastern Poland, the Soviet Union no longer regarded people born there as Polish citizens. Thus, in 1943 the Australian legation in Moscow informed Canberra that exit permits could not be secured for six of the Poles on the list of approved migrants because, 'as inhabitants of Western Ukraine or Belo Russia', they had become 'by Soviet Decree of 29 November 1939 Soviet citizens'.[29]

A few weeks after Germany's invasion of the Soviet Union in June 1941, the Polish government in exile signed a treaty with the Soviet

Union, which provided for the formation of a Polish army in the Soviet Union, and for the release of the Poles who had been incarcerated. As a result of this so-called amnesty, almost 400,000 Polish citizens, about a quarter of them Jewish, were freed. They included a large number of unaccompanied children. Many of the exiles tried to make their way to the south-east of the Soviet Union, where the Polish army – usually referred to by the name of its commander, Władysław Anders – was raised. Between March and September 1942 the Anders Army, accompanied by tens of thousands of civilians, was evacuated to Iran and put under British command. Many of the civilians were then temporarily settled in India, British colonies in Africa, Lebanon and Palestine. Smaller contingents were accommodated in Mexico and New Zealand.

In December 1943 New Zealand's prime minister, Peter Fraser, suggested that his country could take in Polish orphans from Iran until the end of the war. In November of the following year 834 Poles, including 732 children, arrived in Wellington on board an American troopship. They were accommodated at the former Pahiatua internment camp. After the war they were all given the choice to remain in New Zealand, and nearly all did.[30]

In late 1944, after the children's arrival in New Zealand, the Australian government toyed for a while with the idea of emulating the New Zealand model. Its conditions did not seem particularly onerous. 'The Polish Government undertakes to pay for everything, i.e. their full maintenance in Australia,' Polish consul-general Ladislas Adam de Noskowski assured the acting prime minister, Frank Forde. 'There is a chance that a large proportion of them will remain permanently in Australia. They will bring with them their own teachers, a certain number of whom are adults. The only thing that would be required would be for the Australian Government to supply teachers to teach English.'

During the war, Australia also admitted a prominent political refugee, former Russian prime minister Alexander Kerensky, who had been deposed by the Bolsheviks in 1917. Kerensky was stateless and living in exile in the United States. He was married to an Australian, Lydia Ellen

('Nell') Tritton. In 1944 the Kerenskys applied for a landing permit to visit Nell's parents. The Department of the Interior initially rejected Alexander Kerensky's application (while raising no objections to his wife's visit), but in March 1945, after representations by Nell's father, a wealthy Brisbane furniture retailer, and having been assured that the Kerenskys would come to Australia 'purely in a private capacity' and that the United States government had not been 'embarrassed in their relations with the Soviet Union' on account of granting Kerensky permanent residence, interior minister Joe Collings approved the request.[31] A few months after their arrival in Brisbane, Nell Kerensky died; soon afterwards her husband returned to the United States – without having caused embarrassment to the Australian government.

\*

While Australia was not in a position to substantially alleviate the problem of displaced people in Europe and Asia during the war, it contributed generously to a large international humanitarian operation. Even more so than the First World War, the conflicts between 1937 and 1945 were accompanied by mass displacements and caused the large-scale destruction of infrastructure in much of Europe, and in East and South-east Asia. In June 1943 US president Franklin D. Roosevelt therefore proposed the establishment of an international relief organisation to provide assistance to victims of war in areas liberated from the Axis powers. Six months later, delegates of forty-four nations, including Australia, signed a document that established the United Nations Relief and Rehabilitation Administration (UNRRA). The agency, which in 1945 became part of the United Nations, was particularly active in 1945 and 1946, when it provided food and shelter to millions. At the peak of its operations, in mid-1946, UNRRA had nearly 25,000 staff.[32]

UNRRA was largely funded by the United States, which contributed US$2.65 billion of its US$3.65 billion overall budget. In relation to their total government expenditure, other nations also made significant cash and in-kind contributions. Australia was one of them: in November 1944 the government authorised the appropriation of £12 million (approximately US$38 million) for UNRRA; subsequently, it doubled that amount.[33] In fact, Australia was the fourth-largest contributor to UNRRA funds (after the United States, the United Kingdom and Canada), which prompted the government to seek a seat on the organisation's governing council.[34]

The government's decision to be a major donor to UNRRA had significant benefits for the Australian economy. At least 90 per cent of Australia's contribution was spent on purchasing Australian goods, which were then shipped to Europe or China. Australia provided hundreds of commodities to UNRRA, ranging from baby scales to locomotives. In terms of value, raw wool was by far the largest item.[35]

At no stage did the Australian government contemplate resettling some of the people cared for by UNRRA. While it did not side with the Soviet Union, which expected UNRRA to facilitate the repatriation of its citizens and was opposed to their resettlement in third countries, Australia perceived UNRRA as a relief agency, rather than one that was engaged in facilitating population movements to third countries.

*

John Curtin died in office on 5 July 1945. After a one-week interregnum when the country was led by Frank Forde, Ben Chifley, who had been treasurer under Curtin, was sworn in as Australia's sixteenth prime minister. At a first glance, the changes he made to the line-up of his ministry seemed insignificant. Chifley remained treasurer, and the key members of Curtin's last cabinet also retained their portfolios. In one crucial respect, however, Chifley's front bench differed from that of his predecessor: he created a new position, appointing Arthur Calwell as Australia's first minister for immigration.

For several reasons Calwell was an obvious choice. On account of his advocacy for internees, he had a reputation for being interested in the welfare of migrants. In the 1930s, both Chifley and Calwell had been hostile to the idea of immigration-driven population growth. In 1931 Chifley had praised the Labor government of James Scullin for having 'stopped the flood of foreign immigrants into Australia'.[36] Both changed their tune during the war; Calwell, in particular, became a convert to the push for a bigger Australia, not least because he was concerned about Australia's vulnerability to an invasion from the north.[37] In November 1941, before the beginning of the Pacific War, Calwell said in parliament:

> There is no need for the nations to the north of us to cast covetous eyes on Australia and fight a way into it if the present trend continues, because they need wait only a generation or two until we are so reduced in numbers that they will be able to walk into Australia in much the same way as Captain Cook did 150 years ago against the boomerangs and spears of the aborigines.[38]

Ten months later Calwell told his parliamentary colleagues that even if Australia were to win the war, it would not continue to be a 'white man's country' unless it had a population of 40 million.[39]

Calwell was not alone: Curtin, Evatt, Collings and deputy prime minister Forde all supported rapid population growth.[40] And in October 1944, an interdepartmental committee appointed by Cabinet had recommended that Australia pursue a 'vigorous policy of white alien immigration', and in doing so consider 'refugees and displaced persons' as prospective immigrants.[41]

Chifley's decision to put Calwell in charge of the immigration portfolio was an inspired choice also because Calwell was well connected within the union movement, which had historically been opposed to large-scale immigration. As would become evident, Calwell was not easily deterred from pursuing goals he had set himself, however ambitious they might seem. And he was endowed with seemingly boundless energy. In the first months after his appointment, that was put to use as he set up a Department of Immigration.

Its beginnings were modest. Initially, it employed only twenty-four staff, half of them based in London and, according to Calwell's recollections, 'engaged almost exclusively in making arrangements for the British wives and children of Australian servicemen to come to Australia'.[42] Others were facilitating the repatriation of Australians who had become stranded in Europe; in its early days the immigration department was also responsible for providing consular assistance to Australians overseas.[43] There seemed little scope to use the department to inaugurate a new large-scale immigration program.

During Calwell's four and a half years in office, he oversaw the department's rapid expansion, which set Australia on a course to growth through immigration. Since 1945, no Australian government has repudiated the idea that Australia benefits from immigration. Over the years, various leading Australian politicians have publicly demanded that the level of immigration be substantially reduced; during the 2010 federal election campaign, the then prime minister, Julia Gillard, said that the country 'should not hurtle down the track towards a big population'.[44] But only one prime minister authorised a significant deliberate reduction of the immigration program: in the early 1970s, Gough Whitlam oversaw a rapid decline in the level of immigration; by 1975 net overseas migration was at 13,515, which was the lowest since 1947.[45] Whitlam was never a champion of large-scale immigration, but he was not opposed to immigration per se, and the reduction of Australia's immigration program between 1972 and 1975 was due to economic circumstances as much as to any reservations he had.

Calwell and his fledgling department also laid the foundations for Australia's approach to refugees today, which includes the controlled admission of some refugees and the exclusion of others. Ever since its beginnings in 1945, the immigration department has had two key roles: to facilitate population growth through an immigration program, and to exercise tight control over which non-citizens are allowed to enter Australia. Calwell's tenure was marked by a particularly aggressive approach to both tasks. He initiated an unprecedented mass

immigration program, and he was uncompromising in his upholding
of the White Australia policy, even if this meant the deportation of
long-time Australian residents, including refugees, whose cause attracted
widespread popular support.[46]

While Calwell is rightly credited with being the architect of the
post-war mass immigration schemes, the immigration of people from
outside the British Isles was only his third preference. His first was to
increase Australia's birth rate. In his book *How Many Australians
Tomorrow?*, published in 1945, he wrote: 'Our first task is to ennoble
motherhood.'[47] However, by 1945 it had become evident that a rise in
the fertility rate would not substantially increase Australia's population. In 1942 government-commissioned reports by the demographer
W. D. ('Mick') Borrie had found that Australia's fertility was declining
to the extent that births were below replacement levels.[48] Calwell's second preference was to recruit migrants in Britain and Ireland. And only
after both these options proved insufficient to significantly increase
Australia's population, he turned his attention to the recruitment of
immigrants from continental Europe.

In September 1945 Calwell expounded on his third preference in
parliament: 'If we do not get sufficient numbers of immigrants from
Great Britain, we shall look to those other nationals who have fought
in the Royal Air Force and the British Army, and can speak the English
language.'[49] Most of these ex-servicemen were Poles, but they also
included nationals of other countries occupied by Germany during the
war, such as Czechs and Slovaks. Calwell was also flagging the possibility of targeting the blond and blue-eyed populations of north-eastern
Europe. 'There are at least 1,000,000 people who have left the Baltic
states of Latvia, Estonia and Lithuania', he told parliament. 'In Sweden
and Norway, also, there are great numbers of people who would make
admirable Australian citizens.'[50]

But at that time the first priority was to bring Australians home,
and a mass immigration program did not seem to be a prospect in the
short term. 'When we have rehabilitated our own people, and when

the housing problem is approaching solution, we shall bring immigrants here,' Calwell said. 'The worst thing we could do would be to bring to this country people for whom there are no jobs and no accommodation.'[51]

In late August 1945 Calwell had sent a committee led by his parliamentary Labor colleague Les Haylen on a fact-finding mission to Europe to explore the potential scope of European mass migration. The committee found that in a Europe devastated by war there was a lot of interest in emigration, but also that it was not possible to bring migrants to Australia. In his memoir Haylen recalled, for example, how in Switzerland the committee had been besieged by prospective immigrants, but that '[w]e missed getting these fine people. There were no ships and they couldn't wait. This was the trouble everywhere.'[52] The committee reported favourably on the availability of suitable migrants, both in Britain and in continental Europe, but due to a lack of shipping the government was not in a position to follow up on the report's recommendations.[53]

Perhaps a more important consequence of the tour was the fact that, in future years, the men who had visited Europe together in 1945 were able to lend support to the Chifley and Menzies governments' immigration programs. In 1947 members of the fact-finding mission formed the nucleus of the first Commonwealth Immigration Advisory Council. They included Haylen and several highly influential union and industry federation representatives, who could easily have opposed Calwell's policies but had been cleverly co-opted by him, such as ACTU secretary Albert Ernest Monk, ACTU vice-president Robert Arthur King, and the conservative David Olof August Oberg of the Australian Council of Employers' Federations.

Today, Calwell is sometimes credited with single-handedly convincing a reluctant Australian public to accept the immigration of hundreds of thousands of non-British migrants. Admittedly, in the immediate post-war years many Australians were sceptical about immigration from continental Europe. The federal opposition, however, did not need to be convinced of the benefits of mass immigration schemes.

As early as August 1945 Robert Menzies advocated the adoption of an 'adventurous policy of migration'. He said that in order to successfully attract large numbers of migrants, Australia 'must be prepared to take risks with some of our standards of perfection'. He suggested welcoming 'all who have the vigour and enterprise to come here', including immigrants from continental Europe and the United States, rather than just 'a few carefully handpicked people who, we think, are of our own kind'.[54] Arguably, while Calwell was willing to wait until all Australians had been repatriated and the shortage of housing had been alleviated, Menzies was far more impatient; for him, mass immigration could not begin soon enough.

*

In Princes Park in the Melbourne suburb of Caulfield South, a plaque installed in 1995 by the Jewish National Fund of Australia informs passers-by that a small grove of trees there was planted in memory of Calwell, 'whose humanitarian policy opened Australia's shores to the victims of the Holocaust'. Even before the end of the war, representatives of Australia's Jewish community had lobbied the Curtin government to admit Jewish survivors to Australia.

In his memoirs Calwell reported that, soon after his appointment as immigration minister, he was visited by Alec Masel, the president of the Executive Council of Australian Jewry, and asked to facilitate family reunions of Australian Jews and those of their relatives in Europe who had survived the genocide. On 22 August Calwell decided – according to his memoirs, without first seeking Chifley's approval – that the parents, children and siblings of members of Australia's Jewish community would be admitted to Australia, provided that three conditions were met: they had to have spent the war years in labour or concentration camps, they had to organise and pay for their own transport, and their families in Australia had to guarantee their upkeep for five years. The first condition excluded survivors who had fled to the Soviet Union or China, but Calwell successively widened the criteria, and in November extended Australia's invitation to cover all relatives.

Nominations were vetted by Australian Jewish organisations, which also provided secretarial staff to assist with the issuing of entry permits. According to Calwell, he 'automatically approved of each list [of nominees] because I trusted my Jewish friends and they trusted me'.[55] The innovation of Calwell's policy has often been overlooked.[56] It was a significant departure from what had been announced by McEwen in December 1938, both because the immigration authorities did not put an upper limit on the number of migrants who would be accepted, and because they were not prominently involved in the selection process.

Although Calwell tried to keep the details of his decision under wraps, sections of the Australian media soon began criticising his presumed decision to admit Jewish refugees from Europe. In January 1946, before any of the refugees had arrived, *Smith's Weekly* claimed that Calwell was giving preferential treatment to Jewish migrants – the paper referred to them as 'refugees' in quotation marks – while Australian servicemen and their brides were stranded in Britain. As Australia provided neither financial assistance nor shipping berths to Jewish immigrants, these claims were without foundation. *Smith's Weekly* also suggested that a large number of Jewish refugees were about to migrate to Australia. According to the article, 550 refugees had already been granted landing permits, 'and another "selected" 2000 have been signed up for Australia at the earliest opportunity'.[57]

Calwell was initially unwilling to engage with the xenophobic – if not anti-Semitic – critics of his immigration policy, perhaps in the hope that he could thereby deprive them of publicity. It was not until March 1946 that he explained in parliament his policy of making 'a humanitarian gesture to those long-suffering victims of Nazi tyranny'.[58] A few months afterwards he ordered his department to restrict the admission of Jewish immigrants; ships destined for Australian ports were not allowed to carry more than 25 per cent Jewish passengers. However, this quota was difficult to implement, and in at least two instances the government made exceptions.[59]

Throughout 1946, the number of Jewish migrants arriving under the government's policy remained small. The overwhelming majority of those who had survived the Holocaust and wanted to migrate to Australia were in Central and Western Europe. Jews fleeing Nazi Germany or the countries occupied by it had also become stranded in other parts of the world; now that the war was over, they were anxious to move on. About 18,000 Jewish refugees from Germany and Austria had sought refuge in Shanghai, which already harboured a substantial community of recent Eastern European Jewish émigrés. In the early stages of the Pacific War the Japanese had taken to Shanghai more than a thousand Polish Jewish refugees who had reached Japan and failed to secure resettlement elsewhere. From 1943, the vast majority of Jewish refugees in Shanghai were confined to a designated 'restricted area for stateless refugees', which is often referred to as the Shanghai Ghetto.[60]

Eleven refugees from Shanghai had arrived in Australia in late December of 1941 – without prior approval by the immigration authorities. They had worked for the British Ministry of Information and been evacuated on an American ship, the *Cape Fairweather*, just before Japan seized control of Shanghai's International Settlement.[61] They were an illustrious group. Among them was Mark Siegelberg, a Kiev-born Viennese Jew who had been a prominent journalist and imprisoned in the Buchenwald and Dachau concentration camps before escaping to Shanghai; in Australia he became the founding editor of the German language newspaper *Neue Welt*. They also included the actress Eva Schwarcz (née Baruch), and the writer Adolf Josef Storfer, who today is best known as co-editor of the collected works of Sigmund Freud.[62]

After 1941, the route from Shanghai to Australia was closed. Refugees from Shanghai began arriving again from March 1946. For them, as for Jewish survivors in Europe, it was far easier to obtain a landing permit than a berth on a ship bound for Australia. In July 1946, 299 refugees who already held landing permits for Australia travelled from

Shanghai to Hong Kong because they had been told that the Australian troop carrier *Duntroon* would be able to take them to Australia.
However, the Australian government withdrew its offer of transport for
this group of refugees because it felt that the arrival of such a large group
of Jewish immigrants would attract unfavourable publicity.[63] It was only
after they had been encamped for several months in the ballroom of a
Hong Kong hotel that the refugees were eventually able to continue
their journey to Australia.

Throughout 1946, Australian newspapers repeatedly claimed that
'thousands' of Jewish migrants, including 2500 in Shanghai alone, were
in possession of landing permits and were just waiting for an opportunity to travel to Australia.[64] In October 1946 and again in January 1947,
the public's anxieties were aroused by the arrival of ships carrying Jewish immigrants. The first was the P&O liner *Strathmore*, the same ship
that had brought hundreds of European refugees to Australia in May
1939. First news of the *Strathmore*'s arrival in early October 1946 suggested that it was bringing more of the long-awaited British war brides
to Australia. 'Five servicemen's wives and five children and 35 fiancees
of servicemen will disembark at Melbourne,' the *Argus* reported ten
days before the ship's expected arrival in Fremantle, its first port of call
in Australia.[65] 'Record batch of fiancees,' the Adelaide *News* announced
in a headline, and provided the names of all seventeen Adelaide-bound
British fiancées on board the *Strathmore*.[66]

Then, after the *Strathmore* had disembarked passengers at Fremantle and Melbourne and docked in Sydney, newspapers around the
country reported that some of the ship's Australian passengers were
upset about the fact that it had also brought about 200 migrants, supposedly from Eastern Europe, to Australia. According to the *Sydney
Morning Herald*, many of these migrants 'were women who wore
peasant-type shawls draped about their heads. Others wore jackets gaily
decked with patterns worked in silver wire.' Not only did their dress
sense offend some of the Australian passengers, but these non-British
migrants also reportedly spat on the decks, failed to properly dispose

of fruit peelings, 'hung their washing across the promenades' and spoke seventeen different languages, including Hebrew, 'Egyptian', 'Czecho-slovakian', German and 'Austrian'. According to their critics, the ship should not have carried any non-British passengers in the first place.

One of the Australian passengers, a Melbourne car importer, was quoted as saying, 'It staggers me that Australia should have to rely for its population on the type of people that this ship brought.' He believed that '70,000 Australian and British people were on the waiting-list for the earliest possible passages to Australia', but that they had been denied accommodation on the ship.[67]

According to subsequent reports, the decision to allocate 200 places to refugees embarking at Port Said had been made by the Australian high commission in London.[68] Some newspaper articles suggested that some or all of the passengers taken on board in Egypt were Jewish. The *Goulburn Evening Post*, for example, made the fingerprinting of '200 alien Jews' responsible for delays in the disembarkation of British passengers in Sydney.[69] Most of the reports, however, did not specifically mention whether or not any of the passengers were Jewish – but many readers would have equated non-British European immigrants with Jewish refugees.

In Sydney and Melbourne the report prompted a lively debate on the letters pages, with recent European immigrants defending the refugee arrivals and ridiculing their critics, but elsewhere in Australia the reports were not contested.[70] Calwell remained silent until two weeks after the papers had carried reports of 'Austrian'-speaking and 'Jewish'-speaking aliens, when his nemesis, former New South Wales premier Jack Lang, raised the matter in the House of Representatives. Calwell explained that 151 passengers had disembarked at Port Said, which made it possible for the *Strathmore* to take extra passengers on board. He also claimed that all non-Australian passengers had been sponsored by close relatives in Australia, that 180 of them were Greek, and that they had all waited a long time for an opportunity to make the journey to Australia. He antic-ipated a line of argument he would use repeatedly after the arrival of the first DPs in late 1947: 'We shall have to get aliens as well as British subjects to come here if we are to populate the country.' But he also took a swipe at the tone of the criticism: 'The prevailing anti-alienism is a form of racial prejudice which is almost indistinguishable from Nazi-ism.'[71]

The issue was kept alive by Lang and by reports in the papers. On 16 November the secretary of the Air Force Association claimed to know that 17,000 aliens had already been granted landing permits, and that 'a large number was packed ready to leave Port Said'.[72] In parliament, Henry ('Jo') Gullett accused the government of having reserved berths on the *Strathmore* for Jewish passengers at the expense of the wives and children of ex-servicemen. 'We are not compelled to accept the unwanted of the world at the dictate of the United Nations or any one else,' he said, anticipating a popular line of argument against Australia's acceptance of asylum seekers arriving by boat. His attempt to justify why Australia should not admit Jewish immigrants also echoed the language of the Nazis: 'Neither should Australia be the dumping ground for people whom Europe itself, in the course of 2,000 years, has not been able to absorb.' Gullett claimed not to be anti-Semitic, and that his opposition to Jewish immigration was informed by the behaviour of refugees who had been admitted to Australia immediately before or after the Second World War. They 'have been notorious exploiters of labour ... have cornered houses, and evaded income tax,' he said.[73]

Outside parliament, Lang and Gullett had an ally in Ken Bolton, the New South Wales state president of the Returned Servicemen's League (RSL), who claimed that the post-war refugee migrants were 'German Jews of the same ilk as those who came before', and that they would work for their own, rather than Australia's, benefit.[74] He claimed his opposition to 'Australia being flooded with undesirable immigrants' was not informed by racial prejudice; he merely objected to 'those who are past their prime of life and steeped in the traditions of a decadent old world'.[75]

Three weeks after the exchange between Lang and Calwell in the House of Representatives, parliament again debated the issue. This time Calwell provided very different information about the composition and provenance of the *Strathmore*'s human cargo. He also denied that the passengers in Port Said were taken on board after a request from the Australian high commission in London. While the numbers he provided this time do not add up, his statement indicates that only about a quarter of the passengers joining the ship in the Middle East had been Greek nationals. He said that 'not all of them are of the Jewish faith' – which confirmed, rather than contradicted, the suspicion that the passengers embarked at Port Said included many refugees.[76]

The left-wing independent Doris Blackburn had initially seconded Lang's request that the government make the papers related to the *Strathmore*'s passengers public. Now she distanced herself from Lang's anti-alienism, saying that some of the passengers 'are the remnants of scattered families, many members of which did not escape the bestial attacks of Nazi-ism, and who are coming here in an effort to forget the horrible past', and that some had been imprisoned in the Bergen-Belsen concentration camp.[77]

Calwell also tried to refute claims that a large number of British war brides were still waiting to secure a berth on an Australia-bound ship: he pointed out that non-British immigrants were not allowed to travel to Australia from British ports, that 3500 wives of Australian servicemen had already arrived, and that the 137 women still in Britain had decided to postpone their departure.[78] Similar information had earlier been provided in the press,[79] but it had failed to silence allegations that refugee migrants were taking away places from the British wives, fiancées and children of Australian servicemen.

Then, in December 1946, there was news of the impending arrival of the *Hwa Lien*, a forty-year-old ship which had previously served as a ferry between New Zealand's North and South Islands.[80] The ship was said to be bringing 700 Jewish refugees to Australia.[81] Contrary to these reports, the *Hwa Lien* had fewer than 500 passengers on board. Just over 300 of them were Jewish refugees from Shanghai, whose passage had been arranged and paid for by the American Jewish Joint Distribution Committee. The Joint had also subsidised the fares of other passengers, including some Australian ex-servicemen.[82] In turn, the Australian government had waived the requirement that the ship carry at least 75 per cent non-Jewish passengers. That would have been difficult to enforce; of the Britons and Australians booked on the *Hwa Lien*, most had cancelled their passage after seeing the appalling condition of the ship.[83]

The ship's first port of call was Darwin. Its arrival there occasioned some favourable reports; the fact that the stopover was considered at all newsworthy, however, indicated how sensitive the issue of refugee migration had become. Several newspapers commented that the *Hwa Lien*'s passengers were happy to have arrived in Australia and committed to becoming Australians. The *Argus*, for example, quoted several of the refugees praising Australia. 'General opinion was that Australia would be their permanent home, and they would never leave here,' the *Argus* reported from Darwin. 'Those with children said they wanted them to grow up as really good Australians.'[84]

But there was also some panic-mongering: journalists exaggerated the number of refugees aboard the ship, and the words used to describe its Jewish passengers conjured images of a threatening mass of people.[85] Darwin's newspaper, the *Northern Standard*, suggested that the town was being besieged by refugees, and the *Sydney Morning Herald* reported: 'When the ship berthed at Port Darwin hundreds of refugees swarmed along the wharf and overran the town.'[86] The day after the *Hwa Lien*'s arrival in Darwin, the *Courier-Mail*'s editorial suggested: 'Arrival by sea and air from Far Eastern ports of Jewish displaced persons . . . must start the public asking many questions.'[87] The moral panic prompted Calwell to arrange for Walter Brand of the Australian Jewish Welfare Society to fly from Sydney to Cairns to board the *Hwa Lien* and 'prepare the refugees for Australian conditions'.[88]

Calwell had assumed that negative publicity could be kept to a minimum if Brand instructed the *Hwa Lien*'s Jewish passengers how to comport themselves. However, before the ship docked in Sydney on 28 January, the public's response had already been conditioned by the circulation of rumours about the refugees' circumstances. On 21 January the Sydney *Sun* reported that a government probe had uncovered two criminal syndicates facilitating Jewish immigration, 'one Communist-controlled, the other dominated by White Russians'. The paper drew on leaked information from unnamed officials; it did not provide any concrete information but hinted that Jewish refugees in Shanghai had collaborated with the Japanese occupiers, and that there were links between the Jewish refugees from China and the fallout from the Kellock-Taschereau Commission in Canada, which had been established to investigate espionage after the defection of an employee at the Soviet embassy in Ottawa, and which led to the trial and conviction of a prominent Communist Party member of parliament, Fred Rose. The article also highlighted the supposed wealth of refugees from Shanghai, and the willingness of refugees to pay 'any price' for admission to Australia.[89]

'The news that semi-secret organisations, with foreign political backgrounds, are busily shepherding refugees into Australia must cause apprehension to every inhabitant of this country,' the *Sun*'s editorial opined on 22 January. It associated the Jewish refugees' arrival with two issues that were widely reported at the time – the spy trials in Canada, and Jewish terrorism in Palestine – without providing any evidence that proved there was a link between them and passengers on the *Hwa Lien*. 'The danger of infiltration by professional trouble makers, whether Jewish terrorists or Communist agents, will arouse the natural suspicion of all who wish to see Australia kept Australian.' The editorial used quotation marks both to question the bona fides of Jewish arrivals and to lend credibility to a statement (which read like a quote from a government official, but instead was only a reference to an article published by the *Sun* a day earlier): '[W]hen it is revealed that some of these "refugees" were left uninterned by the Japanese, that "any price will be paid for admission" and that many of them possess huge sums of money, most people will suspect that the Minister must have allowed his sympathy to override his judgement.'[90]

On 22 January the press reported the comments of the RSL's Ken Bolton, who wondered aloud why the *Hwa Lien*'s passengers were able to charter a ship when 'thousands of good-type British migrants' were unable to book a passage to Australia. He also recounted the case of a Jewish refugee who evicted a returned soldier from a house he had bought.[91] The RSL was one of two key organisations that lobbied against the admission of Jewish refugees. The other was the Australian Natives' Association (ANA), which had a track record of aggressive advocacy of the White Australia policy.

In January 1947 the ANA president, P. J. Lynch, expressed his surprise about the fact 'that people from foreign countries, even from Palestine, were coming to Australia', and demanded that alien migrants 'not be allowed to have their own schools and newspapers'.[92] In March, Lynch told the ANA's annual conference that 'decent Australians will not allow this country to be used as a tip for the refuse of Europe'. While he denied claims that he was an anti-Semite, Lynch was obviously drawing on anti-Semitic stereotypes when he said: 'We will not allow these people to drag down Australian standards with their black markets and so on.'[93]

Lynch and Bolton were echoing widely shared sentiments. A Gallup opinion poll in March 1947 found that 58 per cent of respondents were against the resettlement of Jewish survivors, even if such resettlement was part of an international effort.[94] The widespread hostility towards Jewish immigration drew on long-standing anti-Semitic prejudices; it was also informed by recent reports of anti-British terrorist acts in Palestine, such as the bombing of Jerusalem's King David Hotel in July 1946 by the Zionist paramilitary group Irgun.

Arthur Calwell was the only member of the Chifley government who tried to publicly counter the rising anti-Semitic panic. There is no doubt that Calwell abhorred the views put forward by people like Lynch and Gullett. 'If we allow ourselves to be influenced by the cruel racial doctrines held by our enemies in the last world war,' Calwell wrote in the foreword to a booklet published in 1949, 'we will have sacrificed a great and noble part of the Australian tradition which has so far kept this country among the most democratic and hospitable in the world.'[95] Yet he was curiously reluctant to vigorously defend the immigration of a rather small number of Jewish survivors.

Rather than arguing for the admittance of refugees for humanitarian reasons, Calwell misrepresented the situation. On 21 January he said that a third of the 15,000 Jewish refugees in Shanghai were leaving for the United States, and that only 200 had landing permits to come to Australia.[96] He also downplayed the size and impact of non-British immigration. On 27 January, in an address at an ANA function, he said he hoped 'we will be able to bring 10 people from England for every one from the continent', and he believed that, 'no matter from what country we bring people to these shores, within one generation they can become good Australians'.[97] Given that it was unrealistic to expect a dramatic increase in the volume of British immigration, Calwell had already decided to curtail the immigration of Jews. On 23 January he terminated the arrangements that had allowed Jewish survivors to enter Australia without having to meet standard immigration criteria. Justifying this decision, he said that the government had 'gone as far as it can reasonably be expected to go for the present in granting landing permits to people of these classes on purely humanitarian grounds'.[98]

Calwell's call for greater tolerance towards immigrants had the support of opposition leader Menzies, who proved less reluctant to defend the government's alien immigration policy than the minister responsible for it. 'Australians must learn from the history of America that when a great country set out vigorously to attract people, it must be prepared to accept risks and criticism,' the Sydney *Sun* reported Menzies saying on 27 January. 'Australia should realise that it was impossible to avoid bringing some people who, at first, might seem unassimilable.'[99]

Meanwhile, the newspapers kept focusing on the Shanghai refugees' presumed 'fabulous wealth', and it was this aspect that came to dominate the press coverage of the *Hwa Lien*'s arrival in Sydney.[100] The

*Canberra Times* claimed those aboard the *Hwa Lien* 'had huge rolls of money', that more than half of them were charged for excess baggage by the shipping company, and that passengers had to pay customs duty on items such as jewellery.[101] The *Sun* reported that 'one man had declared 70 dozen nylon stockings'.[102] In an editorial published the day after the *Hwa Lien*'s arrival in Sydney, the *Sun* declared its support for Calwell's earlier rejection of 'racial and religious prejudices', but immediately qualified its call for tolerance:

> We do not want agitators bringing their old hatreds with them, nor do we want to see non-British arrivals segregating themselves in 'foreign' colonies and implanting the low standards of continental Europe. Australian sympathy for the Jewish refugees is sincere. We know what they have suffered. But we know also that amongst them are some whose standards of education and even hygiene are greatly at variance with ours.

The editorial suggested that it was up to Australians, and particularly those who were the 'co-nationals' of Jewish refugees, to re-educate the new arrivals and make them 'conform to our own way of life'.[103] But the underlying message was clear: the *Hwa Lien*'s passengers were undesirables.

*

The arrival of the *Hwa Lien* was controversial because journalists and the Australian public assumed – correctly, as we know now – that the immigration authorities had not vetted its non-British passengers. They had been granted landing permits because their families in Australia had nominated them, not because they had been selected for migration to Australia by immigration officials. Although the *Hwa Lien* passengers were in possession of appropriate documents, they were perceived to be unauthorised arrivals, much like the 'boat people' of the late 1970s and of the late 1990s were considered to have arrived without prior authorisation by Australian authorities.

Of course, in the late 1940s Australia had almost no experience with migrants entering Australia without prior authorisation and then launching claims for residence permits. There had been the occasional illegal immigrants, particularly from China, who were usually swiftly deported. European stowaways and ships' deserters, on the other hand, were often allowed to remain. Some, such as a handful of German deserters in the late 1930s and Hersz Rozenberg, who stowed away on the *Kasima Maru* in 1941, were evidently refugees, and were allowed to stay also for humanitarian reasons.

Some five months before the arrival of the *Hwa Lien*, Darwin residents had been enthralled by an unauthorised arrival in the strict sense of the term. And although his admission to Australia contravened the White Australia policy at a time when one of the policy's staunchest defenders was in charge of the immigration portfolio, he was allowed to remain in Australia. The migrant in question was a twelve-year-old Timorese boy, Bas Wie, who also became known as the 'kid from Java'.

At Kupang Airport, Wie had climbed into the engine nacelle of a Darwin-bound plane. He was unconscious on arrival and had suffered burns.[104] Initially, the immigration department said that he would be deported back to Timor as soon as he had sufficiently recovered from his injuries, but Darwin residents, including the Northern Territory's administrator, Arthur Driver, rallied in his support. '[P]ublic opinion here is that the boy's courage deserves more than his return to a place he did not like, and which he was prepared to leave in so perilous a fashion,' Melbourne's *Herald* newspaper reported about the mood in Darwin.[105]

Calwell was not easily persuaded by a media campaign, but he was receptive to representations made by Driver, a former public works engineer who had become a senior army officer during the Second World War, and who had offered to employ Wie in his household. A month after his arrival, Wie was granted permission to remain in Australia for twelve months, although the immigration department had reservations. 'The longer this boy remains the more awkward his case is going to become,' a departmental officer noted in October 1947. 'If permitted to remain the decision will be quoted by others as a precedent for many years to come.'[106]

Having left a place he did not like did not make Bas Wie a refugee, and nor was he labelled a refugee either by the Darwin public or by the immigration department. Yet Darwin residents embraced him also because he was thought to have fled an intolerable life, rather than because he was attracted by the prospect of living in Australia. Media reports foregrounded Wie's identity as somebody who had fled to Australia, both in the late 1940s and early 1950s and more recently, when Wie's arrival in Darwin has been remembered as an escape, and his story is mentioned in the context of a history of child asylum seekers.[107] The immigration department was also asked to ensure that he not be exposed to a risk of persecution; from Brisbane, Mohamad Bondan, one of the leaders of the Indonesian independence activists in Australia, asked Calwell to ensure that Wie not be repatriated to Dutch-held territory.[108]

Despite its misgivings, the immigration department periodically extended Wie's permit to remain in Australia. It monitored his education at a convent school in Darwin, his living arrangements – he stayed at Government House with the Drivers until they left Darwin in 1951 – and his social networks. In 1951 a Darwin-based immigration official reported that Wie socialised primarily with 'halfcastes or persons of non-European descent, and it is possible that with or without parental control he may, by gradual degradation, drift into the lesser class of the local halfcaste community'.[109]

In 1952 the immigration minister, Harold Holt, agreed that the best course of action would be for Wie to be adopted by a local family, even though this would mean the department relinquished control over Wie's life. The Northern Territory Supreme Court finalised Wie's adoption in 1954, and he became an Australian citizen three years later.

*

UNRRA was tasked with providing humanitarian relief to refugees and with facilitating their repatriation. However, while the organisation was not expected to promote resettlement, there was nothing in its statutes that barred it from pursuing resettlement as an option. Once it became obvious that many Eastern European DPs did not want to be repatriated, the agency made tentative moves to initiate discussions about resettlement. In May 1946 UNRRA's director-general, former New York mayor Fiorello La Guardia, asked the governments of member countries to propose solutions for DPs who refused to be repatriated, and to advise the organisation of their willingness to resettle DPs.[110]

For the United States government, that was too little too late. It had become increasingly critical of UNRRA because the agency seemed to be interested in repatriation at the expense of other options, and because it effectively provided massive aid to countries in Eastern Europe that were by then under communist control. In 1946 the Truman administration moved to shut UNRRA down.[111] The United States wanted to exclude the United Nations from involvement in refugee resettlement, but the move was opposed by the British government, which preferred a refugee agency that would be directly responsible to the UN General Assembly. The establishment of a specialist agency, the International Refugee Organization (IRO), in place of UNRRA was a compromise.[112]

Although the Soviet Union had also been opposed to entrusting refugee issues to the United Nations, a year after the defeat of Nazi Germany the uneasy wartime alliance between the Western powers and the Soviet Union no longer held. While UNRRA had been the joint creation of all nations fighting the Axis powers, the IRO was already a child of the Cold War and, as the geographer Malcolm Proudfoot observes in his book *European Refugees*, 'from the beginning . . . entirely an instrument of the West'.[113] The Soviet Union and its allies did not sign up to it.

The Soviet Union objected to the IRO also because the organisation's remit was tied to a new understanding of who could be counted as a refugee. Previously, the League of Nations had defined refugees as members of specific political, ethnic or religious minorities; in the 1920s and

1930s the term 'refugee', when used in international agreements, was not generic, nor did it refer to *individual* circumstances. In an appendix to the IRO's constitution of 15 December 1946, a distinction was made between 'displaced persons' and 'refugees'. The former comprised people who had been forcibly taken from their countries of nationality by Germany or its allies. The term 'refugees' was meant to cover, on the one hand, 'victims of the nazi or fascist régimes', Spanish Republicans and 'persons who were considered refugees before the outbreak of the second world war, for reasons of race, religion, nationality or political opinion'. On the other hand, refugees included individuals who were outside their 'country of nationality or former habitual residence' and who were 'unable or unwilling to avail [themselves] of the protection' of the government of their home country. The text also specified that a displaced person or refugee would become a person of concern to the IRO if they raised 'valid objections' to their repatriation. Such objections included '[p]ersecution, or fear, based on reasonable grounds[,] of persecution because of race, religion, nationality or political opinions'.[114]

While this definition was a radical departure from those used in previous international instruments, such as the 1933 Convention Relating to the International Status of Refugees, its genesis had much in common with that of previous definitions, because in all cases the drafters had in mind particular groups of people. In the 1920s and 1930s these included White Russians, Armenians and Germans, and consequently conventions were tailored to meet their circumstances. In 1946 the definition appended to the IRO's constitution was written with former residents of the Soviet Union, the Baltic countries, Poland, Hungary and Yugoslavia in mind, people who were in Western Europe and who, for political reasons, refused to return to their countries of origin.

Australia became a signatory to the IRO's constitution on 13 May 1947, but at that stage the government did not expect the organisation to facilitate migration to Australia.[115] In a joint submission to Cabinet, Chifley and Evatt successfully recommended that Australia join the IRO and contribute £4 million to the organisation in 1947; the submission

also noted, however, that '[p]articipation would not involve us in com-
mitments to take refugees into the country'.[116]

*

In the immediate post-war years, the nation's economy was in need of
labour, and immigration from what had been Australia's principal
source, Britain, was the obvious answer to meet the shortage.[117] The
scarcity of shipping was the single biggest obstacle to increasing the
rate of immigration to Australia from the United Kingdom; in the words
of Noel Lamidey, who was Australia's chief migration officer in London
from early 1946, the question was 'how to beg, borrow or steal shipping
space in sufficient quantities to get them to Australia'.[118] Throughout
1946 and the first half of 1947, Calwell was looking for a means to bring
substantial numbers of British migrants to Australia, but these increasingly desperate attempts to lease ships or make use of the Australian
navy all failed. In early 1947 he identified India as another potential
source of migrants.

Following the British government's decision in February 1947 that
India would be granted self-government, momentum towards independence had quickly gathered pace. Within months of the decision it
was apparent that India would gain independence rather than self-
governing status, that this would happen as early as 1947, and that not
one but two new nation-states would emerge as successors of the British Raj. Calwell and the immigration department believed that white
British nationals in India would be interested in migrating to Australia,
rather than remaining in an independent – and potentially volatile –
India or Pakistan, or returning to a Britain that was still reeling from
the effects of the Second World War; a week after British prime minister Clement Atlee's announcement about self-government on 20
February, Calwell informed Britain's high commissioner in Canberra
that Australia would welcome Europeans evacuated from India, either
temporarily or as immigrants.[119]

The scarcity of shipping affected immigration from India as much as from the British Isles, but at least the voyage from India to Australia was comparatively short, which meant that a ship deployed to ply the India–Australia route could bring far more migrants to Australia than one used on the England–Australia run. In May 1947, the government decided to divert the troop transporter HMAS *Manoora* to India; the plan was to move 850 passengers initially, and to run a shuttle service between India and Western Australia for thousands of prospective immigrants who had registered with shipping companies for a berth on an Australia-bound ship.[120] 'On humanitarian grounds, and because we regarded them as desirable immigrants, we went out of our way to provide facilities to bring them here,' Calwell later explained in parliament; 'they are our own people, and we did not want them to be involved in the troubles in India.'[121] In Australia news of the impending arrival of thousands of British nationals was welcomed enthusiastically. In Western Australia, for example, two Labor members of parliament, Tom Burke and Kim Beazley (senior), led a committee formed to welcome the expected 4000 migrants.[122]

However, in late June, several weeks before the *Manoora* was scheduled to leave Australia for the first of several round trips, it transpired that few of those who had earlier shown an interest in moving to Australia were willing to travel on the troop carrier. 'Troopship travel frightens migrants,' the *Argus* reported on 26 June.[123] By then, Calwell was on his way from Australia to Europe – via India. He had left Sydney by flying boat amidst much fanfare on 19 June, reached Calcutta on 23 June, and arrived in England four days later on a mission to secure shipping for Australia-bound migrants.[124] '[H]undreds of thousands of very desirable migrants were waiting in the United Kingdom, Europe, and America to come to Australia,' he had said before his departure, and it 'was his job to get ships to bring them here'.[125]

Although Calwell would have been deeply disappointed by the lack of interest in berths on the *Manoora* – while in Calcutta he was told that, thus far, there had been only 125 confirmed bookings[126] – he seemed to be thrilled to learn that British expatriates were not the only ones in India who could be enticed to settle in Australia. After 1942, India had accommodated thousands of Poles, including some 5000 in the Valivade refugee camp near Kolhapur, not far from Bombay, the *Manoora*'s port of embarkation.[127] It occurred to Calwell that any berths not filled by British nationals could therefore be offered to Polish refugees.

The presence of a large number of Polish refugees would not have come as a surprise to Calwell. Earlier in 1947, the government of India had lobbied Australia's representative in New Delhi to resettle some of these refugees. The high commission was told informally that the government of India's principal refugee officer was concerned that once India became independent, the refugees' situation would become more precarious, if only because of 'administrative inefficiency'.[128] In April the government of India had submitted fifty-eight applications from Polish refugees for migration to Australia to the Australian high commission in New Delhi.[129] The high commissioner had not been encouraging at the time.[130] Neither had Calwell, who was expecting thousands of British migrants from India and who was determined to reserve scarce shipping capacity for them rather than make it available for non-British migrants. In late May Calwell had decided that the fifty-eight applications could not be considered 'until Australian and other British subjects in India desiring to come to Australia have been provided with berths'.[131]

Calwell's plan to recruit Poles as immigrants was also based on precedent. Earlier that year Australia had agreed to admit Poles from Britain who had served with the Allied forces.[132] Calwell would have remembered that the Curtin government had been willing to admit a small number of Polish deportees during the war, that New Zealand had admitted hundreds of Polish refugee children from Iran, and that Australia had been on the verge of following the New Zealand example.

After his arrival in Europe, Calwell met with representatives of the Preparatory Commission of the IRO (PCIRO), who told him that if Australia were interested in resettling DPs, the IRO would be able to supply the necessary shipping, provided that Australia contributed to the costs. Calwell, with the backing of Chifley, jumped at the opportunity, and in July signed an agreement for the resettlement of 'Refugees and Displaced Persons'.[133] Calwell advised the IRO that Australia would be able to take 4000 migrants in 1947, and 12,000 per year thereafter. In addition to an already agreed annual contribution to the IRO, Australia paid £10 per adult refugee settler as a contribution to the costs of transporting them to Australia.[134] Calwell did not know that the IRO negotiators were stretching the truth about their shipping capacity; at the time, the organisation had only three ships at its disposal.

In 1940 Hope Simpson had found that the refugee 'is an unwanted inhabitant of the world, unwanted in the country of his origin, unwanted in any other country'.[135] In early 1947 that was no longer true for all refugees. Young, able-bodied and single Eastern European refugees living in Central Europe were much sought after, not only by traditional countries of immigration and but also by European countries that experienced labour shortages, such as Belgium and Britain. Immigration officials from various countries in fact competed for those considered to be most suitable among the DPs, and accused each other of 'skimming the cream' by selecting only the most desirable migrants and leaving their dependants behind, often with the argument that housing shortages did not allow for the immigration of entire families.[136]

In February 1947 Emery Barcs had written in an opinion piece for the Adelaide *News* that if Australians wanted to attract large numbers of migrants, they needed to look beyond Britain and the Scandinavian countries, and not base 'admission on unscientific prejudices and insular emotionalism'.[137] Calwell was open to this argument, as long as the integrity of the White Australia policy was not jeopardised. Even before the agreement between Australia and the PCIRO was signed, he decided to make use of the soon to be finalised collaboration. On 8 July Noel Lamidey sent a cable to the immigration department's secretary, Tasman Heyes, in Canberra, advising him that Calwell was trying to have the IRO agree to fund passages for approximately 300 Polish refugees in India.[138] While the immigration department's files do not include a commitment in writing from the IRO to pay for the transport of Polish refugees from India to Australia, the correspondence suggests that Calwell had received such a commitment verbally, and that he acted in the knowledge that the IRO would provide the necessary funds.

From Europe, Calwell tried to spur both the immigration department in Canberra and the high commission in New Delhi to act quickly. For him, the solution was simple enough: a sufficient number of Poles would be selected, they could all be employed by the Hydro Electric Commission in Tasmania (which had already signalled that it would employ Poles recruited in the United Kingdom), and their accommodation could be guaranteed by Catholic welfare agencies. 'I am particularly anxious to ensure that Manoora shall not leave India with empty berths and leave to your discretion to allocate to suitable Polish men, women and children accommodation remaining when requirements for British subjects are fully satisfied,' Calwell instructed the high commissioner on 21 July from Frankfurt.[139] 'Most important Manoora should sail with full complement,' an increasingly impatient Calwell cabled from Dublin five days later, and only eight days before the *Manoora* was to leave Bombay. 'Strongly urge this be achieved by liberal selection of Polish men, women, children . . . Wish to emphasise desirability of including [as] many as possible under 21 years of age particularly children as their successful assimilation can be confidently anticipated.' In fact, he assured the high commission that as everybody under twenty-one could be easily accommodated in Australia, he would accept 'all available within this age group unless something of [a] serious nature [is] known against them'.[140]

For three reasons, the resettlement of Polish refugees from India did not proceed as smoothly as Calwell had imagined. First, the Hydro Electric Commission did agree to take 300 migrants, but stipulated that they had to be men between the ages of twenty and forty, and that a third of them had to be carpenters. The commission also reserved 'the right to discharge from its employment any or all the Poles without obligation to Commission if any of those selected are found to be undesirable or their presence results in dissension or industrial unrest'.[141] The Department of Immigration received a variety of responses from the Federal Catholic Migration Committee and state-based Catholic welfare organisations. While all were willing in principle to assist, they too qualified their offers: they would only accommodate Catholics, they would make accommodation available only for a very limited period, and they would not provide financial assistance to the Polish immigrants. The biggest obstacle, however, was the fact that the Australian official tasked with the selection of 300 Polish migrants was unable to identify more than twenty-three suitable candidates, only twenty of whom actually sailed on the *Manoora*.[142]

Of these, only five were single men between the ages of twenty and forty, and thus acceptable to the Hydro Electric Commission in Tasmania. The group did not include any children, and only three migrants under the age of twenty-one.[143] Calwell directed that all twenty be disembarked in Fremantle. Their arrival was noted in West Australian newspapers but did not generate any publicity elsewhere. On 18 August, three days after the *Manoora*'s arrival, the Perth *Daily News* reported that, according to a Catholic Episcopal Migration and Welfare Association representative, most of the Poles had already found employment, mainly as nursing aids or hospital cleaners.[144] At least one reader took offence at that piece of news. 'I read with amazement that jobs had been found quickly for [them],' a woman from South Como wrote in a letter to the editor. '[I]t is unfair for these migrants to be found light jobs so quickly, while my husband, and other disabled ex-servicemen, are told that there are no light jobs for them in their own country.'

This was not the only complaint directed at the passengers arriving on the *Manoora*. Many among the non-Polish passengers were Anglo-Indians, whose immigration, in the view of many Australians (including, incidentally, the minister for immigration, who had earlier decreed that the *Manoora*'s passengers must be 'of pure European descent'[145]), contravened the White Australia policy. In fact, the *Manoora*'s arrival in August 1947 in Fremantle is today remembered not because it marked the beginning of Australia's collaboration with the IRO, but because of its importance in the establishment of an Anglo-Indian community in Australia.[146]

The experience of trying to recruit 300 Poles in India had a lasting impact. It convinced the immigration department that future recruitments of non-European migrants needed to be undertaken by well-briefed selection missions rather than according to the preferences of a single Australian official. The reluctance of Catholic organisations to take responsibility for the migrants after their arrival must have helped convince Calwell that post-arrival programs needed to be run by the state rather than by non-government agencies. Given the labour shortage in Australia, it also seemed unnecessary to make selections dependent on the requirements of particular employers; subsequently, the Department of Labour was tasked with matching employers with refugee migrants *after* their arrival.[147]

The fact that Calwell's plan failed so miserably could easily make us overlook the fact that the attempted recruitment first of British nationals in India and then of Polish refugees epitomised the minister's opportunistic approach to immigration. His idea to select 300 Poles was not driven by humanitarian considerations, nor by his preference for Poles; he was willing to take whoever was readily available, provided their admission would not contravene the White Australia policy.

*

After the failure of this first attempt to recruit immigrants with the help of the IRO, Australia focused on the refugee camps in the British and American zones in Germany. Once Calwell had agreed with the IRO on the resettlement program's framework, the Australians were keen to move quickly. At the end of August 1947, Tom White, the head of Australia's military mission in Germany, urged the government in Canberra 'to press forward with arrangements' – both because it seemed likely that the first IRO ship to take DPs to Australia would soon be available, and because 'other countries are already at work and unless we act quickly we will miss the best material'.[148]

Calwell and his department had clear views about who constituted the 'best material': young, healthy, non-Jewish DPs from the Baltic countries. The preference for DPs from Lithuania, Latvia and Estonia was not, as has sometimes been assumed, due to the fact that the Australian government wanted blond and blue-eyed immigrants. British and French selection teams also privileged DPs from the Baltic countries over those from Yugoslavia or Poland because of the former's supposed 'hygiene, athleticism, and productivity'.[149]

For the first Australia-bound shipload of refugees, the department imposed particularly narrow criteria: they had to be single, between the ages of fifteen and thirty-five, and physically fit. Vincent Greenhalgh, the most senior of the immigration officials dispatched to Germany, believed that the standard of that first batch was indeed excellent; of 843 DPs, only twenty-three were 'below the Team's best gradings'.[150] (That not all of them were single became apparent when, a few weeks after their arrival, one pregnant 'single woman' asked for her husband, who was still in Germany, to be allowed to join her.[151])

The first transport of DPs left the German port of Bremerhaven on 30 October 1947 aboard the *General Stuart Heintzelman*, a US Army troopship on loan to the IRO. Greenhalgh described their departure for Tasman Heyes:

> I wish you could have seen them coming aboard. We stood near the head of the gangway and watched them. They were a pretty shabby lot, the men at any rate, and very tired and dirty, and they were staggering under the weight of their baggage, but nearly everyone of them looked happy and couldn't quite believe it. It was a moving sight, and I think all the members of the Selection Team were rather touched by it.[152]

When the *Heintzelman* arrived in Fremantle, its passengers were each given a letter from the immigration minister. 'You will find in this country the freedom of life which has been denied to you for years, and I am sure you will soon settle down happily in our midst and become thoroughly Australian in your outlook,' Calwell told them. He believed that the success of the DP program depended on how the *Heintzelman* refugees were viewed. 'You are the first party of displaced persons from Europe to arrive in Australia, and as such, the eyes of our people will be upon you,' he wrote, ignoring the fact that some DPs had already made their own way to Australia. 'I know you will not fail us and we will not fail you.'[153]

The stringent selection criteria were also designed to win over a sceptical Australian public which was unprepared for the arrival of thousands of DPs. Only ten weeks before Calwell signed the agreement with the IRO, the Commonwealth Immigration Advisory Council had warned the government that '[t]he introduction of foreign migrants in considerable numbers before the flow of British migrants reached sub-stantial proportions, would adversely affect the smooth assimilation of foreign migrants in general'.[154] However, Calwell believed he would be able to introduce substantial numbers of non-British migrants if their arrival was supported by a large public education campaign, and if they were people whose appearance and identity would raise no objections in the first place.

The campaign included brochures prepared by the Department of Information, a travel book by the writer Frank Clune, who was paid to travel to European DP camps and write about his impressions, and a film. Concerning Calwell's latter proviso, the immigration department's files include a record of a meeting in July 1947 between Calwell and representatives of the British Control Commission in Berlin, which reveals what he meant. According to that document, Calwell told the British: 'In connection with displaced persons, we want to ensure that they are the very best you have, and people who will be acceptable to the Australian people.' Perhaps remembering the newspaper coverage of the *Hwa Lien*'s arrival earlier that year, Calwell specified that a DP would only be allowed to bring jewellery 'sufficient for his own use'.[155] He ruled out Republican Spaniards: '[w]e do not want refugees . . . who have been engaged in civil wars'. Most importantly, he singled out two classes of DPs who, in his view, would not be readily acceptable: Jews and intellectuals (the latter because their qualifications would not be recognised in Australia). 'As a matter of fact,' Calwell said, his government preferred 'the horny hand of the son of toil'. As for Jews, he assured the British that Australians were not anti-Semites, but insisted that 'we will have to handle this matter carefully'.[156]

As it was in the IRO's interest that Calwell win domestic support for the resettlement of a substantial number of DPs, the organisation agreed that those joining the IRO's first ship destined for Australia would all be non-Jewish Lithuanians, Estonians or Latvians, despite the fact that the agreement between the IRO and Calwell stipulated that Australia would not discriminate against prospective refugee settlers on the grounds of race or religion.[157] However, the IRO thought of the *Heintzelman* selection as an exception; while the organisation never complained about Australia's decision not to resettle Spanish refugees, it was anxious that Australia not impose a Jewish quota, as it had in 1946 in relation to self-funded refugee migrants.

The Australians were unwilling to discount DPs' race and religion when selecting migrants for Australia, but were wary of being called to account by the IRO; Noel Lamidey suspected that the organisation was particularly sensitive about the issue because of its supposed 'Jewish infiltration'.[158] Directives to limit the number of Jewish IRO-sponsored refugee settlers were therefore kept confidential; the IRO was led to believe that Jewish applicants were rejected only because they failed medical tests or were not considered employable.

Occasionally, however, the immigration department's discrimination against Jewish DPs became obvious, both to the IRO and to Jewish organisations such as the Joint and the Australian Jewish Welfare Society, although the latter accepted that of the passengers on Australia-bound

IRO ships, not more than 15 per cent could be Jewish.[159] 'I realise that it is difficult to give effect to our policy . . . without disclosing our hand,' Heyes wrote in 1950 after his department had been embarrassed by instances in which applicants had been told that Australia would not resettle them because they were Jewish. He asked Australia's representative in Germany to issue instructions to selection officers 'that under no circumstances is the selectee to be given as a reason for rejection that he is of the Jewish faith'.[160] Overall, fewer than one out of twenty IRO-sponsored refugees accepted by Australia were known to be Jewish. Australia was not the only resettlement country whose policies were biased against Jewish DPs; the acceptance rates of Canada, Brazil and Argentina were only marginally higher.[161]

DPs wanting to migrate to Australia needed to fill in an expression of interest form. This was processed by the IRO, which also arranged for X-rays (to detect tuberculosis) and for blood tests (to detect syphilis) for applicants who had been shortlisted and were being put forward to the Australian selection team. The Australians would then interview applicants, and complete their medical examinations.[162] They were particularly concerned that a DP be readily employable. Selection officers were therefore to tell applicants about the occupations in demand in Australia, and ask them what they would like to do. The immigration officials would then earmark successful applicants for particular occupations – without, however, letting applicants know about this decision.[163]

The decisions made by the selection teams in Germany were not always self-evident. All the women among the first shipload, for example, were expected to work as domestics, nurses, waitresses or typists. The notes about a 26-year-old Lithuanian reveal that she was a trained nurse, had worked as such for eighteen months in Germany and had a good knowledge of English. In the opinion of an immigration officer who interviewed her in Perth, she was 'more fitted to nursing', yet she had already been earmarked for employment as a domestic. A 36-year-old Latvian, who was to be employed as a waitress, had worked as a clerk but had little knowledge of English (and no experience of wait-ressing).[164] In the view of one contemporary academic observer, 'whether a D.P. immigrant was able to follow his prior occupation was largely a matter of luck and the personality of the employment officer'.[165]

The selection process was fraught because selection officers received little training and were often left to their own devices when deciding whether to accept an applicant.[166] The success of applications therefore often depended on the immigration officers' subjective responses to applicants. The notes compiled by an immigration official in Perth about the designated typists among the *Heintzelman* passengers provide an idea of why some women may have been selected and others not. 'Nice type of woman,' the notes read with regard to one. 'One of the best look-ing girls in party and splendid personality,' the official wrote about another. If he had been a member of the team in Germany, he might not have selected the Estonian woman who looked 'very much older than 31 yrs. of age and not attractive in appearance or personality', although she was fluent in English and German.[167]

Even more importantly, the selection officers had to contend with applicants who were not being truthful about their identity, skills or qualifications. Once DPs knew what selection officers were looking for, they often massaged their biographies to meet expectations. 'The scram-ble of the DPs to get out of Germany was at once heartbreaking and humorous,' wrote Kathryn Hulme, who worked at the Wildflecken DP camp in Bavaria, first for UNRRA and then for the IRO. She described how countries of resettlement called for people with particular quali-fications: 'When, for example, we posted the advance news that Canada would accept qualified tailors, everyone who had ever sewed on a pants' button was a master tailor. Our DP nurses with diplomas from Lenin-grad, Warsaw and Kiev swore they had done a bit of tailoring before they studied nursing.'[168]

As Hulme's anecdote suggests, most DPs, particularly those stuck in refugee camps in Germany, Austria and Italy, were anxious to be accepted for resettlement. Caught up in the initial euphoria over the signing of the agreement with the IRO, Tom White believed that once DPs became aware that Australia was 'in the market, and there are prospects of going to Australia ultimately, then many will be prepared to defer their departure from Germany in the hope of getting to Australia later'.[169] Some did indeed believe that Australia was an excellent option,[170] but for many Australia was not the first choice, either because little was known about it or because unfavourable news about the long voyage or the working conditions in Australia had filtered back to Europe.

The Australian authorities tried to counter these impressions by producing publicity material that presented life 'down under' in glowing terms.[171] In early 1948 the Department of Information produced a booklet in German (by then the lingua franca of the overwhelming majority of DPs), *Glück in der neuen Heimat* ('Happiness in the New Homeland'), which featured the experiences of the migrants who had arrived a few months earlier on the *Heintzelman*, to advertise Australia to prospective settlers. By the end of the year, the first print run of 75,000 copies had been distributed, and the immigration department authorised another 75,000 to be printed.[172]

Despite the immigration department's stringent selection criteria, DPs brought to Australia were not guaranteed resettlement. Of the 843 DPs who arrived on 23 November 1947, four were not allowed to land and were sent back to Europe. Three were considered to be suffering from an illness that could lead to their becoming a charge upon the public purse or a charitable institution: two because they were deemed mentally unstable, and a third because he was suffering from interstitial keratitis, which can be caused by syphilis. According to information received from the IRO in Germany, a fourth passenger, a Latvian woman, was a security risk and was therefore also rejected.[173]

Calwell had told the IRO that Australia would be able to resettle 4000 DPs in 1947, and 12,000 per year thereafter. In 1947 and 1948, however, these targets were not met. Apart from the twenty Poles who had arrived on the *Manoora* in August, the 839 *Heintzelman* passengers were the only IRO-sponsored refugees resettled in 1947. Only four

IRO ships arrived in the first six months of 1948. That did not stop Calwell from pressing ahead with ambitious plans. In July 1948 he announced that Australia would match the US government's decision to resettle up to 200,000 DPs from Europe.[174]

Although the numbers increased in the second half of 1948, the overall number of DPs resettled in Australia by the end of that year was well below that envisaged by Calwell. In 1949, however, more ships became available and the figures of IRO-sponsored migrants rose dramatically. As the number of available places increased, and as other countries began recruiting immigrants in European DP camps, Australia relaxed its selection criteria.

The immigration department's propaganda about the *Heintzelman* arrivals suggested that stringent criteria applied to all DPs destined for Australia, and that all of them passed through Bonegilla or other reception centres and had to work for two years as directed. However, there were different rules, depending on who was responsible for the selection, how migrants travelled to Australia and who paid for their trip. Some DPs were nominated by Australian residents and were paying for their own passage, while in the case of others the IRO funded their passage on privately run ships. About a year after the *Heintzelman*, for example, the *Derna* arrived in Australia from Marseilles. Its passengers, some of whom had boarded only in Port Said, included non-refugee immigrants, IRO-sponsored DPs, Jews whose passage had been funded by the Hebrew Immigrant Aid Society, and self-funded refugee migrants.[175]

Initially, the Australian selection officers were only interested in DPs from the three Baltic states. Successively, the immigration department extended its search for suitable migrants to other nationalities. From September 1947 it began selecting Slovenes and Ukrainians; people from other parts of Yugoslavia and from Czechoslovakia were added to the list of eligible nationalities in January 1948; and, later in 1948, Poles and Hungarians also became eligible. The majority of the 10,793 DPs who arrived through the IRO scheme in 1947 and 1948 were from the Baltic countries, but from 1949 Poles constituted the largest national group, accounting for more than a third of all DPs admitted to Australia through the scheme.[176] Other selection criteria were relaxed as well; as other nations competed with Australia for DPs, the immigration department began accepting people who had served in the German army and single women with children. By March 1950 a senior immigration official was complaining that some of the selected refugee settlers were not employable and that 'we are now dealing with the poorer types'.[177]

Under Calwell, 'Balts' remained the immigration department's ideal non-British immigrants. When in August 1949 the department decided to celebrate the arrival of the 50,000th DP resettled under IRO auspices, it was looking for an 'attractive female child under 10 accompanying parents'.[178] It identified a Latvian girl, Maira Kalnins, who was accompanied by her parents and a younger brother and was due to arrive in Australia on the *Fairsea*. The father, Richard Kalnins, was an engineer and spoke some English. According to the Australian selection team in Germany, he had not been able to complete his university education due to the Russian occupation of Latvia in 1940, and had been 'ordered to evacuate Riga in 1944'.[179] Significantly, the immigration department was not concerned to establish what Richard Kalnins had done between 1941 and 1944, when Latvia was occupied by Nazi Germany, and why the Germans had ordered him to leave Riga.

On 12 August 1949 Calwell welcomed Maira Kalnins in Fremantle. Her arrival and the ceremony involving Calwell were reported both in Australia and in Europe (via Radio Australia's German-language program).[180] According to Calwell's press statement, he had flown across the continent to welcome the 'smiling, flaxen-haired girl of seven from Latvia'.[181] However, the immigration department's attempt to use the arrival of the 50,000th DP to promote the immigration of IRO-sponsored migrants backfired when it transpired that the *Fairsea* was actually bound for Newcastle and had been diverted to Fremantle to allow Calwell to celebrate Maira's arrival.[182] And with the benefit of hindsight one could argue that the immigration department picked the wrong girl: Maira Kalnins did not meet the department's expectations because later in life she returned to live in her native Latvia.[183]

Nine months later, for the next milestone – the arrival of the 100,000th DP migrant – the immigration department once more used a refugee from the Baltic countries. Georges Gross was originally from Estonia, twenty-eight years of age, fluent in English, single and, according to Noël Deschamps, the head of the Australian military mission in Germany, hoping to 'marry an Australian girl'.[184] In this case, however, the arrival received little publicity, apparently because Gross was not considered sufficiently photogenic.[185]

Not all DPs admitted to Australia under the IRO scheme had been displaced as a result of the war. Lithuanians, Latvians, Estonians, Poles and Ukrainians had usually ended up in Germany, having been taken as prisoners of war, forced to work for the Germans or imprisoned in concentration camps, or having volunteered to work for or fight with the Germans. Comparatively few Czechs and Slovaks had been taken to Germany as forced labourers, and when in 1947 Australia's selection of migrants began, the number of Czechs and Slovaks on the IRO's books was negligible. After 1945, Czechoslovakia was also the only Eastern European country whose population seemed to have embraced communism voluntarily: in the April 1946 elections, the Communist Party became the strongest political force, and its leader, Klement Gottwald, was appointed prime minister in a multi-party government. However, in February 1948, following a conflict between communist and non-communist ministers, the communists seized power. In the elections in May, voters no longer had a choice but were asked to vote for a single list. After the February coup, approximately 40,000 Czechs and Slovaks fled to neighbouring Austria and Germany. Australia resettled 9142 of the 34,900 Czechoslovakian nationals who were on the books of the IRO.[186]

Australia also resettled DPs who had ended up in camps outside Central Europe, notwithstanding the earlier failed experiment with Polish refugees who had become stranded in India. For example, in

1949 Australia resettled 913 DPs from Tengeru, a Polish refugee settlement in what was then the British trust territory of Tanganyika (today's Tanzania).[187] Others, most of them Poles deported to the Soviet Union and then dispersed after the evacuation of the Anders Army to Iran, were selected in Greece, Egypt, Lebanon and Uganda.[188]

*

Most DPs found themselves in Germany or Austria because that was where the Germans had brought them, but some had fought in the *Wehrmacht* and entered Germany only at the very end of the war, when trying to evade capture by the Red Army, or they had volunteered to work in Germany. It was sometimes difficult to draw a clear line between voluntary and forced labourers. Some people 'volunteered' to avoid options that appeared worse; others expected to be treated as free migrant labourers. Yet while their initial decision made them appear to be volunteers, their working and living conditions resembled those of forced labourers. The Soviet authorities cared little about such subtleties and considered all forced labourers potential traitors. Once resettled in Australia, most former DPs identified as 'political refugees'.[189] Some glossed over those parts of their biographies that dealt with the war years when giving interviews or writing memoirs later in life.

For the DPs, it was fortuitous that the IRO and the various countries' migrant selection teams were not fussed about the exact circumstances under which a person had ended up as a DP in Austria or Germany. Because the IRO was principally concerned with the fact that somebody could be considered displaced after 1945, it cared as much for a Latvian Jew who had been liberated in Bergen-Belsen as it did for a non-Jewish Latvian who had fought on the side of the Germans. For migrant selection officers, what mattered was whether or not an applicant was registered with the IRO; once that had been established, they turned their attention to the prospective immigrant's age, state of health and skills.

The lack of interest in the question of how exactly somebody had become displaced, and the lack of concern about DPs who reinvented themselves as victims of the Germans, also meant that first UNRRA and the IRO, and then the various countries of resettlement, welcomed some people who had served with the Germans and been implicated in atrocities. It was not until many years later that the true identities of some of the DPs resettled in Australia emerged.

In 1961, for example, the Soviet Union requested the extradition of Ervin Viks. He was an Estonian who in 1947 had moved from Germany to England under the European Voluntary Workers scheme. From there, he and his family were resettled in Australia three years later. When asked by an IRO interviewer in 1950 why he had left Estonia in 1944, he said that his country was being occupied and that he considered himself a political refugee. This was enough for the IRO's eligibility officer – but he could have asked why Viks seemed to consider Estonia's occupation by the Soviet Union altogether different from its occupation by Nazi Germany. Instead, he deemed that Viks fell within the IRO's mandate.[190]

The Soviet authorities accused Viks of having authorised and having been personally involved in the executions of civilians during the war. According to information provided by the Soviet Union, Viks had at one stage been head of the political police in Tallinn. The Menzies government declined the Soviets' request. In parliament attorney-general Garfield Barwick suggested that 'two deep-seated human interests' had come into conflict:

> On the one hand, there is the utter abhorrence felt by Australians for those offences against humanity to which we give the generic name of war crimes. On the other, there is the right of this nation, by receiving people into this country, to enable men to turn their backs on past bitternesses and to make a new life for themselves and for their families in a happier community.

According the Barwick, the government may have been presented with a difficult decision, but if it had to make a choice, it would have decided in favour of the right of asylum.[191] In 1962 Viks was tried *in absentia* in the Supreme Court of Estonia and sentenced to death.[192] He was never prosecuted in Australia, although an investigation by Australia's domestic security service, the Australian Security Intelligence Organisation (ASIO), subsequently confirmed the findings of the Soviet prosecutors.[193]

Another case came to light much more recently. In 2004 the Simon Wiesenthal Centre learned that Károly (Charles) Zentai – a man wanted for the murder of Péter Balázs, an eighteen-year-old Hungarian Jew, in 1944 in Budapest – was living in Perth. At the time of the murder Zentai had been an officer in the Hungarian army. In 1948 two of his fellow officers, who were also implicated in the murder, were tried by a Hungarian court and found guilty; a warrant was issued for the arrest of Zentai, who had been named in court as the third man involved. By then, Zentai was no longer in Hungary. He had left in April 1945, and for the next four years lived in Bavaria, in the American occupation zone, where he was registered as a DP.

In March 1949 Zentai and his wife, two sons and older sister were interviewed by an Australian migration team. His migration selection documents record that he had left Hungary only days earlier as he had 'fled from the Communist Party', and that the Australian immigration official considered him a 'fit worker'. He was accepted for resettlement and arrived in Australia in 1950.[194]

Efforts to extradite Zentai to Hungary failed; in 2012 the High Court decided that he could not be extradited to face a war crimes charge, because in 1944 'war crime' was not an offence under Hungarian law.[195] Unlike in the case of Viks, however, this time the Australian government supported the extradition request.

*

Once DP migrants had embarked on an IRO ship bound for Australia, they were deemed prospective Australian citizens. In on-board lectures they learned what to expect and how to behave. In a lecture on living standards, they were told that '[t]he Australian community is democratic in nature and proud of the fact. There are no hereditary titles and no privileged orders.' How did the audience reconcile this information with that provided in a subsequent lecture, on 'The Australian Aboriginals', from which DP migrants learned that they would 'find a country very like your own, with towns and cities like those of your own country, and with people like yourselves', but that there were also '48,000 blacks in Australia'. According to the lecture notes, 'The wild black of the northern coast is finely built and courageous, but those blacks who have come into contact with white men are poor specimens . . . They eat food which people throw from the train and they beg for cigarettes and clothing.'[196]

Upon arrival, the DP settlers were taken to migrant reception centres, where they had language classes, received further lessons on how to become Australians, and, in Arthur Calwell's words, 'generally [were taught] to take the first important steps towards a happy assimilation of our new fellow-citizens into the Australian community'.[197] The first and most famous of these reception centres was the former Bonegilla army camp, 300 kilometres north-east of Melbourne.[198] When the *Heintzelman* refugees arrived at Bonegilla in December 1947, twenty-two German-speaking teachers recruited from the Victorian and New South Wales education departments were waiting for them. They were directed by Ralph Crossley, the acting head of the Department of German at the University of Sydney, who was an acknowledged expert in the 'direct method' of language teaching. When Crossley surveyed the resources at his disposal, he noted two shortcomings: a piano, with which his students could relax 'after a day's strenuous educational work', and a supply of Australian flags and Union Jacks.[199]

'Strenuous educational work' meant more than English language classes. The minister for post-war reconstruction, John Dedman, was in charge of the Commonwealth Office of Education, which had responsibility for the classes taught at Bonegilla. He insisted that lessons in 'elementary hygiene', where the migrants would be taught about personal hygiene and venereal disease, be part of the curriculum.[200]

The migrant reception centre at Bonegilla seemed also to offer an opportunity for Walter Stolting, the German refugee whose tragic circumstances were featured earlier in this book. In January 1948, while working as a storeman in Sydney, he responded to an advertisement for instructors. He believed that his skills and experience would be of use in an institution where German-speaking immigrants were to be inducted into Australia. The education department wanted to hire him, but before it could do so it had to obtain the immigration department's approval. On account of the fact that Stolting had been interned for four years, Tasman Heyes vetoed Stolting's appointment. This was although he had never been convicted of a crime, had not attracted the attention of the security agencies after his release in 1944, and had by then been naturalised for more than two years.[201]

From the point of view of the Australian authorities, refugee settlers brought to Australia by the IRO had to live and work as directed. Those who did not do as they were told – who, for example, quit the job assigned to them without permission – risked being deported. An idea mooted by Vincent Greenhalgh is illustrative of the mindset of senior immigration officials. In a letter written in 1947, after the departure of the *Heintzelman*, he observed that future recruitment strategies ought to be informed by a good understanding of how the first shipload of DPs experienced their resettlement. And it would be easy to learn about their first impressions, he thought, by reading their letters back to their families and friends in German DP camps.[202] That is, he appears to have believed that the authorities were already monitoring the correspondence of refugee settlers – and he wanted access to it.

The immigration authorities were clearly intent on controlling the lives of refugees resettled in Australia, at least for the first two years after their arrival. They were particularly concerned to enforce the requirement to work in approved employment for two years, because the rules would be ineffective if it became known that they could be broken at will. 'These people have a grapevine service of no mean efficiency, and any weakness or strength in administration is soon generally known,' Heyes told Arthur Calwell's successor as immigration minister, Harold Holt, whom he – rightly – suspected to be less prepared than Calwell had been to enforce Australia's immigration policies at all costs.[203] In 1950, in response to a question in the House of Representatives, Holt said that of the 128,000 migrants who had by then arrived under the auspices of the IRO, forty had been deported 'because they had proved unsuitable as migrants in Australia'.[204] Such unsuitability could include the immigrant's refusal to remain in employment as directed, a security concern or a chronic illness.

The forty mentioned by Holt in parliament probably comprised fewer than half of the IRO-sponsored migrants for whom he or Calwell had signed deportation orders. In 1950, for example, Holt approved the deportation of a man from Yugoslavia who had arrived on one of the first IRO ships, the *Charlton Sovereign*, in 1948. The man had been directed to work for the New South Wales Railways but left his employment in central New South Wales six months later. He was offered alternative work but disappeared and could not be served his deportation order. The archival record reveals that, five years after the department wanted to deport him, he reported the loss of his registration card and was issued a replacement.[205] Others could not be deported because the Italian or German authorities refused to take them back, and Australia was reluctant to deport them to their countries of birth in communist Eastern Europe.[206]

In the late 1930s Central European refugees had been denigrated as 'reffos'. Calwell promoted the use of the term 'New Australians' to refer to the migrants who arrived from 1947 onwards; in 1949 he appealed to Australians to avoid using the terms 'DPs', 'displaced persons' or 'Balts', because 'the expressions could take on unpleasant undertones that would be inimical to the smooth assimilation of newcomers into the community'.[207] By then it had become clear that assimilation was not always smooth. Some observers thought that this was also because Australians had unrealistic expectations of their new fellow citizens. 'We should be tolerant of "New Australians", patient with them if at times they are moody and disheartened,' Frank Clune wrote in his government-funded book about his travels to Europe's DP camps. He wanted Australians to empathise with the new arrivals: 'If we were expelled from Australia by a barbarous invader, and offered sanctuary in Guatemala, Tibet or Turkey, our plight would be similar to theirs. We'd be grateful to those who helped us, but we'd have nostalgia for gumtrees.'[208]

Although the immigration department and politicians used the term 'New Australians' for several years, it did not enter the Australian vernacular in the way intended by the immigration minister. By 1952 it had been officially accepted that 'New Australians' applied only to non-British immigrants, and by the end of the decade the term had taken on derogatory connotations. In 1961 Menzies suggested dropping it altogether.[209]

*

In the second half of 1947, when the Australian selection officers began recruiting migrants among Estonians, Latvians and Lithuanians stranded in Germany, the entire DP population in Germany and Austria comprised approximately 1.2 million people.[210] That was a significant population, particularly in countries devastated by the war. The number of DPs was small, however, in comparison to that of other refugees accommodated in Germany and Austria.

Millions had fled westwards from 1943, when the Red Army began advancing towards the Reich. They included ethnic Germans, so-called *Volksdeutsche*, who had lived outside Germany's pre-1937 borders in countries such as Hungary, Romania and the Baltic states. About 1.2 million had been brought to Germany between 1939 and 1943, following agreements between the German Reich on the one hand, and Italy, the Soviet Union and the Baltic states on the other. Approximately a third of these 'repatriated' Germans settled in German-occupied Poland, but fled west as the Red Army moved inexorably towards Berlin. Other *Volksdeutsche* had left their homelands only once it seemed inevitable that Germany would lose the war, and that they would lose Germany's protection.[211]

The refugees in Germany also included German nationals who had lived in East Prussia, Pomerania or Silesia and been expelled from their homes, as Russians and Poles – many of whom had been displaced themselves – were settled in German territories that became part of the Soviet Union or Poland. The majority of these refugees settled in the three Western zones where they comprised about one-sixth of the total population, but Austria and the part of Germany that was occupied by the Soviet Union – which in 1949 was to become the German Democratic Republic (GDR) – also accommodated substantial numbers of German refugees.[212] East Germany, however, was also a source of refugees: between 1949 and 1961, when the Berlin Wall was built, on average about 200,000 people left the GDR for West Germany each year.

German refugees were the responsibility of the German authorities, rather than of the Allies. They were not always welcome in West Germany, particularly in the immediate post-war years, when they put additional stress on the already tight housing and labour markets. Often their German identity counted for much less than the fact that they were not locals. The latter was particularly true in rural areas, which attracted a comparatively large share of German refugees, because the war-ravaged cities could not accommodate the extra population.

In Germany itself the term *Flüchtlinge* ('refugees') referred to displaced ethnic Germans and, later, to refugees who had fled to Germany from communist Eastern Europe, rather than to DPs who did not want to be repatriated.[213] The Allied occupation authorities and international organisations also distinguished between German expellees and non-German refugees. The former were not part of the remits of UNRRA and the IRO. But that did not stop several Western governments from seeing the pool of German refugees as another potential source of immigrants. The first to actively recruit German refugees was the British government. From an Australian perspective, post-war Britain appeared to be mainly a country of emigration, but between 1945 and 1951 almost a million people migrated to the United Kingdom.

The British government actively encouraged immigration to address labour shortages. It introduced two schemes that targeted single displaced persons: the Balt Cygnet scheme, which was designed to bring single Eastern European women to Britain, and the Westward Ho scheme, which targeted single men.[214] In 1948 the British government extended its European Voluntary Workers program to include single *Volksdeutsche* and Sudeten German women.[215]

In 1949 Calwell and Chifley discussed whether Australia's DP scheme, too, could be extended to *Volksdeutsche* and German refugees. Both agreed that they would make excellent immigrants. At the time, however, the lack of shipping capacity prevented the Australian authorities from recruiting immigrants from among German refugees.

\*

While Calwell was negotiating with the IRO, he oversaw the repatriation of the Asian evacuees who had been admitted to Australia during the war. Most former internees, evacuees and Allied soldiers from the Indonesian archipelago were repatriated in 1946. However, not all of them wanted to go home. Some had married Australians and had Australian-born children. In April 1947 Calwell decided that Australian women married to men from Indonesia would not be allowed to accompany their husbands – with the consequence that the latter then tried to remain in Australia with their wives. But Calwell did not permit any exceptions to the White Australia policy.

Annie Maas Jacob's husband Samuel had died in 1944 in a plane crash while returning from a mission in New Guinea for the

Netherlands East Indies Intelligence Service. Three years later, she married John O'Keefe, who had been the Jacobs' landlord since 1943. The family continued to live at O'Keefe's house in Bonbeach on the Mornington Peninsula, south-east of Melbourne.[216] Notwithstanding her marriage to an Australian of British descent, she too was expected to return to her country of birth. However, in 1947 the government agreed to delay her departure to Indonesia.

Annie O'Keefe took an exceptional course of action, which affected the cases of other wartime entrants determined to remain in Australia. Told to leave Australia by 23 February 1949 or face deportation, she challenged the government in the High Court. The plight of the O'Keefe family featured prominently in the Australia press from January 1949, and was reported largely sympathetically. Newspaper editors, who remembered their altercations with Calwell during his time as information minister during the war, when he was responsible for censorship, played a key role in mobilising public support for the O'Keefes. In February Sydney's *Daily Telegraph* set up a fighting fund to finance her High Court challenge, arguing that 'the people of this country, whatever their politics, will want her to have every chance to prove the rights she thinks she possesses'.[217]

Despite the public outcry, Calwell remained unwavering in his commitment not to allow exceptions. He was convinced that he was justified in taking a hard line, and that the Australian public, if not already behind him, would eventually recognise that. He variously suspected communists, journalists and newspaper proprietors, and the Dutch government of orchestrating the campaign against him. Defending his stance, he frequently used language that could be considered offensive, even at the time. On 9 February 1949, in response to criticism by the Liberals' Harold Holt over his insistence that Annie O'Keefe and her children leave Australia, Calwell declared: 'We can have a white Australia, we can have a black Australia, but a mongrel Australia is impossible, and I shall not take the first steps to establish the precedents which will allow the flood gates to be opened.'[218] He also cast aspersions on the O'Keefes' integrity by insinuating that the only rationale for

Annie's second marriage was to foil the immigration department's attempt to make her leave the country.

In March 1949 the High Court ruled that in order for the Department of Immigration to control Annie O'Keefe's stay in Australia by means of certificates of exemption, she needed to have been declared a prohibited immigrant, which would have required her to have failed a dictation test.[219] But the immigration authorities had not administered the dictation test to either the Asian wartime evacuees or the discharged seamen. The court further decided that she could not become a prohibited immigrant through an administration of the dictation test five years or more after her arrival. The judges therefore upheld her appeal against Calwell's deportation order.

In response to that decision, the government drafted the War-time Refugees Removal Bill, which would allow it to deport wartime refugees regardless of the circumstances under which they had been admitted. When the bill was debated in parliament in June and July 1949, only Calwell's *bête noire*, Jack Lang, who called it the 'Reprisals Against Mrs. O'Keefe Bill',[220] and Doris Blackburn spoke out against its provisions. The Menzies-led opposition did not object in principle to the government's attempt to close a loophole in the administration of the White Australia policy. The War-time Refugees Removal Bill set a precedent (albeit one not much remembered in later years), because from the early 1990s governments have repeatedly introduced legislation to undo High Court rulings that had upheld the rights of refugees and asylum seekers.

While the federal opposition did not oppose the War-time Refugees Removal Bill, its leaders repeatedly attacked Calwell over the uncompromising administration of Australia's non-European immigration policy. In doing so, they joined newspaper editors, church leaders (including the Catholic archbishop of Melbourne, Daniel Mannix, a strong Calwell supporter), unionists and many ordinary Australians who were appalled by what they perceived as the immigration minister's heartlessness.

The *War-time Refugees Removal Act 1949* came into force in July that year, some six months before the federal election that would see Ben Chifley's government voted out of office. In December the High Court rejected a challenge to the Act mounted by several Chinese seamen.[221] But despite Calwell's determination to use the Act to rid Australia of the 'recalcitrant minority'[222] of non-European wartime refugees, it had little effect, because the immigration department deferred the serving of deportation orders.

Calwell is now remembered at least as much for his stubborn attempts to enforce the White Australia policy as for his inauguration of Australia's mass immigration program. That is also because after 1949, with the Labor Party occupying the opposition benches for the next twenty-three years, Calwell continued to rail against attempts to weaken the White Australia policy (as I discuss in more detail in Chapter 4). After Australia gradually abolished the policy between 1966 and 1973, Calwell came to personify the antithesis of a multicultural, tolerant Australia. Notwithstanding the fact that Calwell's 'beautiful Balts' opened the door for hundreds of thousands of Greeks and Dutch, Germans and Italians to immigrate during the 1950s and 1960s, his views were also upheld by those who yearned for an Australia that was essentially white and British. Pauline Hanson, for example, in her 1996 maiden speech in parliament – in which she called for multiculturalism to be abolished and the country's immigration policy to be fundamentally revised – singled out Calwell as a 'great Australian' because of his defence of the White Australia policy.[223]

*

In Ben Chifley's Labor governments, Arthur Calwell and the newly established Department of Immigration designed and implemented immigration and refugee policy. Chifley and several relevant colleagues in cabinet – particularly labour minister Holloway, postwar reconstruction minister Dedman, and Nick McKenna, whose portfolios included health and social services – played little more than supporting roles. Calwell was, however, not the only senior Labor minister whose ideas would have a lasting impact on Australia's refugee and asylum seeker policy. Doc Evatt, who combined the role of attorney-general with that of external affairs minister for the entire time that Labor was in power in the 1940s, had little to do with the recruitment of DPs, but he and the Department of External Affairs were involved in the drafting of the 1948 Universal Declaration of Human Rights.[224]

The drafting committee was chaired by Eleanor Roosevelt, America's first lady from 1933 until the death of her husband in 1945. Its nine members included an Australian, Colonel William Roy ('Hoddie') Hodgson, who had been secretary of the Department of External Affairs from 1935 to 1945, and had taken part in the San Francisco meetings where the United Nations was born. Initially, the Australian government favoured an 'instrument creating legal rights *and obligations*'; it argued for a convention that could be enforced through an international court, and proposed the inclusion of human rights in domestic law – which, in Australia's case, would have required a change to the Constitution.[225]

The draft of the declaration that had been prepared by the Human Rights Commission at its third session in May and June 1948 included two articles of particular relevance to refugee policy. Article 11(2) read: 'Everyone has the right to leave any country, including his own.' This was immediately followed by Article 12(1): 'Everyone has the right to seek and be granted, in other countries, asylum from persecution.' This article had a qualifier: 'Prosecutions genuinely arising from non-political crimes or from acts contrary to the purposes and principles of the United Nations do not constitute persecution.'[226]

Between 30 September and 7 December the Third Committee of the UN General Assembly discussed and amended the draft over the course of eighty-one meetings. As could have been expected, the Soviet Union and its allies objected strongly to the articles enshrining the freedom of movement and a right to asylum.[227] But other delegations also felt that the Human Rights Commission had gone too far. By then, the leader of the Australian delegation was Alan Watt, a seasoned diplomat and at the time Australia's ambassador in Moscow. Evatt had appointed six 'advisers' to assist him, among them the Anglican bishop of Goulburn, Ernest Henry Burgman, and the Catholic bishop, Eris Michael O'Brien.[228]

Watt later wrote that everyone on the Third Committee 'knew perfectly well' that the Universal Declaration 'purported only to embody a set of agreed principles' which would only become binding if they were subsequently enshrined in a covenant, which countries then needed to ratify to commit to the obligations it imposed.[229] Nevertheless, according to the minutes of the meeting on 3 November 1948:

> [The] Australian delegation had more than once pointed out that formulas implying obligation must be avoided in the text of the declaration of human rights. It should be a straightforward, clear and precise statement of the fundamental rights of man and must make no reference to the corresponding obligations of the State.

Echoing concerns raised by the immigration department, the Australian delegation also argued that '[a]s for the right of asylum, each State must be free to decide the form in which that right, having been proclaimed in the declaration, should be applied'. Watt therefore supported a suggestion by the delegation of Saudi Arabia to limit the right to asylum by deleting the words 'and be granted'.[230]

By the time the General Assembly voted on the Universal Declaration on 10 December 1948, draft Article 11 had become Article 14. The Universal Declaration was just that: a *declaration* that imposed no legally binding obligations, rather than a covenant. But it proved to have a moral force, and an influence on subsequent conventions. It did so because, even after its first draft had been watered down, it remained a document that did not fully accept the sovereignty of the nation-state.[231] It powerfully articulated social and economic, and civil and political rights. The latter did not include the right to asylum, because the 'right to seek and enjoy asylum' was meaningless as long as asylees could not claim an enforceable right to be *granted* asylum. The right of asylum had been sufficiently diluted to impose no obligations whatsoever on states granting asylum.

In 1950 Hersch Lauterpacht, who later became a judge of the International Court of Justice, commented that the formula adopted by the General Assembly in 1948 was 'artificial to the point of flippancy', and that it would have been 'more consistent with the dignity' of the Universal Declaration if Article 14 had been left out altogether.[232] He suggested that an international bill of rights needed to include a right to asylum along the following lines: 'Within the limits of public security and the economic capacity of the State, there shall be full and effective recognition of the right to asylum for political offenders and for fugitives from persecution.'[233] Lauterpacht admitted that the limits of the state's duty of asylum made the legal obligation imperfect, but that it would be a legal obligation nevertheless, and that 'its absence would derogate from the authority of a Bill of Rights'.[234]

\*

During the Pacific War, Australia had accommodated far more non-Europeans than at any time since the beginning of European settlement. But rather than heralding a gradual dilution of the White Australia policy, the presence of non-Europeans prompted the policy's reaffirmation in the immediate post-war years. Under the stewardship of Arthur Calwell, Australia was more uncompromising and deported more non-European residents than at any time since the repatriation of Pacific Islanders under the *Pacific Island Labourers Act 1901*. Most of these deportees had been admitted to Australia in the early 1940s as refugees, evacuees or internees.

Over the course of the 1940s, a consensus emerged that Australia needed to substantially increase its population, and that the only realistic means of doing so was through a mass immigration program. The government did not think of refugees as a major source of immigrants until mid-1947, but then took to the idea with gusto, particularly as the IRO was able to facilitate the transport of tens of thousands of refugees at a time when shipping was scarce, and as the immigration department was able to select refugees who could be comfortably accommodated within the parameters of the White Australia policy. The immigration of more than 100,000 European DPs in the late 1940s signalled the end of an Australia that was almost exclusively British, and paved the way for the admission of large numbers of migrants from continental Europe during the 1950s and 1960s.

The admission of IRO-sponsored DPs also set the scene for an immigration program that, henceforth, would always include a significant number of refugee migrants. However, the fact that the Poles, Estonians, Latvians and Lithuanians who migrated to Australia from 1947 were refugees was largely incidental: they were admitted because of the anticipated economic benefits of their immigration rather than out of humanitarian considerations. In fact, the selection criteria excluded prospective refugee migrants who were unlikely to become economic assets.

In the immediate post-war years Australia also experimented with a scheme that was driven more by humanitarian than by economic considerations, when the immigration department freely issued landing permits for Holocaust survivors who had relatives in Australia. The public backlash against the seemingly uncontrolled arrival of a comparatively small number of survivors from Europe, the Middle East and China, however, persuaded the government not only to restrict the immigration of Jews, but also to favour tightly policed immigration schemes for non-British immigrants.

Under Labor prime ministers Curtin and Chifley, Australia adopted a comparatively outward-looking stance. Australia became a key member of UNRRA, joined the IRO and was prominently involved in the establishment of the United Nations. Australian representatives contributed to the drafting of the Universal Declaration of Human Rights. Initially, the Chifley government favoured a binding and far-reaching covenant on human rights, but, like other governments, it became concerned that such a covenant would compromise the sovereignty of nation-states; ultimately, it agreed to a watered-down text that did not entail any international legal obligations.

As the next chapter shows, the policies and practices put in place by the Curtin and Chifley Labor governments with regard to refugees remained largely unchanged under Australia's longest-serving prime minister, Robert Menzies. Unlike his Labor successors, he had to deal with new challenges: asylum claims by people who were already in Australia or in its colony, the Territory of Papua and New Guinea, and the resettlement aspirations of Pacific Islanders.

# DEFECTORS, DESERTERS AND THE 'HARD CORE'

W hen the government of Robert Menzies was sworn in a few days before Christmas 1949, the arrival of DPs had already peaked. Never has Australia accommodated as many refugees in a calendar year as it did in 1949 – not only in proportion to its population, but also in absolute terms. That year 75,486 people arrived under the auspices of the IRO. There were also thousands of displaced people who migrated to Australia after paying their own way. Together, they increased Australia's population by more than 1 per cent.

The Menzies government continued what Chifley and Calwell had begun. Another 70,212 DPs arrived on IRO ships in 1950, and a further 14,209 between 1951 and 1954. Altogether, the number of DPs resettled with the help of the IRO outstripped the total number of non-British immigrants who had settled in Australia in the first four decades after Federation.

As the pool of DPs who met Australia's selection criteria grew smaller, the government revisited the idea of extending the scheme to German refugees. What had initially been conceived of as another option for bringing European refugees to Australia, however, soon morphed into something far more ambitious: an assisted passage scheme for Germans. The metamorphosis of a plan seemingly designed to resettle refugees is further evidence that DPs were resettled in Australia not because they had been displaced, but because they were freely available. In fact, DPs were recruited *despite* the fact that they had been displaced. Australia's immigration policy was not guided by humanitarian sentiment.[1]

By mid-1950 the Australian government had lost interest in a scheme designed specifically for *displaced* Germans. In August the Australian representative in Geneva, Noël Deschamps, told Tasman Heyes that Australia had the opportunity to piggyback onto an arrangement negotiated between the IRO and the US government, whereby the IRO would facilitate the movement of *Volksdeutsche* to the United States. According to Deschamps, the IRO was offering *Volksdeutsche* at the cost of $27.50 per person for processing plus $308.50 for shipping, and demanded the payment of the processing fee in US dollars, and the remainder in pounds.[2] The immigration department was not interested.

In October 1950 Vincent Greenhalgh, who was overseeing Australia's selection of DPs in Germany, outlined the options available to the immigration department, should the government decide to support a mass immigration scheme for Germans. He distinguished between three categories of prospective immigrants from West Germany: *Volksdeutsche*, German refugees (including those from the GDR) and West Germans. 'Among the various elements in the German population, there is no doubt that the indigenous West German is the best potential migrant,' Greenhalgh found. He proffered two arguments. First, non-refugee Germans had 'led a stable normal existence, avoided the demoralisation of refugee movements, and preserved the continuity of [their] economic experience'; second, their 'records and the records of [them] are intact and available'.

In Greenhalgh's view, *Volksdeutsche* were the second-best option: being ethnically no different from indigenous West Germans, they 'have substantially the same characteristics, and have in their favour the historical evidence that they can establish themselves in a new economy'. He wrote that, among *Volksdeutsche*, the unemployment rate was particularly high, 'owing to the facts that having no assets they were unable to withstand the economic shock of the monetary reform in June, 1948, and that they are not particularly acceptable in Germany.' Overall, he was cautious about recruiting *Volksdeutsche*: 'They are, however, a more doubtful quantity from the point of view of records and the recent political history of a good many of them is not much in their favour.'

But they were still a better option than either expellees or refugees from East Germany, who 'are in general a poorer type, involve a larger risk of infiltration, and are the most exposed of all the groups to the degenerative influences of bad social conditions'. He thought that the order of preference was the same from a security point of view:

> The West Germans are easily checked. We could expect about the same degree of effective screening with Volksdeutsche as with DP's. In the case of the refugees from East Germany it would be highly desirable to limit selection to those who arrived in the Western Zones before 1948: with that reservation we could expect no more than the normal DP risk.[3]

That most of the non-British immigrants in the first five post-war years were from Eastern and South-eastern Europe, rather than German nationals, and that most of these immigrants were classified as refugees was not because the Australian government had been guided by humanitarian considerations and wanted to alleviate the refugee problem in Central Europe. DPs were cheaper than Germans because the IRO paid most of the costs associated with bringing them to Australia; moreover, so soon after the war the immigration of large numbers of Germans would have been politically impossible. But that would change very soon, with Australia signing an immigration agreement with the Federal Republic of Germany in 1952, and tens of thousands of non-refugee Germans entering Australia thereafter.

*

In December 1949 the United Nations General Assembly decided that, following the termination of the IRO's activities, a High Commissioner's Office for Refugees be established from 1 January 1951.[4] The Australian government was not enthusiastic about this, or about an international convention to guide the high commissioner's activities, and did not participate in the Ad Hoc Committee on Statelessness and Related Problems, which prepared the convention's first draft. The immigration department, in particular, was sceptical about the benefits of the proposed new body. In May 1950 Heyes warned his counterpart in the Department of External Affairs that:

> [t]here are thousands of non-European refugees, and acceptance by Australia of a convention which provided that such a class of persons should not be discriminated against and should not be subject to any penalty for illegal entry, would be a direct negation of the immigration policy followed by all Australian Governments since Federation.[5]

This was an understatement. In 1950 there were millions of non-European refugees. Following the establishment of the People's Republic of China (PRC), hundreds of thousands of refugees entered Hong Kong – 700,000 in the first six months of 1950 alone – even though the British tried to seal the border.[6] Following the Partition of India in August 1947, some 14 million people fled across the newly created borders between India and Pakistan.[7] But Heyes should not have worried. When negotiating the wording of the draft Refugee Convention, its authors were thinking of European DPs and so-called escapees – refugees from communist Eastern Europe – rather than Chinese refugees in Hong Kong or those displaced on the Indian subcontinent.

In July 1951 the draft Convention was put to a conference of plenipotentiaries in Geneva. The Australian government, which had opposed the convening of this meeting, had to make a difficult call: should it follow New Zealand's lead and boycott the conference to avoid embarrassment over its objections to the draft Convention, or should it try to influence proceedings?

Tasman Heyes argued that Australia's objections to the Convention were unlikely to be met, and were of such a fundamental nature that it made no sense to send a delegation.[8] Objections were also raised by the Queensland and New South Wales governments, which were concerned about their states' ability to impose restrictions on non-citizens – for example, regarding land ownership or the registration of some professionals, such as lawyers.[9] Even the United Nations Section of the Department of External Affairs, which was in favour of attending the conference, found that Australia would 'draw no direct advantages' from the Convention, and thought that it was 'very doubtful, even if the principal objections . . . were removed, that Australia would ever ratify the convention'.[10]

Twenty-five of the United Nations' sixty members, including Australia, were represented at the Geneva conference in July 1951. No Asian country except Iraq, and no communist-ruled country except Yugoslavia, took part in the deliberations. Although the Australian delegation was careful not to highlight Australia's objections, it was comparatively isolated on account of its opposition to key elements of the draft text. Only the United States delegation opposed as many key elements of the draft as the Australians. At one stage in the negotiations, after a US delegate had tried to argue that the Convention would interfere with the right of migrant-receiving countries to select their immigrants, the Danish chairman pointed out 'that the convention had nothing to do with migration'. Thereupon the Australian delegate suggested 'that this should be explicitly stated by a clause to the effect that "nothing in the convention should be regarded as limiting the power of contracting states to legislate in regard to migration"'.[11] The other delegates vehemently objected to the Australian proposal.

It is instructive to consider the proposals put forward by the Australian delegation. For example, Australia wanted to amend Article 2, which obliges refugees to obey the laws of the country of resettlement, because it wanted to commit resettled refugees also to 'observe the conditions upon which [their] entry into the country was permitted'.[12]

This was to allow Australia to require refugees to remain in prescribed employment for two years following their arrival, and not to change their employer without the permission of the immigration department. When its amendment to Article 2 was rejected, the Australian delegation proposed an amendment to Article 3, which stipulates that the Convention applies to refugees 'without discrimination as to race, religion or country of origin'. Australia wanted to add: 'Nothing in this Convention shall be deemed as absolving a refugee from observing the conditions under which he was admitted, or was authorized to stay, in the territory of a Contracting State.' Again, the Australian proposal did not find a majority. Australia also wanted to reserve its right to deport refugees on account of 'lunacy' and other major illnesses, but once more failed to secure the support of a majority of delegates.

With the benefit of hindsight one might suggest that another unsuccessful Australian amendment, this time to Article 5, was tailored to allow for the unlimited detention of prospective refugees, for their deportation to offshore processing centres, and for their removal from a country's territorial waters. At the time, though, neither the Australians nor any other delegation anticipated such an eventuality; instead, the Australian delegation may have been mindful of the internment practices of the Second World War when putting forward the following text:

> Nothing in this Article should prevent a Contracting State in time of war or national emergency or in the interest of national security, from taking provisionally essential measures in the case of any person, pending a determination that the particular person is in fact a refugee and that such measures are still necessary in his case in the interest of national security.

The other delegations did not support Australia's proposal, with the representative of the United Kingdom pointing out that the wording would allow a state to take exceptional measures at any time, and not just during a war or other national emergency.

The Australian and United States delegations were not the only ones attempting to limit the Convention's scope. France suggested amending the definition of refugees in Article 1 by inserting a qualifier designed to exclude non-Europeans. While this proposal was bitterly opposed by the so-called universalists, led by Britain, in the end all delegations except Yugoslavia's agreed to allow contracting states to make the Convention applicable only to people who had become refugees as a result of 'events occurring in Europe'.[13]

This was a better outcome than the Australian government had anticipated. And, as an added bonus, Australia could not be held responsible for the decision to give signatories the option to limit the Convention's geographical focus. The Australian delegation had been instructed not to 'be prominent' in any move to exclude Asian refugees, and more generally to avoid proposing amendments that would 'offend Asian countries'. The delegation was told to play a positive rather than obstructionist role: it was to 'make a strong statement of Australia's good record in the reception and care of refugees', and keep in mind that even if there was a conflict between a particular article of the Convention and Australia's immigration policies, the government could enter reservations later rather than oppose the article at the drafting stage.[14]

When Australia acceded to the Refugee Convention in January 1954, the government made ample use of this option; not only did Australia make a declaration to limit the Convention's geographical scope, it also entered reservations with regards to Articles 17, 18, 19, 26, 28 and 32.[15] The most significant of these was Article 32, which prevented contracting states from deporting refugees except on the grounds of national security or public order.

In 1952 Denmark became the first state to ratify the Refugee Convention. Australia was the sixth, and the first outside Western Europe, to accede to or ratify it. Australia's accession mattered, because, in accordance with Article 43(1), six ratifications or accessions were needed for the Convention to come into force. Of the five states who had ratified the Convention before Australia, only one, the Federal Republic of

Germany – whose 1949 Constitution stipulated that 'persons persecuted for political reasons enjoy the right of asylum' – had neither invoked its right to limit the Convention's geographical scope nor entered a reservation. New Zealand acceded to it only in 1960, and Canada signed on as late as 1969. Thus, in the 1950s Australia's recalcitrance was the norm, rather than the exception.

*

In late 1951 representatives of key countries of immigration (such as the United States, Canada, Argentina, Israel and Australia) and of Western European countries met in Brussels to discuss the future of European migration. They believed their interests would not be served by the UNHCR, and moved to establish the Intergovernmental Committee for European Migration (ICEM). Its activities were not confined to refugees; nevertheless, during the 1950s and 1960s the ICEM played a bigger role than the UNHCR in facilitating the migration of refugees to Australia.

In its early years the UNHCR was not in a position to coordinate the resettlement of large numbers of refugees. It was poorly resourced and had very limited operational capacities, not least because the governments that underwrote the creation and resourcing of ICEM were unwilling to provide further funds to the UNHCR. By contrast, the ICEM received generous financial support from its members; during its first ten years of operations, it was able to spend about US$145 million on refugee operations.[16]

The Australian immigration department continued to be interested in refugees largely because they were available and willing to settle permanently. Those classified as refugees were treated no differently from many other, non-refugee migrants after their arrival in Australia. It is therefore difficult to identify those who were admitted to Australia *as refugees* during the 1950s and 1960s.

According to the immigration department's statistics, 73,729 humanitarian migrants were financially assisted to enter Australia between

1 July 1950 and 30 June 1960, and another 40,699 arrived in the next decade.[17] These numbers may include migrants who were classified as refugees to fill a particular ICEM-administered contingent; they almost certainly exclude many whose circumstances were identical to those officially regarded as refugees, except that their passage to Australia was not funded by the government. For example, DPs who were recognised as refugees by the IRO, yet who came to Australia not through the IRO scheme but because they were sponsored by relatives, were not included in the official number of refugee arrivals. Often the only indication that somebody would have been considered a refugee was their place of residence at the time of their recruitment.

One group of migrants whom the Australian authorities deemed to be refugees were Slovenes in Italy. At its meeting on 10 January 1947 the United Nations Security Council had approved a provision in the proposed peace treaty between the Allies and Italy which called for the establishment of the Free Territory of Trieste.[18] According to that peace treaty, the Free Territory was 'recognized by the Allied and Associated Powers and by Italy, which agree that its integrity and independence shall be assured by the Security Council of the United Nations'.[19] The Free Territory, an area of 738 square kilometres bordering the Gulf of Trieste in Istria, had an ethnically mixed population, which included an Italian-speaking majority and Slovenian- and Croatian-speaking minorities.

The rationale for establishing the Free Territory was to neutralise a potential source of future conflict between Italy and Yugoslavia. However, when the Free Territory was officially established after the ratification of the peace treaty in September 1947, the idea of a self-governing buffer zone between Italy and Yugoslavia was not realised; instead, the Free Territory was split into a smaller but more populous Zone A, which included the city of Trieste and was administered by the British and American military, and a larger Zone B, administered by the National Yugoslav Army.

In 1954 the fiction of an independent Trieste was finally laid to rest when Italy took control of most of Zone A, and Yugoslavia incorporated Zone B and the remainder of Zone A into its territory. About a fifth of the approximately 300,000 inhabitants of Zone A were ethnic Slovenes; when Zone A fell to Italy, many became displaced as they were not welcome in Italy and did not want to migrate to Yugoslavia. The displaced also included Italians, Croats and Slovenes who had left Istria either immediately after the war or in 1954.

The admission in 1954 of refugees from Trieste attracted little attention in Australia. The fact that most of the people from Eastern and South-eastern Europe who migrated to Australia in the early 1950s were classified as refugees hardly registered. Neither the Australian public nor the government conceived of DPs primarily as freedom fighters or as people who had escaped communist Eastern Europe, but rather as workers who provided much-needed labour to a growing post-war economy. That was very different in the United States, where the government responded to the refugee problem in Europe largely out of foreign policy concerns, and where the public, associating 'American' with 'anti-communism', supported the government's policy because its beneficiaries were supposedly being rescued from communist persecution.[20]

\*

The image of the brave but hapless victim who needed to be rescued from Moscow's clutches and offered a sanctuary in Australia made its first appearance in 1954. On 3 April that year Vladimir Petrov, third secretary of the Soviet Union's embassy in Canberra, formally sought political asylum in Australia.[21] Officially, Petrov was a diplomat; however, what made his defection so attractive to the Australian government was his unofficial role as a high-ranking intelligence operative with the Soviet Ministry for Internal Affairs (MVD). Thus, when Menzies announced Petrov's defection in parliament on 13 April, the focus was not so much on the protection granted to Petrov but on the insights he could offer concerning Soviet espionage in Australia.[22]

There had been previous defections in Australia. Following the 1948 communist coup in Czechoslovakia, three members of the Czechoslovakian consulate-general in Sydney resigned from their positions and asked to remain in Australia. They included the consul, Karol Tököly, who told the Australians that he did not recognise 'the Czechoslovak Government as a true Government of our people' and could therefore not serve it any longer;[23] according to a newspaper report, ten days later the immigration department announced that it 'had thoroughly investigated his case and could see no reason why he should not be allowed to stay here'.[24] In 1951 the acting consul-general, Josef Felix, also defected and successfully applied for political asylum; he had learned that he would soon be replaced by another consular official and transferred to the foreign affairs ministry in Prague.[25] Elsewhere, there had been other defections in the aftermath of Stalin's death in 1953 and the fall from grace of the feared head of the Soviet secret police, Lavrentiy Beria. In late 1953, for example, Józef Światło, a senior officer with the Ministry of Public Security in Poland, defected while on a mission in West Berlin. Yuri Rastvorov, an MVD officer stationed at the Soviet embassy in Tokyo, defected in January 1954.

While Petrov was being debriefed in an ASIO safe house, his wife, Evdokia Petrova, was under house arrest at the Soviet embassy in Canberra. As soon as the embassy had become suspicious about Petrov's disappearance, two armed diplomatic couriers had been dispatched to Australia. On 19 April they were to escort Petrova back to Moscow. The Australian authorities were not in a position to prevent her departure, unless she clearly indicated that she, too, wanted to seek asylum.

The government had decided to encourage her to seek asylum not while in Australia but during a stopover in Singapore, because it did not want to put additional strain on Soviet–Australian relations or imperil the safety of Australian embassy staff in Moscow. However, by the time Petrova was led on board the plane that was to take her from Sydney to Darwin, and from there to Singapore, the public had become aware of her impending departure. A large crowd, much of it composed of recent immigrants from Eastern Europe, gathered at Sydney's Mascot airport and witnessed the two couriers compelling a clearly frightened Petrova to board the plane. Some in the crowd believed they heard Petrova crying out for help.

One of the onlookers was William Wentworth, a Liberal member of federal parliament; later that evening he told the Menzies cabinet that the government had to act if it did not want to pay a high political price for being seen to collude with the Soviets. On Wentworth's urging, and no doubt influenced by other reports of the chaotic scenes at Mascot, the government changed its plans. At Darwin the two couriers were disarmed, and Petrova accepted the offer of asylum made to her by the acting administrator of the Northern Territory, Reginald Leydin.

The events surrounding the granting of asylum to Evdokia Petrova were significant in two respects. First, images of a clearly distraught woman being manhandled by two bulky Soviet agents, splashed across the front pages of newspapers and featured prominently in newsreels, left a powerful impression on Australians. As Robert Manne observed in his book about the Petrov affair, it was an image 'of what most Australians still believed the Cold War to be about – the struggle between the forces of Evil and Good'.[26] The image also suggested that Australia had the capacity to rescue individuals who were at risk of becoming the victims of Soviet thugs. Second, the rowdy demonstration on the evening of 19 April made the government realise the extent to which some New Australians – including many former DPs – were unwilling or unable to discard their old-world political passions.

The 1951 Refugee Convention came into force two days after Petrova accepted Australia's offer of political asylum, but it had played no role in the government's deliberations. The Petrovs were not considered refugees in the terms of the Convention's Article 1. Article 14 of the 1948 Universal Declaration of Human Rights may have been considered more relevant, but it did not guide government policy because, as we saw in Chapter 2, it did not impose any obligations on states. The government was bound by neither domestic law nor established policies, and since it considered the case of the Petrovs to be exceptional and did not anticipate many similar defections, it did not formulate a policy that might be applied in future.

Two years later, in July 1956, Cabinet suddenly saw the need to develop a policy to guide Australia's approach to asylum seekers. The government's initiative was prompted by expectations that Eastern European athletes and officials would attempt to defect during the 1956 Summer Olympic Games, which were due to begin in Melbourne on 22 November. The negotiations between the relevant government agencies are interesting for two reasons: for the lack of references either to the 1951 Refugee Convention or to Article 14 of the Universal Declaration of Human Rights, and for the views put forward by the Department of Immigration and its minister, Harold Holt.

In 1951 Holt had been responsible for granting political asylum to Josef Felix; at the time he justified his decision by reference to Felix's war record and his democratic convictions.[27] Five years later the immigration minister thought that asylum requests were not a matter for him and his department but for external affairs and the Prime Minister's Department.[28] The immigration department's representatives were concerned that an asylum policy might encourage non-Europeans to claim asylum in order to gain permanent residence, and objected to the suggestion that they should be responsible for the welfare of asylees. Any government assistance would only encourage people to seek asylum, they argued; asylees should be put in touch with sympathetic compatriots who could care for them.[29]

On 16 October 1956 Cabinet 'approved of the principle that political asylum and refuge should be available in appropriate instances to various categories of aliens namely Olympic Games visitors, members of visiting trade and other delegations, members of diplomatic and consular missions in Australia, certain other defectors and Asian leaders'.[30] The prediction that athletes and officials would use the Melbourne Olympics to seek asylum in Australia came true. A total of fifty-nine members of Olympic delegations, most of them Hungarians, decided not to return home at the conclusion of the games. Forty went from Australia to the United States to claim political asylum there. The remaining nineteen were processed as 'political refugees' by the committee established in accordance with the Cabinet decision, but they were granted the same residence permits as other immigrants, rather than political asylum.

The 'political refugee' whose case attracted most attention in late 1956 was not an athlete but a Ukrainian stewardess, Nina Paranyuk, who was working on the liner *Gruzia*, which had brought the Soviet Union's Olympic team to Melbourne. On 18 November, four days before the games' opening ceremony, she disappeared while on an organised visit to the Melbourne Zoo. As groups of New Australians had frequently visited the *Gruzia* and challenged its crew to defect, it was assumed that she had made an attempt to leave the ship for good and had been assisted when doing so.

The Soviet Union's diplomatic representatives were suitably outraged, to the extent that the external affairs official who spoke to them the day after Paranyuk's disappearance thought that the Soviet Union might consider withdrawing from the Games.[31] Paranyuk reappeared two months later, long after the *Gruzia* had returned home. She told the ASIO officers interviewing her that she was dissatisfied with the poor living conditions and lack of freedom in the Soviet Union, but she did not apply for political asylum. The government's Committee of Review dealt with her case regardless, and recommended that she be classified as a refugee. This classification was immaterial, in the end, as the positive outcome of health, security and character checks meant her application for a conventional residence permit was successful.[32]

*

The noisy demonstration at Mascot airport had shone a spotlight on the political passions of some refugees accepted by Australia for resettlement. On their way to Australia, DPs had been told: 'We enjoy your music, your folk dancing and the rich culture you have brought with you. We hope you will continue to develop your own national pursuits as well as mingle with us and enrich our national life.'[33] However much Australians empathised with the anti-communism of many of the DPs, they and the government also believed that the politics of immigrants' home countries had no place in Australia. And while folk dancing was appreciated as a form of entertainment, it was something to be reserved for special occasions. On all other days, immigrants were expected to assimilate: to speak, dress and comport themselves like other Australians.[34]

In the eyes of the government, one of the preconditions for successful assimilation was for migrants formally to become Australians. In 1948 the *Nationality and Citizenship Act* created the legal basis for Australian citizenship (as distinct from British subjecthood).[35] The Act had no immediate consequences for how 'New Australians' were expected to identify; as Ann-Mari Jordens has observed, 'Australians only slowly developed an understanding of citizenship based on equality of rights rather than on British culture and ethnicity.'[36] In 1951 a leaflet prepared by the Empire Youth Movement, in collaboration with the immigration department, told its intended audience that it was important to remember 14 November as the birthday of Prince Charles, by then 'a fine, healthy, handsome little baby boy looking out upon the world about him with the direct gaze of truth and with an expression of good humour and merriment'.[37]

Refugee migrants have been expected to apply for citizenship as soon as possible after they become eligible, and many have done so, not least to have access to a passport and the ability to travel overseas. Ordinarily, refugee migrants who arrived after 1947 needed to have been resident in Australia for five years before they could take out citizenship, but in January 1951 the first DP to arrive under the auspices of the IRO scheme was naturalised in Canberra. She was the twenty-year-old Erna Okaite from Lithuania, who had arrived in Australia in 1949 as an unaccompanied minor.[38] Later that year the immigration minister reduced the waiting period for all migrants between the ages of sixteen and twenty-one from five to two years.[39]

Although there had been no Australian citizens before 1948, a refugee migrant applying for citizenship after 1948 joined an established polity, most of whose members had acquired citizenship at the stroke of a pen, and who expected the newcomer to fit in and adopt their language and culture.[40] Given the level of non-British immigration, that expectation became increasingly unrealistic. The more non-English-speaking migrants arrived in Australia, the more opportunities were created for immigrants to establish communities that were linguistically and culturally distinct from the Anglo-Celtic model.

Moreover, the newcomers could not always be sure precisely which cultural traits they were meant to follow. 'Should you attempt to align yourself with Irish-Catholic Australia and its (to the newcomer) largely incomprehensible mythology of ancient wrongs?' Andrew Riemer, who arrived in Australia as a refugee in 1947, once asked. 'Or should you try to throw in your lot with what Manning Clark referred to as the Protestant Ascendancy?' He concluded: 'The demand that newcomers must assimilate, promoted at a time when Australian society began to realise that it harboured considerable numbers of "DPs", "refs", "balts", "dagoes" and "wogs", was entirely self-defeating.'[41]

*

When Calwell tried to convince a sceptical public that it ought to welcome those arriving on the *Heintzelman* and other IRO ships, he emphasised that they possessed all the qualities of good immigrants: they were hard workers and keen to assimilate. He rarely dwelled on the fact that they had signed up for resettlement because they did not want to return to communist Eastern Europe. Even after the beginning of the Cold War, Eastern European refugees were accepted for pragmatic rather than ideological reasons. That changed in 1956 with the suppression of the Hungarian uprising and the exodus of hundreds of thousands of Hungarians.

Although it won only 17 per cent of the vote in the national elections of November 1945, the Hungarian Communist Party had slowly been able to bring the government under its control. By mid-1948 Hungary was effectively a communist state, led by the Communist Party's general secretary, Mátyás Rákosi. In June 1956 the Soviet bloc was shaken by violent anti-government protests in Poland, which in mid-October led to the appointment of the reformist Władysław Gomułka as first secretary of the Polish United Workers' Party. In July, following pressure from a Soviet leadership intent on reining in some of the excesses of Stalinism, Rákosi was forced to resign, but his replacement was a long-time associate and fellow Stalinist, Ernö Gerö.

On 23 October an anti-government protest rally in Budapest triggered a nationwide revolt. The following day the Soviet Union intervened militarily to prop up the government, but its troops met with strong resistance, and initially agreed to withdraw from Budapest. Both Gerö and prime minister András Hegedüs fled the country to seek refuge in the Soviet Union.

When the newly formed government of Imre Nagy declared that Hungary would leave the Warsaw Pact and become neutral, the Soviet leadership decided to launch a second military intervention. Between 4 and 10 November Soviet troops seized control of Hungary and installed a new government. Over the next couple of years hundreds of presumed opponents of the new regime, including Nagy, were executed, and thousands more were sentenced to lengthy prison terms.

In late 1956 about 200,000 people fled Hungary to Austria, where they were initially accommodated in hastily set up refugee camps. There is no doubt that nearly all were compelled to leave Hungary, but such compulsion did not necessarily make them refugees in the sense of the 1951 Refugee Convention. 'In the narrow legal sense, then, it seems certain that most of the Hungarians who fled their homeland in 1956 and 1957 possessed no "well-founded fear of persecution" and were not technically refugees when they left Hungary,' Gil Loescher and John Scanlan write in their book about post-war US refugee policies, 'although it seems likely that because of their departure and subsequent activities in the West, some would have faced harsh treatment had they elected to return'.[42] Similar observations might be made about others in the 1950s and 1960s who, in the West, were regarded as refugees simply because they had left an Eastern bloc country.

Most Hungarian refugees were subsequently resettled in Western countries, including about 40,000 in the United States. Towards the end of 1956, as it became increasingly difficult to cross the border from Hungary to Austria, some Hungarians fled to Yugoslavia. Initially, the Yugoslav government was determined to care for them without outside assistance, but in late December 1956 it formally sought help from the UNHCR, which in turn appealed to Western governments to resettle them.[43]

Australia offered to assist with the humanitarian crisis triggered by the exodus of Hungarian refugees almost as soon as the Soviet Union invaded Hungary. On 6 November the Department of External Affairs' United Nations Section reported that 15,000 people had so far fled Hungary. It recommended that Treasury be approached to authorise a contribution of £10,000 to the UNHCR. An annotation in the margins of the memorandum noted that New Zealand had already contributed £10,000 to the Red Cross.[44] In this and other instances, the Australian government's response to a refugee crisis was influenced by what other governments, particularly those of New Zealand, Canada and the United Kingdom, were doing; evidently, the government was often as interested to gain intelligence about the reactions in Wellington, Ottawa and London as it was in the size and nature of the crisis itself.

On 8 November immigration minister Athol Townley announced that the government had agreed 'to provide sanctuary for up to 3,000 refugees from Hungary'.[45] This time, the Australians were ahead of the government in Wellington, which announced the following day (after its immigration minister, Ralph Hanan, had emphasised the 'advantage

in getting in early') that New Zealand would take 500 Hungarian refugees.[46] In a departure from the policy that had governed the admission
of DPs, Townley told parliament that 'it is anticipated that the group
will include a number of compassionate cases, such as children and
people of ages exceeding the normal age limits imposed for other assisted
migrants. If necessary, normal selection standards may be modified for
the group.'[47]

The Labor federal opposition, led by Doc Evatt, welcomed the
announcement. Arthur Calwell, Evatt's deputy, used the opportunity
to suggest to the government that it should also show compassion to
DPs still living in camps in Germany 'under deplorable conditions',
who earlier, 'because of the loss of an eye, an arm, or a leg, or because
of some other physical defect, deformity or injury, were not able to come
to Australia when we selected only the fittest and ablest persons'.[48] In
the late 1940s it had of course been Calwell himself who had insisted
on accepting only young and able-bodied DPs.

On 5 December Townley announced that an additional 2000 Hungarians would be accepted under assisted passage arrangements.[49] In
1957 Australia kept selecting Hungarian refugees in excess of the 5000
it had first agreed to admit. Between November 1956 and December
1957 about 14,000 Hungarians arrived in Australia. Most had fled from
Hungary to Austria. In March 1957 Australia agreed to accept 2000 of
the Hungarians who had sought refuge in Yugoslavia – with the proviso, however, that they would not arrive in Australia before 30 June
1957, to allow the government to charge the costs involved in the operation to the 1957/58 budget.[50] The selection of this group of refugees is
particularly well documented; the government files, held by the National
Archives in Canberra, provide a window into the policies, politics and
practicalities of selecting refugee migrants at the time.

The decision to select Hungarian refugees in Yugoslavia was not without irony. After all, Australia regularly resettled Yugoslav citizens who
had left their country for Austria or Italy as refugees; it was prepared to
rely on the cooperation of one refugee-producing communist-ruled

country to resettle citizens from another refugee-producing communist-ruled country. Yet the proposal was supported by the external affairs and immigration departments; the former expected there to be 'political advantages', and the latter was convinced of the 'probability of our getting good types', as Tasman Heyes put it in a submission to his minister.[51]

However, the idea met with opposition from the head of ASIO, Charles Spry. He thought that it would be next to impossible to perform adequate security checks on prospective immigrants because the Yugoslav authorities, unlike their counterparts in Austria, would be unwilling to cooperate with the Australian selection mission.[52] His misgivings were also 'based upon the knowledge that the first batch of Refugees from Hungary would have been the Communist element which in the early days was fleeing from the so-called freedom Government'.[53] Spry thought that these people were more likely to seek refuge in another communist country than in Austria.

Once again, the Australian security services were proving themselves to be exceptionally ill informed about events taking place in Europe. In fact, Spry's reasoning is nothing short of staggering. Not only did he incorrectly assume that the installation of the Nagy government had triggered a significant refugee movement; he also believed that refugees loyal to the regime of its predecessor would have wanted to emigrate to Australia rather than return to Hungary. In the end, Spry reluctantly agreed to the mission, while Townley and the immigration department committed themselves to proceeding with the selection of refugees in Yugoslavia only if Australia could run security checks on applicants.[54]

The other government agency with serious misgivings about a selection mission in Yugoslavia was the Department of Health. It believed that incidents of tuberculosis and mental illness were higher among Hungarians in Yugoslavia 'than in any other section of migrants from Europe hitherto examined' – tuberculosis because of the very poor conditions, including severe overcrowding, in the refugee camps, and mental health problems because the refugees allegedly included former patients of psychiatric institutions who had been released during the uprising, and because 'many of the Hungarians in Yugoslavia have had a bad time so that they have been under some considerable mental strain'.[55]

By comparison, the views of the Department of Labour and National Service were positive. Its officers had been impressed by the Hungarian refugees who had arrived in Australia up to that time. 'Very few of them appeared to be what might be regarded as peasant types,' the department's Hal Cook wrote. 'They appeared to be alert, industrious and they have satisfactory standards of personal hygiene.' Cook nevertheless requested a modification of the selection criteria. In his view, the selection officers ought to privilege applicants with some knowledge of English, and should not select unaccompanied young men and women under the age of twenty-one.[56]

Australia's deputy chief migration officer in Athens, Gordon Brooks, was appointed to lead the mission. His team also included a medical doctor, two ASIO officers and two other immigration officials. In early June, Brooks and Bruce Campbell, one of two ASIO officers stationed at the Australian migration office in Vienna, travelled to Yugoslavia for negotiations with the local authorities and to visit the refugee camps.[57] Campbell introduced himself as the mission's 'co-ordinating officer'.[58] Brooks told the government in Belgrade that Australia would be prepared to resettle 2000 refugees, provided that five conditions were met: they needed to be 'anxious to emigrate and resettle permanently in Australia'; they had to meet Australia's normal immigration criteria of age, health and family composition; they had to be in possession of documentation to allow the Australians to determine that they would not pose a security risk; the Yugoslav authorities had to make a processing centre available to the Australian team; and the costs of the operation must be kept to a minimum.

According to Brooks' report of his initial visit, the authorities in Belgrade were at first 'disturbed' by these conditions but eventually agreed to them. By then, several European countries and Canada had already sent selection teams to Yugoslavia; while they had selected only small numbers, they had been comparatively indiscriminate in accepting refugees for resettlement.[59]

While Australia and other resettlement countries applied different selection criteria in relation to applicants' age, family size, presumed employability and general state of health, none paid much attention to the criteria of Article 1 of the 1951 Refugee Convention. The fact that a Hungarian was in a refugee camp in Yugoslavia and willing to settle in a third country was considered sufficient evidence for her status as a refugee; she did not have to demonstrate that she had been persecuted in Hungary or that she would be persecuted if she returned there. And while the UNHCR was involved in providing relief to Hungarian refugees, it played no role as far as Australia's mission in Yugoslavia was concerned. It was the ICEM that provided logistical support and preselected applicants, much as the IRO had in Germany in the late 1940s.

The Australian mission had been provided with facilities to set up a processing centre close to the Osijek refugee camp in eastern Croatia. On 7 August 1957 it began assessing prospective immigrants. The ICEM had compiled a shortlist of refugees who had expressed a strong interest in being resettled in Australia. Almost immediately, however, the selection ran into practical difficulties.

The mission was told that it needed to approve 100 applicants by 9 August, and a further 429 by 20 August, to fill berths booked on two ships sailing from the northern Italian port of Genoa. The medical officer complained that he could not examine more than thirty applicants per day without compromising the requirement that the examination be 'complete and thorough'.[60]

The next problem arose because the ICEM had not anticipated that the Australians would accept only about 60 per cent of the cases presented to them, and was therefore struggling to preselect enough candidates. The Australians, in turn, blamed the ICEM for presenting 'some extremely poor material'.[61] A third of the applicants were rejected because they failed to meet Australia's standard selection requirements: unsuccessful applicants included single women with children, people over the age limit, and large families. Ten per cent were excluded on security grounds.

More than half of those rejected by the mission did not meet Australia's stringent medical criteria: the most common reason for a rejection on medical grounds was suspected tuberculosis; other medical issues that ruled out applicants included obesity, potential psychosis and hypertension. The medical criteria were designed to exclude anybody who might be a burden rather than an asset; for example, 'suspected tuberculosis' could refer to scarring that was the result of tuberculosis suffered a long time ago. For some medical conditions there were no objective criteria. A medical doctor who vetted applicants in Austrian refugee camps in 1958 recalled: 'If a person wasn't the full quid or slightly off beam, even personality-wise, we were asked to think very carefully about selecting him.'[62] Since so many refugees were desperate to be selected, applicants had good reason to be anxious and appear 'slightly off beam'.

By 21 October the Australians had selected 1325 refugees from Yugoslavia and were preparing to close down their operations. The mission was unable to meet the target of 2000 recruits; of the almost 20,000 Hungarian refugees originally in Yugoslavia, fewer than half were left by the time the Australian mission began its work, and that number shrank quickly once the United States, whose criteria were comparatively liberal, began selecting migrants very soon after the Australians had arrived.

The international organisations involved could consider the resettlement of Hungarian refugees stranded in Yugoslavia a success story. By January 1958, 16,409 refugees had been resettled and 2773 had been repatriated; the remainder, 675, had been integrated locally.[63] While Australia resettled a significant proportion of refugees, it could not claim to be responsible for the success of the overall operation. That credit belonged to countries such as Sweden, Belgium and France, which did not exclude applicants on the basis of their medical condition.[64]

*

By the time the IRO ceased its operations, the vast majority of those Eastern Europeans who had become stranded in Germany or Austria in the aftermath of the Second World War and had refused to return to their countries of origin had been resettled. However, some refugee camps could not be closed because selection teams from Australia and other countries of immigration had approved only those they considered to pose no risk and to constitute an economic gain. The elderly, the disabled, the chronically ill, single mothers (who were sometimes referred to as 'socially handicapped cases') and others who did not fit the stringent selection criteria remained behind. Often, entire families could not be resettled because one family member was considered a liability – for example, because she had once had tuberculosis or was an amputee. The IRO had referred to refugees who were unattractive to countries of resettlement as the 'hard core'. The UNHCR inherited the problem of some 25,000 'hard core' refugees, most of whom were still housed in camps in Germany.[65] Its initial attempts to interest resettlement countries in accepting applicants who belonged to the 'hard core' met with no more success than had earlier attempts by the IRO.

In 1959 some 25,000 people were still living in refugee camps in Europe. From the late 1950s, however, the attitude of countries of resettlement slowly shifted. Two interrelated factors were responsible. First, there was a marked increase in the general awareness about refugee issues due to World Refugee Year, a highly successful private initiative which gained the backing of the UNHCR and, eventually, many governments, including that of Australia (which had initially been one of a handful of Western countries that did not support World Refugee Year in the United Nations).[66] Partly in response to World Refugee Year, some governments announced they would henceforth also admit refugees whose resettlement ostensibly did not make economic sense. These gestures then prompted others to follow suit; as would happen in response to the Indochinese refugee crisis in the late 1970s, for example, displaced people became the beneficiaries of competitive humanitarianism.

In 1957 several European countries had already relaxed their selection criteria as part of a concerted effort to resettle Hungarian refugees from Yugoslavia, but of the traditional countries of immigration it was New Zealand which first responded to the UNHCR's appeal to resettle the 'hard core' when in 1959 it accepted twenty families that each included somebody with a disability.[67] Despite having a larger population and a more substantial immigration program, Australia initially only matched New Zealand's offer, but later announced it would accept 200 families under its refugee program, and an additional 300 if they were sponsored by the non-government sector.

When the UNHCR suggested that Australia publicise the arrival of the 250,000th refugee in the context of World Refugee Year, the Department of Immigration decided to select a refugee with a physical disability to emphasise Australia's contribution to the resettlement of the 'hard core'. But the selection of a suitable person proved complicated. The first two candidates were Poles who had had tuberculosis. One had contracted the disease in a German concentration camp and had long since been cured. Neither was acceptable to the immigration department because it was not prepared to admit TB cases above a small quota, which had already been filled.[68] Three further candidates were also rejected – in one case, apparently, because the applicant had lost a leg after rather than during the war.

The department finally chose Otto Kampe, a 41-year-old Latvian who could walk only with the help of crutches because he had suffered from bilateral hip disease as a child. It says much about the department's confidence in its selection process that it was not afraid that the publicity surrounding Kampe's arrival would highlight his previous failed attempts to immigrate. Kampe was a designer. His physical disability did not affect his capacity to earn a living. His sisters and his mother had migrated to Australia in 1950 and 1951, respectively, and for ten years Kampe had tried to follow them. Yet it was only when the immigration department was looking for an attractive family to publicise Australia's decision to accept disabled refugees as part of its contribution to World Refugee Year that his application was finally successful.

Kampe was accompanied by his wife and five children. In a press statement announcing their arrival, the minister for immigration, Alick Downer, made much of the fact that Australia had not simply accepted a 'permanent cripple' but had gained seven settlers who would benefit Australia: 'In accepting the Kampe family we will gain not only five fine, healthy young future Australians, but two courageous people who have shown by their fortitude and their strength of character in the most unfortunate circumstances that they will make truly worthy citizens.'[69]

Six weeks after the Kampes' arrival, the *Canberra Times* devoted a full page to World Refugee Year. Several articles encouraged the public to donate money.[70] They were illustrated by a photo of Downer, of barracks in Lager Kapfenberg, a refugee camp in Austria, and of an anonymous middle-aged woman, captioned 'One of the tens of thousands of European refugees looking to World Refugee Year for deliverance'. The Kampes featured in an article that emphasised the benefits of refugee resettlement – not for the refugees but for the countries of resettlement. 'The refugees have contributed at least as much to their new homeland as they have received,' the article claimed. 'They have added new skills and woven new threads into the cultural pattern.'[71] The article implied that, so far, Germany had been the beneficiary of Kampe's work as a designer and maker of musical instruments; Australia's offer to resettle him could thus be seen as a move to secure his talents rather than as a humanitarian gesture.

*

The selection of Kampe and of other 'hard core' refugees during World Refugee Year marked a departure from Australia's refugee resettlement policy, although refugees like Kampe remained the exception to the rule and were only selected as part of a small quota. World Refugee Year was not the first time, however, that Australia had agreed to waive 'normal immigration criteria' on humanitarian grounds. Calwell had done so in 1945 with respect to Jewish survivors. The Menzies government did so again in the 1950s, when it agreed to admit European refugees from China. In both cases the migrants' admission to Australia was sponsored by non-government agencies: international Jewish organisations, such as the Joint, which paid for travel costs, and Jewish organisations in Australia, which provided resettlement services, in the first case, and the World Council of Churches and the resettlement agencies of the Australian churches in the second.

At the end of the Second World War, China accommodated two large and distinct groups of European refugees: people from the Soviet Union who had emigrated between 1917 and the mid-1920s, and people who had become displaced in the late 1930s and early 1940s, largely on account of Nazi Germany's policies. Most of the latter were Jewish and sought refuge in Shanghai. The first, larger group included members of the Old Believers,[72] Russian Orthodox Christians who had rejected the church reforms of the mid-seventeenth century, had been persecuted under the Tsars, and then faced persecution again under the Bolsheviks, as well as members of the White Russian armies who had fled to China at the end of the civil war. Many of these exiles had settled in the north and north-east of China. After 1946, some registered with the IRO and as a result received limited financial support. When the high commissioner for refugees submitted his second report to the United Nations General Assembly, in 1953, he drew particular attention to the European refugees in China, who, according to UNHCR estimates at the time, numbered 15,000 and who mainly lived in and around the city of Harbin.[73]

In the 1920s Harbin had received more than 100,000 Russian refugees, which had earned it the name *Belyi Harbin* ('White Harbin') in the Soviet Union. The Chinese government tolerated, if not welcomed, the Russian exiles. The number of 'Harbintsy' (Russians in Harbin) dropped to about 30,000 in the 1930s, when Harbin became part of the Japanese puppet state of Manchukuo and tens of thousands returned to the Soviet Union – often only to be imprisoned in the Gulag or shot upon their return. When the Red Army liberated Harbin in April 1945, some 10,000 Harbintsy were arrested and taken to the Soviet Union. A year later, the Chinese People's Liberation Army assumed control of Harbin, and in 1949 the city became part of the People's Republic of China. The communist government barely tolerated the Russians in Harbin and elsewhere in China, and in the 1950s encouraged them either to let themselves be repatriated to the Soviet Union or be resettled in countries such as the United States, Canada, Brazil and Australia.[74]

Australia's authorities were wary of admitting Russians from China. Unlike DPs in Germany and Austria, Russians in China could not be selected by Australian immigration officials. Most importantly, it was difficult to do thorough security checks on them. While some of the Russians were stateless, others had taken out Soviet citizenship in the mid-1920s, often in order to be able to work for the Chinese Eastern Railway. They often tried to hide the fact that they held Soviet passports – which only added to the Australian suspicions.[75] Because of these concerns, on several occasions Australia suspended the issuing of landing permits to Russians in China.

Given the difficulties of subjecting Russians in China to thorough health and security checks, and the ease with which European immigrants could be recruited elsewhere, it is the more remarkable that Australia admitted more than 11,000 European refugees from China between the late 1940s and the early 1960s – more than 40 per cent of the total number of those resettled from China during that period.[76] One explanation for the government's willingness to put aside the serious reservations expressed by the Department of Health and ASIO is that Russians in China had powerful advocates, including international organisations such as the ICEM, the UNHCR and the World Council of Churches. In Australia, the churches successfully lobbied members of the Commonwealth Immigration Advisory Council, which requested not only that the government consider applications from Europeans in

China sympathetically, but also that it accommodate some of them in migrant reception centres, which were normally reserved for assisted passage migrants.[77]

The council's views were in stark contrast to those of Colonel Spry, the ASIO director-general, who – under sufferance – attended several meetings of the council to brief its members about his organisation's concerns. An indignant Spry told Heyes in 1955 why he refused to provide the council with further briefings: 'Whilst I confess to being unaware of the real place which the Advisory Council occupies in the Departmental machinery, I have some doubts as to whether it is correct for me to be placed in a position where I must justify my recommendations to a body which is purely advisory and apparently not part of the Executive Government.'[78] However, in 1955 the immigration minister, Holt, who had earlier been dismissive when informed of Spry's concerns, decided to follow the recommendations of this 'purely advisory' body, although his department had endorsed only some of them, and done so only reluctantly.[79] The minister also ruled that – in stark contrast to standard policy regarding migrants nominated by sponsors in Australia – applications were to be accepted 'irrespective of the nominees' ages'.[80]

Spry remained at loggerheads with the immigration department, its minister and the Commonwealth Immigration Advisory Council, and repeatedly railed against what he consider 'virtually unscreened migration from China'.[81] In the 1950s, however, ASIO seems to have been in a far weaker position than in recent years, when refugees with adverse security findings against them remain in indefinite detention – not least because the then immigration department was often sceptical of the security agency's claims that people who posed seecurity risks might infiltrate Australia disguised as refugees.

Arthur Calwell, Harold Holt, Athol Townley and Alick Downer did not publicise the immigration of Russian refugees from China, which they oversaw while in charge of the immigration portfolio. In March 1962, however, all four were given the opportunity to briefly share the limelight with a former Russian refugee who, a few months earlier, had become famous as Miss Australia 1961.[82] In 1952 eleven-year-old Tatiana (Tania) Verstak, her sister and her parents – who, incidentally, both held Soviet passports when they applied for a visa – had arrived in Australia from China.[83] Five years later, Tania had applied for Australian citizenship.[84]

As Miss Australia and, in 1962, Miss International Beauty, Tania Verstak highlighted her personal history as a comparatively recent non-British migrant who had managed to become a true Australian. While she was not shy to be critical of official attitudes to migrants when demanding that the term 'New Australian' no longer be used,[85] she was the kind of ambassador Calwell and Downer had been looking for when they selected the '50,000th DP migrant' or the '250,000th refugee' to arrive in Australia. According to the *Australian Women's Weekly*, which twice featured her on its cover, Verstak told an international audience: 'The sky is the limit for migrants to Australia.'[86]

By then, the immigration department had long realised the potential advantages posed by the crowning of Verstak. When the UNHCR's Executive Committee met in Geneva in November 1961, the department sent pictures of Verstak to the other delegations. Each photo was accompanied by a note, part of which read: '[In] the context of our discussions here on refugees, you might be interested to hear about the story behind the attached photograph. Ten years ago, this girl's family arrived in Australia penniless and homeless. Today Miss Verstak has been chosen by her new compatriots to be "Miss Australia".'[87]

*

Neither the nineteen Eastern European athletes who had sought asylum at the conclusion of the Melbourne Olympics nor the *Gruzia* stewardess Nina Paranyuk had tested Australia's new asylum seeker policy. Their cases were examined by the government's Committee of Review, but eventually they were treated much like other prospective immigrants: they became the sole responsibility of the immigration department and were granted residence permits. Their requests to remain in Australia had been widely publicised, but they were uncontroversial. With news about Soviet tanks in the streets of Budapest still fresh in Australians' minds, there was no opposition to their requests.

Over the following years there were a few more cases of Eastern Europeans seeking asylum in Australia. Usually, they were sailors who had jumped ship. Their cases were not publicised, and they, too, were allowed to stay. In the 1950s the only high-profile asylum seekers were the Petrovs and Paranyuk – the latter because the media were attracted to the human interest aspect of her case, rather than because of the politics involved. The first case in the 1960s that attracted a lot of attention, both from the government and from the media, was that of a Polish diplomat. On 14 January 1961 Prime Minister Menzies announced that the Polish commercial consul in Sydney, Ryszard Stanislaw Zielinski, and his Hungarian-born wife, Marta, had asked for political asylum for themselves and their children. The request featured prominently in the Sunday papers the next day – although it was not deemed as important as the tumbling wickets during the cricket test between Australia and the West Indies at the Sydney Cricket Ground – but subsequently attracted comparatively little attention, either in Australia or overseas.[88]

Zielinski had been recalled to Poland some six weeks earlier – according to his own account, because he had not cultivated left-wing Australians – and had then approached the Australian government. His approach was not unexpected; he had been considered a potential defector as early as November 1957, six months after his arrival in Australia.[89] Zielinski was willing to provide intelligence about the operations of the Polish and other Eastern European missions in Australia, but, unlike the Petrovs, he was a career diplomat rather than a member of the intelligence service posing as a diplomat, and thus the Australians were not overly excited about the prospect of debriefing him. ASIO's Charles Spry approved of the idea to grant the Zielinskis asylum, but after interviewing the diplomat in mid-December he proposed to delay the announcement until after the Polish consulate had completed its annual audit, anticipating that 'an attempt will certainly be made to smear the character of Dr Zielinski by alleging mishandling of Polish funds'.[90]

As Spry had expected, the Polish consulate did indeed accuse Zielinski of misappropriating funds, but otherwise lodged only a mild protest.[91] By March the affair had blown over; according to a newspaper report, the Zielinskis had come out of hiding and resumed a normal life in Sydney. They kept a low profile, however, and declined all media requests for interviews.[92]

Zielinski's case was similar to other asylum requests received by the government after 1956. There was no indication that he had been, or would be, persecuted on account of his views. He wanted to stay in Australia not only because he did not want to return to Poland, but also because his family evidently liked living in Australia. It therefore seems surprising that Menzies decided to formally grant the Zielinskis political asylum, rather than invite them to apply to remain in Australia as regular immigrants. I suggest he did so because he could afford to: Poland was not a major power, and Zielinski was not prominent enough for his defection to hurt the Polish government.

Occasionally, Australia was asked by one of its allies to accommodate people who had sought asylum elsewhere. Thus, in 1957 the British high commission wanted Australia to admit a Greek-Cypriot shepherd who had provided the British authorities with information that led to the killing of a leading member of Ethniki Organosis Kyprion Agoniston (EOKA), a nationalist group in Cyprus that was waging an armed campaign against the British colonisers.[93] Two years later the United States government enquired whether Australia would be willing to accept Fulgencio Batista, the former Cuban dictator who had fled to the Dominican Republic in January 1959 to pre-empt the overthrow of his regime by Fidel Castro's rebels. The Australian government politely declined the latter request, not least to avoid giving ammunition to critics 'who would be ready to draw a contrast between our willingness

to admit an ex-dictator from Latin America, with a record of violation
of human rights, and our general restrictive immigration policies regarding Asians'.[94] Batista was eventually offered asylum by the Portuguese
government.

*

In the first five years after its introduction, the government's asylum
seeker policy had only been used in relation to people from communist
Eastern Europe. In fact, those drafting it in 1956 had not conceived of
the possibility that people from authoritarian regimes aligned with the
West might seek asylum in Australia. In Europe at the time there were
two such regimes: the dictatorship of *Generalísimo* Francisco Franco
in Spain, and António de Oliveira Salazar's *Estado Novo* ('New State')
in Portugal.

Both Franco and Salazar persecuted their political enemies. Both
had been in power for a long time: Franco since the end of the Spanish
Civil War in 1939, and Salazar since 1932. Despite the contempt of each
for democracy and the rule of law, they were considered allies by the
Western powers. In fact, both Spain and Portugal were founding members when the Western military alliance NATO was established in 1949.

In the 1950s and early 1960s Australia had no close relationship with
either Spain or Portugal. There was little immigration from the Iberian
Peninsula, and the volume of trade was insignificant. Australia's interests were represented by the British ambassadors in Lisbon and Madrid.
Portugal was of some interest to Australia because of its colony East
Timor. It was this colonial presence in the region that led to regular
visits to Darwin by Portuguese navy ships.

On 7 December 1961 the frigate *Gonçalves Zarco* arrived in Darwin
on one of its routine visits. On 10 December three sailors – Joaquim
Teixeira, Jose Manual da Costa and Norberto Andrade – jumped ship
and went into hiding in Darwin, where they may have made friends
during previous visits.[95] In line with the policy regarding desertions,

the authorities informed a representative of the ship's owner – in this case the Portuguese chargé d'affaires in Canberra, Manuel d'Almeida Coutinho – of the desertion and asked that he arrange for the sailors' repatriation once they had been apprehended. In turn, Coutinho requested that the Australians undertake the necessary steps for their apprehension and deportation. On 11 December the *Gonçalves Zarco* left Darwin without the three men. On 14 December the sailors came out of hiding and asked the Northern Territory's administrator for political asylum.

In accordance with the government's 1956 asylum seeker policy, it was ASIO's responsibility to assess the men's claims, while the Department of External Affairs would make the final decision. ASIO concluded that the men 'could not be regarded in any sense as "defectors"'.[96] On 19 December the external affairs secretary, Arthur Tange, after reporting this finding to his minister, recommended that they be deported. Menzies, who was at the time also responsible for foreign affairs, endorsed Tange's recommendation two days later. It was now up to the Department of Immigration to enforce that decision. Minister Downer thought it would be a mistake to deport the sailors but did not convey his views to Menzies in time. Thus, Downer had no choice but to sign the deportation orders.

Menzies remained in the dual roles of prime minister and minister for external affairs only for one more day. Australians had gone to the polls on 9 December. The results were close, and it took more than a week to confirm that the conservative Liberal–Country Party Coalition had won the elections by a whisker. On 22 December the new ministry was sworn in, with Sir Garfield Barwick continuing as attorney-general and also taking charge of external affairs. Barwick agreed with Menzies' decision. In his memoirs, he wrote: 'I thought that we owed it to a friendly power – Portugal is the oldest (and continuing) ally of Great Britain – to return to its custody deserting members of its defence force.'[97]

On 4 January Coutinho was informed of the decision not to grant the men's asylum request, and told that the men would be deported to

Dili, the administrative capital of Portuguese Timor, on the next available flight. They were apprehended and placed in Darwin's Fannie Bay Gaol. A few days later, a Darwin lawyer instituted habeas corpus proceedings and challenged the deportation orders in the Northern Territory Supreme Court. On 28 March the court upheld the immigration department's right to deport the Portuguese, whereupon their lawyers applied for leave to appeal the decision in the High Court.

The asylum seekers had many supporters, particularly in Darwin. They included the Northern Territory's sole representative in federal parliament, Labor's Jock Nelson, and the influential editor of the *Northern Territory News*, Jim Bowditch. According to an ASIO officer, Bowditch 'seems to champion those people who, because of colour, creed or their own inability, have failed to achieve their ambitions or have in some ways been baulked by authority'.[98] Trying to divine what fuelled Bowditch's fight for social and political justice, a senior immigration officer wrote at the time that his 'views were undoubtedly influenced by the fact that he was married to a mixed blood girl'.[99] The territory's administrator, Roger Nott, a former Labor member of the New South Wales Legislative Assembly, whose appointment in Darwin had been designed to force a by-election for his seat of Liverpool Plains, was evidently also sympathetic, although he could not make his views public.

In 1961 Darwin residents had clashed with the Department of Immigration over the planned deportation of three Malay pearl divers who had lived in Australia for many years; they had been served with deportation orders because their employer had gone out of business. By the time the story of the Portuguese sailors broke, people in Darwin were ready for another fight to support these presumed underdogs against bureaucrats and politicians in distant Canberra. As had happened in the case of the Malay pearlers – who became known as the 'Stayput Malays' – the cause of the three sailors also attracted interest and sympathy in the southern states. Newspapers in Sydney and Melbourne ran articles about Salazar's brutal rule, students organised protest meetings and many Australians wrote to the government to express their concerns.

Meanwhile, Barwick was in two minds about how to proceed. In his capacity as foreign minister he sympathised with the Portuguese government's request to have the men deported to Portugal. But as attorney-general he came to realise that it would be 'wrong in law' to use the deportation provisions of the *Immigration Act* and hand the sailors over to the Portuguese authorities.[100] He therefore persuaded the Salazar government to dismiss the sailors from the navy and drop its request for their deportation to Portuguese territory, with the argument that the Australian media ought to be discouraged from dwelling on the nature of the Portuguese regime. Having accomplished this, he told Coutinho 'that the communists, who might have otherwise continued their efforts to cause embarrassment over the ratings', had now turned their attention to other causes.[101] Barwick was still intent on deporting the men but planned to send them to Brazil, which had previously accommodated a prominent Portuguese dissident, the former air force general and candidate in the 1958 presidential elections Humberto Delgado.

On 30 April the High Court rejected the sailors' application for leave to appeal the Northern Territory Supreme Court's earlier decision. Now Downer could enforce the deportation order. But the next day the government announced that it had allowed the three Portuguese to remain in Australia. That decision was the result of some horse-trading between Downer and Barwick. The immigration minister and his departmental secretary, Peter Heydon, a former diplomat who had replaced Tasman Heyes in 1961, had all along been lukewarm about implementing Menzies' decision. Heydon had told his minister that Barwick's decision to deport the sailors to Brazil would 'put us in a ridiculous light in many countries',[102] and that only a reversal of the original decision would protect the Australian government 'from all sorts of emotional and illogical Press exhortation and criticism'.[103]

Barwick and the external affairs department, on the other hand, were opposed to enforcing the White Australia policy by deporting the

'Malay Stayputs'; that case had already attracted widespread criticism among Australia's South-East Asian neighbours, and their deportation was likely to further damage Australia's reputation. Thus, Downer agreed to let the Malays stay, and in return Barwick revoked Menzies' ruling regarding the Portuguese.

*

New Zealand was ahead of Australia not only when it came to admitting refugee migrants with health problems; it also pioneered the resettlement of non-European refugees. In 1962 the government in Wellington announced that New Zealand would admit twenty Chinese orphans from Hong Kong for resettlement.[104] This was a controversial gesture – and not only because it ran counter to New Zealand's long-established racially discriminatory immigration policy. The UNHCR criticised the placement of the orphans in non-Chinese families. Australian diplomats followed these arguments closely, because the offer had the potential to enhance New Zealand's humanitarian credentials and thereby once again upstage Australia's approach to refugee resettlement.

Although there was no pressure on Australia to admit Chinese who had fled the People's Republic for the British colony of Hong Kong, in 1962 the government was confronted with the Chinese refugee issue in an unexpected way. Since Federation, the Australian authorities had struggled to control the illegal immigration of Chinese, who entered the country with the help of people smugglers or traffickers. In 1959 this became a much publicised issue when the bodies of two men were found floating in Sydney Harbour.[105] They had stowed away on the cargo ship *Taiyuan*. A crew member later confessed that five stowaways had been taken on board in Hong Kong. Two had suffocated in the purpose-built secret locker where they were hiding while the ship was searched by customs officials.[106]

Some three years after these tragic deaths, on 9 February 1962, Willy Wong (aka Willie Wong, aka Wong Bee Lee, aka Billy Wong) was apprehended by an immigration officer at a market garden in Matraville, Sydney.[107] He claimed to have been born on 25 July 1926 in the Go Yiu District near Canton (Guangzhou), and to have crossed into Hong Kong in about 1954. He was part of the large exodus of people from the People's Republic to Hong Kong during the 1950s.[108] According to his account, he stowed away to Sydney on the *Changsa* within a fortnight of arriving in the crown colony, but he was unable to speak English and could not produce any documentary evidence supporting his claim of a seven-year residence in Australia.[109]

Wong was arrested and legal proceedings began. As soon as he was detained, Wong, his friends or his employer sought the help of the Sydney lawyer William Lee, who twenty-four years earlier had been the first Chinese-Australian to be admitted to the New South Wales bar. Lee at once wrote to the immigration department, asking for his client to be allowed to remain in Australia.[110] Three non-Chinese Sydney residents submitted statutory declarations in which they professed to having known Wong for seven years. On 12 February Wong was taken before a magistrate, who directed that he be held in detention. He was then taken to the immigration detention facility at Sydney's North Head quarantine station. On 22 February immigration minister Downer signed a deportation order for him, having been advised by his department that Wong was 'a very doubtful quantity in so far as his claim to seven years residence here is concerned'.[111] On 24 March Wong was placed on board the Hong Kong-bound *Anshun*.

Lee pursued the case vigorously. He contacted the prominent Liberal backbencher Sir Wilfrid ('Billy') Kent Hughes, who passed Lee's concerns about returning Wong to the PRC on to Downer. On 5 April the latter informed Kent Hughes that he had reviewed Wong's case but had not varied his original decision: Wong was deported 'because he entered Australia illegally and did not come within the classes eligible to remain'.[112] On 12 April, having received further communication from Lee, Kent Hughes and a second concerned Liberal backbencher, the anti-communist crusader William Wentworth, spoke to Downer. Following their meeting, Downer instructed the Australian Trade Commission in Hong Kong to intercept Wong. By the time the trade commission received the late-night cable the following day, however, it was too late. On 12 April Wong had been escorted across the border into China.

In a press statement released on 14 April, Downer tried to contain the damage. He referred to the *Taiyuan* tragedy to argue that 'illegal entry by stowaways and other acts of deception require constant action to ensure compliance with our laws'. He attempted to lay some of the blame at Wong's feet, implying that the latter had lied in his statement about a seven-year residence in Australia, and claiming that Wong himself 'did not suggest any other destination than Communist China'. Downer also played down the likelihood that Wong would have been persecuted upon his return: 'Allegations regarding how he will be treated are, at best, assessments – various factors suggest that, in fact, a returning deportee is allowed to resume normal life.' If Wong were to be mistreated, Downer suggested, then it would be the fault of those in Australia who had publicised his fate, whose actions 'could unnecessarily and dangerously direct to this man attention by the Chinese authorities which otherwise might well not arise'.[113]

At the height of the Cold War, less than a year after the erection of the Berlin Wall, news of Wong's deportation prompted an outcry in Australia and Hong Kong, as well as elsewhere in the region. 'Sunday newspapers howl about Wong,' the immigration department's secretary, Peter Heydon, noted in his diary on 15 April.[114] The Melbourne *Herald*'s Richard Hughes claimed to have access to an eyewitnesses account when he wrote on 16 April:

> Willie Wong came to Australia as a stowaway. He was deported.
>
> On Wednesday, unhappy, bewildered, apprehensive and apologising to his Chinese police 'escort', bowing respectfully to sympathetic English police officers at the border, he was transferred across the 'no man's land' bridge at Lowu, to waiting armed Chinese Communist guards.[115]

In the public debate about Wong's deportation, the *Herald*'s version of events, or variations thereof, prevailed over Downer's. 'Unless there are some special conditions that have not been made known to the public . . . there can be little doubt about the fate of the unfortunate Willie Wong,' the author of a letter to the editor of the *Sydney Morning Herald* asserted confidently. 'Within an hour of his being handed over to Communist China he joined his ancestors, having been either beheaded or shot.'[116]

Yet there was no credible evidence that Wong (or other deportees before him) had been taken into custody by PRC border guards or police. Bert Furler, an Australian immigration officer stationed with the trade commission in Hong Kong, commented:

> [T]here may be an impression in Canberra of beetle-browed Chinese border guard thugs prodding the poor helpless and inoffensive Chinese traveller with sub-machine guns or bayonets and that there is a background of tanks and what not looming over all. This is an impression that could perhaps be gained from films and lurid newspaper reports on Berlin and Iron Curtain countries.
>
> Nothing could be further from the truth . . . The flow of people through the control point could perhaps be compared to the traffic over the Sydney [Harbour] bridge, where one buys a ticket and proceeds. At the border here a traveller shows his documents to the Hong Kong and Chinese officers and, if O.K., just walks on. It's just a routine.[117]

News of Wong's deportation broke at a time when the immigration department and its minister had been under sustained attack for more than six months over the implementation of the White Australia policy. One day before Kent Hughes and Wentworth spoke to Downer about Wong, on 11 April 1962, the minister had received the prominent Melbourne lawyer Zelman Cowen, who represented two of the 'Stayput Malays'; he had urged Downer to back down and let the men stay in

Australia. When Australia's newspaper journalists were reporting Wong's deportation in mid-April 1962, stories about the deportation orders against the Portuguese asylum seekers and the pearlers, which were then being challenged in the High Court, were fresh in their readers' minds.

At the time, several other illegal immigrants from mainland China were awaiting deportation. As a result of the furore caused by Wong's return, the government decided to suspend all deportations to communist China. For many years Wong remained the last person deported from Australia to the PRC.

Journalists referred to Wong as somebody who had fled communist China and was being returned to that country. Had Lee been able to prosecute the case while Wong was still in Australia, he may have advised his client to lodge an asylum claim. When lobbying Kent Hughes to intervene on behalf of Wong, Lee pointed out that '[m]any Chinese are actuated by the desire to escape from Communist oppression and seek a land in the free world where vast opportunities exist for advancement'.[118]

One of the detainees at North Head (all of whom were allowed to remain in Australia following the Cabinet decision of 17 May 1962) did in fact claim political asylum. 'We consider our client to be a refugee from Communist China who, after residing in Australia for a period of eight years, has established himself in the social system and has made many friends among the Chinese community,' Fun Cheung Wong's lawyer submitted to Garfield Barwick, recognising that his client's assimilability mattered to the Australian authorities. 'He fears that he will be punished and possibly executed if he is forced to return to Communist China,' the lawyer wrote, but he recognised that his client could not invoke a right to asylum: 'I realize that Mr. Wong is an illegal immigrant within the meaning of the Immigration Act and any decision to allow him to remain in this country would be an act of mercy by the Government.'[119] The government declined the request for asylum, but Fun Cheung Wong was among those allowed to remain in Australia.

*

Officially, Australia was categorically opposed to the resettlement of non-European refugees. But since the late 1940s the immigration authorities had struggled to determine whether a prospective immigrant was barred from entering the country on racial grounds. 'European' was often taken to mean 'light-skinned northern European'. In the 1950s prospective immigrants from southern Italy were occasionally rejected because they were considered to be too dark.[120] An immigration officer involved in the selection of Hungarian refugees in Austria recalled rejecting a man who 'really was a very dark gypsy with crinkly black hair'.[121]

In the late 1940s and 1950s Australia had admitted thousands of Ceylonese Burghers, who had mixed Dutch (or Portuguese) and Sinhalese ancestry. After 1957, the relevant policy required immigrants to be 75 per cent European by descent, and to be acceptable as Europeans in Australia. For migrants from South-East and South Asia who were of mixed ancestry, it was not always possible to prove that they fit these criteria, and it was therefore left to Australian consular staff to determine their eligibility.

In the early 1960s the number of applications from Burghers rose because of the increasing marginalisation of people of part-European descent in Ceylon. Following the 1962 military coup in Burma, which ushered in a single-party state propped up by martial law, Anglo-Burmese also increasingly sought to migrate to Australia. Apart from their skin colour, Ceylonese Burghers and Anglo-Burmese were desirable immigrants: they were native English speakers and were often highly qualified professionals.

In 1964 the so-called mixed descent policy was revised, not least to make it easier for applicants who experienced 'hardship on grounds of discrimination' to meet Australia's requirements.[122] This change of policy was prompted by humanitarian considerations, but they were not publicised. Although the government did not refer to Burghers and Anglo-Burmese as refugees, this was only the second instance in Australia's history – after Calwell's relaxation of the rules for Holocaust survivors in 1945 – in which an established immigration policy was changed in the interests of people whose human rights were threatened, if not violated, in their home countries.

*

Until 1962 the island of New Guinea was divided between two colonial powers: the Netherlands and Australia. The 800-kilometre border between the Dutch and Australian territories was largely defined by a meridian, 141° longitude east. Dutch and Australian government officials did not always know for sure whether a particular village sat on this or that side of the border. In 1949 the Dutch had retained West New Guinea when they formally relinquished control over the remainder of their former colonial empire in South-East Asia, which then became the Republic of Indonesia. In response to Indonesian demands for a Dutch withdrawal from West New Guinea, the Dutch made significant investments in New Guinea, improving its infrastructure and upgrading the education system to create an indigenous elite capable of eventually taking charge of an independent West New Guinea.

As a result of Indonesian pressure, the support of the United Nations General Assembly for decolonisation and the interests of US foreign policy, the Dutch became increasingly isolated and in the New York Agreement of 15 August 1962 had to agree to hand over control of their territory to a United Nations interim administration (UNTEA). This administration was formally in control of West New Guinea from 1 October 1962 to 30 April 1963, after which the former Dutch territory became part of Indonesia.[123]

As soon as the Dutch decided to withdraw from West New Guinea, the Australian government began making contingency plans for an anticipated influx of refugees. Following a request from the Dutch government to accommodate a limited number of political refugees from West New Guinea, Cabinet decided on 6 August 1962 that, in the case of Dutch-sponsored civilian refugees of Papuan extraction who wished to remain as residents in Papua and New Guinea, 'each case be decided upon its merits by the Minister for Territories in consultation in view of the political aspects with the Minister for External Affairs'. It was Cabinet's understanding that the Dutch would bear the costs incurred in accommodating these refugees, and that there would be approximately 1200 Indonesian and Papuan refugees, 150 of whom were thought to want to remain in Papua and New Guinea.[124]

After the Dutch withdrawal from West New Guinea, several West Papuans who were openly critical of the Indonesian takeover applied to the Australian representative in Hollandia (today's Jayapura) to be allowed to settle in Papua and New Guinea as refugees; in many cases permission was granted. For several years the Dutch government supported these refugees financially. A small number of West Papuan tertiary students in Port Moresby, who had asked for political asylum, were initially also allowed to remain in Papua and New Guinea.

From late 1962 significant numbers of West Papuans crossed into Papua and New Guinea without first seeking Australian permission. Leaving aside the small group of Dutch-sponsored refugees, the Australian authorities distinguished between three types of 'border crossers': (a) 'Ordinary inland village people, still fairly primitive, who cross the border for purposes such as hunting, subsistence agriculture or visiting people of their clan'; (b) 'Unskilled, semi-sophisticates generally with limited primary school education who are half-heartedly looking for employment and a higher standard of living'; and (c) 'Genuine refugees'.[125]

In the first year after the Indonesians took control of West New Guinea, between June 1963 and May 1964, the Department of Territories counted 377 'non-political native refugees' who crossed the border without a valid visa – mainly, according to the department, for either of two reasons: 'general dislike of [the] Indonesian administration' or 'avoidance of conscription'.[126] All these people were turned back. In addition, there were 323 people from the south-east of West Irian who crossed into Australian Papua after at least one village had been pillaged by Indonesian troops. As Papuan villagers in the border region offered them land and invited them to stay, and as attempts by Australian and Indonesian patrols to persuade them to return across the border failed, the Australian administration treated these refugees as if they were locals who had crossed the border for social reasons.[127]

In March 1964 Charles Edward ('Ceb') Barnes, Paul Hasluck's successor as minister for territories, reviewed the issue and decided that the 1962 Cabinet ruling was still applicable. He also approved of the following statement: 'The fact is that, by an international decision to which Australia was party, West New Guinea is under Indonesian administration and the people of West New Guinea and the Administration of Papua and New Guinea alike have to learn to live with that situation.'[128] But the implementation of the government's policy was fraught with difficulties. The terrain and the constraints imposed by Australia's very limited presence in the border region made it impossible for patrol officers to police the border effectively. Those sent back sometimes returned to Australian territory and remained in hiding for as long as they were tolerated by local villagers.

While police were used to escort refugees to the border, illegal 'border crossers' were not sent back at gunpoint, and refugees probably knew that the Australian territory's police or army would not shoot at them if they decided to slip back across the border. Patrol officers sometimes took pity on refugees. In September 1964, assistant district officer A. M. Bottrill judged three refugees to be 'in such a dejected and desperate mood' that he sent them to a border village rather than back to West Irian.[129] But they, too, were eventually returned, after the district commissioner found that '[Bottrill's] heart got the better of him'.[130]

The first refugees who were not sponsored by the Dutch but nevertheless allowed to remain in the Australian territory were a family originally from the Moluccas and a West Papuan accompanying them: Benjamin Nikijuluw, his wife, their six children and their West Papuan servant, Djoni Jakedewa, crossed the border in September 1964.[131] Three months later, Jakedewa, whose father, mother and uncles had been killed by the Indonesians – possibly because of the father's association with

West Papuan nationalists – was granted permissive residence, even though his case was not covered by the Cabinet decision of August 1962.[132]

Several members of Benjamin Nikijuluw's family were living in exile in Holland. They were associated with the self-proclaimed Republic of South Maluku, an attempt to create an independent state comprising Seram, Buru, Ambon and some smaller islands in the west of the Indonesian archipelago. Nikijuluw and his wife and children were initially allowed to remain in Papua and New Guinea because the Australian government hoped the Dutch would accept them too. Nikijuluw's claims to have been persecuted were not as strong as those of some of the West Papuans who had been returned to West Irian in 1963 and 1964.

But the director-general of ASIO, Charles Spry, was not concerned that Nikijuluw's fear of persecution may have been difficult to prove; he felt that Nikijuluw was a genuine refugee because he had left considerable assets behind without any hope of recovering them once he entered the Australian territory.[133] In February 1966, after the Dutch government had declined Nikijuluw's application for permission to settle in Holland, he and his family were granted permissive residence in Papua and New Guinea – despite Indonesian protests, Indonesian claims that Nikijuluw had embezzled public money and had sex with his uncle's stepdaughter, and Indonesian demands that Nikijuluw be deported to Indonesia to face criminal charges.[134]

*

When responding to Hungarian athletes seeking asylum during the 1956 Melbourne Olympic Games, the Petrovs and the Zielinskis, the three Portuguese sailors deserting the *Gonçalves Zarco* in 1961, and West Papuan 'border crossers', the Australian government was not bound by international law to grant them asylum or to offer them protection as refugees. In signing the 1951 Refugee Convention, Australia had opted for the version that applied only to people who had become refugees as a result of events occurring before 1951 and in Europe. The

Universal Declaration of Human Rights, while not having similar geographical or temporal limitations, included the right to seek and enjoy asylum but did not oblige states to grant asylum to people fleeing persecution. Its wording was a far cry from that adopted earlier by the Commission on Human Rights. But for international lawyers and others involved in the push for a legally binding international human rights instrument, this was merely a temporary setback.

From the early 1950s, attempts resumed to devise an internationally binding instrument that would guarantee the right of asylum.[135] These centred initially on an attempt to include a right of asylum in the draft Covenant on Human Rights. In 1957 France submitted a draft declaration on the right of asylum to the thirteenth session of the Commission on Human Rights. In assigning the responsibility for granting asylum to the United Nations, this draft tried to circumvent the problem that nation-states were reluctant to agree to an instrument that would oblige them to grant asylum.

For the Australian government, this compromise was still unacceptable: the French proposal amounted to a 'substantial inroad on national sovereignty', as former crown solicitor Fred Whitlam, who had represented Australia at the Commission on Human Rights and continued to advise the government on international legal matters, wrote in 1958.[136] However, at the same time the Attorney-General's Department was comparatively relaxed about the Commission's initiative. 'So far as Australia is concerned, the matter of asylum is not one of great practical moment. Individuals who flee from other countries to seek asylum are rarely likely to reach Australia,' a departmental officer noted. He also assumed that if they did reach Australia, Australia would be bound by its domestic policies rather than by international agreements: 'Our nearest neighbours, too, are Asians and our immigration policy would probably prevent us from admitting Asians even for the purposes of asylum.'[137]

In October 1959 the Sixth Committee of the UN General Assembly passed a resolution calling upon the International Law Commission 'to undertake the codification of the principles and rules of international law relating to the rights of asylum'.[138] Australia was among a small minority of member states (led by the Soviet Union) which abstained. Among Canberra's policy-makers, opinions were divided about the stance to be adopted by Australia should a declaration on the right of asylum be put to a vote. The immigration department feared that such a declaration would impinge on Australia's sovereign right to decide whether or not to admit a non-citizen to its territory, but was eventually persuaded that a declaration would not be legally binding.[139] The Department of Territories, which was responsible for the administration of Papua and New Guinea, was concerned that Australia would be obliged to accommodate large numbers of West Papuans.[140] The Department of External Affairs, on the other hand, had as early as 1959 expressed misgivings about Australia's opposition to a declaration, if only because there were 'political grounds for our voting with the majority', particularly if that majority included the United States and the United Kingdom.[141]

Given that a United Nations declaration is not a binding agreement, and that the government had no intention of codifying the terms of that declaration in Australian domestic law, the case in favour of voting for a declaration, however much its terms privileged the rights of asylum seekers over the rights of nation-states, seemed clear-cut. However, Australia's at times fractious relationship with various United Nations bodies over its human rights record suggests that matters might be more complicated. The potential for such complications was recognised during discussions about a draft Declaration on the Right of Asylum. In 1965 Ted Hook, secretary of the Attorney-General's Department from 1964 to 1970, told his counterpart in the Department of External Affairs:

> [Simply] because the instrument is not, nor does it purport to be, an international agreement or convention, it must be borne in mind that this assessment of the legal effect of the instrument is made from the Australian viewpoint and by the application of Australian standards: it may be that countries outside the Anglo-American system of law would take a contrary view and maintain that a

Declaration of this kind, once arrived at, had legal value and, in fact, formed part of the general body of international law . . .

[Even] if the Australian view that such a Declaration has no legally binding force were accepted, it would not necessarily follow that criticism of Australia for failure to give effect to its provisions would be likely to be less.

Assuming that the Declaration on the Right of Asylum is adopted, with Australia voting in favour of its adoption, then it seems to me to be likely that if for any reason Australia in the future refused to grant asylum in a particular case it could be criticised internationally, and perhaps in Australia itself, if the refusal was thought to be contrary to the provisions of the Declaration. In such a situation, the distinction between principles to which Australia is legally bound is likely, it seems to me, to be regarded as a fine one and as not affording a substantial defence to the criticism.[142]

On 14 December 1967 the UN General Assembly adopted a Declaration on Territorial Asylum.[143] Australia voted in favour of the resolution. The Declaration did not go substantially further than Article 14 of the 1948 Universal Declaration on Human Rights and was not legally binding. Hook's fears that it might subsequently play a role in debates, either in Australia or in international fora, about how the Australian government ought to respond to refugees, proved unfounded. Ironically, the international instrument that has been regularly referenced by critics of Australia's response to asylum seekers is the 1951 Refugee Convention, although that instrument was not drafted to define an individual right to asylum, and in fact does not mention the term *asylum* except in its preamble.

\*

During the 1950s and 1960s, the Australian government was opposed to the idea of resettling refugees – or other immigrants, for that matter – in groups, because it wanted to avoid the creation of ethnic enclaves. However, in 1963–1964, the Menzies government seriously considered resettling a large, ethnically distinct group of people en masse on an island in Queensland. Although the people in question did not meet the requirements of the White Australia policy, it was not for want of goodwill on part of the government that the plan did not come to fruition.

The people in question were the 2600 inhabitants of Nauru, an island of 21 square kilometres in the Central Pacific. Nauru had become a German colony in 1888, was annexed by Australia during the First World War, in 1920 was entrusted to Australia, New Zealand and the United Kingdom under a League of Nations mandate, and in 1947 became a United Nations Trust Territory. Nauru was attractive to Western colonial powers because of its reserves of high-grade rock phosphate. Under the League of Nations and United Nations arrangements, the mined phosphate was shared between Australia (42 per cent), the United Kingdom (42 per cent) and New Zealand (16 per cent).

Phosphate mining was lucrative for the Western powers, but it created a barren wasteland unsuitable for agriculture and left much of the island uninhabitable. From the early 1950s, when the end of phosphate mining on the island was still thought to be a few decades away, the United Nations and the three trustees became increasingly convinced that the Nauruans needed to be resettled.[144] The trustees did not question their responsibility to provide the rapidly expanding population of Nauru – which was projected to reach 6000 by 1980 – with an economically sustainable alternative once mining was no longer an option, although they did not spell out its precise provenance or nature.

There was a precedent for resettlement. About 300 kilometres from Nauru lies another once phosphate-rich island, Banaba. Called Ocean Island in the 1950s, it was part of the British Gilbert and Ellice Islands colony, today's independent states of Kiribati and Tuvalu. Because of the environmental havoc wrought by the mining, the Banabans were resettled to Rabi Island in Fiji. (In turn, the indigenous Rabi Islanders were resettled on nearby Taveuni.)[145]

The first plans that the trustees drew up envisaged the *gradual* resettlement of Nauruans, possibly in a range of locations, including Australia. Even at a time when the Australian government was still vehemently opposed to suggestions that Australia be opened up to non-European immigration, the settlement of Nauruans was considered acceptable. 'The Nauruans are an intelligent people of good physique and likable character and during their visits to and residence in Australia they have been well received by the Australian people,' noted a paper prepared by the Department of Territories in 1952.

> They have a higher standard of living than the Papua New Guinea native and are generally much more advanced and would more easily fall into the Australian way of life . . . it would be in the interests of the natives of Nauru to be admitted to Australia for permanent residence should they so desire.[146]

The Nauruans themselves preferred to be resettled as a community on an island; however, neither of the two sites considered briefly in the 1950s – Laucala in Fiji and Woodlark in Papua and New Guinea – was deemed suitable.

In 1960 Dudley McCarthy, an assistant secretary of the Department of Territories, visited Nauru for two weeks to negotiate a solution that would be acceptable both to Australia and to the Nauruans. He did not come empty-handed; he had been authorised by his minister, Paul Hasluck, to make a generous offer. He told the Nauruan Local Government Council:

> We ask you to live with us; to become part of us and to allow us to become part of you; to accept completely and absolutely without reservations of any kind all the privileges which we ourselves achieved with painful struggle for our own people; to share with us common responsibilities; to build your homes on our land without restriction as to how much of that land you can ultimately

acquire for yourselves as individuals except the restrictions which are imposed by the system of justice which we will share and by the abilities of each individual; to make complete and unrestricted use of all our centres of learning and development; to accept the opportunity to gain for yourselves the highest offices in our country; to rest as securely under our protection as the most powerful and the most humble of our own people alike rest securely; to mix your blood with ours if you wish; to inherit with us everything of which we ourselves are the inheritors.[147]

McCarthy offered Nauruans cultural autonomy – 'You can preserve your traditions or national pride in any proper ways which seem fit to you' – but cautioned them that political autonomy would not be possible, since they would all become citizens of Australia.[148] He acknowledged that '[i]n a curious way you identify yourself with people for whom you work; and for whom you are responsible; and with whom your ways lie', but he denied that Australia, by offering to accommodate Nauruans in Australia, was discharging a debt or acting out of a moral obligation.[149]

The Nauruan councillors – led by Nauru's head chief, Hammer DeRoburt, an Australian-educated former teacher and since 1956 chairman of the Local Government Council – responded without much enthusiasm. They knew enough about Australia to be aware of the racism they might encounter if they settled there. They also insisted on being given a home to replace, as DeRoburt put it, 'a home given to them by God'.[150] 'A home must be a home at all times, in all circumstances, and in all aspects a home,' he said.[151] This home was to allow them to remain Nauruans. The head chief's counter-proposal was deceptively simple: the Australian government 'could cut us a slice of Australia and give it to us to be our own'.[152] For the Nauruan negotiators, political autonomy would guarantee racial homogeneity. They rejected McCarthy's offer and instead asked the Australian government to be given Fraser Island off the Queensland coast, or any other comparable island, as their new home.

Over the next four years the Nauruans remained unwavering in their demands, while the Australian government searched for a compromise that would be acceptable. In 1963 the government offered to resettle the Nauruans on Curtis Island, whose land area is well in excess of that of Nauru and which is within easy reach of the Queensland town of Gladstone. The Nauruans declined. They liked the location but were unhappy with the proposed political arrangements.[153] Curtis Islanders were also opposed to the plan; 'I'm going to walk up to the first nigger who comes ashore and punch him right in the eye,' one local resident, Frank Grant, was quoted as saying.[154] The federal government nevertheless persevered with its plans.

In January 1964 Cabinet authorised the purchase of the island from the Queensland government (subject to the latter exercising 'powers of acquisition to acquire all existing land interests'), and in April agreed that the Commonwealth's powers under Sections 51 and 52 of the Constitution be used to acquire the land if the Queensland government was not willing to sell it.[155] The government was confident that the Nauruans would agree to the proposed solution; Cabinet was more concerned about the response of the Queensland government.[156] By the second half of 1964, however, the negotiations reached a dead end, as the Nauruan negotiators kept insisting on political sovereignty.

In the early 1960s the Australian government went out of its way to pre-empt a scenario whereby the Nauruans would become environmental refugees due to the destruction of their home by phosphate mining. It did not want to be accused in the United Nations of neglecting its duty of care towards the Nauruans, but it also recognised a moral obligation. In 1962 Menzies told Queensland premier Frank Nicklin: 'The availability of a source of cheap rock phosphate at Nauru has been of very great importance to the primary industries of Australia, the United Kingdom and New Zealand and there is a clear obligation on the Governments of these countries to provide a satisfactory future for the Nauruans.'[157]

Such sentiments may appear surprising at a time when industrialised countries fail to recognise the obligations arising from the emission of greenhouse gases that cause climate change, which are likely to force the peoples of Pacific Islands nations such as Tuvalu and Kiribati to seek new homes because of rising sea levels.

\*

Under Menzies, Australia continued the policies introduced by the Chifley government. Mass immigration continued apace, but the composition of the migrant intake changed. As more shipping became available, and as Australia signed immigration agreements with several European countries, it no longer needed to recruit a large proportion of its immigrants from among European refugees. At the same time, the number of refugees of interest to Australia declined; as Australia did not want to resettle non-European refugees, and as most of the DPs had been resettled by the early 1950s, the pool of available and attractive refugees shrank. That changed only briefly, after the suppression of the Hungarian uprising in 1956, and then Australia was once more one of the key resettlement destinations.

Under Menzies, Australia gradually adopted a more humanitarian approach to refugee resettlement. Russian refugees from China, whose maintenance was guaranteed by the churches, were resettled throughout the 1950s and 1960s. At the end of the 1950s, in the course of World Refugee Year, Australia also agreed to accommodate some refugees who earlier had not been selected for resettlement for medical reasons. But in relation to Australia's overall migrant intake, the admission of so-called handicapped refugees was symbolic rather than substantial.

In the 1940s and 1950s migrants were expected to assimilate and, ideally, to become naturalised. Gradually, the idea that assimilation could be a two-way process, whereby migrants also changed the nature of Australian society, took hold. In 1959 immigration minister Downer praised the contributions of European migrants to 'our rather stodgy Anglo-Saxon communities'.[158] In 1964 the government dropped the term 'assimilation' and instead began promoting 'integration'.

The Menzies government had to deal with two new challenges. First, it responded to people seeking asylum *after* arriving in Australia. In 1956 Australia developed a comprehensive asylum seeker policy, which would remain in place until 1977. Second, Australia – or, rather, its Territory of Papua and New Guinea – became a country of first asylum after Indonesia occupied the Dutch colony of West New Guinea. Australia did not recognise the so-called 'border crossers' from West Papua as refugees in the terms of the 1951 Refugee Convention, nor did it grant them political asylum, but it allowed some of them to remain in Papua and New Guinea on temporary visas.

The Australian government was adamant that the West Papuan 'permissive residents' not be allowed to settle in Australia, because their admission would have contravened the White Australia policy, which during the Menzies era remained largely intact. The government was, however, prepared to resettle non-European environmental refugees from another colonial possession, Nauru, because it recognised that their displacement was the direct outcome of the mining of phosphate, which had benefited the three colonial powers, Australia, New Zealand and Britain.

In the next chapter I discuss how Australia's response to refugees and asylum seekers evolved after Menzies' retirement, which led to a relaxation of the White Australia policy.

# BORDER CROSSERS, EVACUEES AND POLITICAL REFUGEES

On Australia Day 1966 Harold Holt succeeded Robert Menzies as prime minister. Unlike his predecessor, Holt had a strong interest in immigration policy. For seven years, from 1949 to 1956, he had served as immigration minister under Menzies. He had overseen the continuation of the mass immigration program initiated by Arthur Calwell, but did not share Calwell's zealous commitment to the White Australia policy. Although the High Court had upheld the Labor government's *Wartime Refugees Removal Act 1949*, Holt did not make use of the legislation. During his tenure as immigration minister, the most famous victim of Calwell's hardline stance, former US Army sergeant Lorenzo Gamboa, was finally able to join his wife and children; the Japanese wives of Australian servicemen, who had previously been barred from entering the country, were also allowed to settle in Australia.[1] In the mid-1950s Holt oversaw tentative moves to reform the White Australia policy.[2] In 1964 immigration minister Hubert Opperman made another, bolder attempt to change Australia's discriminatory immigration policy, but failed because Menzies was unsupportive.[3]

When Holt assumed the prime ministership, he immediately revisited the issue of immigration reform. In his first public statement as prime minister he foreshadowed changes to the White Australia policy to make room for what he called a 'spirit of humanity'.[4] He had the support not only of Opperman, but also of the secretary of the Department of Immigration, Peter Heydon. A few days before Menzies' departure, Opperman met with Heydon and other senior departmental officials to map out a plan for reforms. The public servants were impatient to act; according to Heydon, Opperman felt the need to caution them that 'we must not appear to have been waiting for the old man to go'.[5] On 2 March 1966 Cabinet agreed to significant changes to the White Australia policy, which paved the way for its abolition seven years later. The decision was also a response to a shift in public opinion: by 1966 the majority of Australians wanted to see a liberalisation of the policy.[6]

After the end of the Menzies era, Australia continued to resettle European refugees. During Holt's prime ministership, however, the numbers were comparatively small. In a paper published in 1965, Heydon observed: 'What is called the problem of the "old" refugees in Europe has virtually been solved. Apart from residual problem cases and a trickle of refugees, the camps are almost empty.'[7] That was not to say that large populations of displaced people were a problem of the past. According to the UNHCR, in 1965 there were some 850,000 refugees in Africa alone.[8] Overall, however, in the mid-1960s there were far fewer displaced people globally than there were in the second half of the 1940s – or in the first half of the 2010s, for that matter.

From the 1960s Australia had to contend with growing expectations that it would resettle non-European refugees. Beginning in the middle of the decade, Vietnam emerged as the most obvious country of origin of such people. One of Australia's best known foreign correspondents, Denis Warner, was among the first to suggest that the government in Canberra consider putting the White Australia policy aside to assist Vietnamese refugees. In November 1964, several months before the first Australian and American combat troops were deployed in Vietnam, Warner told readers of the Melbourne *Herald* that people fleeing communist North Vietnam were looking to Australia as a country of resettlement: '[H]igh among the desirables, a country that has been second only to the adequately populated United States in encouraging these people to fight the Communists, is sparsely populated, under-developed White Australia.' According to Warner, Australia had an obligation to resettle people who had been told 'that they are holding the line in Asia, our line as well as theirs'.[9]

Similar suggestions were made throughout the second half of the 1960s and the first half of the 1970s. While the government never publicly countenanced the idea of resettling large numbers of Indochinese, it took note, and the issue was periodically the subject of correspondence involving the immigration and external affairs departments.

Despite the relaxation of the White Australia policy, it long remained unthinkable for the government to resettle non-European refugees. Commenting on the 'new refugee situations in Africa and the Middle East', Heydon wrote that 'resettlement in Australia is rarely an appropriate solution'.[10] In the mid-1960s Australia was directly dealing with only one group of non-European refugees: West Papuans fleeing former Dutch New Guinea to seek refuge in the Australian-controlled Territory of Papua and New Guinea. The number of West Papuan refugees gradually increased. There had been a total of 573 'border crossers' between 1963 and 1966. There were 866 in 1967, and 801 in 1968. Only a minority of these were allowed to remain in the Territory on five-year permissive residence visas; between 1962 and 1969, only seventy-five West Papuans and their families were granted visas.

Writing about West Papuans who crossed the border into Papua and New Guinea in 1968 and 1969, June Verrier astutely observed that most of them 'undoubtedly did so for political reasons, just as most of them were undoubtedly sent back also for political reasons'.[11] It may have been the case that only a small proportion of the West Papuan 'border crossers' returned by the Australians to Indonesian-held territory were political refugees. But the colonial administration in Port Moresby was not in a position to know for certain why West Papuans decided to cross the border. It was up to individual Australian patrol officers, the so-called kiaps, to decide if the protection claims of a particular 'border crosser' warranted further investigation, or if it appeared unlikely that he or she was a 'genuine refugee' – the label Territory officials tended to use to describe those whose protection claims merited recognition by the Australian government – and so could be swiftly returned to Indonesian-occupied territory.

The Territory's colonial administration often had only a very limited understanding of issues affecting Papua New Guineans; it knew even less about what went on in the former Dutch colony. When questioning West Papuans who had been provisionally allowed to remain in Papua and New Guinea, Territory officials were therefore often more interested in gathering intelligence about West Irian than in ascertaining the extent of a refugee's persecution at the hands of the Indonesian security services. Notwithstanding such attempts to learn about developments in the Indonesian-controlled half of New Guinea, however, the Australian authorities were generally in a poor position to anticipate future developments.

In June 1968, for example, the administration became excited about what it believed to be an imminent and large-scale influx of West Papuans. It had intelligence which suggested that there would be demonstrations against the occupiers on Indonesian Independence Day, 17 August 1968, that the Indonesian authorities would then overreact, and that this would trigger a refugee exodus. The Territory administration drew up detailed contingency plans;[12] they were shelved when the forecast events did not happen, to be revisited the next time the administration was gripped by panic.

The 1951 Refugee Convention applied only to persons who became refugees 'as a result of events occurring before 1 January 1951'. From the late 1950s, the UNHCR had been increasingly able to provide relief to people who were excluded by this qualifier and who had little in common with the DPs resettled in the late 1940s and early 1950s. From 1957, for example, the UNHCR assisted refugees in Tunisia, who had been fleeing the war in Algeria.[13]

Under high commissioners Auguste Lindt (1956–1960) and Félix Schnyder (1960–1965), the UNHCR expanded its reach, but it did so without a firm legal footing. In the mid-1960s the organisation decided that in order to be able to initiate interventions in refugee crises, it needed states to agree to the removal of both the temporal qualifier and (where applicable) the optional geographical limitation, and that such agreement would best be secured by a protocol rather than by an amend-ment of the original convention. The Protocol Relating to the Status of Refugees, which is often referred to as the Bellagio Protocol (named after the small town on the shores of Lake Como in the far north of Italy where its draft was discussed), entered into force on 4 October 1967. By the end of 1969 Australia's key allies, the United States and the United Kingdom, had both signed up to it.

Australia had been one of the very first states to accede to the 1951 Convention, yet in the late 1960s and early 1970s it was reluctant to ratify the 1967 Protocol. In interdepartmental discussions initiated by the Attorney-General's Department, both the Department of Immi-gration and the Department of Territories raised objections. The concerns of the latter, in particular, persuaded the Australian govern-ment to stay clear of the Protocol: by signing it, Australia would have implicitly invited the UNHCR's involvement in attempted solutions to the West Papuan refugee problem, since Article 2 of the Protocol obliges signatories to cooperate with the Office of the High Commissioner in the exercise of its functions, in particular to facilitate its duty of super-vising the application of the Protocol.[14]

Prince Sadruddin Aga Khan, who served as high commissioner for refugees from 1965 to 1977, repeatedly tried to convince the Aus-tralian government of the advantages of the UNHCR's involvement. Not only could the UNHCR assist the Australians in determining whether or not a 'border crosser' was a refugee under the terms of the 1951 Refugee Convention, it could also use its authority to assure those critical of Australia's approach 'that Australia was behaving properly'.[15] Despite his misgivings about the Australian practice of letting patrol officers decide whether or not to return somebody across the border, Sadruddin was an ally: in return for receiving confiden-tial briefings about the West Papuan refugee issue from the Australian government, he kept quiet (at least publicly), he advised members of his staff who questioned Australia's approach that the matter was not their concern as he was dealing with it personally, and he largely ignored the representations of West Papuan political activists.[16]

*

On 17 December 1967 Holt died while swimming at an ocean beach near Melbourne. After a twenty-five-day interregnum in which the nation was led by the Country Party's John ('Black Jack') McEwen, who twenty-nine years earlier had taken responsibility for the decision to admit up to 15,000 refugees from Europe, John Gorton became prime minister. It was on Gorton's watch that Australia once again responded to a refugee crisis unfolding in Europe.

On the night of 20 August 1968, the Prague Spring was brought to an abrupt end when troops of five Warsaw Pact countries – the Soviet Union, Bulgaria, Poland, Hungary and the German Democratic Republic – invaded Czechoslovakia. The Australian government was quick to denounce the invasion. Two members of cabinet, Malcolm Fraser and immigration minister Billy Snedden, attended a public protest meeting in Canberra. At the largest protest, held at the Olympic swimming stadium in Melbourne, Billy Kent Hughes delivered a personal message from Gorton.[17]

Unlike in Hungary twelve years earlier, there was no armed resistance to the invasion. Nevertheless, scores of people fled the country. Others who had gone abroad temporarily, taking advantage of the relaxation of travel restrictions during the Prague Spring, chose not to return. On 27 August Snedden assured parliament that if a refugee crisis eventuated, the government 'would respond as it has in similar situations in the past and as I am sure the Australian people would wish it to do'.[18] The next day, although there was no news yet of a major exodus of Czechs and Slovaks, Snedden said that he had 'instructed immigration posts overseas that they are to offer all possible help to Czechoslovakians wishing to come to Australia for resettlement'.[19]

The Department of Immigration moved fast. On 10 September Snedden announced that it had already approved 260 applications from

Czechs and Slovaks wishing to resettle in Australia.[20] Ten days later the first group of refugees arrived in Sydney. It was the first time that the government had chartered a plane to bring refugee migrants to Australia. Over the next couple of years, about 6000 of the 240,000 Czechs and Slovaks who had left their country in 1968 were resettled in Australia. They joined thousands of Czechs and Slovaks who had arrived in Australia following the 1948 coup, as we saw in Chapter 2.

As Snedden had predicted, most Australians welcomed the arrival of refugees from Czechoslovakia.[21] There were exceptions. In federal parliament Bert James, the Labor member for the New South Wales seat of Hunter, invoked the humanitarian crisis created by the war between Nigeria and Biafra, which had seceded from Nigeria in 1967. He suggested it was 'more important to fly food to the people of Biafra than to fly Czechs out here'.[22] Before entering parliament, James had been a policeman; perhaps that was why he chose a law-and-order argument to justify his opposition to the resettlement of Czechs and Slovaks. He claimed that the Hungarians who had been resettled after 1956 could not have been 'freedom fighters' because 'the true Hungarian freedom fighter died underneath the Russian tanks'.[23] Instead, according to James, they included 'some of the most skilled housebreakers and burglars this country has known'. He predicted that, in the case of refugees from Czechoslovakia, 'after a time it will be proved that a fair percentage of scum will have been allowed into Australia by the immigration authorities and by the security police'.[24]

Revelations that were made several years after James's death offered another perspective on his disdain for Hungarian dissidents: according to a Soviet intelligence dossier, James had been an informant for the KGB secret service.[25]

*

Since the first West Papuan refugees crossed into Papua and New Guinea, the Australian administration had been anxious that the Indonesian government not see their presence in the Territory as a provocation. Of particular concern were refugees who used the Territory as a base from which to agitate against Indonesian rule in their homeland, or from which to launch hit-and-run attacks on the Indonesian military. The obvious solution was to deny West Papuan permissive residents easy access to their supporters in West Papua and to likely sympathisers in Papua and New Guinea – that is, local and expatriate elites in the Territory's urban centres. In October 1968 a senior Territory bureaucrat assured his colleagues from the external affairs and external territories departments that all West Papuans granted permissive residence would be resettled away from the border area 'and, preferably, nowhere near other Irianese. The more difficult the new settler appears, the more isolated will be the area in which he is settled.'[26]

On 30 October 1968 the first thirty-eight refugees were transferred from the border area to Manus, a large island some 300 kilometres from the New Guinea mainland and more than 800 kilometres from Port Moresby. They were initially housed in police barracks on the edge of the district's administrative capital, Lorengau. They included both single men and families with children. In early 1969 work began on a purpose-built camp at Salasia, a government-owned coconut plantation a few kilometres outside Lorengau. The men selected to be accommodated at Manus tended to be well educated. They had been among those trained by the Dutch to run West Papua after the departure of the colonial administration. After crossing into Papua and New Guinea, they had settled in either Wewak or Vanimo, small coastal towns in the Sepik district, on the north coast of Australian New Guinea. Some of them had been employed in Dutch-owned shops.

In May 1969 the *South Pacific Post* journalist Jack McCarthy visited the camp at Lorengau. In a full-page article, titled 'Refugee "prisoners" live without hope', he painted a bleak picture.[27] 'For six months, they have sat on this island coast, limited by language and isolated by distance and their own inability to help themselves,' he wrote. 'As far as these people are concerned, this has become their Devil's Island.'

According to McCarthy, the West Papuans' main problems were that the men among them were unemployed and that the families were living on rations provided by the administration, whereas in Vanimo or Wewak they had had 'steady incomes and wages' and had been 'economically secure and happy'. McCarthy found the men 'sullen and silent, with six months of decaying idleness behind them and an indefinite period of the same ahead'.

The colonial administration was sensitive to that kind of public criticism, if only because it could be taken up by the indigenous elites in Papua and New Guinea and by the Australian public, sections of which had already begun to think of Australia's colonial commitment in the Pacific as an anachronism. An official was dispatched to Lorengau to investigate whether there was any substance to McCarthy's allegations. He concluded that the West Papuans' accommodation conditions were 'quite a degree better than [those of] many Public Servants in the town' – which could of course also be read as a comment on the standard of accommodation provided for the latter, particularly if they were locals.[28] The official did not dispute McCarthy's claim that the men were idle but did not think this was the administration's fault. He reported that they had 'shown no enthusiasm for work' and had in fact 'no intention of working except under their own terms'. He did recommend, however, that 'future camps be established in situations with more job opportunities'.

The question of whether or not the West Papuans on Manus were willing to work continued to exercise the colonial administration. By moving people who had been able to fend for themselves in places such as Vanimo and Wewak into a camp, the administration had created a situation in which refugees became dependent on government rations and donations from supporters overseas. From the government's point of view, the Salasia camp turned out to be counterproductive also for another reason. As the local district commissioner, Des Ashton, put it in 1971: '[T]hese people, if they are to remain in the Territory, must lose their identity as a group of West Irianese permissive residents and partake in communal affairs in other parts of the Territory as individuals.'[29]

In other words, by sequestering the West Papuans in a remote location, the authorities sabotaged what successive Australian governments had thus far regarded as the ultimate outcome of refugee settlement: assimilation.

While the administration had directed the West Papuans to live in the camp on Manus, it did not imprison them there. The children attended local schools, and the adults were encouraged to find employment. They were not living behind barbed wire; thus, their situation was very different from that of asylum seekers accommodated on Manus between 2001 and 2004, and again since 2012. There are nevertheless intriguing parallels: both in 1968 and in 2001 and 2012 the comparative remoteness of Manus made the island an attractive location for a camp. The authorities' decision was informed by the desire to move a group of displaced people out of sight, and away from potential support networks. In all three cases the government paid little attention to the specific local conditions on Manus, and ordered the refugees' transfer well before the facilities to accommodate them had been built.

In 1968 the decision makers in Port Moresby and Canberra had no experience of setting up and administering camps for asylum seekers and refugees. The same could not be said of those who devised the Pacific Solution in 2001. In fact, in 2001 policy-makers could have drawn on the experience of Australia's first refugee camp on Manus. They might have found that, even in an open camp, uncertainty about the future, a lack of meaningful work, and isolation from the local population took their toll on people who were particularly vulnerable because they had experienced forced displacement and, at least in some cases, imprisonment and physical abuse in their homeland.

\*

Compared with Holt, Gorton was a staunch defender of the White Australia policy. In April 1968, and then again in June 1969, his immigration minister, Billy Snedden, submitted proposals to Cabinet that would have extended the 1966 reforms, but on both occasions Cabinet, with the prime minister's backing, rejected Snedden's ideas.[30] 'I would want to see Australia remaining homogeneous, overwhelmingly homogeneous, as I think that this is the only way one can avoid racial tensions,' Gorton told an interviewer in January 1971.[31] Thus, he was even less likely than his predecessor to set a precedent by allowing non-European refugees to settle in Australia. Australia remained committed to supporting the work of the UNHCR, but as far as refugee crises outside of Europe were concerned, such support consisted of monetary contributions rather than offers of resettlement.

The White Australia policy could be easily enforced when refugees were in a third country. While non-European refugees had entered Papua and New Guinea, thus far none had arrived uninvited in Australia itself. That changed on 16 February 1969, when Australia's first eight 'boat people' (or, rather, 'raft men', as they were dubbed) landed on Moa (Banks) Island in the Torres Strait. They were West Papuans who had travelled by raft from a village near Merauke, a coastal town about 100 kilometres from the border between Indonesian-occupied West Irian and Australian Papua. From there, it is less than 200 kilometres to Moa, but because of unfavourable winds their journey had lasted more than a month. One of their party had died while they were drifting between the New Guinea mainland and Cape York Peninsula.

There are two written accounts of interviews held with the men in the days after they landed in Australia. Thursday Island resident Roland ('Rolly') Cantley interviewed the men a day after their arrival. He recorded a first-person narrative from Alexander Toembay, the leader of the West Papuans. Toembay spoke of Indonesian persecution. He also shed light on the men's decision to head for Australia. 'I hope that Australian people give us political protection and allow us to live in peace,' he told Cantley. 'But I also hope that people of Australia help us to get independence that was promised in the United Nations for people of West Irian. Then we would like to go back and help make it a good country to live in.'[32]

The other account was provided by a sub-collector of customs, who on 18 February had spoken to the men on behalf of the Department of Immigration and arranged for their transfer to Thursday Island. His report includes a description of their harrowing journey. He also noted that the men were members of the Organisasi Papua Merdeka (OPM), a West Papuan independence movement which had been waging a guerrilla war against the Indonesian occupiers.[33] He later added that they had not explicitly requested political asylum, 'but when asked if they would return to West Irian they became depressed and said that "this would mean the end"'.[34]

Unbeknown to those who interviewed him on Moa, Toembay had already been found to be what Australian government officials often referred to as a 'genuine refugee'.[35] He had first entered Papua and New Guinea in 1963, been granted permissive residence, and worked for Radio Daru. In April 1968 Toembay returned to West Irian of his own volition. He was accompanied by ten other West Papuan émigrés (including two who would be with him on his 1969 trip to Australia). At the time he claimed:

> that his decision to return to West Irian was influenced by a Radio Australia news broadcast in Bahasa Indonesia which stated that the United Nations was going to 'move back' into West Irian on 1st May 1968 in order to supervise and prepare the country for the 'plebiscite' in 1969.[36]

Five days after the arrival of the eight West Papuans, representatives of the external affairs, external territories and immigration departments conferred in Canberra. The immigration department's representative favoured the men's removal to the Territory of Papua and New Guinea (TPNG), where their claims for protection could be assessed in line with the procedures in place for West Papuans seeking asylum there. He argued that 'it would be undesirable to encourage future refugees to make for Australia by allowing this group to settle there'.[37] An external affairs official pointed out that, '[i]f settled in Australia, refugees would be much more accessible to the press whereas it would be possible to isolate them to some extent in TPNG'.[38] He may have been thinking of the Salasia camp. His department was mindful of Prime Minister Gorton's policy directive that there must be 'no trouble with Indonesia over West Irian',[39] but he did not think the directive warranted deporting the men to West Irian (although he did not want to rule out deportation as an option).

External territories minister Ceb Barnes believed that the eight West Papuans were not his responsibility. A representative of his department therefore argued against transferring them to Papua and New Guinea. He said that a forcible removal to the Territory 'could lead to unfavourable comment' in the parliament in Port Moresby, 'to the effect that they were not good enough to be allowed to live in Australia'. He too thought that their deportation to West Irian, on the other hand, was an option, if only because it was guaranteed to please the Indonesian government.[40]

In the end, the arguments of the immigration and external affairs departments and their respective ministers, Billy Snedden and Gordon Freeth, prevailed, and it was decided to process the West Papuans in Papua and New Guinea and, in the case that their asylum applications were successful, to settle them there in the same way in which some of the 'border crossers' had been granted temporary visas. But the government also acknowledged the validity of a point made by one of the public servants involved in the interdepartmental discussions: 'that the refugees had indicated that they did not wish to go to TPNG and . . . that they should not be moved against their will'.[41] This argument was presumably given additional weight by the fact that, probably thanks to Rolly Cantley, the Australian news media had become aware of the West Papuans' landfall on an Australian island.[42]

As the government ruled out the enforced removal of the eight West Papuans from Thursday Island, it had to rely on their cooperation. The task to persuade them that their own interests were best served by their transfer to Papua and New Guinea fell to an immigration official. He was instructed to inform the men that 'the Australian Government had decided they will not be allowed to remain in Australia', that the government had offered to hear their cases in Papua and New Guinea, and that, alternatively, 'serious consideration will have to be given to their departure for West Irian'.[43] The men's response to the government's offer was 'lukewarm' but the implied threat of deporting them to Indonesian-controlled territory was eventually effective. 'After much deliberation,' the immigration official reported, 'the group decided to go to Papua New Guinea on my assurance that their cases would be properly heard on their arrival there.'[44]

On 24 February 1969, the day after their meeting with the immigration official, the men were flown to the Weam patrol post, near the border between West Irian and Papua's Western District. A sympathetic full-page article by Rolly Cantley in the *Australian Women's Weekly*, which humanised their story and was illustrated by photos depicting the eight men and their raft, might have mobilised public support but was published two days after their removal to Weam.[45] Ten days later, in parliament, external affairs minister Freeth was able to tell the Labor Party's Jim Cairns that the men – whom he referred to as 'refugees' – 'voluntarily went to Papua and New Guinea to have their request for permissive residence examined'.[46] He also commented more generally on those crossing the border into the Australian territory, suggesting that they included people who came 'with the intention of carrying out aggressive tendencies against the Territory'.[47]

Freeth later asked for his statement to be corrected in Hansard: in the edited version he refers to West Papuans entering Papua and New Guinea 'with the intention of carrying out aggressive or political activities against the area they have left'.[48] The slip of tongue was understandable: the government believed that attempts to attack or embarrass Indonesia from the safety of Papua and New Guinea were damaging Australia's relations with its northern neighbour and jeopardising the Territory's future as an independent nation.

The Territory's administration moved quickly to assess the eight men's claims for political asylum. Two days after their transfer from Thursday Island, a Special Branch officer interviewed them at Weam. His findings were then evaluated by the administration in Port Moresby. On 17 April 1969 the Territory's administrator, David Hay, found that:

> On political grounds it is not considered that the situation in West Irian has deteriorated since April, 1968 when [Toembay and two others] voluntarily elected to return. In fact, it is only because of their continued anti-Indonesian attitudes, unwillingness to adapt to the regime there, that their future may be compromised. In view of the Indonesian offer to West Irianese abroad it is not unlikely that if they returned to West Irian and settled down to make an honest attempt to work and live, they could do so without much hindrance . . . The circumstances do not clearly warrant the grant of permissive residency on humanitarian grounds. That is, we are not convinced that the eight persons would be in danger of loss of life or serious loss of liberty.[49]

The administrator was mindful that, 'largely resulting from the sympathy and widespread publicity following their raft trip, it could be politically embarrassing to return them'. But he cited another reason for not granting the men permissive residence permits. He pointed out that the behaviour of five of them, who had been living in the small Papuan town of Daru before returning to West Irian in 1968, had been 'most unsatisfactory'. '[T]hey are lazy, unwilling to work or assimilate, have an exaggerated opinion of their own importance and capabilities, and hold the Australian government responsible for much of what has happened to them,' Hay complained. 'They regard it as a right to be fed, clothed and housed – without working.'[50]

Following Hay's line of argument, the Department of External Territories recommended that the eight applications for permissive residence in Papua and New Guinea be refused, that the men be removed to West

Irian unless the Dutch government offered to resettle them in the Netherlands, and that the Indonesian government be informed of the decision
prior to the men's return to West Irian. The ministers responsible for the
granting of residence to asylum seekers in the Australian territory, Freeth
and Barnes, concurred with this recommendation.[51]

Eighteen months earlier, the Australians had deported a West
Papuan refugee, Adrian Dedda, because he had become mentally ill.
Dedda had been sponsored by the Dutch government to study medicine in Port Moresby, had refused to return home when the Indonesians
occupied the Dutch colony, and had successfully sought asylum in Papua
and New Guinea. During his time in Port Moresby, he had been an
outspoken critic of the Indonesian government, yet Australian government officers had flown him to Indonesian territory and watched him
being taken away by Indonesian officials.[52]

Toembay and his companions were spared such a fate: neither were
they directly handed over to the Indonesian authorities, nor did the
Australians notify the Indonesians that the West Papuans were sent
back across the border. In fact, two days after Ceb Barnes had approved
of Toembay's deportation, the Indonesians came looking for him. A
group of ten soldiers crossed the border into Papua and New Guinea
near the Weam patrol post, abducted three adults and six children, and
questioned them about refugee movements, the number of West Papuans at Weam and Toembay's whereabouts.[53] Despite what their interest
suggests, Toembay, at least, does not seem to have been victimised by
Indonesia's security services after his deportation in 1969. A year later
he reappeared in Papua and New Guinea – not to stay, but with the
intention of 'just passing through to go on to Thursday Island'.[54]

In July and August 1969 the Indonesians conducted the so-called
Act of Free Choice, a United Nations–sanctioned vote in which the people of West Papua were invited to decide whether they wanted the former
Dutch colony to become part of Indonesia. However, rather than organ-
ising a referendum, as suggested by Fernando Ortiz Sanz, the Bolivian
diplomat appointed by United Nations Secretary-General U Thant to

supervise the vote, the Indonesian authorities selected 1025 'elders' to act on behalf of all West Papuans. Not surprisingly, the outcome was a vote in favour of incorporation with Indonesia, and at the conclusion of the Act of Free Choice, West Papua became the Indonesian province of Irian Jaya. The Gorton government recognised the legitimacy of Indonesia's claim to West Papua – as have all subsequent Australian governments, for that matter.

Prior to the Act of Free Choice, Indonesia had invited West Papuan exiles to return to West Papua to participate in the vote, but only one family living in Australian New Guinea decided to accept that invitation, returning to West Papua in May 1969.[55] West Papuan nationalists did not accept the outcome of the Act of Free Choice, and the OPM intensified its guerrilla warfare against the Indonesians. This led to an increase of refugee movements across the border to Papua and New Guinea. Rather than settling the issue, the Act of Free Choice only strengthened the claims of West Papuan nationalists that Indonesia's rule was illegitimate.

\*

In March 1971 William McMahon successfully challenged for the Liberal Party leadership and replaced Gorton as prime minister. McMahon's approach to West Papuan refugees did not depart from that of his predecessors. With hundreds of West Papuan activists now living on permissive residence visas in Papua and New Guinea, and an at times tense situation at the border between Irian Jaya and the Australian colony, the issue of 'border crossers' had only become more delicate.

That same year the Australian authorities were faced with a particularly thorny case when they received an application for permissive residence from Mozes Weror – in the words of a foreign affairs official, it was 'perhaps the most difficult such application that Ministers have had to consider to date'.[56] Unlike previous applicants, Weror was known personally to some of the decision-makers in Canberra. In 1962 he had accompanied Barwick and Townley on their tour of Indonesia. For the next five years, from June 1962, he had been third secretary at the Indonesian embassy in Canberra. The Australians knew that he was critical of Indonesia's annexation of West Papua. When Weror left the diplomatic service in 1967, apparently after disagreeing with his superiors over Indonesia's policy in West Papua, he was already rumoured to be considering a request for asylum rather than a return to West Papua.[57] In 1969 Weror was arrested by the Indonesians for his part in a protest against the Act of Free Choice in Jayapura, and jailed without trial for seven and a half months.[58]

In September 1971 foreign minister Nigel Bowen granted Weror's request for permissive residence, although his department had told Bowen that Weror's claim was 'weaker than that of the more active dissidents'. The government, however, was wary of the attention he had attracted when arriving in the Territory – Jack McCarthy had written a sympathetic full-page article about him in Port Moresby's *Post-Courier*, and a week later the *Sydney Morning Herald* had reported his asylum request on its front page, and had then published a lengthy article based on an interview with him. The Department of Foreign Affairs feared that 'there could be widespread criticism of the government in TPNG and Australia if he were sent back'.[59]

As it allowed Weror to remain in Papua New Guinea, the Australian authorities emphasised that he was under no circumstances to criticise Indonesia from the safety of his exile; a foreign affairs official recommended 'quickly and thoroughly' dampening any interest Weror had in getting the Australian and Papua New Guinean public interested in the issue of West Papua.[60] Like other permissive residents, Weror was required to sign an undertaking which committed him and his family to refrain from engaging 'in political activities or public comment to the press, or any other media against the activities of the authorities in West Irian'.[61] Over the next couple of years, the Territory administration anxiously watched Weror, hoping he would abide by its rules.

*

McMahon and his immigration minister, Jim Forbes, also had to deal with a major international refugee crisis in 1972, when Uganda's dictator, Idi Amin, expelled tens of thousands of Asians. Apart from the events along Papua and New Guinea's border to Indonesian-controlled West Papua, this was the first refugee crisis affecting only non-Europeans that prompted Australia to respond other than by providing funds for humanitarian aid.

Like other countries in Eastern and Southern Africa, Uganda had a small but visible South Asian minority.[62] Many had been brought to Uganda by the British to serve in the colonial army or build the country's railways. Others had come to work as clerks or mechanics, or set themselves up as traders. At the time of Uganda's independence in 1968, Asians comprised about 1 per cent of the population. About a quarter of them applied for Ugandan citizenship at the time, with about half of those unsuccessful in their applications.

From the late 1960s the Ugandan and Kenyan governments encouraged Asian residents to leave. Most were entitled to British passports, and many would have been only too willing to migrate to the United Kingdom, but in 1968 the British parliament passed the *Commonwealth Immigrants Act* to curtail the immigration of British passport holders from East Africa; many of East Africa's Asians therefore stayed put.[63]

On 4 August 1972 President Amin announced that all Asian residents holding British passports had to leave the country. Over the next few days, he extended his decree to include residents of India, Bangladesh and Pakistan, and set midnight of 8 November 1972 as the deadline. Between August and November 1972 more than 50,000 Asians fled Uganda. They included many Ugandan passport holders – either because their citizenship had been revoked or because they feared for their lives.

The Conservative British government of Edward Heath acknowledged its obligation to admit at least those Asians who were entitled to British passports, but had to contend with a public that was largely opposed to the admission of tens of thousands of Asians. It therefore appealed to other Commonwealth countries – in particular, India, Pakistan, Canada and Australia – to take some of the expellees.

When it became public knowledge that the British government was hoping, if not expecting, that Australia would take some of the expelled Asians from Uganda, Forbes declared that the government was not intending to invite anybody from Uganda to resettle merely because they were refugees. In other words, there were to be no exceptions to Australia's restrictive immigration policy. 'Applications by Asians in Uganda will continue to be considered on their individual merits in accordance with our non-European immigration policies,' Forbes said in parliament on 17 August. 'These policies reflect the firm and unshakeable determination of the Government to maintain a homogenous society in Australia.'[64] Five days later the issue was on Cabinet's agenda: Forbes' colleagues backed him and decided that Australia would not depart from its established immigration policy. There would be no special treatment for Asians forced out of Uganda, as there had been for Czechs and Slovaks four years earlier.

'The Australian Government's lack of response, though understandable in terms of domestic policies, is very disappointing and in marked contrast to the generous Canadian offer,' foreign secretary Alec Douglas-Home cabled the British high commission in Canberra on 30 August.[65] He suggested that the Australians might be lobbied on two fronts: Heath could approach McMahon, and former Labour prime minister Harold Wilson could talk to Whitlam. The high commission did not think that McMahon was likely to change his mind, and advised against approaching the leader of the opposition: the Australian Labor Party was divided, and aware that 'advocacy on relaxed line could be electorally damaging'.[66]

Earlier, the foreign office had tried to enlist the help of a member of the Heath government: Margaret Thatcher, then secretary of state for education and science, was scheduled to travel to Australia in late August, and before her trip received a briefing from a British foreign affairs official. Her response indicates that she may not have tried to lobby the

Australians, and it demonstrates that the ruling Conservatives were themselves divided over the question of how to respond to the crisis in Uganda. '[She] opened our conversation by telling me that she hoped she would *not* be asked to press the Australians on [accepting refugees from Uganda]', the official briefing her reported. 'She made it very clear that, in her view, Australian immigration policy is in the best interests of that country and that this is not the case with our policy.'[67]

Among the approximately 3000 migrants admitted to Australia under its revised non-European policy each year since the 1966 immigration reforms, the number of Asians from East Africa was negligible; they included only forty-five non-European families (totalling 180 persons) from Uganda. In 1970, when the Kenyan government had threatened to discriminate against residents of Asian ancestry, the Australian government had in fact been careful not to encourage applications from Asians living in East Africa. This was despite the fact that, according to the immigration attaché at the Australian high commission in Nairobi, 60 per cent of applicants met Australia's requirements.[68]

The immigration department, however, was willing to fast-track applications from Asians in Uganda. On 20 September, with six weeks of Amin's three-month ultimatum already gone, John Paddick, the immigration attaché at the Australian high commission in Nairobi, travelled to the Ugandan capital, Kampala, where Australia did not maintain a permanent diplomatic mission, to hand out forms and interview applicants. He had planned to stay one week, but due to the high level of interest in migration to Australia he remained for six.

Paddick found that '[i]f [Australia's] policy was relaxed I consider we could select 1000 good types with useful trade and semi-professional qualifications'.[69] But the government was unwilling to waver. By the time the ultimatum had expired, Australia had approved 190 applications covering 491 persons; more than twice that number were rejected. A fortnight into his stay in Kampala, Paddick confided to a Canadian colleague that he was 'utterly frustrated' at the number of times the immigration department in Canberra rejected applicants he had interviewed.[70] Furthermore, according to Paddick, during the Ugandan crisis a total of some 2000 enquirers were told not to bother submitting an application.[71]

The majority of the expellees who had been approved by the Department of Immigration did not make use of their visas; by the time Amin's deadline expired, only forty-six of the 491 had arrived in Australia. Many of those who were approved by Australia had other options. Their qualifications and skills meant they were sought after as immigrants also by Britain, the United States and Canada; many applicants went 'visa-shopping', and those with transferable skills and qualifications often ended up with offers from several countries. The most highly qualified, who had the best chances of being resettled, were not even required to leave Uganda. Two-thirds of those approved by Australia in September and October 1972 belonged to categories that Amin had exempted from the expulsion order.

Other countries were more generous than Australia. Canada issued visas to 6175 Asians from Uganda, and flew 4200 of them to Canada on government-funded charter flights. New Zealand announced that it would take 200 expellees, and offered to cover the cost of fares from London. Several Western European countries also provided resettlement places.

British diplomats thought they knew why Australia was reluctant to accommodate Asians from Uganda; in late August they reported that they had 'been told privately that with elections pending Ministers do not feel they could risk forfeiting votes by being more forthcoming'.[72] The Labor Party's foreign affairs spokesperson, Don Willesee, said on 22 August that 'Australia should not stand by with eyes closed to suffering which is being so heartlessly thrust on these people', but neither he nor his leader, Gough Whitlam, campaigned for a change of Australia's approach.

That was partly to do with internal divisions within the Labor Party. Since 1971 its platform had called for a non-discriminatory immigration policy, but some senior Labor politicians openly disagreed with their party's official position. These included Fred Daly, who had been the party's immigration spokesperson until 1971, when he had to be sacked by Whitlam after defending the White Australia policy in contravention of Labor's platform. Former party leader Arthur Calwell was another prominent dissident. In October he claimed that 'the overwhelming majority of Australians do not want to see any Ugandan Asians brought to Australia', and asked Forbes in parliament:

> Will he tell the do-gooders who have been pressuring his Department on African and Asian migration to exhaust themselves in doing something practical to help fair dinkum Australians to do something worthwhile for the Australian Aborigines who alone have a claim for justice and fair treatment by the Australian people[?][73]

A variant of this argument was resurrected in the late 1990s by Pauline Hanson and her One Nation party. Hanson's racism would prove even more offensive than Calwell's, but not because the latter had been any less crass. A few months before speaking out against the admission of Asians from East Africa, Calwell had criticised the immigration of Mauritians, Ceylonese Burghers, Anglo-Burmese and Anglo-Indians who had been admitted under Australia's 'mixed race' policy. He said that he did not want a 'chocolate-coloured Australia', and claimed that some of the recent immigrants of mixed descent 'live on the smell of an oily rag and breed like flies'.[74]

While the Labor leadership was largely indifferent to Forbes' intransigence, the government was not without its detractors. They included church leaders and three prominent state politicians: the Labor premiers of South Australia and Western Australia, Don Dunstan and John Tonkin, and the Liberal premier of Victoria, Rupert Hamer. The *Australian* newspaper was also a strident critic of the government's policy. But the government may have agreed with Calwell's assessment that most voters did not want Asians from Uganda to be resettled in Australia, and that it could afford to ignore the 'do-gooders'. The government's attitude was encapsulated by the remark of a foreign affairs official in mid-September 1972, that the 'predictable people and papers quickly said and printed the predictable things'.[75]

The only argument that seems to have been acceptable to McMahon and his cabinet was put forward by former immigration minister Alick Downer, who by then was Australia's high commissioner in London. He thought that the refusal to admit refugees outside the criteria of established immigration policy was damaging Australia's international reputation. Downer reiterated a pragmatic view, which many external affairs officials had held throughout the 1950s and 1960s: they objected to the White Australia policy not because it was racist but because it gave Australia a bad name. Downer's argument was also reminiscent of that put forward by one of his more illustrious predecessors: as we saw in Chapter 1, Stanley Bruce had urged the government in 1938 to announce a generous quota for European refugees in the interests of Australia's reputation.

Days before Amin's November deadline, the UNHCR, with the help of the ICEM and the Red Cross, evacuated the remaining expellees to five transit camps in Europe. Most were stateless and therefore had no claim to being resettled in Britain. In December the Labor Party won Australia's federal election, and Whitlam became prime minister. The new government swiftly announced that it had dispensed with the remnants of the White Australia policy. Whitlam appointed Al Grassby, the son of Spanish and Irish parents and since 1969 the member for Riverina, as minister for immigration. Grassby stood for what Labor's last immigration minister, Arthur Calwell, had despised with a vengeance: a multicultural and multi-ethnic Australia. Grassby was credited with saying during a visit to the Philippines, where many remembered the saga surrounding Sergeant Gamboa's attempts to join his wife in Australia, that the White Australia policy 'is dead – give me a shovel, and I will bury it'.[76]

On 2 February 1973 Whitlam and Grassby decided to depart from their predecessors' policy, offering resettlement places to fifty families of stateless Ugandans in transit camps. At the same time, Grassby instructed his department to relax its selection criteria. By the end of June, however, of the 4416 persons initially accommodated in the five transit camps, Australia had resettled only nine. By then the United States had resettled 1308, while Canada, which had already accepted thousands directly from Uganda, had taken in another 438.

Even after the change of government in December 1972, Australia's response remained miserly in comparison with that of other Western countries because the immigration department paid little attention to Grassby's policy directive. Any piece of evidence suggesting that applicants would experience difficulties finding a job or would not readily integrate into Australian society counted against them. The department turned down applications also on health grounds. A widow and her five children, for example, were rejected because one of the daughters 'has epilepsy which brings her under Section 16 of the Migration Act and she is not suitable for entry any category'.[77]

Other countries explicitly suspended similar provisions of their immigration policies. New Zealand's prime minister Norman Kirk, for example, said at a press conference in April 1973:

> I don't think we can stand aside and say we'll only take the best apples in the barrel and that's all we are interested in. And I am sure that most New Zealanders will agree that the families who have handicapped members are probably the ones who need the bit of consideration more than the others, at the present time.[78]

Although Kirk's choice of words may have been unfortunate, the sentiment behind it was far more generous than that which informed the approach of the Whitlam government. Kirk's stance was partly a response to lobbying, particularly by the churches, for a relaxation of the selection criteria; the general secretary of the National Council of Churches, for example, had said in January that New Zealand had acted slowly and selfishly, 'taking the cream and leaving the others to flounder'.[79]

Kirk's statement also reflected his personal conviction that New Zealand had a responsibility to act as a good international citizen. In March 1973 he had met with a senior UNHCR representative, Ole Volfing, who had asked for New Zealand's intake of Ugandan Asians to increase. Volfing was anxious not to overplay his hand, telling Kirk that the UNHCR 'would not submit for entry to New Zealand an elderly couple without a breadwinner'. According to a record of the conversation kept by Kirk's staff, 'The Prime Minister asked why not. Mr Volfing replied that they would rather have New Zealand take increased numbers of people than concentrate on such handicapped.' Kirk seemed surprised by this explanation and remarked that 'it may be the handicapped who need New Zealand's help more than the others'.[80]

On the other side of the Tasman Sea there was little enthusiasm for an increased intake of Asians from Uganda, particularly if they included refugees who were unlikely to secure employment. Besides, the staff of the Department of Immigration were slow to embrace the policy changes, even though the White Australia policy had been officially abolished. The fact that an applicant from the transit camp in Malta had 'African appearance, dark complexion, frizzy hair' was, almost a month after Grassby's announcement of a change in Australia's policy, still noted – presumably because the man's African appearance was considered a detriment.[81]

The immigration department's persistent commitment to the White Australia policy is exemplified in an anecdote Grassby told in 1984 about a tour of the department's state offices soon after he became immigration minister:

[I]n the Sydney office I explained, as I did in every other office, that the new policies would be totally non-discriminatory. That would be reflected in the filing, in the terminology and everything else. So, one very senior officer told my private secretary, he said 'He can't do that. It's against departmental policy.'[82]

Grassby himself and the Department of Foreign Affairs, which had a particular investment in a non-discriminatory policy, knew that the immigration department was dragging its feet in implementing the policy changes. In fact, it was not until the late 1970s that 'many procedural and legal obstacles' to the implementation of Grassby's reforms were removed.[83]

Despite Al Grassby's good intentions, the Whitlam government's approach to Asians from Uganda was in stark contrast to that of its counterpart in New Zealand, but barely differed from the McMahon government's. In fact, the positions of McMahon and Whitlam themselves were remarkably similar. In October 1972 an ABC journalist asked McMahon whether, as far as the expelles from Uganda were concerned, immigration policy ought to be guided by compassion. 'I think our own interests must come first,' the prime minister replied, 'and consequently we should be able to choose those migrants that are going to make the greatest contribution to the development of this country.'[84] Six months later, during a visit to London, Whitlam was asked whether the abolition of the White Australia policy meant that now Australia would accommodate more Asians from Uganda. He replied: 'If they have got qualifications such as entitle people to come to Australia then certainly they can come.'[85]

While McMahon was reluctant to admit refugees from Uganda because he remained committed to the fantasy of a White Australia, Whitlam was merely indifferent to the plight of East Africa's Asians – but as would soon become clear, the flipside of Whitlam's indifference towards the fate of Uganda's Asians was not a heightened concern for refugee populations elsewhere. In this instance, however, his indifference was perhaps understandable. Australia agreed to resettle some Asians from Uganda not so much because the Ugandan expellees had nowhere else to go but because it tried to share the burden carried by the United Kingdom, which had a moral obligation to resettle them – or, rather, because it did not want to be seen as immune to British appeals to share that burden.

In comparison with most other significant refugee crises in the twentieth century, that in Uganda was dealt with exceptionally swiftly and comprehensively and through a concerted effort of Western governments and international organisations. By the end of 1973 all but 100 of those forced to leave Uganda had been resettled, and a year later they too had been offered new homes.

At around the same time as the UNHCR was trying to find resettlement places for Asians from Uganda, it was dealing with the aftermath of the conflict between Pakistan and India. Hostilities had ceased in December 1971, when the Pakistani forces surrendered and East Pakistan became Bangladesh, and soon after the UNHCR was able to assist in the repatriation of millions of people who had become displaced during the conflict. More than four decades later, a permanent solution has yet to be found for hundreds of thousands of Biharis and members of other Urdu-speaking minorities in Bangladesh, who in 1971 became stranded in Bangladesh. They are not wanted by Pakistan or India, and are often not entitled to citizenship and voting rights in Bangladesh.[86]

*

On 11 September 1973 the Chilean military, led by General Augusto Pinochet, staged a coup against the democratically elected government of Salvador Allende. The coup had been supported by the CIA – which, in turn, had received some assistance from its Australian counterpart, the Australian Secret Intelligence Service (ASIS). ASIS had had two operatives stationed at the embassy in Santiago. Whitlam later claimed that, upon learning about them in April 1973, he ordered their immediate withdrawal, but that the head of ASIS, Bill Robertson, possibly in collusion with Australia's ambassador, Noël Deschamps (referred to later as 'our despicable diplomat' by Whitlam),[87] defied the prime minister's orders. Robertson disputed this version of events, but all sources agree that ASIS had two men stationed in Santiago, and that one of them left only after the coup.[88]

The 11 September coup was accompanied by a wave of arrests of officials and supporters of the Allende government. Trade unionists and members of leftist parties went into hiding or fled abroad. Some sought refuge in diplomatic missions in Santiago, including the Australian embassy. This was the first time that Australia dealt with requests for extra-territorial – or diplomatic – asylum. Like most other Latin American countries, Chile had signed the 1954 Caracas Convention on Diplomatic Asylum, but because Australia was not a signatory, the Chilean government was under no obligation to recognise and respect Australia's decision to grant asylum to somebody calling at its Santiago mission. Chile was, however, obliged to respect the inviolability of diplomatic missions – much as the United Kingdom authorities must not enter the Ecuadorian embassy in London to arrest Julian Assange, who was granted asylum by Ecuador and has been holed up in its embassy in London since 2012.

Australian embassy staff, however, told enquirers that because Australia was not a party to relevant conventions, it could not guarantee the safety of asylees. Instead, the Australians 'discreetly' arranged for those who sought Australia's protection to enter other embassies.[89] On 5 December one of those seeking refuge at the Australian mission called the Australians' bluff and refused to leave. The chargé d'affaires, Ian James, reported to Canberra:

> The man was terrified and exhausted and with armed police passing in the street between other embassies nearby I had no option but to offer him temporary shelter, after my explaining that we could not grant him diplomatic asylum nor any final solution to his problem. And his polite but firm reiteration that he would not leave voluntarily.[90]

In this case, James was able to persuade the Norwegian ambassador to accommodate the man, and arranged for his transfer to Norway's Santiago embassy the next day.

The reason given by Australia's diplomatic representatives may have appeared spurious to people seeking its protection. The embassies of other Western countries which had not signed up to the Caracas Convention were still harbouring refugees. These included the Canadian mission, which was sheltering dozens of asylees, and the embassy of West Germany, which gave refuge to more than 200 refugees and put them up in the ambassador's residence and in accommodation specifically rented for that purpose.[91] Australia was not alone, however; the United States embassy also refused to harbour asylees.

While most of the people seeking refuge in foreign diplomatic missions were Chilean, many were nationals of other Latin American countries. They had been among the 15,000 refugees who had fled to Chile from other authoritarian regimes, including those of Brazil, Uruguay and Paraguay, and been granted asylum by the Allende government.[92] In many instances the Chilean junta preferred to rid itself of foreign exiles and Chileans opposed to the regime by allowing them to leave the country rather than by imprisoning or murdering them. The junta therefore initially recognised and respected 'safe havens' for foreign refugees and granted safe-conduct passes to people who had sought refuge in embassies; within a month of the coup it had issued 4761 such passes for Chileans and foreign nationals.[93] The 1954 Caracas Convention provided for such passes; it stipulated that '[o]nce asylum has been granted, the State granting asylum may request that the asylee be allowed to depart for foreign territory, and the territorial State is under obligation to grant Immediately . . . the necessary guarantees'.[94]

Eventually, Whitlam, in his capacity as acting minister for foreign affairs, intervened and instructed the Australian embassy in Santiago to offer protection to those who requested it.[95] He was told that his directive arrived too late: from 11 December, the junta issued safe conduct passes only for refugees holed up in embassies of countries that were co-signatories of the Caracas Convention.

Whitlam now decided to pursue the matter in principle. In August 1974 Australia successfully requested that a convention on diplomatic asylum be placed on the agenda of the United Nations General Assembly. When invited a few months later to table its views on the matter, the Australian government argued strongly for such a convention. It noted that its advocacy of a binding global agreement was 'moved by humanitarian considerations'; an answer to the question whether a convention would impose 'an *unacceptable* limitation on the power of a State within its territory' would not determine 'whether or not the rule is worth having'.[96] However, only a handful of other countries supported Australia's initiative, and it was shelved.[97]

Meanwhile, the UNHCR asked Australia to pledge a resettlement target for Chilean refugees. The organisation knew from experience that governments could sometimes be persuaded to engage in a competitive bidding process, and to try to match each other's targets. The Whitlam government told the UNHCR, however, that it was unwilling to set a target because it put two conditions on the resettlement of refugees from Chile: they would be selected 'against the normal migrant criteria', and they had to show a genuine commitment to Australia.[98] This was a contentious issue within Cabinet. Even Whitlam himself supposedly thought that Australia could and should do more, and foreign minister Willesee told Grassby in a letter:

> I was especially disappointed to note that 14 families [from Chile] have been rejected for migration to Australia on grounds of 'drunkenness, mental disturbance, previous migration rejections and generally below reasonable personal standards'. Most of these, standing alone, seem to me rather flimsy reasons for rejection in a refugee type of situation.[99]

In the late 1960s the immigration department had identified Chile as a potential source of immigrants, not least, as one immigration officer assessing prospective countries of emigration wrote, 'from an ethnic point of view'.[100] In turn, many Chileans had identified Australia as a country to migrate to. One Chilean applying to migrate to Australia at the time was Maximo Alberto Bachelet. 'European looks, outlook, manner & dress. Positive migrant gain,' the interviewing officer at the Australian embassy in Santiago noted on the file covering him, his wife and their young son, and approved the family's admission under the government's assisted passage scheme.

After the coup, the government allowed for 'some flexibility'[101] but did not formally relax the 'normal' criteria, as Grassby had done in early 1973 for Asians from Uganda: it seemed possible to assist some Latin American refugees while at the same time gaining particularly suitable immigrants. But if the government had wanted to resettle a sizeable number of Chileans who met its normal migrant selection criteria, it should have properly resourced the selection process. In January 1974 alone, the embassy in Santiago received 5132 applications, but it was still working its way through a backlog of 12,000 applicants who had to be interviewed.[102]

The question of who should be accepted from Chile raised two important issues. The first concerned the distinction between refugees and other migrants. The rate of applications from Chile for migration to Australia rose sharply after the coup: from 520 persons in September 1973 to 13,754 in January 1974.[103] But only a tiny proportion of these were 'mandated' refugees – that is, people who had been granted refugee status by the UNHCR because they had sought to be formally recognised as refugees and met the criteria laid down in Article 1 of the 1951 Refugee Convention. In the first four months after the coup, Australia received only eight applications (covering twenty-two persons) from refugees in Chile who had been officially recognised as such.[104]

There were others who had managed to leave Chile and applied from neighbouring countries. In some of those instances the Australian authorities questioned whether somebody granted mandated status by the UNHCR was indeed a refugee. Australia's ambassador in Buenos Aires, for example, queried the assessment made by the UN refugee agency, claiming that applicants were screened not by the UNHCR but by welfare agencies, which tended to believe whatever applicants told them.[105]

In the past, the issue of whether or not somebody had been officially recognised as a refugee by the UNHCR had not usually been a problem, both because Australia was interested in refugees as migrants and did not care too much about their official status, and because of the size of the migrant intake. Under Whitlam, however, the government was trying to reduce the country's overall migrant intake; it therefore tried to tighten the 'normal' criteria, and consequently rejected many applicants who would have been accepted in earlier years. Arguably, they included some refugees. They certainly included many people who identified as refugees and who were considered refugees by many Australians. It would be left to the Fraser government to distinguish clearly between refugees, humanitarian entrants who were not refugees according to the 1951 Convention, and other immigrants.

The overwhelming majority of Chileans who were admitted either before or after September 1973 had to meet the normal migration criteria; in other words, most Chilean applicants were treated just as prospective immigrants from other countries were. The archival evidence suggests that, under Whitlam, fewer than one in seven of all Chilean immigrants were admitted as refugees and irrespective of whether they met the normal migration criteria.[106] They included a handful of political prisoners whose release was subject to their resettlement, and so-called 'political duress cases' whose lives were endangered because of their association with the Allende government.[107]

One of these bona fide refugees was the daughter of a high-ranking military officer and Allende loyalist, Alberto Bachelet Martínez, who had been arrested after the coup, was tortured and died in prison. His daughter, Michelle Bachelet, and her mother were detained in early 1975 but released a few weeks later, after Australia had provided the Chilean authorities with a guarantee that they would leave the country. The fact that Michelle Bachelet ended up in Australia was due to representations made by her brother, Maximo Alberto, who had arrived in Australia some six years earlier.[108] Michelle Bachelet did not remain in Australia long, but moved on to the German Democratic Republic, which resettled about 2000 Chilean refugees, including the leadership of the Socialist Party of Chile. She returned to Chile in 1979 and became the country's president in 2006.

The second issue raised by the admission of Chilean refugees would eventually also lead to a significant change in Australia's response to refugees. When Willesee complained to Grassby about the rejection of a refugee on account of 'drunkenness', he could hardly have found a more sympathetic ear. 'The need for a compassionate approach to the plight of these people is accepted without reservation,' Grassby wrote in reply. Unlike many other countries, however, Australia did not have government-funded settlement services specifically for refugees. As Grassby pointed out, applicants rejected on account of being alcoholics could well have been accepted 'if we were able to arrange institutional care for them, fund this care and provide for on-going full-time maintenance and care for the breadwinner and dependants if any'.[109]

The Australian public was unaware of the restrictions imposed on applicants from Chile; many suspected that the Whitlam government was admitting scores of Chileans because of its political sympathies with Allende and his supporters. To allow the immigration minister to refute this suspicion, in October 1975 Labor senator Tony Mulvihill asked a 'Dorothy Dixer' question in the Senate about the numbers of Chilean migrants admitted to Australia. Immigration minister Jim McClelland informed senators that 3237 Chileans had been accepted in the first two years after the coup, but that 4343 had been admitted during the previous three years, when Chile had been ruled by the Allende government. 'Many of the people who left Chile during the period when the Opposition was in Government did so to better their economic prospects or because they disliked the Allende Government,' McClelland explained. 'Today many who leave Chile do so for similar reasons.'[110] That was arguably incorrect, as the Allende government had not persecuted its political opponents, and as the number of applicants had skyrocketed after September 1973. But it was correct in the sense that the nature of Australia's Chilean immigration program barely changed after 1973.

*

Whitlam had long pushed for Papua New Guinea's independence, and helped to speed up the process that eventually led to it becoming reality in September 1975. 'If history were to obliterate the whole of my public career, save my contribution to the independence of a democratic PNG,' he wrote, 'I should rest content.'[111]

The Whitlam government had inherited the problem of West Papuan refugees from its predecessor. But with Australia's colony being put on an accelerated path towards independence, on 1 December 1973, less than twelve months after the Labor Party's 1972 election victory, Papua New Guinea became self-governing. While Australia retained control over foreign affairs and defence, the government of Papua New Guinea was now effectively in charge of most policy areas. West Papuan 'border crossers' and permissive residents were no longer Australia's responsibility. Thus, the reservations that had been raised previously by the Department of External Territories and its predecessor, the Department of Territories, became irrelevant, and in December 1973 Australia acceded to the 1967 Refugee Protocol, as well as to the 1954 Convention Relating to the Status of Stateless Persons and to the 1961 Convention on the Reduction of Statelessness.

Australia's binding commitment to a host of international instruments has been one of the most important legacies of the Whitlam government. 'If orderly and humane arrangements are to be made for [refugees] to secure homes and status,' Whitlam wrote in 1985, 'then affected or interested countries must at least ratify the conventions which are already available and conclude further conventions as circumstances dictate.'[112] Indeed, today it would arguably be easier for the Australian government to negotiate humanitarian solutions for displaced people if all countries in the region had signed up to the 1951 Refugee Convention and the 1967 Protocol. Referring to the decision to accede to the Protocol, Whitlam also observed that '[o]ur farsightedness was demonstrated at the conference on refugees in Geneva in July 1979' (when Australia and other countries tried to negotiate a concerted response to the Indochinese refugee exodus).[113]

With the benefit of hindsight, the decision to sign the 1967 Protocol may indeed appear to have been forward-looking, but from the perspective of 1973 it appeared that Australia was lagging behind, as it had in the 1950s and 1960s when it signed the 1951 Convention only after recording numerous reservations, which it was subsequently slow to withdraw.

*

In 1974 a military coup d'état on the other side of the world triggered another refugee exodus. On 15 July the Greek military helped to overthrow the government of Cyprus in order to unite Cyprus with Greece. The coup backfired badly when, five days later, Turkey invaded Cyprus and the Greek forces were unable to put up any effective resistance. The successful Turkish invasion had two dramatic consequences: the restoration of democracy in Athens, and the division of Cyprus, which was accompanied by the expulsion of ethnic Greeks from the part of the island claimed by Turkey, and vice versa.

The Australian government did not recognise the victims of ethnic cleansing as refugees; 'Cypriots who have fled to the hills on Cyprus because of the present situation are *not* refugees – they might more accurately be termed "displaced",' a circular advised all Department of Foreign Affairs staff.[114] But the government dispatched a migrant selection team to Cyprus and resettled Greek Cypriots displaced as a result of the island's partition, provided they were sponsored by relatives or friends in Australia.[115] Only 1.5 per cent of Cypriots, however, were given access to assisted passages.[116] Although the arrangements for

Cypriots were less generous than those for Czechs and Slovaks in 1968, who had mostly been brought to Australia on assisted passages and accommodated in migrant hostels upon their arrival, thousands of Greek Cypriots migrated to Australia at the time. As a result, Australia is, according to the High Commission of the Republic of Cyprus, now home to the second-largest Cypriot community outside Cyprus.[117]

Al Grassby was no longer a minister by the time the crisis in Cyprus unfolded. In April 1974 Whitlam had called a double-dissolution election. In May his government was returned with a slightly reduced majority, with the member for Riverina having been one of the casualties. Grassby had been genuinely concerned to make a distinction between humanitarian and other migrants, but his good intentions had been stymied by a declining economy and the perceived need to cut the overall migrant intake, and by an immigration department wedded to ideas of a White Australia and committed to upholding 'normal' migrant selection criteria.

Some in the department may have been glad to see their minister lose his seat, but his loss turned out to be theirs as well. After the election Whitlam decided that the immigration department be absorbed into the labour department, which was renamed the Department of Labor and Immigration. On 12 June 1974 Clyde Cameron, who had been labour minister in the previous Whitlam government, was appointed minister for labor and immigration. Both he and his successor, McClelland, focused on the labour aspects of their portfolio;[118] not since the mid-1930s, well before the creation of the Department of Immigration under the last Labor prime minister before Whitlam, had a government paid as little attention to immigration issues.

*

The Australian government was able to observe the refugee crises in Uganda, Chile and Cyprus from afar; Australians played no significant direct or indirect role in the events preceding Amin's expulsion order, Pichochet's coup (the meddling of two ASIS operatives aside) or the Turkish invasion of Cyprus. The same could not be said about the flight of West Papuans, but their numbers were always small. The next refugee crisis to affect Australia – the flight of people from Vietnam, Laos and Cambodia – made the displacement that occurred in West Papua, Uganda, Chile and Cyprus pale into insignificance. The question of whether Australia was obliged to accommodate Vietnamese refugees because it had been a party to the conflict in Vietnam, as Denis Warner had suggested as early as 1964, however, would be bitterly contested.

The Vietnamese refugee crisis began when hundreds of thousands of people fled from the advancing North Vietnamese army as it rapidly moved southwards in the first months of 1975. The speed of the offensive came as a surprise to many, including the South Vietnamese government, its American ally and even the leadership in Hanoi. On 30 March Da Nang fell, which at one stage accommodated 600,000 refugees. By then it had become obvious that the fall of Saigon was only months away, if not weeks. The American military had left the country in 1973, and while many people in the south hoped it would return in time, such expectations were unrealistic. With the collapse of the regime in Saigon on the horizon, Vietnamese who were afraid of a communist victory knew they would have to leave the country if they wanted to feel safe.

Those most fearful of vengeful victors included Vietnamese who had worked for – or, even worse, *with* – the Americans and their allies. They therefore appealed to their erstwhile employers and comrades-in-arms to take them in. Most of these appeals were directed at the United States, but Australia too was expected to provide a refuge for Vietnamese desperate to get out of the country. The Australian embassy in Saigon was inundated with requests for visas, and, increasingly, pleas that Australia evacuate those most at risk.

Australia provided Hercules planes to move refugees out of the immediate reach of the North Vietnamese forces, but, exceptions aside, the government was most reluctant to resettle refugees from Vietnam; as a Senate committee found later, it 'generally refused until the last moment to use its transport resources to evacuate Vietnamese nationals from South Vietnam'.[119] Its stance was unpopular and harshly criticised by the conservative state premiers, the churches, most of the media, and the federal opposition and its newly minted leader, Malcolm Fraser.

The prime minister personally devised and defended the government's stance. Since the 1974 election Clyde Cameron had held the immigration portfolio, but on 2 April 1975 Whitlam assumed responsibility for all issues concerning Vietnamese refugees. Thereafter, his cabinet colleagues, including the immigration minister, had no significant input into the making of Australian refugee policy.[120] Later, Cameron bitterly complained about Whitlam's meddling in the immigration portfolio; he wrote that he did not raise the issue with Cabinet for fear that Whitlam would realise an earlier threat and put the foreign affairs department in charge of the issuing of visas.[121]

One of the exceptions to Whitlam's uncompromising stance towards Vietnamese anxious to escape before the inevitable North Vietnamese victory concerned children in South Vietnamese orphanages. The Australian interest in these children resembled that of other Western governments, including those of the United States and Canada.[122] Whitlam seemed to hope that the highly symbolic gesture of 'rescuing' hundreds of small children and flying them to Australia might deflate accusations that his government lacked compassion. The evacuation of 283 children from Vietnam and their resettlement in Australia in April 1975 became known as the 'babylift'.[123]

Before announcing the scheme, Whitlam wrote to the state premiers, asking them to commit to receiving some children. Maybe he was hoping the premiers would be unable to match words with deeds; if so, the answer he received from one of his fiercest critics, New South Wales premier Tom Lewis, must have come as a disappointment. The premier told Whitlam, who envisaged admitting at most a few hundred Vietnamese orphans, that the New South Wales government would accept responsibility initially for 2000 children, and for more if needed, irrespective of their state of health. He cabled: 'Suggest your government take immediate although now belated action to get the children here.'[124]

While the federal government went out of its way to facilitate the evacuation of children from Vietnamese orphanages, it put up administrative hurdles for other Vietnamese. On 14 April Whitlam told the immigration department to suspend the processing of Vietnamese applicants who would be eligible 'within the normal guidelines of Australian immigration policy'.[125] On 22 April the prime minister announced Australia would only accept the spouses and children of Australian citizens and of Vietnamese students living in Australia, and, on a case by case basis, Vietnamese 'with long and close associations with the Australian presence in Vietnam' whose lives were in danger; he confirmed these criteria again six weeks later.[126] Those accepted were to be given temporary rather than permanent resident status. These criteria were intentionally restrictive, and indeed, as Malcolm Fraser was quick to point out, 'narrower than those that apply under the normal immigration program';[127] in the words of one foreign affairs officer, the immigration department was refusing 'persons entry into Australia who would be approved if they had any nationality except Vietnamese'.[128] Foreign minister Willesee opposed this restrictive approach and tried to change Whitlam's mind, but Whitlam could count on the support of other senior Labor figures. Clyde Cameron, for example, 'saw no reason why we should take the risk of opening our doors to war criminals'.[129]

On 24 April Australia decided to close its embassy in Saigon. The next day a RAAF Hercules evacuated the embassy's non-local staff and seventy-eight Vietnamese refugees from Vietnam. The refugees included a group of thirty-four nuns. Of the remainder, forty were the spouses, children or fiancées of Australian citizens or permanent residents. By then, another 342 persons had been approved for entry but were unable to leave Vietnam (some were subsequently evacuated by the United States military).[130] Many of those who had been approved by Australia had not been able to obtain the necessary exit permit and passport from the Vietnamese authorities; in mid-April the going rate for a Vietnamese passport was said to be A$16,000.[131]

'During the morning [of 25 April 1975] I made last minute inquiries through the Embassy to discover whether some Vietnamese whose lives might be endangered could not be taken out,' Denis Warner told a Senate committee some four months later.

> I was instructed that this was not possible. As an alternative, I passed on lists of names, addresses and occupations of those who were felt to be in special danger to the American Embassy, where the promise was made that it would do its best. Members of the Australian Embassy privately made similar application for other Vietnamese.[132]

As Warner's story suggests, the Australian response contrasted starkly with that of the United States, which was taking in tens of thousands of people who had fled or been evacuated from South Vietnam. The same day that Whitlam restricted the immigration of Vietnamese, the United States Senate's judiciary committee agreed to the admittance of more than 150,000 Vietnamese, and the American military launched a massive evacuation.

The Whitlam government's policy was, however, in line with that adopted by New Zealand. There, the National Party opposition had tried to use the Australian response to shame the government into allowing more Vietnamese into the country, even though the Labor government in Canberra was hardly more generous than the Labour government in Wellington.[133] Much like Whitlam, Bill Rowling of the New Zealand Labour Party, who had become prime minister after Kirk's death in office in 1974, had opposed Australia's involvement in the Vietnam War, had been a critic of the American execution of that war, and was now reluctant to commit his government to admitting a sizeable number of refugees from Vietnam.[134]

On 6 May 1975, a week after the United States military had evacu-ated some 7000 people from Saigon in the course of Operation Frequent Wind, the *Australian* ran the following headline on its front page: 'Flee-ing Vietnamese ships may risk voyage to Australia'.[135] The article referred to the exodus of refugees from southern Vietnam. It reported that 5700 had already arrived in Singapore, where thirty-two vessels carrying refugees could be counted in the harbour. But the Singaporean authori-ties, while willing to provide food, water and medical aid, were adamant that the refugees had to move on.

Other South-East Asian nations were equally opposed to letting Vietnamese refugees land, including those rescued in the China Sea by cargo ships. As Singapore, Malaysia, Hong Kong and Thailand were trying to shut their doors to people fleeing Vietnam, other countries in the region became obvious destinations. According to the newspaper article, 'there were unconfirmed reports that a tanker with 200 refugees aboard was heading for Australia'.

The previous day the *Age had* cited a letter from sixty-three Viet-namese refugees, among them sixteen children, who had left Saigon on 20 April, reached Singapore and were said to be heading to Sydney. 'After landing in Singapore Harbour for refuelling and supply we plan to sail to the Royal Australia,' the letter said. 'We strongly believe that the generous Government and people of the Royal Australia will accept us with pity as refugees in their country.'[136] Andrew Peacock, the oppo-sition's foreign affairs spokesperson, who had visited Saigon the previous month and so had some first-hand experience of the desperation driv-ing the Vietnamese exodus, immediately seized upon the newspapers' predictions of the arrival of refugees by boat, and amplified the alarm-ist sentiments that informed some of the press coverage.[137] Foreign minister Willesee told Whitlam 'that the question of the Vietnamese refugees in Singapore and the "spectre of an armada" sailing for Aus-tralia will now become the issue which will most attract public opinion and potentially present the greatest problems'.[138]

A paper drafted in the Department of Foreign Affairs three days later painted a picture that was even more alarming than that conveyed by the newspapers. According to information received by the department, one of the ships in Singapore Harbour, which was carrying 'several hundred Vietnamese', intended to proceed to Sydney, while another with 287 refugees on board was also headed for Australia. The paper noted that 'the Singaporean authorities have provided the refugee ships with water and charts for Australia', and concluded that 'it is only sensible to assume that some smaller craft will also make the attempt'.[139]

The Department of Police and Customs was also alarmed about the prospect of 'Vietnamese war refugees' arriving by boat, although for a very particular – and, with the benefit of hindsight, rather peculiar – reason. As a senior officer told the responsible minister, Kep Enderby, 'it was assessed that 500 pounds of heroin and morphine and 15 tons of opium were in South Vietnam shortly before the end of the war', but his memorandum did not explain why people escaping Vietnam by boat might be expected to move large quantities of those drugs to Australia.[140]

On 19 May 1975 the Department of Labor and Immigration convened an interdepartmental meeting 'to consider contingency planning in case sea craft carrying South Vietnamese . . . should arrive in Australian waters or make landfall on the Australian coast without approval'.[141] The meeting was attended by representatives from the Departments of Labor and Immigration, Foreign Affairs, Prime Minister and Cabinet, Health, Police and Customs, Transport, Defence, Northern Territory, Social Security, and Housing and Construction. Its main outcome was the decision that the Departments of Labor and Immigration, Foreign Affairs, and Prime Minister and Cabinet should jointly draft a paper assessing the situation and exploring the options available to the government, should the anticipated arrival of Vietnamese refugees eventuate.

The authors of that paper noted Australia's international legal obligations under the United Nations Convention Relating to the Status of Refugees, the Agreement relating to Refugee Seamen, the Convention for the Safety of Life at Sea, the Declaration on Territorial Asylum, and Article 14 of the Universal Declaration of Human Rights. They also outlined two 'political considerations': first, that the arrival of a boat carrying Vietnamese refugees could not be kept a secret; and, second, that:

> It must be expected that if the Australian Government allows people arriving in small boats to land and remain in Australia this would create a precedent which would not go unremarked by people in a number of countries to the north of Australia. Even if it did not lead to an influx of South Vietnamese it could have future implications in the event of internal political or economic crises developing in other countries to our north.[142]

The authors discussed two options: the boat arrivals could either be prevented from landing in Australia (by preventing refugee boats from entering Australian territorial waters, or by refusing to let their passengers and crew disembark), or they could be allowed to land. They counselled against the first option on account of Australia's international legal obligations and of the anticipated 'weight of public opinion' in favour of Vietnamese refugees, and pointed out that the second option entailed several possibilities: the refugees could be allowed to land without granting them entry permits, they could be issued with limited permits, or they could be disembarked 'into custody' in order to be able to return them to their boat 'for the purpose of departing them from Australia'.[143] The paper did not explore to what extent any of these options was practicable, nor did its authors advocate a particular course of action. It was left to Whitlam to identify a solution.

Whitlam decided that, should Vietnamese refugees reach Australia by boat, they would be disembarked 'into custody'. He added that the Australian authorities ought to ensure 'that the boat is not made deliberately unseaworthy so that any Operation Phoenix or like types can be returned to the boat before other passengers are permitted to remain'.[144] The government never publicised the policy. Nor did it ever use it. In 1975 not a single Indochinese refugee arrived on Australia's shores by boat.

Whitlam's policy may not have found favour with the opposition or the Australian news media if it had become public, but those likely to criticise him for lacking compassion for 'boat people' shared his government's concern about the prospect of their unbidden arrival. 'There are within sailing distance of Australia populous nations where the political situation in the future may not be as stable as it is at the present time,' the Liberal Party's immigration spokesman, Michael MacKellar, said in October 1975, conjuring up the spectre of 'a situation where large numbers of people sail to Australia . . . and say: "Here we are. What are you going to do with us?"'[145] Two years later it would be up to him and Fraser to decide what to do, when the threat of uncontrolled arrivals of Indochinese refugees on Australia's northern shores at last became reality.

Thus far, Australia had always been concerned to ensure, as far as was feasible, that refugees would not use Australia as a platform from which to agitate against the governments of countries they had fled, irrespective of the relationship these governments had with Australia. This expectation extended also to Vietnamese refugees, perhaps the more so since the Whitlam government's political views aligned more closely with those of the government in Hanoi than with the views expressed by hard-line anti-communists loyal to the former regime in Saigon. According to Whitlam, 'refugees who were forced to leave their homeland will resent the fact and long remember it. But it cannot be accepted that this is justification for using Australia as a base for futile political activity intended to change political arrangements in their native land.'[146] Following an idea attributed to Willesee,[147] the government required a handful of refugees to commit themselves in writing not to engage in political activities directed against the Vietnamese government. They had to 'solemnly declare that if admitted to Australia for permanent residence' they would not 'engage in political activity of any kind'.[148]

The opposition cried foul when it became aware of this practice (and Fraser would release signatories from their commitment once he became prime minister).[149] It made much of the fact that not a single Chilean refugee had been asked to sign such an undertaking. Whitlam pointed out that while only a tiny minority of Vietnamese refugees were affected by his government's policy, all West Papuan refugees had to commit in writing to abstain from anti-Indonesian political activism. The gagging of West Papuans had never been an issue of public concern in Australia, however, and Whitlam's reference to this long-standing practice was therefore not an effective means to take the heat off the government.

While the Whitlam government was miserly in its approach to Vietnamese refugees who tried to enter Australia, it was comparatively generous with regard to Vietnamese (and Laotians and Cambodians) already in the country. Indochinese students – 445 from Vietnam and seventy-five from Cambodia – many of them in Australia courtesy of the Colombo Plan, had their visas extended until 31 December 1975. Staff of South Vietnam's embassy were also allowed to remain in Australia.

In late May the government succumbed to diplomatic and domestic pressure and sent a team of immigration officers to Hong Kong, who selected 201 refugees for resettlement in Australia.[150] A further 323 were selected in Singapore and Malaysia in July and August. In the context of the size of the exodus from Vietnam and the efforts of comparable countries, these were token gestures. The number of refugees admitted to Australia was also much smaller than the intake proposed by the Department of Foreign Affairs, which in May had suggested admitting 2000 refugees in addition to those whose applications had by then already been approved.[151]

The admission of the Vietnamese refugees from Hong Kong, Malaysia and Singapore was nevertheless significant, as for the first time in Australian history the selection officers deliberately privileged applicants who had no prospect of being resettled elsewhere. The selection team included two prominent public servants: Michael Delaney, Whitlam's senior adviser, and Wayne Gibbons, the private secretary to the minister for labor and immigration, who was later to become the coordinator of the Indochinese resettlement program. When giving evidence to a Senate inquiry, Gibbons said that the team tried to select those who 'were most in need of the humanitarian assistance that resettlement in Australia would provide', and that, as a consequence, 95 per cent of those selected would have been ineligible for migration to Australia if the standard criteria had been applied.[152]

Whitlam's reluctance to admit Vietnamese refugees was informed by several assumptions. He thought that at least some of those fleeing Vietnam had been the agents of highly dubious South Vietnamese and United States policies (such as the notorious Operation Phoenix) and were now escaping retribution at the hands of the victors. In July he told Frank Bauman, the UNHCR's representative in Australia, that he did not know of any persecutions occurring in Vietnam at the time – in other words, that while Vietnamese refugees may have been fearful, their fear was unfounded. He was also unsympathetic to requests by Vietnamese students to let their parents come to Australia; according to Bauman, Whitlam believed that the students had been sent to Australia by their relatives 'with a view to having a place to go to themselves in the event of a drastic change in circumstances in Vietnam'.[153]

*

In August 1968 the Portuguese dictator António Salazar, whose regime had received bad publicity in Australia after the asylum claims of the three Portuguese naval ratings in 1961, suffered a stroke. He was replaced as prime minister by Marcello Caetano. While Caetano's powers were more limited than Salazar's had been, the nature of Portugal's authoritarian *Estado Novo* regime hardly changed.

In the 1960s and early 1970s, that regime came increasingly under pressure not so much domestically as in Africa, where Portugal fought independence movements to hold on to its colonies: Angola, Mozambique, São Tomé and Príncipe, Cape Verde and Guinea-Bissau. The war against pro-independence forces in Angola and Mozambique consumed more than a third of Portugal's budget and was unpopular with many in the Portuguese military who were expected to execute it. On 25 April 1974 the Movimento das Forças Armadas (Armed Forces Movement), a group of junior officers who identified with the political left, staged a bloodless coup, which became known as *Revolução dos Cravos* (the Carnation Revolution, named after the flowers that soldiers stuck into the muzzles of their rifles), deposed Caetano and installed a military junta, pending the formation of a democratically elected government. Following the coup, Portugal withdrew its administrative and military personnel from Africa.

Portugal also had colonies in Asia: Macao and Portuguese (East) Timor. The junta was intent on relinquishing all of Portugal's colonial possessions, but took little account of the fact that the situation in East Timor was very different from that in Angola or Mozambique. Following the Carnation Revolution, two major political forces emerged in East Timor: the left-leaning Frente Revolucionária de Timor Leste Independente (Fretilin), which advocated independence, and the conservative União Democrática Timorense (UDT), which initially championed a continuing association with Portugal. A third, much smaller group, Associação Popular Democratica Timorense (Apodeti), favoured integration with Indonesia. In Timor the period of liberalisation made possible by the Portuguese revolution was marked by bitter conflict – not between the metropolitan government and a Timorese pro-independence movement, as might perhaps have been expected, but between the three Timorese political factions and their respective expatriate supporters.

Australia did not support any of the political groupings in East Timor. On 8 September 1974 Whitlam met with Indonesian president Suharto to discuss East Timor; according to a foreign affairs background briefing about the meeting, Whitlam told Suharto that 'Australia felt an independent Timor would be an unviable state'. But he also stressed 'that the people of the colony should have the ultimate decision on their future'.[154] These two views characterised the government's approach to Timor for the remainder of Whitlam's prime ministership.

On 10 August 1975 the UDT attempted to seize control of the country through a coup. This sparked a civil war, in which Fretilin held the upper hand, not least because it captured the local Portuguese military's armoury. On 12 August the Department of Prime Minister and Cabinet learned that East Timor's governor had 'ordered the evacuation of all Portuguese people', and that two ships in Dili Harbour were taking on board evacuees. One, the *Macdili*, was said to be preparing to sail to Darwin to offload 300 passengers.[155] News of the impending arrival of hundreds of refugees took the Australian government by surprise. A few days later Portugal formally sought humanitarian assistance from Indonesia, Australia and the Red Cross.

On 25 August the first ship with evacuees from East Timor, the *Lloyd Bakke*, arrived in Darwin. It carried 1155 evacuees, including relatives of Australian residents. The government assumed that the majority of the evacuees would be accommodated by Portugal, but agreed to approve relatives of Australian residents 'for admission without regard to their occupation, subject only to health clearance'.[156] The following day a jumbo jet chartered by the Portuguese government arrived in Darwin. Much to the surprise of the Australian authorities, only about 250 of the evacuees decided to fly to Portugal, with the remainder opting to stay in Australia for the time being. The majority were ethnic Timorese or Chinese, rather than Portuguese expatriates. The prime minister's department told Whitlam that Australia was dealing with an unforeseen problem:

> It is not clear whether the 'unwillingness' [to fly to Portugal] reflects anything more than a reluctance to travel at this early stage after the trauma of evacuation from Dili. There are, however, the seeds of a problem here which could mean the presence in Darwin of an undue number of evacuees over a period longer than had been anticipated . . . [T]here are now 250 nominations

of Timorese relatives by Australian residents and the figure may rise to about 300.[157]

On 29 August the *Macdili* disembarked another 732 evacuees at Darwin. Considering how anxiously the arrival of 'boat people' from Vietnam had been anticipated about three months earlier, it is surprising that the disembarkation of large numbers of refugees from Timor was not a cause of public concern. Excluding people who immediately proceeded to Portugal, Australia eventually accommodated almost 2000 evacuees from East Timor.[158] The Whitlam government granted all of them permission to remain in Australia temporarily until 30 June 1976, and allowed them to nominate close relatives to join them in Australia.[159]

Throughout his last seven months in office, Whitlam was under enormous pressure to increase the number of Indochinese refugees admitted to Australia for resettlement. Domestically, the pressure was piled on by the federal opposition, most state premiers, large sections of the media, the churches and many ordinary Australians. The government was also lobbied by the UNHCR and admonished by its counterpart in Washington. In a conversation on 7 May Whitlam had promised US president Gerald Ford that Australia would take in about half as many Indochinese refugees as Canada, but it became soon evident to the Americans that Australia was falling well short of that target.

The crisis in East Timor provided Whitlam at last with an argument to deflect diplomatic pressure to take a greater share of refugees from Indochina. On 28 August a foreign affairs officer telephoned the American chargé d'affaires, who a few days earlier had reminded the Australian government of Whitlam's commitment to Ford.[160] The diplomat was asked to convey a message from Whitlam to the United States government:

With the collapse of the situation in Portuguese Timor, Australia had suddenly been presented with a new refugee problem of some proportions ... Already quite a number of these refugees had been admitted to Australia, and undoubtedly a lot more would be

presenting themselves requesting permission . . . The Prime Minister considered that in these circumstances it would be impossible
for the Australian Government to respond positively to the requests
of the United States Government at the present time. The Australian Government simply had to give first priority to the refugees
who had already arrived from Portuguese Timor and to further
refugees who would be arriving in the near future.[161]

A similar message was conveyed to the UNHCR's representative in
Australia.[162]

At the same time, Whitlam drew on offers of help his government
had received with regards to the Vietnamese. 'My Government believes
we could and should do more than we have done as a nation so far,'
Victorian premier Rupert Hamer had written. Comparing the Vietnamese refugees to other displaced people accommodated by Australia,
such as refugees from Nazi Germany in the late 1930s and Czechs and
Slovaks in 1968, Hamer suggested that '[i]n terms of human misery and
suffering', the Vietnamese 'rank at least equal in need, are geographi-
cally closer, and more of a direct responsibility for us due to our civil
and military involvement in Vietnam'. He told Whitlam that Victoria
would provide accommodation and other services.[163] Whitlam responded
by saying that 'I assume that this offer similarly applies to Timorese
refugees'.[164]

The Americans were told that the East Timorese evacuees 'were asking to be given residence in Australia', implying that granting residence
to a large number of Timorese would prevent Australia from accommodating a sizeable number of Vietnamese. If the American diplomats
had looked closely at this claim, however, they would have realised that
the number of evacuees accommodated by Australia in 1975 was comparatively modest, and that the Whitlam government was not granting
them permanent residence status.

The number of Indochinese refugees admitted to Australia under
Whitlam was equally modest. On 24 October 1975, less than three weeks

before Whitlam was sacked by the governor-general, somebody in the Department of Foreign Affairs put together a table in order to lend credence to his suggestion 'that we should be cautious in proclaiming Australia's record in this area'. According to his memorandum, which used the latest figures provided by the UNHCR, 150,238 Indochinese refugees had been settled or were awaiting a determination of their claim in the United States, 6275 in Canada, 2347 in Belgium and only 707 in Australia.[165] However, archival evidence suggests that by the time the foreign affairs official compiled these figures, the government had agreed to raise its intake. According to a document submitted to Andrew Peacock, Fraser's foreign minister, in December 1975, the Department of Foreign Affairs had convinced Peacock's predecessor, Don Willesee, to endorse a UNHCR request to resettle 840 refugees from Thailand, most of them Cambodians, and Whitlam had approved the proposal; it had not been implemented because of his dismissal.[166]

*

At the Labor Party's Terrigal conference in February 1975, the platform concerning immigration policy had been amended: a Labor government was now required to allow for '[s]ympathetic consideration of people who for political and other reasons would face danger to life and liberty upon return to their country of origin'.[167] The Department of Labor and Immigration was also under pressure from non-government agencies involved in caring for refugees resettled in Australia, including the Resettlement Department of the Australian Council of Churches, the Catholic Immigration Office and the Federation of Australian Jewish Welfare Societies. In July 1974 they had complained to Cameron that the Whitlam government had 'very largely discarded the application of compassionate and humanitarian considerations to refugee and near-refugee cases', and observed that '[a]t the present time Australia does not have a good reputation amongst international agencies and some foreign governments for its refugee work'.[168]

In response to lobbying from welfare organisations and the decision made at Terrigal (which also reflected that lobbying), the immigration minister initiated discussions about the parameters of a generic refugee policy. Not much came of them in the short term, for two reasons: the government's time was running out, and those involved in formulating the new policy, including Cameron and, from 6 June 1975, Jim McClelland, had to exclude Vietnamese and Cambodians, 'where decisions of acceptability have been made by the Prime Minister',[169] from their discussions. Cameron endorsed a recommendation that mandated refugees be accepted 'without regard to occupational status', that 'non-mandated cases involving persons in a refugee type situation be accepted without regard to occupational status where outstanding compassionate circumstances exist', and that in both cases assisted passages be made available. But given that Vietnamese refugees were not his responsibility, and that the Timorese evacuees and Cypriots were not considered refugees, there was no opportunity to test the new approach.

In any case, the Whitlam government's tentative moves to design a refugee resettlement policy were soon brought to a halt by the installation of Malcolm Fraser as prime minister. It was left to Michael MacKellar, Fraser's second immigration minister, to develop a comprehensive refugee policy; it ought to be acknowledged, however, that MacKellar was able to build on ideas raised by Grassby, pursued – against the odds – by Cameron, and supported both by Willesee and, after 11 November 1975, by Peacock.

Whitlam's response to Indochinese refugees is often characterised by reference to two quotes attributed to him. Clyde Cameron reported that Whitlam had told him and Willesee during a discussion about the Vietnamese refugee issue on 21 April 1975 that he was 'not having hundreds of fucking Vietnamese Balts coming into this country with their hatreds against us'.[170] Nancy Viviani, who was Willesee's private secretary and is particularly knowledgeable about the Whitlam government's Indochinese refugee policy, quoted Whitlam as saying that 'Vietnamese sob stories don't wring my withers'.[171]

Even Gerard Henderson, who conducted an acrimonious exchange with Whitlam over his response to the Vietnamese crisis, in which the first quote featured prominently, has admitted that Cameron is not a particularly reliable source.[172] It seems anyway doubtful that Whitlam's policy response was determined by his antipathies towards the political views espoused by many of the Vietnamese refugees, or by the anticipation that Vietnamese refugees would eventually vote for the conservative Coalition parties rather than the Labor Party, although he did tell the UNHCR's Frank Bauman that he was afraid that the Catholics among the refugees admitted to Australia would align themselves with the Democratic Labour Party.[173] Surely Whitlam's political preferences would have led him to argue for an increase in the admission of Allende supporters from Chile, who could be expected to favour Labor.

I consider the sentiment underlying the second quote far more relevant. Unlike Willesee, for example, Whitlam was unlikely to let compassion dictate his policy response. He was opposed to the admission of a large number of refugees for pragmatic reasons; most importantly, he was convinced both that the settlement of Vietnamese refugees would put a strain on Australia's relationship with a reunified (and communist) Vietnam, and that the fear which drove tens of thousands of Vietnamese to flee the country was unfounded.

Whitlam's approach to Vietnamese refugees – as well as to Chileans and Cypriots – was also in line with his broader approach to immigration. The 1971 Labor Party conference has been remembered mainly for its decision to commit to a non-discriminatory immigration policy. At the same time, the party agreed to another principle that distinguished its policy from that of the Coalition government. As Whitlam put it when launching the 1972 election campaign: 'We removed the assertion that a primary national objective must be to increase population. We removed the commitment to expand the immigration program. We related our immigration needs specifically to the capacity of Australia to provide "employment, housing, education and social services".'[174]

The Labor government became even more determined to reduce

the size of Australia's immigration program when the post-war economic boom finally came to an end. Since the refugee intake was conceived as an integral part of the immigration program, it was only logical that the number of refugees who were offered resettlement declined as Australia cut its overall migrant intake in response to the worsening economic conditions.

Between 1972 and 1975 Australia resettled comparatively few refugees. Were there fewer per year than under any other post-war prime minister? The answer to that question depends on who is counted as a refugee. Since 1947, most refugees had been brought to Australia under an assisted passage program; under Whitlam, there were on average only 600 assisted passages for refugees per year, while in the previous twenty years there had been 4260 per annum on average.[175] However, under Whitlam, many immigrants who could be considered refugees – for example, the Cypriots – did not qualify for assisted passages. And the East Timorese had come without having been invited.

Whitlam's response to the Vietnamese refugee problem could be easily portrayed as being morally wrong, and as contributing to his eventual downfall. It gave the opposition an opportunity to argue that it was its *duty* to remove a morally bankrupt government. In the weeks immediately before and after the fall of Saigon, many Australians pleaded with their government to admit more refugees from Vietnam; on 9 May 1975 the Department of Foreign Affairs reported that relevant letters and telegrams were 'running at about thirty to one in favour of the Government admitting more refugees'.[176] Many of those letter-writers believed the government's policy was wrong because of its perceived cold-heartedness. They could not see the merits of Whitlam's attempts to put Australia's relationship with Vietnam on a new footing. When Fraser was prime minister, Australians supported a more compassionate policy. That is not to say, however, that they would have supported a mass resettlement scheme in May or June 1975. As the public response to 'Operation Babylift' demonstrated, compassion is a fickle emotion: while the arrival of the first planeload of Vietnamese children on 5 April 1975 was almost universally celebrated as a self-evident humanitarian response to human suffering, the arrival of the second contingent on 18 April elicited a much cooler, and far less critical response. Within only two weeks Australians seemed to have sobered up.

Much like Malcolm Fraser would later do, Gough Whitlam tried to have a say in how his government would be remembered. On many occasions he provided his version of the events of 11 November 1975. With *The Whitlam Government 1972–1975*, his 788-page tome covering all aspects of public policy, he offered a detailed appraisal of the achievements of his prime ministership. Given Whitlam's personal interests, it is unsurprising that the chapter on international affairs takes up more than 150 pages, while immigration is dealt with in only twenty-two pages. Although Whitlam made refugee policy a prime-ministerial matter in 1975, he barely mentioned refugee and asylum seeker issues. While he wanted to be known as a champion of international human rights conventions, he was less interested in discussing his government's record with regards to the application of the 1951 Refugee Convention in Australia. *The Whitlam Government* remains silent on West Papuan refugees, Vietnamese boat people, Timorese evacuees, Asians expelled from Uganda, and Chileans fleeing Pinochet's dictatorship.

Fraser, too, wanted to be remembered as having a strong commitment to human rights. Unlike Whitlam, though, he often and at great length revisited his government's approach to asylum seekers and refugees. Much of the next chapter will be taken up by a discussion of Australia's initial response to Indochinese 'boat people' under Fraser. Fraser's own detailed accounts of Australia's response are helpful for an understanding of his government's stance, but, as I will show, they have much in common with Whitlam's silence about key aspects of his government's approach to refugees. Neither should be taken at face value.

'BOAT PEOPLE'

In terms of Australia's response to refugees and asylum seekers, the governor-general's installation of Malcolm Fraser as prime minister on 11 November 1975 was more significant than any previous or subsequent change of government.

The death of John Curtin had also heralded a radical turn-around of the Australian government's approach to refugees. But the change of leadership from Curtin to Chifley in July 1945 was not responsible for the new approach. Chifley and Calwell oversaw the immigration of hundreds of thousands of European immigrants; the fact that many of them were refugees was relevant mainly because the IRO was able to provide the ships that brought them to Australia. The government's new immigration policy was made possible not so much by Chifley's elevation to the prime ministership as by the end of the war; Curtin, too, had been convinced of the need to substantially increase Australia's population, but could not act on his conviction while the war was in progress.

The transition from Whitlam to Fraser brought about a change in the government's attitude to immigration *and* in Australia's response to refugees and asylum seekers. Whitlam saw no need for a substantial increase of Australia's population; under his tutelage, the overall migrant intake sank to its lowest level since 1947. Fraser, on the other hand, had long favoured population growth through immigration. Long before becoming prime minister, he said he hoped Australia would reach a population of 25 million in his lifetime.[1] In this regard his dreams were similar to those of Arthur Calwell. But in two other respects his approach differed radically from Calwell's, and instead resembled Al Grassby's: Fraser favoured a multicultural and, if need be, multiracial Australia, and he believed the government's response to refugees should also be guided by humanitarian considerations.

The first Fraser government went into caretaker (and campaign) mode as soon as it was sworn in, and there were no immediate changes to Australia's refugee policy. Fraser retained the structure introduced by Whitlam after the 1974 election, and included a minister for labor and immigration in his cabinet. It was only after the Liberal–National Country Party Coalition won the election of 13 December 1975 that Fraser was able to put his stamp on the ministerial division of labour. Tony Street, who had been responsible for immigration in the caretaker government, became minister for employment and industrial relations. Significantly, the government did not simply resurrect the immigration department abolished by Whitlam the previous year, but on 22 December 1975 established a Department of Immigration and Ethnic Affairs. By the end of the 1975/76 financial year, it employed a total of 1462 staff in Australia and overseas – about 60 per cent of the number before the disestablishment of the department in 1974, and about 15 per cent of the 9614 staff employed by the Department of Immigration and Border Protection on 30 June 2014.[2] Michael MacKellar was appointed minister for immigration and ethnic affairs.

Like Fraser, MacKellar had been comparatively young when he first entered parliament, in 1969, to represent the seat of Warringah. MacKellar was thirty-seven when he became immigration minister, two years older than Fraser had been when Holt had appointed him minister for the army in 1966. MacKellar was an agricultural scientist by training, but had been the opposition's spokesman for immigration since June 1974 and was therefore familiar with the relevant issues.

Fraser and other leading politicians of the conservative Coalition had criticised Whitlam's handling of the Indochinese refugee crisis while in opposition. John Carrick, a New South Wales senator and senior Liberal politician, on 23 April 1975 referred to the government's 'extremely narrow and restricted guidelines for the admission of refugees from South Vietnam' and suggested that the 'division of families by wilful act of the Commonwealth Government' would 'cause terrible anguish to all concerned' and 'threaten the very lives of those forced to remain in South Vietnam'.[3] MacKellar had claimed that the Whitlam government had 'acted with shameful indifference to the plight of thousands of South Vietnamese'.[4] And a couple of weeks before the fall of Saigon Fraser had said that Australia ought to be prepared to accommodate 'some thousands of refugees'.[5] Later, he wrote to Whitlam, pleading with him to reconsider a 'narrow and inhumane policy'.[6]

In its first months in office the Fraser government sent out mixed signals about its intentions regarding Indochinese refugees. One was the logical consequence of a particular line of attack against the Whitlam government. On 23 January 1976 Fraser asked MacKellar to instruct his department to contact the Vietnamese refugees who had been required by the previous government to sign an undertaking that they would not engage in political activity. They were to be told the new government considered that request 'inappropriate', and the undertaking would be cancelled.[7]

Then, on 3 February 1976, Cabinet terminated a research project about the settlement of Indochinese refugees.[8] The day after his second ministry was sworn in, Fraser had told his ministers that the government's overriding goal was to rein in government spending.[9] One small step in that direction was a review of fifty inquiries initiated by the Whitlam government, which resulted in the termination of about a third of them. One was a longitudinal study of the settlement needs and experiences of Indochinese refugees, to be carried out by the sociologist Jean Martin. As the author of the 1965 classic *Refugee Settlers*, Martin was well qualified to undertake this work. She was commissioned to do the research a few weeks before Whitlam's dismissal, and received an initial payment of $10,000. She wasted no time, appointed three staff, and began collecting data. However, by 11 November, when Fraser replaced Whitlam, her contract had still not been signed – which made it comparatively easy for the incoming government to cancel the study.

Cabinet's decision came as a shock not only to Martin but also to the Senate Standing Committee on Foreign Affairs and Defence, which in June 1975 had begun looking into Australia's response to the Indochinese refugee crisis. The committee drew extensively on Martin's preliminary findings in its 1976 report, 'Australia and the Refugee Problem', and reproduced them in an appendix.[10] Arguing that a detailed understanding of the resettlement process would be invaluable to the government, the committee also recommended that funds be made available to allow Martin to continue her work.[11]

The Senate Standing Committee did not make recommendations about the number of Indochinese refugees Australia ought to resettle per year, but it made it clear that it considered the Whitlam government's response to the refugee crisis precipitated by the military collapse of South Vietnam woefully inadequate. Among the policy responses criticised by the committee was the Whitlam government's decision not to provide relief and settlement assistance to refugees in Thailand.[12] The Fraser government appeared to share the committee's views about the need to respond to the crisis in Thailand. In January MacKellar announced that a team of immigration officers would select 800 Indochinese refugees from Thai camps. However, this was an initiative that emerged out of discussions in the Department of Foreign Affairs, rather than in MacKellar's own department.

On Christmas Eve 1975, two days after the new government was sworn in, foreign affairs revived an idea which had already been successfully put to Don Willesee, when it made an eight-page submission to its new minister, Andrew Peacock. It strongly argued for the admission of Indochinese refugees from Thailand (without, however, mentioning a specific number), and 'for widening the criteria for family reunion'. Peacock's annotation on the submission reads, in part, 'I believe we should approach the matter as generously as possible.' He also told his department that he would discuss the issue with MacKellar.[13] A team of immigration officers left for Thailand in March but did not meet the announced target. The selection of refugees in Thailand remained the only dedicated selection mission that year. It was responsible for two-thirds of the 1976 intake of Indochinese refugees.

Thus, the government initially did little to increase the number of Indochinese refugees admitted to Australia. In 1975, under Whitlam, Australia admitted a total of 1086 refugees from Indochina. The following year, under Fraser, it took in only 865. This was remarkable for several reasons: first, people continued to flee Vietnam, Laos and Cambodia in large numbers well past April 1975; second, Australia's key ally, the United States, kept resettling large numbers of Indochinese; third, the federal opposition would not have opposed a modest increase of admissions from Indochina, and Fraser himself had of course advocated such an increase before November 1975; and, finally, Australia increased its overall migrant intake from 52,748 in the 1975/76 financial year to 70,227 in 1976/77.[14]

*

In November 1976 Australia's first purpose-built immigration detention centre opened at Villawood, in Sydney. The facility was designed for forty-eight people and, according to the immigration department, combined 'security with a reasonable standard of comfort', including two common rooms with colour television sets.[15] The Villawood centre was not built with 'boat people' in mind; it was to house people awaiting deportation. It was intended to provide more appropriate accommodation than the detention facilities used in New South Wales in the 1960s and early 1970s, such as the old North Head quarantine station. Previously, the department had at times resorted to housing detainees at the Long Bay gaol; it hoped that the opening of the Villawood facility would put an end to that practice.

Immigration detention facilities were considered necessary to ensure that illegal immigrants who had been served with deportation orders would not abscond before their departure from Australia. A very small proportion of people who were in Australia without a valid visa had entered the country illegally: either as stowaways or as crew members who deserted their ships. Hersz Rozenberg, Bas Wie and Willy Wong, whose stories we have encountered in previous chapters, all fell into that category. The overwhelming majority of illegal immigrants, however, were people who entered Australia on temporary permits and failed to leave the country within the period stipulated on their visas. The immigration department estimated that on 31 December 1975, there were 39,500 prohibited immigrants.[16]

Countries of immigration such as Australia and the United States have often been more interested in regularising the status of overstayers than in deporting them. In order to be able to regularise their status, governments needed to assure overstayers that they would not be prosecuted for visa breaches if they came forward. That is what the Fraser government did in early 1976: it announced an amnesty and gave overstayers until the end of April to apply for permanent residence. Overstayers were promised that their applications would be granted if they met the normal health and character requirements. Altogether, 8614 applications were received, about 15 per cent of them from Greek nationals, and another 10 per cent from British passport holders. By the end of November 7228 applications had been approved; only eleven had been rejected on health or character grounds.[17]

Indonesians made up the third-largest group of applicants; another 247 were either Timorese or Portuguese.[18] Thus, it was no surprise that, by 27 April 1976, 150 prohibited immigrants had applied in Darwin alone, which had sizeable Indonesian, Timorese and Portuguese communities. That day, in an article published in the local newspaper, the immigration department reminded others who had not yet submitted applications that time was running out.[19] The department was promptly confronted with five more requests for residence visas, but they caught immigration officials – and everybody else in Australia – by surprise.

On 27 April 1976 the *Kein Giang*, a 'decrepit wooden fishing boat', entered Darwin Harbour with the first Vietnamese 'boat people' on board.[20] They said they had sailed to Australia after having been refused permission to land in Thailand, Singapore and Malaysia. After the West Papuan 'raft men' in 1969, this was only the second time that 'boat people' identifying as refugees had entered Australia unauthorised. With the benefit of hindsight, the arrival of 25-year-old Lam Binh, who captained the boat, his brother Lam Tac Tanh, and their three companions, Gip Chong Pau, Nguyen Van Chen and Ngo Son Binh, seemed to herald a new era in Australian history, but at the time only few observers would have considered the *Kein Giang*'s arrival momentous. A photo depicting the five men with big smiles on their faces and a story about their arrival made it onto the front page of Darwin's *Northern Territory News*.[21] Neither the government nor the media in the southern states paid much attention.

The five 'boat people' were looked after by the local St Vincent de Paul Society, were issued with one-month temporary visas the day after their arrival, and were eventually granted permanent residence – again, without any fanfare. The low-key response was sensible. The panic of May 1975, which had led Whitlam to decide that 'boat people' would be taken into custody upon arrival, had long subsided. There were no indications that the *Kein Giang* was the first of an armada of boats sailing to Australia.

In fact, for months it remained the only refugee boat to reach Australia. The next boat came in November, and there was another one in December. But that year, a mere 111 'boat people' arrived;[22] even by current-day Australian standards, this was a negligible number. There was never any mention of locking them up in Villawood or one of the other immigration detention facilities; instead, those arriving in the late 1970s in Darwin or Broome by boat were flown to migrant reception centres such as Wacol in Brisbane.

\*

While the Fraser government was initially slow to admit Indochinese refugees, it responded generously to other refugee crises. From April 1975 Australian refugee and asylum seeker policy seemed to focus on the Vietnamese. But in 1975 and 1976 the Vietnamese were not the largest group of refugees admitted to Australia. Like other governments before and after it, Fraser's took a flexible approach to the question of who should and who should not be considered a refugee and deserving of resettlement in Australia. In its 1976/77 annual review the immigration department referred to 'refugee situations' that 'involve humanitarian action to alleviate suffering and hardship' but did not concern refugees as per the definition of the 1951 Refugee Convention. The department provided three examples of such refugees: East Timorese evacuees, displaced people from Cyprus, and Lebanese who were admitted to Australia under relaxed migration criteria.[23]

In the two years from 1 July 1975 to 30 June 1977, Australia accepted 10,618 people classified as refugees, 34,096 people under its family reunion program, 49,988 migrants who were 'occupationally eligible' and 28,273 others.[24] Lebanese made up the largest proportion of 'others'. The anthropologist Michael Humphrey, who has done extensive research among Australia's Lebanese community, estimates that more than 20,000 civil war refugees from Lebanon migrated to Australia; he claims they were 'largely poor' and 'sometimes destitute'.[25]

In 1975 clashes between the Lebanese National Movement and the Phalange escalated into a full-blown civil war. By November the security situation in Beirut was so precarious that it became necessary to relocate the Australian embassy to a hotel, and to significantly reduce the number of its staff. On 28 March 1976 the embassy was evacuated. This happened at a time when many Lebanese residents tried to escape the civil war. By the middle of the year, more than 1 million people, about half of them Syrians who had been working in Lebanon, had fled the country. However, both the UNHCR and the Australian government referred to them as 'displaced persons' rather than as refugees, which meant that in the case of those admitted to Australia, the government did not pay for their passage, as it would have if they had been classified as refugees.

Australia already had a sizeable Lebanese population, with 24,218 Lebanese-born people counted in the 1971 census.[26] Australia had had a migration office in Beirut since 1965. In the late 1960s the number of Lebanese immigrants increased significantly, despite attempts by the Lebanese government to discourage emigration, and Australia became the second-most important destination of Lebanese emigrants (behind Canada). At that time, most Lebanese in Australia were Maronite or Melkite Catholics. By 1971 Lebanese migration to Australia had reached such levels that the immigration department decided to suspend the acceptance of unsponsored applications from people living in Lebanon.[27] On account of the immigration of large numbers of Lebanese in the late 1960s and early 1970s, Australia became a preferred destination for Lebanese emigrants when the civil war began.

In July 1976, in response to lobbying by Lebanese migrants in Australia, the immigration department relaxed its entry requirements for Lebanese. It now processed the spouses, dependent children and parents of Australian residents without nomination, and no longer required that Lebanese immigrants meet occupational criteria. Within one month the department had approved 853 Lebanese applicants who were outside the normal family reunion or occupational criteria.[28] The Lebanese communities in Australia were invited to 'present to the [immigration department] lists of acceptable sponsored people who [were] close relatives of Australian residents and the Lebanese communities subsequently arrange[d] for their assembly overseas, for their documentation and for their group travel to Australia';[29] this procedure closely resembled that used by Calwell some thirty years earlier to facilitate the migration of Jewish survivors to Australia.

On 23 September Cabinet decided to send a special taskforce to Nicosia to speed up the processing of Lebanese applicants who had fled to Cyprus.[30] After less than ten weeks, however, Cabinet had second thoughts; on 30 November the government decided to withdraw the

taskforce by Christmas, and, after 31 December, to end the special con-
cessional arrangements and approve applications from Lebanese
nationals only if they met the normal immigration requirements. This
was despite the fact that only half of those issued with a visa proceeded
to Australia, either because applicants had considered a visa 'a form of
insurance', as one foreign affairs official put it, or because they lacked
the funds for the fare to Australia.[31]

Two arguments were put forward to justify that change of policy.
The immigration department was concerned about a 'marked deterio-
ration in the quality of applicants'. Its officers also thought that many
of those applying, who were being approved under the relaxed criteria,
were not refugees but were simply taking advantage of the opportunity
to migrate to Australia. Foreign affairs officials readily supported those
arguments; they told Peacock that the Cypriot authorities had complained to Australian diplomats in Nicosia about the 'poor quality' of
Lebanese entering Cyprus in order to apply for Australian visas. For
the Department of Foreign Affairs, however, another argument had
more weight: it was concerned that the admission of large numbers of
war refugees from Lebanon restricted Australia's capacity to accept
Indochinese refugees, for whom there had been no relaxation of selection criteria.[32]

Post-1975 Lebanese immigrants belonged to communities aligned
with different sides in the civil war. In the same manner in which the
immigration of Polish Jews had outstripped that of German or Austrian
Jews in the immediate post-war period (because Melbourne's Polish
Jewish community had sponsored a proportionately large number of
migrants), the composition of Australia's Lebanese population changed
during the civil war, with Sunni Muslims and Orthodox Christians
sponsoring proportionately more members of their families than Maronite and Melkite Catholics. In fact, of the Lebanese arriving in Australia
between 1975 and 1977, 60 per cent were Muslim.[33]

\*

The Fraser government was willing in principle to relax the normal migration criteria or extend the visas of temporary entrants in response to political turmoil and natural disasters. However, the government's announcements suggest a compassionate response should not be taken at face value. For example, after the Thammaset University massacre of 6 October 1976, when members of the police and of paramilitary groups killed dozens of students and other protesters in Thailand, MacKellar announced in parliament that applications from Thai students to extend their stay in Australia would be 'treated with utmost sympathy'.[34] That did not mean, however, that the Fraser government was following the precedent established by its predecessor in 1975 in relation to Vietnamese students; then, *all* those in Australia at the time of the fall of Saigon were offered an extension of their visas, and those who took up that offer were eventually allowed to remain in Australia permanently.

There were two reasons why the Fraser government was unwilling to allow all Thai students to remain in Australia. The first had to do with diplomatic considerations. Many Thai students in Australia were sponsored under the Colombo Plan, and thus had an obligation to return home at the end of their studies. The foreign affairs department argued that Australia's credibility as an aid donor was at risk if it did not insist that these students fulfil their part of the bargain, because of the precedent such a decision would create. '[T]here is no determining where this trend should stop,' the department argued in a submission to its minister, fearing that Colombo Plan students with obligations towards other undemocratic governments, such as Indonesia's, might follow the Thai students' example.[35] No such precedent had been set in 1975 because the South Vietnamese government had ceased to exist; thus, all obligations towards it were extinguished. The other diplomatic consideration concerned Australia's relations with the government in Bangkok, which had come into office after the military had forced the elected government of Seni Pramoj out of office. The Fraser government was not willing to unnecessarily offend the new rulers in Thailand, who, according to an assessment by the Department of Foreign Affairs, would regard the granting of asylum to Thai students 'with disfavour'.[36]

The second reason was ideological. Australia's diplomats conceded that, following the 6 October massacre and the military's coup, thousands of students had been arrested, and acknowledged that the fears expressed by Thai students in Australia were genuine. But they had little sympathy for 'hardcore radical critics of the Thai political scene' and found the suggestion credible that Thai students in Australia had been subjected to a 'well orchestrated left-wing campaign' aimed at installing a communist government in Thailand.[37]

The government itself was conflicted about the issue. MacKellar appeared sympathetic but had to defer to the minister for foreign affairs. In January 1977, when the foreign affairs department was seeking a ministerial ruling on the issue, however, its submission landed on the desk of the minister for trade and commerce, New South Wales Liberal Senator Bob Cotton, who at the time was acting foreign minister. Cotton approved of a policy that was informed more by foreign policy considerations than by concerns for the welfare of individual students.

Foreign minister Peacock did not share Cotton's views, and once back at the helm told his department that Australia's approach was not 'as sympathetic as it could be'.[38] The archival record suggests that while the 'utmost sympathy' which MacKellar had invoked in October 1976 was not extended to all Thai students in Australia, and although no applications for political asylum were granted, some students were allowed to remain in Australia. There were also cases, however, in which the immigration department took out deportation orders against students.[39]

*

The arrival of the first Vietnamese 'boat people' and Australian discussions about how to respond to Thai students who feared returning home after the October 1976 military coup coincided with a renewed attempt by the UNHCR and several non-government organisations to enshrine the right to asylum in international law.

As we have seen in Chapter 3, previous attempts had culminated in the 1967 Declaration on Territorial Asylum, which once more privileged the right of nation-states to admit – or refuse to admit – non-citizens over the right of refugees to seek and be granted asylum. In 1971 the UNHCR and the Carnegie Endowment for International Peace launched a fresh attempt. At a colloquium in Bellagio in 1971, and at the meeting of a working group in Geneva the following year, a draft text for a convention on asylum was drawn up. Article 1 of that draft spoke of refugees in terms that were very similar to those of the 1951 Refugee Convention, and stipulated that '[a] Contracting State, acting in an international and humanitarian spirit, shall use its best endeavours to grant asylum in its territory' to persons who met that definition.[40] The High Commissioner for Refugees subsequently submitted this draft to the United Nations General Assembly for consideration. It was then referred to a group of experts, which represented twenty-seven states, including Australia, and which in 1975 produced a report on the draft text.

This report makes it clear that even the rather vague terms of the original draft were seen by some governments as an infringement of the right of states to decide whether or not to admit a person to their territory. Article 1 now read: 'Each Contracting State, acting in the exercise of its sovereign rights, shall use its best endeavours in a humanitarian spirit to grant asylum in its territory to any person eligible for the benefits of this Convention.'[41] A working group formed by several non-governmental organisations put forward an alternative draft, which was less concerned with the rights of nation-states to grant asylum than with the right of asylees to be afforded protection. '[This draft] will be given most careful consideration,' Australia's ambassador in Geneva, Owen Lennox Davis, told the UNHCR executive in October 1976, but he left no doubt as to his government's preferred position: '[A] realistic and satisfactory solution can be achieved only

by the adoption of a text that carefully balances the legitimate expectations of claimants for asylum against the rights and duties of a state
in the exercise of its sovereign power.'[42]

In January and February 1977 the UNHCR convened a conference
of plenipotentiaries in Geneva. A brief prepared by Australia's immigration, foreign affairs and attorney-general's departments outlined the
limits set by the government : 'From Australia's point of view, if a Convention on territorial asylum is to be acceptable it is important that it
should not impose *legal duties* on Parties to accept into their territories,
whether provisionally or conditionally, persons who have well founded
fear of persecution or prosecution on inadmissible grounds.' Reiterat-
ing a point that had been made by numerous previous governments – and
that would be made again and again – the brief explained that the Australian government 'will wish to retain its discretion to determine
ultimately who can enter Australian territory and under what conditions newcomers may remain'. The Australian delegation knew that,
unlike during the discussions of the 1951 Refugee Convention, this time
its views would not be considered exceptionally restrictive, and that it
could rely on others to ensure that a convention on asylum did not go
too far. 'As an influx of asylees or refugees can create serious political,
social and economic problems,' the brief said, 'it would be surprising if
States were prepared to deprive themselves of ultimate freedom of action
when considering applications for entry into their territory'.[43]

There were no such surprises at the Geneva conference, which,
according to the Norwegian international lawyer Atle Grahl-Madsen,
who attended it as an observer, was 'spectacular' but 'did not come to
much'.[44] In fact, if anything, the conference achieved less than expected.
It failed to reach a consensus about the overall aim of a convention, as
well as about individual articles of the draft text. The Australian delegation had been in favour of creating a legally binding instrument on
asylum, and remained 'hopeful about the final outcome of the Conference's work'.[45] Few others shared that optimism. The UNHCR made it
known that it wanted the conference to be deferred indefinitely, most

likely because it had hoped for something far more ambitious than what had been palatable to the meeting in Geneva, and had no interest in continuing a discussion that might have ended only in a document affirming states' rights.[46]

Australia's commitment to arrive at a binding agreement – which would not have advocated an abrogation of states' sovereignty – was shared only by a small minority, which included a handful of Latin American countries as well as Tanzania, Senegal, Ghana and Nigeria. The majority of the ninety-two governments represented in Geneva – and most of Australia's Western allies – were unwilling to continue working towards a convention that would create legally binding obligations for them.

In 1977 governments were even less prepared to sign off on anything that resembled a right to asylum than they had been in the early 1950s and mid-1960s. Over the next decades their attitudes hardly changed. In fact, the increase in asylum applications in the 1980s, and then again in the second decade of the twenty-first century, made them only more wary of an international instrument that would limit states' prerogative to decide who was allowed to enter, and remain in, their territories.

*

At the same time as the government was responding to East Timorese evacuees, the first Vietnamese 'boat people' and Lebanese displaced by the civil war, the Senate Standing Committee on Foreign Affairs and Defence was investigating Australia's response to refugees. Chaired first by Victorian Labor senator Cyril Primmer and then, from March 1976, by West Australian Liberal Peter Sim, the committee had been asked in June 1975 to explore the following issues:

a) The plight and circumstances of refugees and other persons forced to leave South Viet Nam following the occupation of that area by North Vietnamese forces, together with the existing and future circumstances of all South Vietnamese students now in Australia and their close relatives;

b) The response of the Australian Government to the requests made both from within Australia and at the international level for assistance in the matters of resettlement and rehabilitation; and

c) The areas of operation in which the Australian nation could render appropriate and effective assistance.[47]

The committee held hearings in October 1975 and in April 1976. It soon interpreted the second and third issues very broadly; rather than being preoccupied with the Whitlam government's response to the collapse of South Vietnam, it explored the possible tenets of an Australian refugee resettlement policy. It explored who could and should be considered a refugee, and whether the settlement needs of refugees were distinct from those of other immigrants. In a question directed at a senior official of the immigration department, Sim summed up one of the key insights the committee had gained. 'Is it a fact,' he asked, 'that the intake criteria are varied for refugees, but that the settlement criteria are rarely varied at all?'[48]

The Standing Committee's report was tabled in December 1976. Unsurprisingly, the formulation of a refugee settlement policy was the first of a long list of recommendations for the Fraser government. The committee considered 'it essential that there exist an approved and comprehensive set of policy guidelines', and urged the government to tackle the formulation of such guidelines as a matter of priority.[49]

The members of the 1975–1976 Senate committee set an important precedent: many subsequent parliamentary inquiries have regularly produced reports highly critical of the government's approach, made crucial interventions in debates about Australia's response to asylum seekers and sometimes brought about changes to policies and administrative practices. Noteworthy reports include the 1982 findings of a Senate inquiry into the resettlement of Indochinese refugees, the 1992 report by a joint standing committee on migration regulations on Australia's refugee and humanitarian system, the report 'A Sanctuary Under Review', tabled in 2000 by a Senate committee inquiring into Australia's refugee determination process, and the report of the Senate Select Committee into a Certain Maritime Incident, which investigated the so-called children overboard affair in 2002.[50]

In 1976 a second parliamentary committee echoed some of the concerns expressed by Senator Sim and his colleagues. Chaired by Labor's Kim Beazley (senior), the Joint Committee on Foreign Affairs and Defence had explored the humanitarian aspects of the crisis in Lebanon. In July 1976 Beazley had written to MacKellar, demanding that '[in] order for Australia to be seen to be taking its fair share of refugees . . . Australia must develop a clear-cut policy on refugees'.[51] The committee's final report echoed this demand:

> The Committee believes that a world which appears to be increasingly intolerant will continue to create refugee situations for many years to come and that Australia is well placed to be imaginative in its policy and generous to refugees . . . The Committee believes that need especially consequent upon persecution and danger, and the ability to integrate are the important criteria, and that refugee policy should not be an area of party politics.[52]

In March 1977 the government-appointed Australian Population and Immigration Council published a Green Paper on immigration, which included a chapter devoted to refugees.[53] It was another two months before MacKellar was able to announce in parliament that the government had decided on a policy and arrangements 'to enable refugee and analogous situations to be dealt with promptly, equitably and effectively'.[54] Not only did it thereby heed the calls of two parliamentary inquiries, it also implemented a policy the Coalition parties had announced two years earlier while in opposition: the establishment of 'a refugee mechanism to cater for emergency situations instead of making ad hoc responses as at present'.[55] MacKellar's statement on 24 May 1977 marked a watershed in Australia's response to refugees. Admittedly, the government had developed policies and devised procedures to deal with displaced people on previous occasions, such as in late 1938, when McEwen had announced that Australia would admit up to 15,000 European refugees, and in 1956, when the government had formulated a policy to deal with asylum requests. But MacKellar's statement constituted a new approach in three respects: first, it was not designed with one particular group of refugees in mind; second, it covered Australian contributions to the UNHCR, the resettlement of refugees selected off-shore and the response to on-shore requests for protection; and third, it was made public (unlike all previous asylum policies, including that of 1956, the 1962 policy regarding West Papuans, and Whitlam's 1975 'boat people' policy).

According to MacKellar's statement, the government's refugee policy would be guided by four considerations: that Australia acknowledged its responsibility to admit refugees for resettlement; that the government retained the ultimate say over who would be resettled; that some refugee settlers required special post-arrival assistance; and that the needs of some refugees were best met by solutions other than resettlement in Australia.[56]

In many respects MacKellar followed the Senate Standing Committee's recommendations. However, while acknowledging the role of voluntary organisations, he did not envisage them playing a central role in the provision of resettlement services, as the committee had suggested. Nor did MacKellar make any reference to some concrete proposals for post-arrival services that the committee had put forward. His announcement on 24 May was a statement of intent and a broad outline of policy principles; it did not include a catalogue of policy measures.

MacKellar's statement was remarkable for other reasons as well. He began by emphasising that the policy applied also to 'analogous situations', and then referred to natural disasters and the effects these had 'for people with associations with Australia'. He mentioned asylum requests by deserting seamen and people who had entered Australia on visitors' visas, but made no reference to either the Indochinese 'boat people' or the East Timorese who had fled to Darwin in 1975.

One of MacKellar's policy innovations concerned the division of labour between immigration and foreign affairs: it would henceforth be the responsibility of the immigration minister to propose responses to refugee crises, which suggested that Peacock and his department had effectively been sidelined. This was a curious outcome: after all, the immigration department more so than the Department of Foreign Affairs had been in the firing line of the Senate Standing Committee's report. Between Whitlam's dismissal and May 1977, Peacock and his department had been in favour of Australia's resettling more Indochinese refugees from camps in South-east Asia, while the immigration department had privileged the immigration of displaced people from war-torn Lebanon who had family in Australia, and of Chileans who met the normal immigration criteria.

By far the most significant policy innovation was contained in MacKellar's admission that some refugees needed special assistance. This was an issue that had featured prominently in the hearings of the Senate Standing Committee: Vietnamese refugees needed extra support in order to settle successfully, both because their cultural background did not prepare them for life in Australia and because of the hardship they had suffered as refugees. Donald Whitelum, secretary of the Australian Society for Inter Country Aid, had told the committee that they needed help, particularly during the first six months after their arrival in Australia, 'to get over the emotional crisis that they would be suffering'.[57] Another witness who appeared before the committee, the director of the Christian and Missionary Alliance of Australia, Robert Thomas Henry, emphasised 'the intensity of the trauma through which these refugees have come'.[58]

Not only did MacKellar's statement make it clear that it was the responsibility of the government to provide the required assistance; it

also suggested that Australia would no longer automatically reject refugee settlers on account of their age or employability. '[T]he Government
readily accepts that there will be people in urgent need of resettlement
who will have major problems of resettlement in Australia,' MacKellar
said. 'It would be inconsistent with the humanitarian nature of refugee
resettlement not to accept some people in this category.'[59] This was a far
cry from the policies that had guided not only the resettlement of DPs,
but which, more recently, had also informed the selection of Ugandan
Asians and Chileans.

The federal opposition welcomed the fact that the government had
formulated a refugee policy but was unhappy with some of its features.
In particular, the Labor Party's immigration spokesman, Ted Innes,
criticised that the government had not taken up the Standing Committee's suggestion to establish a Refugee Policy Council, whose members
would be drawn from government agencies, non-government organisations and the UNHCR.[60] However, it was obvious that he was
concerned not so much that organisations such as the Red Cross were
excluded from the refugee policy arena, but that the government did
not intend to formally consult 'representatives of the various ethnic
groups in our society'.[61]

Innes, who had succeeded Calwell as the Federal Member for Melbourne, singled out three ethnic groups which, in his view, had been
neglected by Australia's refugee policy: people from Chile, Cyprus and
Lebanon. Regarding the latter, he thought the government had failed
to facilitate the immigration of enough 'refugees from this sorry nation'.[62]
Rather than objecting to the principles of the government's refugee
policy, Innes was concerned that the admission of some refugees (presumably those from Indochina, although he did not spell that out) would
make it more difficult for members of Labor's ethnic constituency to
sponsor family members.

*

Whitlam had been concerned that the admission of South Vietnamese refugees from Indochina would create problems for Australia's relations with a reunified Vietnam. Initially, though, the Fraser government did not encounter any major difficulties in that regard – neither with Vietnam nor with Laos, which since the end of 1975 was ruled by the Pathet Lao, who had emerged as victors of a decades-long civil war, and which became another major source of refugees.

In mid-1977, however, Australia's relations with the government in Vientiane were thrown into jeopardy by a request for political asylum. Chansamone Vongsaphay was the deputy head of the Non-Aligned Department in the Laotian foreign ministry. Earlier in his career, in 1971 and 1972, he had served as Laos' chargé d'affaires in Canberra.[63] Although he had been a foreign affairs official under the previous government, he had retained a senior position after the Pathet Lao came to power. However, in early 1977 he told Australian embassy staff in Vientiane that he wanted to get out of Laos.[64] When his superiors learned of his intentions, his position became untenable, and Vongsaphay and his family crossed the border into Thailand. From there, he again approached the Australians. Australia was an obvious destination not only because of his previous posting in Canberra but also because members of his family, including his mother, two brothers and a daughter, were already living in Australia.

Vongsaphay's request put the Fraser government in a difficult position. The authorities in Vientiane were holding Australian ambassador John Forsythe responsible for Vongsaphay's departure, and warned him that Australia's admission of Vongsaphay 'could lead to a "clouding over" in relations' – not least because they feared that his defection might entice other leading officials of the previous government to follow.[65] Forsythe's protestations that he had been unaware of Vongsaphay's intentions, who had 'thrust himself' upon the embassy's second secretary in the ambassador's absence, made no impact.[66] The Australian government therefore decided to ignore Vongsaphay's request for political asylum and instead process it as an application for migration to

Australia. To demonstrate to the government in Laos that Vongsaphay and his family were ordinary immigrants, the Australians told them they were ineligible for an assisted passage (which would have been available to them if they had been considered refugees).[67]

Notwithstanding its ideological differences with the Pathet Lao, the Fraser government was not prepared to jeopardise its diplomatic relations with the government in Vientiane by granting political asylum to a high-ranking defector. It was also careful not to publicise the fact that Vongsaphay had been allowed to migrate to Australia. This was not because Fraser and his cabinet were opposed in principle to the granting of asylum; in 1980, in a decision that surprised some of the government's own supporters, they granted political asylum to the East German ballet dancer Heidi Giersch.[68]

*

In late 1976, after the third boat with Vietnamese refugees reached Darwin, the first rumblings about unauthorised arrivals appeared in the press. In December the Melbourne *Sun* warned of a 'tide of human flotsam' lapping the shores of northern Australia, and speculated about an invasion of Australia's far north 'by hundreds, thousands and even tens of thousands of Asian refugees'.[69] However, notwithstanding occasional sensationalist reporting in some tabloids, politicians, the media and the general public largely paid little attention to the arrival of 'boat people' in 1976 and early 1977. The immigration department was still unperturbed about the unauthorised arrivals at the time. In its summary of significant events between 1 July 1976 and 30 June 1977, it reported that '204 people of various ages in 7 small boats reached northern and north-western Australia unheralded after hazardous journeys from Indo-China'. According to the department, all these people were given permanent residence permits.[70]

In the first nine months of 1977, 167 'boat people' arrived in Australia: there were two boats in May, three in June, one in July and two in September. At that stage it was still only in Darwin that the arrival of the refugee boats was a prominent topic of conversation. But even there most Australians were still relaxed. In fact, if the coverage in the local newspaper is any indication, the feat of steering fairly small fishing boats from South-East Asia to Australia sparked admiration rather than fear. 'Eight brave sea to achieve dream,' read the headline of a front-page article in the *Northern Territory News* on 26 September.[71] Perhaps people in Darwin were kindly disposed towards these boat arrivals also because earlier that month they had closely followed the exploits of the *Can-Tiki*, a boat made from beer cans, which a group of local residents had sailed from Darwin to Singapore to promote tourism to Australia's Top End.[72]

In October 1977, with 102 arrivals, the numbers of 'boat people' sailing to Australia picked up. That month, MacKellar discussed refugee issues with his counterparts in the various state governments. 'There is growing disquiet,' he told them, 'particularly . . . about people arriving unannounced off Australian shores . . . [P]eople are concerned that in the future there is the possibility that massive numbers may be involved.'[73]

Some of MacKellar's state colleagues shared his concerns. Walter Jona, Victoria's first minister for ethnic affairs, told the meeting that many Australians from both sides of the political divide had suggested to him that 'we should just slash the refugee program to nil and to hell with refugees'. Jona himself was appalled by such attitudes; while he argued that the meeting needed to be realistic and recognise them as 'an unfortunate fact of life', he also thought that 'State governments, responsible citizens and Ministers ought to be trying to create a climate . . . where the Australian community will much more readily accept its duty and its obligations to take its rightful share of refugees'.[74]

Views about what would comprise such a 'rightful share' varied. Neil Batt, a minister in Tasmania's Labor government, advocated the most extreme position. 'Australia, probably more than any other nation on earth, has a particular responsibility to . . . become a place where refugees from either natural disaster or political problems can come as a first stopping place, even though subsequently they might be transferred elsewhere,' he argued.[75] MacKellar disagreed and raised two points that were already well-worn in 1977, but whose appeal has not diminished several decades later. 'Australia can really be quite proud of what it has done and what it is doing,' the immigration minister said, referring specifically to having just beaten Canada with the release of a government statement on refugee policy. He also drew attention to the enormity of the problem: there were millions of refugees in the world.[76]

Batt was not easily deterred: 'The fact that there are six million refugees in the world indicates that our response ought to be more substantial than it is at the moment, not that it ought to be less.' He argued that Australia was 'uniquely placed' to contribute to the problem's solution: 'we can hardly point to Thailand or Pakistan or wherever and say that they have a greater international responsibility than we have . . . It is an international problem and we have to be part of it.' None of the other ministers shared Batt's enthusiasm.

In another crucial respect, however, Batt's views conformed to those expressed by his state colleagues and MacKellar. He said that 'no government can ultimately tolerate a situation of self-selection', and that if Australia had a far more generous refugee policy, it would in fact be in a stronger position to reject some of the 'boat people' arriving spontaneously.[77]

The spontaneous arrivals continued. Another two boats arrived in the first half of November, and the issue of how to respond to Indochinese asylum seekers arriving by boat gained in prominence. In Darwin, community attitudes shifted.[78] Concerns about the introduction of exotic diseases and about the effectiveness of the authorities' surveillance of Australia's northern coastline grew louder, particularly when a boat was found to have entered Doctor's Gully in Darwin under the nose of – but unnoticed by – the Australian military.[79] On 16 November the immigration department for the first time did not immediately grant thirty-day temporary entry permits to a group of 'boat people', and initially did not allow them to disembark. While the department issued them with visas twenty-four hours later, the initial refusal and an accompanying statement by MacKellar, in which he announced that his department would 'assess the implications of unauthorised entry as a matter of urgency', suggested the government was adopting a tougher line.[80]

Three weeks earlier, Fraser had ended speculation about an impending federal election by announcing that Australians would go to the polls on 10 December. The question of how Australia ought to respond to Indochinese refugees had been hotly debated between April and August 1975 but had been overshadowed by the death throes of the Whitlam government. It had not featured in the election campaign of November/December 1975. Those who supported Malcolm Fraser did so because they were tired of the scandal-ridden Labor government and did not trust it to steer Australia through a time of economic crisis. The fact that Fraser favoured the admission of more refugees from Indochina, while Whitlam did not, was not a significant issue in the 1975 campaign.

Initially, it seemed the 1977 campaign would be no different. For the government it began badly when Fraser was forced to demand the resignation of the treasurer, Phillip Lynch, who had been implicated in shady land deals in Victoria and criticised for the use of a family trust to minimise his tax obligations. These issues dominated the first half of the campaign, and Fraser later confided that he would not have called an election had he known about Lynch's troubles.[81] (Lynch was subsequently cleared of any improper conduct.)

Halfway through the 1977 election campaign, however, the reception of Vietnamese refugees became a highly contentious issue that featured prominently on the front pages of the nation's newspapers. On 20 and 21 November, less than three weeks out from the elections and coinciding with the Coalition's official campaign launch, six boats carrying 218 people arrived in Darwin.[82] In one newspaper report they were dubbed 'the second fleet'.[83] One of them was the *VNKG 1062*, called *Tự Do* ('Freedom') by its owner. It was less than twenty metres long and had thirty-one people on board, including seven children under the age of ten.[84]

Today the boat is in the collection of the Australian National Maritime Museum in Sydney; in 1977 it was owned by a thirty-year-old businessman, Tan Than Lu, who had meticulously planned his escape from Vietnam and had the boat built specifically for that purpose. Together with family, friends and neighbours, he left Vietnam on 16 August 1977. The *Tự Do* initially made landfall in Malaysia, from where Tan Than Lu unsuccessfully tried to be accepted for resettlement in the United States. After a month in Malaysia he decided to push on towards Australia. The boat made landfall again in Java, where the refugees were reprovisioned and told to move on by Indonesian officials. Off Flores, they encountered another refugee boat, which had run aground; the *Tự Do* towed it across the Timor Sea all the way to Darwin.[85]

News of the arrival of the boats came as MacKellar and the federal opposition's acting immigration spokesman, Senator Tony Mulvihill, were discussing immigration issues on *The Policy Makers*, an ABC Radio program which was exploring the key themes of the campaign. The minister took the opportunity to announce the establishment of a committee to assess refugee claims; Mulvihill flagged the introduction of an upper limit on the number of refugees accepted by Australia, should Labor win the election.[86] He criticised the government for accepting 'boat people' indiscriminately, suggesting that not all of them were genuine refugees who deserved to be resettled in Australia. He also claimed that many refugees in Latin America were 'under worse political duress' than the people fleeing Indochina.[87]

The next day, 23 November, the Northern Territory's Labor senator, Ted Robertson, urged the government to 'spread the word' that Vietnamese refugees arriving by boat were unwelcome. The government must 'make it clear', he said, 'that Australia is not going to open the floodgates . . . We will have to try and find a way of showing our sympathy while stopping the flood of what basically are illegal immigrants.'[88] Both sides of politics in the Northern Territory Legislative Assembly, including the Country Liberal Party's majority leader, Paul Everingham, and Labor's Jon Isaacs, publicly deplored the unchecked arrival of refugee boats.[89] So too did the mayor of Darwin, Dr Ella Stack. 'I think some of the last boatload of refugees are pseudo-refugees,' she told ABC Radio's *AM* program. 'They just don't look like refugees or people who have suffered, or have had the trauma of that long trip.'[90]

Australians in the southern states had to rely on the alleged first-hand testimony of Stack and others in Darwin who could claim to have witnessed the arrival of the Vietnamese. Newspapers drew on these presumed eyewitness reports uncritically. The *Australian*, for example, quoted an unnamed 'health department official' involved in processing boat arrivals in Darwin, who had observed that they looked 'as though they've been on an excursion cruise'; he had 'seen people in much worse condition after the Sydney to Hobart yacht race'.[91] At that stage, in the first four or five days after the arrival of the six boats on 20 and 21 November, neither journalists nor the immigration department seemed to be interested in verifying this or similar statements. The majority of the first media reports suggested that Australians had good reason to be alarmed about the boat arrivals; only the *Sydney Morning Herald* published an editorial that bucked the trend. 'Australia must take all that it can,' the paper argued. 'These people deserve our admiration, our compassion and our help.'[92]

The idea that people who were not destitute and were not visibly suffering could not possibly be refugees also featured prominently in statements made by officials from the Waterside Workers' Federation, which had called on its members in Darwin to strike in protest against the 'preferential treatment' allegedly given to refugees.[93] A resolution passed by the Federation's Darwin branch immediately after the arrival of the six boats referred to the Vietnamese arrivals as 'illegal immigrants' and cast aspersions on their 'moral fibre' because they supposedly 'could finish up at the end of a very long war with gold bars and servants'.[94] On 24 November the federation's president, Curly Nixon, categorically declared that the recent boat arrivals were not refugees because they supposedly had 'pressed trousers, gold, and in one case three servants'.

Nixon also claimed to know why the 'boat people' were able to afford pressed trousers. 'Who makes money out of a civil war?' he asked. 'Black marketeers, dope runners, and brothel keepers. You've got the lot here. If they said good morning to me, I'd put my pyjamas on and go to bed, that's how far I trust them.'[95] The same day, Senator Mulvihill repeated Nixon's claim that the recent arrivals were wealthy and included brothel owners.[96] Darwin waterside workers proved responsive to such incitements. According to a *Times* correspondent, some of them hurled insults at 'boat people'.[97]

Much of the 'information' on which Nixon and others were drawing was little more than hearsay and speculative gossip. An article in the *Northern Territory News* used an unnamed 'reliable' source when suggesting that the movement of Indochinese refugees from Thailand to Australia was part of a racket.[98] In the Legislative Assembly Jon Isaacs said that 'there is concern that the refugees are part of a well orchestrated organisation' because some of the boats had new engines and modern navigation instruments.[99] (It was later established that only one of the boats arriving in November had a new engine, which had been taken from an American tractor owned by one of the refugees.[100])

Fraser's government was unprepared for the strength of the reaction against the arrival of 'boat people'. Detailed speaker's notes compiled by the Liberal Party's federal secretariat refer briefly to the government's 'far-reaching and humanitarian' refugee policy, but otherwise do not mention either refugees or unauthorised arrivals; the party had not anticipated that 'boat people' would feature in the election campaign.[101] The government nevertheless presented a united front. In the first week after the arrival of the *Tự Do* and the other five boats, senior Liberal politicians who commented publicly on the issue echoed the concerns voiced by unionists, the Labor Party and local leaders in the Northern

Territory. Fraser and his colleagues appeared to be intent on placating those anxious about boat arrivals, and on not allowing Labor to exploit the issue.

On 22 November MacKellar issued a statement in response to the resolution passed the previous day by the Darwin wharfies. While he stressed 'Australia's obligation to deal in the most sympathetic terms with people who, to the best of the ability to determine the facts, were genuine refugees', he seemed anxious not to appear too critical of the waterside workers' outrageous claims. MacKellar 'well understood that there could be differing views held about the movement of refugees into Australia by these means'. According to his press release, '[t]here was no question that a rising flow of small boat migration would require a continuing review and tightening of the surveillance procedures'.[102]

MacKellar's half-hearted defence of the admission of 'boat people' who were found to be refugees, coupled with his professed empathy with Australians who voiced strong and evidently irrational objections to unauthorised arrivals, anticipated a position taken by Labor prime minister Julia Gillard during the 2010 election campaign: she legitimised similar objections when she repeatedly assured Australians hostile to asylum seekers that she fully understood their concerns.[103]

Also on 22 November, in a speech to the New South Wales branch of the Institute for International Affairs, the immigration minister warned that 'no country can afford the impression that any group of people who arrive on its shores will be allowed to enter and remain'. He painted a dire picture of the consequences of an unchecked arrival of refugee boats. 'We have to combine humanity and compassion with prudent control of unauthorised entry, or be prepared to tear up the Migration Act and its basic policies,' he said.[104] Foreign minister Andrew Peacock said that Australia could not 'continue to indefinitely accept Asian refugees arriving unannounced by sea', and that 'Australia could not be regarded as a dumping ground'.[105]

Fraser had allegedly been told by his advisers to treat the refugee issue with caution because of its potential to be a 'campaign "sleeper"'.[106]

Both he and MacKellar warned that asylum seekers arriving by boat would not necessarily be resettled in Australia, and might indeed be sent back.[107] 'Limit on refugees says P.M.,' read a front-page headline in the Brisbane *Courier-Mail* on 26 November, while on the same day a *Sydney Morning Herald* front-page headline said: 'Fraser warns refugees'.[108]

The government was rattled also because it knew that more boats were on their way. On 23 November the immigration department told its minister that at least twelve boats were en route to Australia; it feared that another forty boats would soon set out from Thailand, and that some 2000 people wanted to come to Australia from Malaysia.[109]

The increase in boat arrivals in Australia was partly due to a hardening of the position of South-East Asian nations. In Thailand, which then housed the largest number of Indochinese refugees, a new policy had come into effect on 15 November, according to which refugees were pushed back across the border wherever possible. Only when that proved impossible would their claims be investigated by district-level committees. According to Australia's ambassador in Bangkok, who toured northern Thailand a month later, those found to be refugees were housed in camps which were not supervised by the UNHCR; the others were 'prosecuted for illegal entry and then sent to one of the three new camps on a "temporary" basis pending return to their country of origin whenever that becomes possible'.[110]

MacKellar and his department recognised that in order to get an anxious Australian public off the government's back, it was important to stem the flow of unauthorised arrivals. This, they knew, would require a substantial increase in Australia's off-shore selection of Indochinese refugees, which up to that point had still been comparatively low (with a total of 2958 Indochinese refugee arrivals, including those who had come by boat, in 1977). On 23 November the ministers for immigration and health, MacKellar and Ralph Hunt, announced that a team of immigration officials would be dispatched immediately to Malaysia and Singapore.[111]

Only two days later the Department of Foreign Affairs was able to tell its minister that the strategy seemed to be working. According to information provided by UNHCR representatives, some Indochinese refugees had decided, following MacKellar's announcement, to postpone their departure from Malaysia.[112] On 30 November an immigration officer in Malaysia was reported as saying that he had been able to dissuade people from four boats from continuing their voyage to Australia with the argument that an immigration selection team would visit Malaysia the following week.[113] MacKellar and Hunt's statement did not mention how many refugees Australia would be prepared to resettle. The immigration department had been instructed to select 1000 refugees from Malaysia and 500 from Indonesia; however, a senior immigration bureaucrat told a meeting of immigration and foreign affairs officials that Australia ought to be thinking of resettling 10,000 Indochinese in the 1977/78 financial year.[114]

MacKellar and Hunt also announced that 'urgent consideration was being given to surveillance requirements essential to safeguard Australia against unauthorised entry', but did not say how such surveillance would have an impact on unauthorised entry. Obviously, surveillance in itself would not stop boats from reaching Australia, but it would provide the government with more advance notice and prevent a repeat of the embarrassment caused when the authorities became aware of refugee boats only after they had tied up at the wharf in Darwin. In fact, none of those who demanded that 'boat people' be stopped from entering Australia made any practical suggestions as to what a 'stop the boats' policy might look like. 'Would not some of them be likely to sink on the return voyage?' the *Sydney Morning Herald* asked in an editorial in early December. 'Would any government risk the hostile public reaction which would be bound to follow?'[115]

Meanwhile, sections of the media and senior Labor politicians continued to pour petrol on the flames. 'Illegal immigrants masquerading as refugees should be returned to their countries of origin – and billed, where possible, for the cost of their passage home,' the *Courier-Mail* demanded in an editorial on 24 November.[116] The next day the *Australian* suggested that 'troublesome political arrivals' be sent 'straight back', and that 'criminal bully boys (it is said that some recent refugees slit throats to get the riches they are arriving with) should be sent packing, too'.[117] Also on 25 November, Gough Whitlam claimed that Australia needed to do more to police its northern borders if it wanted to prevent unauthorised immigration, the importation of drugs and the spread of infectious diseases, thereby subtly associating asylum seekers with illicit drugs and dangerous viruses.[118]

Whitlam also doubted the legitimacy of refugee claims made by Vietnamese, suggesting it was 'not credible, 2½ years after the end of the Vietnam war, that these refugees should suddenly be coming to Australia'.[119] Three days later he conceded that 'genuine refugees' should be accepted (while insinuating that not all of the recent boat arrivals were genuine refugees), but warned the government not to put refugees 'ahead in the queue' over applicants who were sponsored by their relatives.[120] The imaginary queue was soon to become one of the most powerful images in the anti-'boat people' discourse; it served to distinguish 'good' from 'bad' prospective immigrants.[121]

Because of the temporary absence of Labor's immigration spokesperson, Ted Innes, it fell initially to Mulvihill to represent the federal opposition's stance. He called on the government to 'make an example' of some of the unauthorised arrivals: 'We have to turn a few of them around, and send them back to South-East Asia under naval escort.'[122] Throughout his political career, which included a stint as chair of the Commonwealth Immigration Advisory Council, Mulvihill had championed the rights and interests of migrants.[123] That did not make him an unlikely critic of the government's response to 'boat people' – to the contrary. Recent immigrants were concerned about the potential impact of boat arrivals on Australia's family reunion program, and their representatives were therefore more likely to oppose the admission of people who had not been processed off-shore.

Labor politicians portrayed themselves as advocates of people who were supposedly disadvantaged by Australia's acceptance of 'boat people'. According to Innes, Australia's Lebanese community was particularly aggravated about refugees 'jumping the queue' because many Lebanese had supposedly been 'left for dead in Nicosia'.[124] This was a curious argument, given that in 1977 the intake of Lebanese was considerably higher than that of refugees from Indochina, including those who arrived under their own steam.

For almost a week, the government did not contradict the Labor Party. Nor did it challenge journalists who reported the hostile views of unnamed government officials, such as the 'authorities in Darwin' who said that many recent boat arrivals 'do not appear to have suffered in refugee camps' and that some of them 'have substantial quantities of gold',[125] or an unnamed Australian official in Bangkok who had used the term 'armada' (which had already been bandied about in May 1975) when talking about refugee boats on their way to Australia.[126] 'Reports say at least 60 boats are on the way to Darwin,' the *Sun-Herald* claimed, but it did not reveal who had authored these reports.[127]

Then, on the weekend of 26 and 27 November, the tenor of the public debate began to shift. MacKellar denied that an 'armada' was on its way and said that the possessions of the last 220 Vietnamese boat arrivals were worth a total of $10,000.[128] Church leaders and fifty-seven Sydney academics wrote an open letter to the government, invoking Australia's obligations 'as a stable and relatively prosperous nation' and the responsibility of individual Australians 'to receive refugees and other migrants into the community'. They called for a substantial increase of the country's refugee intake.[129] Don Chipp, a former Coalition government minister who had quit the Liberal Party in March 1977 and was now leader of the newly formed Australian Democrats, became the first prominent politician to speak out against the idea that 'boat people' could be turned back.[130]

At the same time, some newspaper editors remembered that journalists were obliged to critically interrogate claims before publishing them. An editorial in the Hobart *Mercury* on 28 November ridiculed suggestions that the Vietnamese had somehow been able to bring substantial quantities of gold to Australia without attracting the attention of the customs department, and observed that some Labor spokespeople were 'seizing on the refugee question with the same sort of enthusiasm formerly reserved for extremists propounding the danger of the Yellow Peril to our North'.[131] (The editorial did not mention that Labor leaders had once been prominent among these 'extremists'.) Both the *Mercury* and, on the same day, the *Sydney Morning Herald* warned against making the refugee problem into an election issue. The *Herald* questioned claims of a 'flood' or 'horde' of Vietnamese descending on Australia: 'How many hundreds of refugees are there in a flood or a horde?'[132]

While the government was scrambling to deal with the influx of refugees who had arrived on 20 and 21 November, it was also monitoring the movements of a ship bound to pose bigger problems than any of the boats that had arrived thus far. The *Song Be 12* was a refrigerated trawler which, after April 1975, had been nationalised by the Vietnamese government. To prevent its crew from using it to escape Vietnam, armed soldiers had been placed on board. However, the crew had seized control of the ship after overpowering and imprisoning the guards, and set a course for Australia.

The *Song Be 12* carried 181 people – the largest number arriving in a single boat thus far – including three soldiers who initially insisted they be repatriated. As far as was possible on the basis of the sketchy intelligence it could obtain from local sources in Indonesia and the US State Department, the Australian government monitored the progress of the ship through the Indonesian archipelago. On 17 November the *Song Be 12* was reported anchored at Surabaya; local church groups were said to be providing food and medicine to its passengers and crew.[133] The ship left the Indonesian port on 22 November.[134] A week later, HMAS *Ardent* escorted the *Song Be 12* into Darwin Harbour.[135]

The *Song Be 12*'s arrival added another argument to the repertoire of those anxious about the arrival of 'boat people': not only were they too well fed and too wealthy to qualify as refugees, they were also no less ruthless than the regime whose clutches they were supposedly escaping. The Australian government was now under pressure from two sides:

domestically from a Labor Party trying to capitalise on fears about the unchecked invasion of 'boat people' and hostile journalists purporting to represent public opinion, and externally from the government in Hanoi, which claimed that Australia was condoning an act of piracy.[136]

At last, the Fraser government went on the offensive. At a joint press conference in Adelaide on the day the *Song Be 12* arrived, Peacock and MacKellar appealed to their fellow politicians '*not* to subordinate the issues [raised by the arrival of Vietnamese asylum seekers] to electoral considerations, *not* to exaggerate the dimensions of the problem, *not* to attempt to exploit the assumed fears of sections of the Australian public, and *not* to forget the human tragedy represented by these few small boats'. In a reference to Mulvihill's earlier statement, the two ministers committed their government not to '"make examples" of boat refugees by indiscriminately turning some of them back', and not to 'risk taking action against genuine refugees just to get a message across'; doing so 'would be an utterly inhuman course of action'.[137]

Why did the government change tack? From the perspective of 2015, it is tempting to believe that Fraser was concerned that the fears of 'boat people', if condoned by his government, would get out of control – that the genie of xenophobia, once out of its bottle, could not be put back in. But Fraser could not have known what would happen in 2001, when the nation seemed to be gripped by a collective paranoia that was stoked by the government of John Howard and not challenged by the Labor opposition led by Kim Beazley (junior), or in 2013, when a desperate Labor prime minister signed a deal with his Papua New Guinean counterpart for the processing and resettlement of asylum seekers who had sought Australia's protection.

By 1977, the argument used by Fraser himself in 1975 in favour of the admission of Vietnamese refugees – that Australia had a moral duty to help its former allies – had lost much of its traction. Politicians and commentators who defended the indiscriminate admission of 'boat people' invoked the need to be compassionate; given that the majority of Australians had never been swayed by this argument, I doubt that

Fraser would have risked the backlash of voters in order to be able to claim the high moral ground.

Following MacKellar and Peacock's statement, Father Jeff Foale of the Indo-China Refugee Association, the key advocacy group that had been lobbying the government to admit more Indochinese refugees, heaped praise on the immigration minister: 'Australia is emerging as a country of compassion and good sense. The Minister for Immigration and Ethnic Affairs stands as something of a hero, being the only politician who did not lose his cool under fire.'[138] But the archival evidence suggests that MacKellar could not claim credit for the press conference on 29 November. The fact that it was not Fraser, nor MacKellar by himself, who announced that the government would not change its approach towards 'boat people' suggests that Peacock and his department were the driving force behind the government's stance.

It was also Peacock who rejected suggestions that the government ought to be guided by public opinion on the issue. In a radio interview on 1 December, in response to the interviewer's suggestion that Darwin residents had 'expressed concern about the numbers of people coming in', Peacock said: 'Indeed they have but they are not the government.' And when pressed by the interviewer – 'You have no suggestions at all that we should be stopping these boats from coming in?' – Peacock's response was unequivocal: 'None whatsoever.'[139]

Peacock and MacKellar's statement suggests that when the government decided to take on the panic-mongers, it was concerned about how the parochial Australian debate was being perceived in South-East Asia. 'The problem is a regional problem and the validity of Australia's credentials as a good neighbour will depend largely on a willingness to meet our regional obligations by bearing part of the burden,' the ministers' statement read, closely reflecting Peacock's views on Australia's role in the region and in an increasingly globalised world.[140]

The potential diplomatic fallout of the kind of policy favoured by senior Labor politicians was also being noted by other informed observers. The *Sydney Morning Herald*'s South-East Asia correspondent,

Michael Richardson, for example, who had tried to convey the complexity of the refugee crisis in the region to his readers, wrote on 29 November that the decision to turn back refugee boats 'would raise a chorus of protests from neighbours whose friendship Australia wants to retain'.[141] In fact, news of the public response in Australia to boat arrivals in the last week of November had already generated unfavourable headlines in the region.[142] And on 25 November Thailand's ambassador to Australia, Wichet Suthayakhom, had issued a statement in which he defended Thailand's response to Indochinese refugees while deploring the Labor Party's stance. He was particularly incensed by a suggestion made by Mulvihill that Australia cut its foreign aid to Thailand to discipline the Thai government for refusing to accommodate more Indochinese refugees.[143]

The Fraser government had reason to be concerned about the damage its lack of response to the populist anti-'boat people' rhetoric was doing to Australia's reputation as a defender of human rights and an advocate of humanitarian solutions. On 29 November the deputy high commissioner for refugees, Charles Mace, and the UNHCR's acting director of assistance, Franz-Josef Homann-Herimberg, called on Australia's ambassador in Geneva to express the organisation's concern that the Fraser government might be willing to turn back Vietnamese refugee boats. They argued that such a course of action would be irresponsible on two counts: for humanitarian reasons, the boat arrivals could neither be sent back 'nor sent on elsewhere', even if they were not, strictly speaking, refugees; and an Australian policy to turn boats back would weaken the position of the UNHCR, which was appealing to Thailand, Malaysia and the Philippines to allow 'boat people' to land.[144]

Some of Australia's allies were also concerned about the public hostility to 'boat people' landing in Darwin, and about the mixed messages being sent out by the government. In December the Australian embassy in Washington, for example, warned that Australia risked 'being singled out in Congress, and elsewhere, as a country which is lagging in humanitarian concern for Asian refugees'.[145]

Judging by the indignation it engendered, the negative publicity in London and Washington that was (or that threatened to be) generated by the government's apparent capitulation to *vox populi* troubled Fraser and his ministers. One scathing London newspaper column, in particular, caught their attention. It appeared on 30 November in the *Times*, whose views Australian governments tended to take very seriously. To make matters worse, its author was Britain's most famous columnist at the time, Bernard Levin. Although his column was published after MacKellar and Peacock's joint press conference, it was obviously written before the Australian government had clarified that it would not turn back Vietnamese refugee boats; thus, Levin's criticism was directed at what appeared to be the government's pandering to popular opinion. Levin did not mince his words: Fraser's warning to Indochinese refugees was an unparalleled 'swinery' designed to placate the xenophobic vote. And while Australia was not alone in telling Indochinese 'boat people' that they were not welcome, unlike its poor South-East Asian neighbours, it had no excuse for doing so because it did not lack the capacity to accommodate refugees. 'What is more,' Levin wrote, 'there would still be no excuse for Australia if the Vietnamese refugees were counted in hundreds of thousands, instead of in ones and tens.'[146]

The impact of Levin's article can be gauged by the fact that two of Fraser's former colleagues came to his defence on the letters pages. Gordon Freeth, in 1977 Australia's high commissioner in London, and Malcolm Mackay, a former minister for the navy, both tried to rebut Levin's arguments, the former by drawing on the statement issued by MacKellar and Peacock on 29 November, and the latter by claiming that Australia was a 'country with enormous problems . . . torn by fire, drought and exotic cattle disease, as well as the man-made problems of industrial upheavals'.[147] No doubt Mackay's defence would have confirmed Levin's view that Australia was 'apparently determined to retain, and indeed strengthen, her reputation as the armpit of the Southern Hemisphere'.

When Peacock and MacKellar jointly committed the government to hold the line, they had reason to be confident that the Coalition would be returned with a majority at the 10 December election.[148] The government might have thought it could afford to let Labor pander to Australians' fears of an Asian invasion, while hoping that Whitlam and his colleagues would temper their rhetoric after the election. It was, however, concerned about the mood in Darwin, where Stack and Everingham continued to paint alarmist pictures and demand that the government stop the boats from landing.[149] MacKellar eventually dispatched a senior immigration official, Derek Volker, to talk to local leaders in Darwin. The report of this visit must have reinforced the government's view that the situation should not be allowed to spiral any further out of control. Darwin people were genuinely concerned about an invasion from Indochina and South-East Asia, Volker found. The local response to 'boat people' was uninformed, even at the highest level, and tended to be exacerbated by the sense that Darwin was isolated from and neglected by the rest of Australia.[150]

While the government had, somewhat belatedly, decided to resist the temptation of adopting a populist approach, senior Labor Party figures continued to try to exploit the arrival of 'boat people' for electoral gain. Bill Hayden, who was touted as the next Labor leader (and who would indeed succeed Whitlam within two weeks of the election), told the Perth Press Club that sailing into Darwin was as easy as crossing Sydney Harbour on a Manly ferry.[151] Of all senior Labor politicians, it was the ACTU and Labor Party president, Bob Hawke, who was most openly opposed to the admission of Indochinese 'boat people'. On 28 November, while campaigning for Labor in Hobart, he demanded that they be subject to normal immigration requirements, and that those who failed to meet such requirements be deported.[152] On 1 December he suggested that Australia only accept refugees selected off-shore.

Hawke also anticipated two lines of argument used by John Howard in 2001 during the *Tampa* crisis. Hawke said that Australians were renowned for their compassion, and would show it to refugees 'who have gone through our formal process of screening and . . . meet our requirements'. Unauthorised refugee arrivals, however, did not have 'a total monopoly on our compassion'.[153] In Hawke's view, Australia, as a sovereign nation, had 'the right to determine how it will exercise its compassion and how it will increase its population'.[154] Hawke's efforts to make the boat arrivals into a key election issue were unsuccessful (and may have been half-hearted in the first place), however, and after a few days in which 'boat people' dominated the front pages of newspapers around the country, the issue lost traction.

Three days out from the election, there was one last attempt to exploit Australians' fear of uncontrolled boat arrivals. This time it was made not by a senior opposition figure but by a government minister. As if to demonstrate that not everybody in the government agreed with the line adopted by Peacock, MacKellar and Fraser after 29 November, the minister for transport, the National Country Party's Peter Nixon, announced that, henceforth, 'boat people' would only be allowed to land in Australia if they had been cleared by Australian immigration officials in refugee camps in Thailand or Malaysia. 'If they leave the camps without going through Australian immigration checks, then their boats will be sent back to where they came from,' he was reported to have said in Darwin.[155] The next day MacKellar flatly denied that the government would turn back boats, and Nixon's office scrambled to retract his statement.[156] By then, however, it had been widely reported, both in Australia and overseas, and elicited another concerned response from the UNHCR in Geneva.[157]

The 1977 federal election was the first in Australian history in which one of the major parties appealed to the public's unease about unauthorised boat arrivals. In fact, much of the anti-'boat people' rhetoric to which Australians became accustomed during the Howard years made its first appearance in late 1977. Particularly in the second half of the campaign, the issue of the Indochinese refugee boats featured prominently on the front pages of Australian newspapers. But when, less than two weeks out from the election, voters were asked to name the issues most important to them in the campaign, they nominated unemployment, inflation and economic management, rather than immigration and border control.[158] In fact, political scientists agree that the issue of unauthorised refugee arrivals did not influence the election outcome.[159] It helped that there were no further arrivals in the final week before the polls. The 1977 campaign was also the first in which a senior government minister advocated a policy response to refugees that was not populist, and forcefully asserted the government's right, if not responsibility, to pursue such a response.

On 10 December the Coalition lost two of its seats in Queensland to Labor, but overall won a comfortable majority. In the House of Representatives its primary vote dropped by almost 5 per cent, but Labor's primary vote dropped too: Don Chipp's Australian Democrats, contesting their first federal election, attracted 9.38 per cent of the primary vote. The Coalition's election win, the approaching silly season and the fact that there was a lull in the arrival of refugee boats defused the issue that had excited politicians and commentators in late November and early December.

Given that the 1977 campaign was otherwise widely held to be boring, and in light of the experience of subsequent federal election campaigns (particularly those in 2001, 2010 and 2013), it seems paradoxical that the debate died away almost as soon as the government defended its policy. After all, the refugee issue would have allowed the Labor Party to distinguish its line clearly from that of the government, and to seek electoral gain by playing to a latent fear of invasion and harnessing xenophobic sentiments. Labor was clearly hesitant to do so – perhaps because its leaders knew about the potency and dangers of fear-mongering, and because both sides of politics had traditionally taken a bipartisan approach to immigration matters and were hesitant to abandon that.

The fact that Labor did not (or did not manage to) make unauthorised boat arrivals into a dominant election issue also raises another interesting possibility. During the *Tampa* election of 2001, and then again in 2010 and 2013, the Labor Party assumed that there would be disastrous consequences if it did not match the anti-asylum-seeker

rhetoric of the Liberals and Nationals – that a considered and princi-
pled approach similar to that taken (albeit belatedly) by Fraser, Peacock
and MacKellar in 1977 would severely damage its standing at the polls.[160]
It would be fascinating to see one of the major political parties test this
orthodoxy. The experience of 1977 suggests that such a test might not
be as risky as a line of Labor leaders, from Kim Beazley to Bill Shorten,
have readily assumed.

*

The Fraser government's response to refugees is now remembered largely
for the resettlement of tens of thousands of Indochinese refugees. Fraser
himself has highlighted his government's contribution to resettling refugees from Indochina and thereby giving 'substance to the ending of the
White Australia policy'.[161] His claim is correct overall, but not in relation
to his first two governments – from November 1975 to December 1977 –
when the number of Indochinese refugees who were resettled in Australia
was small in absolute terms and small relative to both the total migrant
intake and the resettlement of displaced people from Lebanon.

This period nevertheless marks an important turning point in Australia's response to refugees and asylum seekers. First, beginning with
the selection of Vietnamese refugees in Hong Kong in mid-1975 under
Whitlam, the government acknowledged that refugees were different
from other immigrants in two crucial respects: their selection ought to
be governed by specific criteria, and their settlement in Australia ought
to be assisted to account for their specific needs. Second, Australia experienced the first wave of 'boat people'. Third, the period marked the end
of the bipartisan consensus that had underwritten Australia's response
to refugees since Federation: in 1975 the Fraser-led opposition demanded
that Australia resettle far more Vietnamese refugees than the few hundred admitted by the Whitlam government, and in 1977 the Fraser
government and the Labor opposition disagreed on how to respond to
refugees arriving by boat. Finally, in 1977 the government for the first

time defended its approach to refugees by drawing on the language of humanitarianism *and* by invoking Australia's responsibilities in the Asia-Pacific region. Significantly, its defence did not draw on the language of human rights and did not include prominent references to Australia's international legal obligations.

At one level, the events of the late 1970s appear familiar, because they seem to anticipate later developments. In particular, Whitlam's image of an orderly queue and of queue-jumping 'boat people' would be recycled again and again. Following the 1977 election, Moss Cass, the grandson of Moses Cass – who, as we have seen, had arrived as a refugee from Tsarist Russia in 1906 in Perth – replaced Innes as the federal opposition's spokesman on immigration. On 26 June 1978 Cass wrote in an opinion piece in the *Australian*: 'There is no policy covering the Boat People and the problem will not go away by being ignored. Between April 1976 and January this year 1,037 Boat People arrived in Australia: none were sent back. The implications of a government policy which accepts queue-jumping on this scale are obvious.'

It is perhaps ironic that Cass's objections to 'queue-jumping' were similar to some voiced against the acceptance of Jewish refugees in the late 1930s and in the immediate aftermath of the Second World War: namely, that their admission would lead to a rise of anti-Semitism. Cass wrote:

> The word is out in Indo-China that if you make it to Australia you can expect to gain resident status. Who can blame these people for trying? Many Australians, however, have already reacted strongly to this continued entry of what they perceive as illegal immigrants. Unless the situation is handled effectively, we run the risk of a backlash of prejudice against all Indo-Chinese people here, regardless of whether they are legal immigrants, selected refugees or Boat People.[162]

At another level, however, some of the arguments deployed at the time now appear decidedly odd; recognising that there was nothing peculiar about them if viewed from the vantage point of the 1970s might help us de-familiarise the present. Take, for example, the suggestion by the Tasmanian state politician Neil Batt that Australia become a staging post for large numbers of refugees from Indochina and elsewhere. Or take the views expressed by those in charge of the Department of Immigration and Ethnic Affairs: in its 1977/78 review the department acknowledged that the arrival of 'boat people' was 'of enormous concern' because 'the unscheduled, uninvited boat challenges the adequacy of the Migration Act and the resources available to police it'.[163] The department observed that 'Australian sentiments' had been 'greatly stirred by the Indo-Chinese refugee question', but pointed out that Australia had little choice but to play its part in solving a crisis that was not of its making. 'We are locked into international obligations towards refugees which, we dare say, never envisaged the movement of people on the large scale now being experienced,' the review stated; it warned that 'Australia's credibility and status as a civilised, compassionate nation are under test'.[164]

The department emphasised that the 'boat people' were not illegal entrants, and that their claims for protection had been properly assessed. However, it could point to only one case in which a claim was determined to be unfounded and the person making it was deported. Presumably, this reference was to an Indonesian man who, in MacKellar's words, had 'hitched a ride' on a boat passing through Indonesia.[165] The department tried to put the boat arrivals into perspective: the 1650 'boat people' who had arrived thus far were the equivalent of only 2.5 per cent of people who had overstayed their visas or deserted from a ship and were therefore in Australia illegally. The department also put forward an argument that might appear highly unusual to readers in the twenty-first century:

> It is sobering to consider how easily today's well-established and confident citizen can, by the overnight imposition of an unacceptable political and economic regimen, become tomorrow's refugee. All available evidence suggests that the Indo-Chinese refugees

exhibit the range of skills, attitudes and backgrounds which might be found in a similar number of Australians in like distressed circumstances.[166]

These were not the musings of a junior officer. The text of the annual review would have been approved by the department's then secretary, Lou Engledow, who led it from 1977 to 1980. It represented departmental policy, which in turn could be expected to be in tune with the approach taken by the government and, in particular, the responsible minister, Michael MacKellar. While Calwell (and, after him, Holt) had tried to suggest that European DPs selected for resettlement in Australia would, in time, exhibit the skills and attitudes of Australians, the 1977/78 review tried to make the opposite claim: Australians would be like Vietnamese 'boat people' if they found themselves in a situation that forced them to become refugees.

The text did not call upon its readers to extend compassion to refugees, which would have been predicated on a hierarchical relationship between them and the suffering refugees. Instead, it called into question the idea that refugees are fundamentally different from 'us' and that they constitute a problem which needs to be managed, and which sometimes needs to be kept at bay (by, for example, 'turning back the boats').

# CONCLUSION

Reeferences in the public debate to Australia's historical response to refugees and asylum seekers tend to deploy history in order to endorse or to criticise the status quo. Either the past is seen as an imperfect precursor of the present or it is regarded nostalgically, as a time to recall fondly. In either case pasts that did not apparently go anywhere – that could not be readily interpreted as an earlier version of the present – are neglected. In either case history is often used to buttress a patriotic stance: one that points to a proud record continuing into the present, or one that allows critics of the present to identify with something that has been lost, and criticise current circumstances as an aberration. Finally, in either case the present is taken for granted.

At the beginning of this book, I suggested that history can help us to make the present appear strange, that we can use history to achieve a Brechtian *Verfremdungseffekt*. I hope that my account of Australian responses to refugees and asylum seekers might have unsettled some ideas about the status quo, and that histories of episodes that appear surprising from the vantage point of today might have prompted readers to be unsettled by what is happening today.

Little can be gained from using this or any other history to establish whether or not Australia's response to displaced people in the late 1970s was 'superior' to that in, say, the late 1930s, or whether the government's current policies are 'better' or 'worse' than those of the Fraser or Lyons governments. The latter comparisons tend to reduce the past to a yardstick by which to measure the present, and make it difficult to think about it in its own right. Besides, there is no clear-cut 'better' or 'worse'. The episodes, at least in the way I have told them, in fact suggest not so much historical progression or decline, but rather continuity. That continuity has two key features: parochialism, that is, the tendency for public debate about refugee and asylum seeker issues to be largely oblivious to developments outside Australia and its immediate neighbourhood; and what the historian Frank Crowley, writing about the response to Vietnamese 'boat people' in the 1970s, called 'the perennial attitude of White Australians to aliens'.[1]

I would like to illustrate aspects of this continuity by briefly revisiting two episodes: the arrival of the *Hwa Lien* in January 1947, and the arrival of Vietnamese 'boat people' in November 1977. On both occasions those critical of Australia's admittance of Jewish survivors and Vietnamese 'boat people' made prominent use of the idea that the arrivals could not be refugees because they were not visibly suffering and seemed in fact comparatively well-off, and that their arrival was the work of an illegal racket. On both occasions unauthorised arrivals were seen as queue jumpers (although that term was not yet used in 1947) who were taking away places from legitimate migrants (be they British war brides, as in 1947, or Lebanese displaced people, as in 1977).

In 1947 and again in 1977 the government claimed that it and the Australian people had been generous and compassionate in the past, but that a purely humanitarian response could not continue. This claim was, of course, also made by the Gillard and Rudd governments as they introduced increasingly harsh asylum seeker policies from 2009. The ideas that 'boat people' jump queues, that they help sustain unscrupulous people-smuggling syndicates, and that many of them are too affluent to qualify as refugees have featured prominently in debates about Australia's response to asylum seekers since the early 1990s.

Crowley's remark about the anti-alienism of 'white Australians' should not be taken literally. Whiteness signifies not simply a skin colour but a sense of belonging, to the extent that one can legitimately demand the exclusion of 'non-white' others. Thus, in 1947 to be 'white' meant to be from the British Isles. Then, 'non-white' immigrants included not just Chinese and Japanese but also Jews, particularly if they were from Eastern Europe, and Southern Europeans. In 1977 the 'non-whites' par excellence were Indochinese; by then, Southern European and Jewish immigrants had become part of White Australia. In more recent years, to be 'non-white' meant to be from Southern Sudan, Somalia or Afghanistan. Lebanese Australians and Vietnamese Australians could demonstrate their belonging to White Australia not least by joining the chorus that demanded the exclusion of Hazara, Iranian and Tamil 'boat people'.

In 1947 and in 1977 the suffering associated with the group of people vilified in sections of the media and by Australian politicians counted for nothing. The *Hwa Lien* episode happened less than two years after the Holocaust. There had also been newspaper reports about the appalling situation of refugees in Shanghai, both during and after the war. In 1946 a 21-year-old German Jewish stowaway arriving on a ship from China was reported to have said that conditions in Shanghai were so bad that he would rather have died than stayed there. When the *Song Be 12* arrived in Darwin, Australians knew that many Indochinese refugees leaving Vietnam by boat perished during the journey, that the women on these boats were often raped by pirates, and that the 're-education' camps run by the Vietnamese government were designed to punish people associated with the former South Vietnamese regime at least as much as to educate them. In more recent years Australians have easily been able to know about the atrocities committed during the last stages of the civil war in Sri Lanka, and about the continued marginalisation of Tamils, yet few objected when the government introduced accelerated processing procedures, aimed at quickly returning asylum seekers to Sri Lanka.

If we look at the two episodes in isolation, the response to the *Hwa Lien* seems to be informed by anti-Semitism, while the response to the *Song Be 12* seems to have more to do with fears of an Asian invasion. (Anti-asylum seeker angsts after 2001 might easily be interpreted primarily as the outcome of islamophobia and a fear of terrorism.) If viewed together, however, particular forms of racism can be seen as historically contingent manifestations of a broader anxiety.

A third and no less important feature of continuity is the idea that particular responses to refugees and asylum seekers can usefully be considered in isolation from previous responses. In 1977 the discussions about the admission of Vietnamese refugees – which had excited Australians two years earlier – had already been forgotten, and nobody remembered that the Vietnamese who arrived in Darwin by boat in April 1976 had not been the first 'boat people' in Australian history. Today, contributors to the debate about Operation Sovereign Borders assume that the Abbott government's policies are so unique that it would make no sense to discuss them in the context of earlier policies. I hope this book might draw attention to the potential benefits of an historically informed discussion.

I am not suggesting, however, that things have not changed. Remember Bruce Wilson's rhetorical questions, which I quoted in the Introduction? In 1947 the Chifley government did not consider refusing to let the *Hwa Lien*'s passengers land. The Fraser government did not deploy the *Ardent* to turn around the *Song Be 12*. In 1947 the Menzies-led opposition did not endorse the anti-Semitic hysteria fanned by large sections of the press, organisations such as the ANA and political leaders such as Jack Lang. Unlike in 1947 and 1977, today the government's asylum seeker policy has the backing of both major parties. Broader claims about the universal and timeless nature of refugee issues, such as that most non-Indigenous Australians are descended from 'boat people', or that '[there] have been refugees almost since man was placed on the earth', as immigration minister MacKellar once said,[2] are particularly unhelpful for gaining an understanding of today's problems.

Nor am I suggesting that we ought to dismiss the benefit of hindsight. Hindsight allows us to recognise that Fraser and his government may have erred when they waited a week before distancing themselves from the Labor Party's scaremongering. Hindsight allows us to recognise that Calwell let himself be spooked, and that he squandered the opportunity to make an argument for the admission of Holocaust survivors.

*

Even a critical account of Australia's response to refugees and asylum seekers might be misunderstood as a patriotic history if it took for granted the proposition that refugees and asylum seekers must have been attracted by Australia's and Australians' (supposedly self-evident) qualities.

The current discussion about asylum seekers rightly emphasises the fact that many have gone to great lengths to be able to resettle in Australia. Those who set out in barely seaworthy fishing boats from Indonesia have known about the dangers of the crossing; at least since the sinking of the SIEV X, asylum seekers have been aware they are risking their lives – and, in many cases, the lives of their children. Of course, other routes asylum seekers have taken to get into countries in the industrialised West are no less dangerous: thousands of people have drowned trying to reach Spain or Italy from Morocco, Tunisia, Algeria or Libya, or the Canary Islands from the West African coast. Others have perished trying to cross the borders between Mexico and the United States, or between Turkey and Greece.

It is important to be mindful of the death toll associated with irregular migration elsewhere in the world, lest we mistakenly assume that the decision to make Australia as unattractive a destination as possible provides a genuine solution. From an Australian vantage point, we might also be lured into thinking that Australia is at the top of the list of resettlement destinations. It is true that the services provided by the Australian government to settle refugees who have been selected offshore are better than those of many other countries, that there is a higher degree of social mobility in Australia than in many European countries, and that Australian living standards are comparatively high.

Refugees sometimes had other reasons for considering Australia an attractive destination. Emery Barcs remembered being fascinated by Australia as a child, after reading Jules Verne's novel *In Search of the Castaways*.[3] Andy Csorba, who fled Hungary in 1956, recalled that he opted for Australia because he had learned at school that 'Australians had built long fences to stop the rabbits from going from place to place. I could not imagine a country with so many rabbits that they had to build fences to keep them out . . . At least we would never be hungry with so many rabbits to eat!'[4] Cecile Kunrathy, a former DP from Hungary, remembered that while waiting to be resettled, she and her family 'studied the flora, fauna, climate, population, agriculture, commerce, constitution and social structure of each country that could be considered for emigration purposes, and, during these studies, we created a Utopia-like state, taking for granted the best of each country in question'.[5]

Historically, many refugees have come to Australia because they had no other choice, or because Australia was the first option that presented itself. Australia is 'the land to which no one went of his own free will', the narrator of David Martin's novel *Where a Man Belongs* is told by his father, a German Jewish refugee who had fled to London. The narrator ends up in Australia – not of his own free will but courtesy of the British government, which decided to send him there to be interned for the duration of the war.[6]

\*

Since the 1950s the Australian government has persistently claimed that Australia's acceptance of refugees has been exemplary. Often such statements have been intended to counter domestic or international criticism of a particular aspect of Australia's refugee and asylum seeker policies. In the late 1950s, for example, Australia had to defend itself against accusations that it was not contributing to the resettlement of the so-called hard core of refugees languishing in European refugee camps.

In the 1960s and 1970s the government referred to Australia's tradition-ally generous acceptance of displaced people to neutralise criticism of its refusal to resettle non-European refugees. In more recent years the government has implied that Australia's generous resettlement program somehow gives it the moral right to treat asylum seekers harshly.

Australia's claim to be a model international citizen on account of its response to refugees since the Second World War is usually sup-ported by statistics. There are many figures that can be cited in support of this claim. For example, in 2013, the most recent year for which rel-evant statistics were available from the UNHCR at the time of writing, Australia ranked first for the number of resettled UNHCR-nominated refugees on a per capita basis (with proportionately more than twice the number of refugees resettled as Sweden and Norway, and more than three times as many as New Zealand, Canada and the United States), and second in absolute terms (behind the United States).[7] In 1960 Aus-tralia claimed that, relative to its population, it had 'led the world in accepting refugees for resettlement'.[8]

In a booklet published by the Department of Immigration in June 2009, the then minister, Chris Evans, wrote that Australia had accom-modated approximately 700,000 refugees since the end of the Second World War; this is a remarkable figure, considering that it is equal to 10 per cent of Australia's total population in 1949.[9] It is tempting to highlight such figures. After all, are they not hard evidence of Austral-ia's exemplary humanitarian record? Yet figures such as this are little more than rough estimates. 'It is one of the striking features of the his-tory of refugee movements that statistical information is so unreliable and contradictory,' John Hope Simpson wrote in his preliminary report on the global refugee problem in 1938.[10] His observation is still valid – both in terms of the number of people fleeing a given country, and in terms of the number of people accommodated in first countries of asy-lum or in countries of resettlement, including Australia. In its 2008 Statistical Yearbook, for instance, the UNHCR reported that the num-ber of Colombian refugees in Ecuador and of Iraqis in Syria was 1 million below that reported in the preceding year – not because the situation for Colombians and Iraqis had dramatically improved, but because the UNHCR had revised its estimates downwards by more than 30 per cent.[11]

Hope Simpson recognised that the unreliability of relevant statistics was partly a problem of definition. We do know how many migrants came to Australia through the IRO scheme in the late 1940s and early 1950s. All these people were in possession of IRO-issued cards that identified them as displaced persons. If they had come to Australia as 'boat people' in the past twenty years, however, a significant proportion of them would not have been recognised as refugees because the immigration department would have argued that they faced no persecution in their home countries. The case of Ervin Viks suggests that the protection claims of others could have been rejected because they fled prosecution for crimes committed during the war rather than persecution on account of their politics or faith.

On the other hand, at the same time as Australia accepted IRO-certified migrants, it also admitted people from continental Europe who had been sponsored by their relatives. Many would easily have qualified as refugees under the terms of the 1951 Convention. For example, a Holocaust survivor from Poland, living in a refugee camp in Germany, would have had a strong case to be recognised as somebody who, owing to a well-founded fear of being persecuted for reasons of race or religion, was unwilling to avail herself of the protection of her country of nationality; she could have cited the Kielce pogroms of July 1946 as evidence that she would not be safe if she returned to Poland. It is difficult to estimate the proportion of IRO-sponsored immigrants who could thus have been considered refugees, and perhaps even more difficult to establish how many refugees came to Australia in the late 1940s and early 1950s outside the IRO program.

Since the 1950s the Australian government has often let its refugee and asylum seeker policy be informed by the criteria of Article 1 of the Refugee Convention, but on many other occasions it paid little

attention to them. In 1976 and 1977 Australia admitted a large number
of people from Lebanon who had fled their homes because of the civil
war engulfing their country, rather than because they had experienced
or feared persecution. The government nevertheless recognised that
they were in a particularly vulnerable position and relaxed its entry
requirements. In later years, the immigration department either modified its selection criteria or extended the visas of temporary visitors in
response to devastating earthquakes (in Italy in 1980, in Chile in 1985
and in Turkey in 1999).[12] Should people affected by natural disasters be
counted among the number of refugees resettled by Australia?

Finally, the question of who could be counted as refugees cannot
be divorced from the question of why refugees were admitted to Australia. In the late 1940s and early 1950s Australia admitted more refugees
than during any other period in its history. Yet their classification as
refugees was purely incidental. DPs happened to be available; more
importantly, it was possible to bring them to Australia at little cost.
Their admission is therefore barely comparable with the acceptance of
Indochinese refugees in the dying days of the Whitlam government,
who were selected on account of their presumed neediness, rather than
because they were expected to make an immediate contribution to the
Australian economy.

Australians who got to know refugees – for example, as neighbours,
workmates or fellow students – have usually accepted them and often
made them feel welcome. That is true for Jewish refugees in 1939 as
much as for Vietnamese 'boat people' in 1977 and Hazara asylum seekers in 2015. Nevertheless, throughout the history of federated Australia
the majority of Australians have had, at best, a mixed response to the
admission of refugees. In 1948, for example, the arrival of the *Heintzelman* migrants met with a positive response. At the same time, most
Australians were opposed to admitting more Jewish refugees. Today,
Australia's humanitarian program is comparatively uncontroversial,
but most Australians support the draconian measures adopted by successive governments to keep out 'boat people'.

Refugee advocates sometimes claim that today's hostility towards refugees – both by the government and by many in the community – is unprecedented. It is not. There were, proportionately, at least as many virulent xenophobes in 1939 or in 1947 or in 1977 as there are now. Then and now, however, many advocates have campaigned tirelessly for the admission of refugees.

Throughout Australian history the government's response has been mixed: in 1939 it was more intent on keeping out refugees than on welcoming them, but it did not waver in its commitment to accommodate an (admittedly small) number of refugees from Europe. It did not let itself be intimidated by a largely hostile press. In 1947 Calwell was responsible for an extensive publicity campaign to support the government's decision to admit DPs. At the same time, he failed to vigorously defend his decision to admit Jewish survivors from Europe, the Middle East and East Asia. In 1977 the Fraser government was initially reluctant to resettle Indochinese refugees and succumbed, albeit only for a short while, to the temptation of adopting a populist rhetoric.

*

I am afraid this book does not provide straightforward 'lessons' for Australia's current response to displacement in other parts of the world. In fact, my most important lessons might be that the issue of forced migration is complex (and was complex throughout the period covered in this book), and that it is not easy to neatly distinguish between genuine refugees and economic migrants; that it is therefore a fallacy to expect lessons that translate into easy solutions; and that, rather than seeking such solutions, we ought to try to learn to live with a complex and often uncomfortable problem.

This book has tried to suggest that there is nothing self-evident or natural about Australia's current response to asylum seekers and refugees. I hope to have encouraged you, my reader, to imagine alternative futures – which take into account Australia's capacity to assist people in need of a new home, its responsibility as a regional power, its legal obligations as a member of the international community, and, most importantly, the precarious circumstances of the men, women and children who are seeking Australia's protection.

# ABBREVIATIONS AND ACRONYMS

| | |
|---|---|
| ABC | Australian Broadcasting Commission [later Corporation] |
| ACTU | Australasian [later Australian] Council of Trade Unions |
| AJWS | Australian Jewish Welfare Society |
| ANA | Australian Natives' Association |
| ANZ | Archives New Zealand |
| Apodeti | Associação Popular Democratica Timorense (Timorese Popular Democratic Association) |
| ASIO | Australian Security Intelligence Organisation |
| ASIS | Australian Secret Intelligence Service |
| BAKIN | Badan Koordinasi Intelijen Negara (State Intelligence Coordinating Agency) [Indonesia] |
| CIA | Central Intelligence Agency [United States] |
| CIB | Commonwealth Investigation Branch |
| Convention | United Nations Convention Relating to the Status of Refugees (1951) |
| CPD | *Commonwealth Parliamentary Debates* |
| DP | displaced person |
| EOKA | Ethniki Organosis Kyprion Agoniston (National Organisation of Cypriot Fighters) |
| Fretilin | Frente Revolucionária de Timor Leste Independente (Revolutionary Front for an Independent East Timor) |
| GDR | German Democratic Republic |
| ICEM | Intergovernmental Committee for European Migration |
| IRO | International Refugee Organization |
| ITO | Jewish Territorialist Organization |

| | |
|---|---|
| JEAS | Jewish Emigrant Aid Society |
| Joint | American Jewish Joint Distribution Committee |
| KGB | Komitet gosudarstvennoy bezopasnosti (Committee for State Security) [Soviet Union] |
| MUA | Musicians' Union of Australia |
| MVD | Ministerstvo Vnutrennikh Del (Ministry of Internal Affairs) [Soviet Union] |
| NAA | National Archives of Australia |
| NATO | North Atlantic Treaty Organization |
| NLA | National Library of Australia |
| NZPD | *New Zealand Parliamentary Debates* |
| OPM | Organisasi Papua Merdeka (Free Papua Movement) |
| PCIRO | Preparatory Commission of the International Refugee Organization |
| PRC | People's Republic of China |
| Protocol | United Nations Protocol Relating to the Status of Refugees (1967) |
| RSL | Returned Servicemen's League |
| SIEV | suspected irregular entry vessel |
| TNA | The National Archives [United Kingdom] |
| TPNG | Territory of Papua and New Guinea |
| UDT | União Democrática Timorense (Timorese Democratic Union) [East Timor] |
| UN | United Nations |
| UNHCR | United Nations High Commissioner for Refugees |
| UNRRA | United Nations Relief and Rehabilitation Administration |
| UNTEA | United Nations Temporary Executive Authority [West New Guinea] |

# ACKNOWLEDGEMENTS

My warm thanks go to the many people and institutions whose support made this book possible.

My history of Australia's response to refugees draws heavily on unpublished sources. I was fortunate to receive advice and assistance from librarians and archivists at the National Library of Australia, the National Archives (United Kingdom), Archives New Zealand, the State Library of Victoria and the Department of Immigration and Border Protection, among others. The National Archives of Australia is by far the most important repository of archival records relevant for this book, and I thank the Archives – and, in particular, Rod Covell, Michael Wenke and Kerri Ward – for assisting me over many years. Government files on asylum seeker and refugee policies are deemed to be sensitive, and unfortunately it can take many years for access requests to be actioned; I am therefore grateful that shortly before my manuscript was due, the Archives made a valiant effort to tackle a large backlog of outstanding applications for access examination.

I thank my employer, Swinburne University of Technology, for giving me the time to pursue this project. I also gratefully acknowledge the Australian Research Council and the MacArthur Foundation, which provided funding at crucial points in the journey.

The German playwright Heinrich von Kleist once suggested that in order to arrive at an idea, we must try articulating it in conversation with others. I have certainly benefited from having had attentive and inquisitive audiences and interlocutors at seminars, workshops and conferences, and at the Swinburne Institute for Social Research. I am particularly indebted to my colleagues Sandy Gifford and Peter Browne, and to other members of the Melbourne 'dinner group', for their interest in my work, their advice and their willingness to challenge my assumptions.

I thank the people at Black Inc., particularly Nikola Lusk, who commissioned the book, and Julian Welch, who saw it through to publication. He was meticulous but respected my voice; I could not have wished for a better editor.

This book is dedicated to the memory of Hank Nelson – extraordinary teacher and good friend – who would no doubt have closely read, and scribbled all over, its manuscript.

# NOTES

## INTRODUCTION

1. Bruce Wilson, 'It's the Yellow Peril Again', *Courier-Mail*, 29 November 1977.

2. David Marr & Marian Wilkinson, 2003, *Dark Victory*, Crows Nest, Allen & Unwin, chapter 6.

3. Wilson, 'It's the Yellow Peril Again'.

4. For example, volume 5 of *The Oxford History of Australia* devotes less than two (out of 342) pages to Australia's response to refugees, although the period covered by the book includes the late 1940s and early 1950s (when Australia admitted more than 170,000 DPs [displaced persons]) and the 1970s and 1980s (when Australia resettled more than 100,000 refugees from Indochina); see Geoffrey Bolton, 1996, *The Middle Way 1942–1995*, second edition, South Melbourne, Oxford University Press, pp. 54–55, 238, 255.

5. For example, a 361-page biography of John McEwen does not mention his crucial role (as minister for the interior) in the government's decision in 1938 to admit up to 15,000 European refugees: Peter Golding, 1996, *Black Jack McEwen: Political Gladiator*, Carlton South, Melbourne University Press; Adam William Martin's two-volume biography of Robert Menzies is silent on Menzies' response to refugee issues: A. W. Martin, 1993, *Robert Menzies: A Life: Volume 1: 1894–1943*, Carlton, Melbourne University Press, and A. W. Martin, 1999, *Robert Menzies: A Life: Volume 2: 1944–1978*, Carlton South, Melbourne University Press; the 349-page account of Whitlam's prime ministership in the second volume of Jenny Hocking's Whitlam biography includes only one page that deals with his or his government's response to refugees: Jenny Hocking, 2012, *Gough Whitlam: His Time*, Carlton, Miegunyah Press, pp. 219–220.

6. Eric Richards, 2008, *Destination Australia: Migration to Australia Since 1901*, Sydney, UNSW Press.

7. Peter Gatrell, 2013, *The Making of the Modern Refugee*, Oxford, Oxford University Press, p. 11.

8. Tony Kushner, 2006, *Remembering Refugees: Then and Now*, Manchester, Manchester University Press, p. 1; see also Philip Marfleet, 2013, 'Explorations in a Foreign Land: States, Refugees, and the Problem of History', *Refugee Survey Quarterly*, vol. 32, no. 4, pp. 16–17.

9. Convention Relating to the Status of Refugees, www.unhcr.org/3b66c2aa10.html.

10. Paul Hasluck, 1976, *A Time for Building: Australian Administration in Papua and New Guinea*, Melbourne, Melbourne University Press, p. 371.

11. Eilhard Schlesinger, 1933, *Die griechische Asylie*, Giessen, Töpelmann; Kai Bammann, 2002, *Im Bannkreis des Heiligen: Freistätten und kirchliches Asyl als Geschichte des Strafrechts*,

Münster, Lit; Martin Dreher (ed.), 2003, *Das antike Asyl: kultische Grundlagen, rechtliche Ausgestaltung und politische Funktion*, Köln, Böhlau; Léopold Bolesta-Koziebrodzki, 1962, *Le droit d'asile*, Leiden, A. W. Sythoff, pp. 36–37; Linda Rabben, 2011, *Give Refuge to the Stranger: The Past, Present, and Future of Sanctuary*, Walnut Creek, Left Coast Press, pp. 48–49.

12. See, for example, A. Hellwig, 1903, *Das Asylrecht der Naturvölker*, Berlin, R. v. Decker's Verlag; Albert Hellwig, 1906, *Beiträge zum Asylrecht von Ozeanien*, Stuttgart, Verlag von Ferdinand Enke; Ortwin Henssler, 1954, *Formen des Asylrechts und ihre Verbreitung bei den Germanen*, Frankfurt am Main, Vittorio Klostermann.

13. Universal Declaration of Human Rights, www.un.org/en/documents/udhr.

14. Fredrik Stang, 'Award ceremony speech', 10 December 1922, www.nobelprize.org/nobel_prizes/peace/laureates/1922/press.html.

## Chapter 1: Undesirables

1. On the following, see Myra Willard, 1923, *History of the White Australia Policy to 1920*, Melbourne, Melbourne University Press; H. I. London, 1970, *Non-White Immigration and the 'White Australia' Policy*, Sydney, Sydney University Press.

2. John Howard, speech to launch 2001 election campaign, 28 October 2001, http://museumvictoria.com.au/immigrationmuseum/discoverycentre/identity/videos/politics-videos/john-howards-2001-election-campaign-policy-launch-speech.

3. Richards, *Destination Australia*, p. 2.

4. For example, Scott Holmes, 'Why Not House "Boat People" Right Here?', *Newcastle Herald*, 19 November 2012; Melissa Reid, 'Closed Borders Spur Closed Minds', *Right Now*, 14 January 2013, http://rightnow.org.au/topics/asylum-seekers/closed-borders-spur-closed-minds.

5. Anne-Maree Whitacker, 1994, *Unfinished Revolution: United Irishmen in New South Wales, 1800–1810*, Darlinghurst, Crossing Press; Bob Reece, 2001, 'Irish Convicts', in James Jupp (ed.), 2001, *The Australian People: An Encyclopedia of the Nation, Its People and Their Origins*, Cambridge, Cambridge University Press, pp. 448–449.

6. Ian Harmstorf, 'German Settlement in South Australia until 1914', in Jupp (ed.), *The Australian People*, p. 360; W. D. Borrie, 1954, *Italians and Germans in Australia: A Study of Assimilation*, Melbourne, F. W. Cheshire, pp. 159–161.

7. Simon Collier, 2003, *Chile: The Making of a Republic 1830–1865: Politics and Ideas*, Cambridge, Cambridge University Press, p. 51, n. 13.

8. Alice Bullard, 2000, *Exile to Paradise: Savagery and Civilization in Paris and the South Pacific, 1790–1900*, Stanford, Stanford University Press, pp. 133–134.

9. Juliette Rastoul, 'The Escaped Communists' (letter to the editor), *Argus*, 8 May 1875.

10. Ann Stephen & Charles Pickett, '"To the Youth of Australia"', in Ann Stephen (ed.), 2001, *Visions of a Republic: The Work of Lucien Henry – Paris – Noumea – Sydney*, Sydney, Powerhouse Publishing, pp. 59–60.

11. John Docker, 2001, 'Arabesques of the Cosmopolitan and International: Lucien Henry, Baroque Allegory and Islamophilia', *Australian Humanities Review*, http://australianhumanitiesreview.org/archive/Issue-June-2001/docker3.html; Arthur McMartin, 1972, 'Henry, Lucien Felix (1850–1896)', *Australian Dictionary of Biography*, volume 4, http://adb.anu.edu.au/biography/henry-lucien-felix-3755; Terry Irving & Rowan Cahill,

2010, *Radical Sydney: Places, Portraits and Unruly Episodes*, Sydney, UNSW Press, pp. 67–74.

12. Michael R. Marrus, 2002, *The Unwanted: European Refugees from the First World War Through the Cold War*, second edition, Philadelphia, Temple University Press, pp. 27–39.

13. Hilary L. Rubinstein, 1986, *The Jews in Victoria 1835–1985*, Sydney, George Allen & Unwin, pp. 84–91; Hilary L. Rubinstein, 1987, *Chosen: The Jews in Australia*, Sydney, Allen & Unwin, pp. 79–81; Hilary L. Rubinstein, 1991, *The Jews in Australia: A Thematic History: Volume One: 1788–1945*, Port Melbourne, William Heinemann Australia, pp. 116–117; Suzanne D. Rutland, 1988, *Edge of Diaspora: Two Centuries of Jewish Settlement in Australia*, Sydney, Collins Australia, pp. 93–98.

14. David Carter, 2012, 'Waten, Judah Leon (1911–1985)', *Australian Dictionary of Biography*, volume 18, http://adb.anu.edu.au/biography/waten-judah-leon-14884.

15. Quoted in Stuart Macintyre, 1998, *The Reds*, St Leonards, Allen & Unwin, p. 278.

16. Judah Waten, 1964, *Distant Land*, Melbourne, F. W. Cheshire.

17. Judah Waten, 1981, *Alien Son*, South Yarra, Currey O'Neil, pp. 74–75.

18. Naturalisation file for Moses Cass, National Archives of Australia (hereafter 'NAA'): A435, 1949/4/257.

19. Moss Cass, interviewed by Mara Moustafine, n.d., *Making Multicultural Australia*, www.multiculturalaustralia.edu.au/library/media/Video/id/1454.Moss-Cass-reflects-on-his-Jewish-identity-as-a-young-man.

20. Elena Govor, 2005, *Russian Anzacs in Australian History*, Sydney, UNSW Press in association with National Archives of Australia, pp. 58–59.

21. Elena Govor, 1997, *Australia in the Russian Mirror: Changing Perceptions 1770–1919*, Carlton South, Melbourne University Press, pp. 156–157; Olga Doubrovskaya, 1993, 'Political Characteristics of Russians in Brisbane in the 1900s', in Rod Fisher & Barry Shaw (eds), *Brisbane: The Ethnic Presence Since the 1850s*, Kelvin Grove, Brisbane History Group Incorporated, pp. 71–81.

22. Tom Poole & Eric Fried, 1985, 'Artem: A Bolshevik in Brisbane', *Australian Journal of Politics and History*, vol. 31, no. 2, pp. 243–254.

23. Tom Keneally, 2009, *The People's Train*, North Sydney, Knopf.

24. S. Stedman, 1959, 'From Russia to Brisbane, 1913', *Australian Jewish Historical Society Journal and Proceedings*, vol. 5, no. 1, p. 22.

25. Marett Leiboff, 2011, '"The Main Thing Is to Shut Them Out": The Deployment of Law and the Arrival of Russians in Australia', *Law Text Culture*, vol. 15, pp. 234, 245–253, 261.

26. Govor, *Australia in the Russian Mirror*, p. 158.

27. Claudena M. Skran, 1995, *Refugees in Inter-War Europe: The Emergence of a Regime*, Oxford, Clarendon Press, p. 21.

28. Roger Daniels, 2004, *Guarding the Golden Door: American Immigration Policy and Immigrants Since 1882*, New York, Hill and Wang, pp. 46–56.

29. Brisbane Hebrew Congregation to J. Mahon, 13 April 1916, NAA: A1, 1916/10708; Atlee Hunt to Brisbane Hebrew Congregation, 10 May 1916, NAA: A1, 1916/10708.

30. High Commissioner's Office to Prime Minister's Department, 19 May 1921, NAA: A434, 1949/3/3196; Marrus, *The Unwanted*, pp. 65–66.

31. A[lbert] R[obert] P[eters] to Acting Secretary, 23 May 1921, NAA: A434, 1949/3/3196.

32. Secretary, Department of Home and Territories, to Prime Minister's Department, 24 May 1921, NAA: A434, 1949/3/3196.

33. Prime Minister's Department to High Commissioner's Office, 1 June 1921, NAA: A434, 1949/3/3196.

34. F. J. Quinlan to Official Secretary, 3 October 1925, NAA: A434, 1939/3/3196.

35. Gatrell, *The Making of the Modern Refugee*, pp. 25–31.

36. Annemarie H. Sammartino, 2010, *The Impossible Border: Germany and the East, 1914–1922*, Ithaca, Cornell University Press, p. 179.

37. Joseph B. Schechtman, 1946, *European Population Transfers, 1939–1945*, New York, Oxford University Press, pp. 16–22.

38. Nevzat Soguk, 1999, *States and Strangers: Refugees and Displacements of Statecraft*, Minneapolis, University of Minnesota Press, pp. 31–35.

39. John Torpey, 2000, *The Invention of the Passport: Surveillance, Citizenship, and the State*, Cambridge, Cambridge University Press.

40. Skran, *Refugees in Inter-War Europe*, 16–17.

41. Claudena M. Skran, 1988, 'Profiles of the First Two High Commissioners', *Journal of Refugee Studies*, vol. 1, no. 3–4, pp. 277–288; Vincent Chetail, 2003, 'Fridtjof Nansen and the International Protection of Refugees: An Introduction', *Refugee Survey Quarterly*, vol. 22, no. 1, pp. 1–6; Ivor C. Jackson, 2003, 'Dr. Fridtjof Nansen: A Pioneer in the International Protection of Refugees', *Refugee Survey Quarterly*, vol. 22, no. 1, pp. 7–20.

42. Skran, *Refugees in Inter-War Europe*, p. 284; Natasha Saunders, 2014, 'Paradigm Shift or Business as Usual? An Historical Reappraisal of the "Shift" to Securitisation of Refugee Protection', *Refugee Survey Quarterly*, vol. 33, no. 3, p. 81.

43. Skran, *Refugees in Inter-War Europe*, pp. 281–282.

44. Otto Hieronymi, 2003, 'The Nansen Passport: A Tool of Freedom of Movement and of Protection', *Refugee Survey Quarterly*, vol. 22, no. 1, pp. 36–47; Alessandra Roversi, 'The Evolution of the Refugee Regime and Institutional Responses: Legacies from the Nansen Period', *Refugee Survey Quarterly*, vol. 22, no. 1, pp. 21–35.

45. James C. Hathaway, 1984, 'The Evolution of Refugee Status in International Law: 1920–1950', *International and Comparative Law Quarterly*, vol. 33, no. 2, pp. 348–380.

46. Skran, 'Profiles', pp. 281–284.

47. Skran, *Refugees in Inter-War Europe*, pp. 91–92, 106–107, 210–211.

48. B. Christa, 2001, 'Russians', in Jupp (ed.), *The Australian People*, p. 639.

49. Susan D. Rutland, 2001, 'Jewish Immigration 1881–1933', in Jupp (ed.), *The Australian People*, p. 531.

50. Richards, *Destination Australia*, p. 120.

51. Robert Menzies, *Commonwealth Parliamentary Debates* (hereafter '*CPD*'), Representatives, vol. 145, 14 November 1934, p. 256.

52. Thomas Walter White, *CPD*, Representatives, vol. 145, 14 November 1934, p. 265.

53. *R v Carter; Ex parte Kisch* [1934] HCA 50 (16 November 1934), www.austlii.edu.au/au/cases/cth/HCA/1934/50.html.

54. Heidi Zogbaum, 2004, *Kisch in Australia: The Untold Story*, Melbourne, Scribe Publications; Glenn Nicholls, 2007, *Deported: A History of Forced Departures from Australia*, Sydney, UNSW Press, pp. 65–69; Egon Erwin Kisch, 1969, *Australian Landfall*, translated by John Fisher & Irene and Kevin Fitzgerald, Sydney, Australasian Book Society, pp. 7–147; Peter Monteith, 1991, 'Kisch and the Jews', *Journal of the Australian Jewish Historical Society*, vol. 11, no. 3, pp. 450–457.

55. W. Stölting, 1930, *Australien: Das Land von morgen*, Berlin, Deutsche Buch-Gemeinschaft; see Manfred Jurgensen, 1992, *Eagle and Emu: German-Australian Writing 1930–1990*, St Lucia, University of Queensland Press, pp. 17–19.

56. Walter Stolting, n.d., autobiography, National Library of Australia (hereafter 'NLA'): MS 4650, folder 7.

57. Walter Stolting to Minister for Home and Territory, 4 November 1935, NAA: B741/5, V15423.

58. J. A. Carrodus to Secretary, Department of External Affairs, 20 December 1937, NAA: A981, LEAGUE REFU 1.

59. Andrew Markus, 1983, 'Jewish Migration to Australia 1938–49', *Journal of Australian Studies*, no. 13, p. 19.

60. Michael Blakeney, 1985, *Australia and the Jewish Refugees 1933–1948*, Sydney, Croom Helm Australia, p. 76; Paul R. Bartrop, 1994, *Australia and the Holocaust 1933–45*, Melbourne, Australian Scholarly Publishing, pp. 144–148.

61. Marrus, *The Unwanted*, pp. 172–174.

62. John Hope Simpson, 1938, 'Refugees: Preliminary Report of a Survey', London, Royal Institute of International Affairs, p. 193.

63. Ibid., p. 188.

64. Ibid., p. 190.

65. Ibid., pp. 194–195.

66. R. A. Wiseman to Official Secretary, Commonwealth of Australia, 1 April 1938, attachment, NAA: A981, REF 4 PART 1.

67. Department of External Affairs, 'United States Proposal for Committee on Austrian Political Refugees' (submission to minister), 6 April 1938, NAA: A981, REF 4 PART 1.

68. Bruce to Prime Minister, 5 April 1938, NAA: A981, REF 4 PART 1.

69. Marrus, *The Unwanted*, p. 171.

70. H. Rothmund, quoted in 'Proceedings of the Intergovernmental Committee, Evian, July 6th to 15th, 1938: Verbatim Record of the Plenary Meetings of the Committee: Resolutions and Reports' (1938), p. 37.

71. T. W. White, quoted in 'Proceedings of the Intergovernmental Committee, Evian', p. 20.

72. C. B. Burdekin, quoted in 'Proceedings of the Intergovernmental Committee, Evian', p. 25.

73. Hume Wrong, quoted in 'Proceedings of the Intergovernmental Committee, Evian', p. 20.

74. Henry Bérenger, quoted in 'Proceedings of the Intergovernmental Committee, Evian', p. 16; see Timothy P. Maga, 1982, 'Closing the Door: The French Government and Refugee Policy, 1933–1939', *French Historical Studies*, vol. 12, no. 3, pp. 436–438.

75. F. Strahan to Secretary, Department of External Affairs, 1 December 1938, NAA: A981, REF 4 PART 1; file note, 28 March 1939, NAA: A981, REF 4 PART 1.

76. Alfred Stirling to W. R. Hodgson, 17 July 1938, NAA: A981, REF 4 PART 1.

77. Suzanne D. Rutland, 1985, 'Australian Responses to Jewish Migration Before and After World War II', *Australian Journal of Politics and History*, vol. 31, no. 1, p. 32.

78. Alfred Andermann to Prime Minister of Australia, 15 October 1938, NAA: A461, MA349/3/5 PART 1.

79. Naturalisation records for Arthur Andermann, The National Archives (United Kingdom) (hereafter 'TNA'): HO 334/188/31494 and HO 405/719; naturalisation records for Alfred Andermann, TNA: HO 334/222/48046 and HO 405/1299.

80. Bartrop, *Australia and the Holocaust*, pp. 96–98.

81. Paul R. Bartrop, 1989, '"Not a Problem for Australia": The Kristallnacht Viewed from the Commonwealth, November 1938', *Journal of the Australian Jewish Historical Society*, vol. 10, no. 6, p. 492.

82. Bruce to Prime Minister, 21 November 1938, NAA: A433, 1943/2/46.

83. John McEwen, *CPD*, Representatives, vol. 158, 1 December 1938, p. 2535.

84. Ibid.

85. Ibid., p. 2536.

86. John Curtin, *CPD*, Representatives, vol. 158, 1 December 1938, p. 2536.

87. Extract from Cabinet minutes, 30 November 1938, NAA: A461, M349/3/5 PART 2; A. R. Peters, 'Refugees', 27 April 1939, NAA: A433, 1943/2/46.

88. Bartrop, *Australia and the Holocaust*, p. 120; David Lee, 2010, *Stanley Melbourne Bruce: Australian Internationalist*, London, Continuum, p. 128.

89. 'Homes for the Refugees' (editorial), *Times* (London), 2 December 1938.

90. Quoted in Blakeney, *Australia and the Jewish Refugees*, p. 145.

91. Irving M. Abella & Harold Martin Troper, 1982, *None Is Too Many: Canada and the Jews of Europe, 1933–1948*, Toronto, Lester & Orpen Dennys, p. 47.

92. Arthur Calwell, *CPD*, Representatives, vol. 190, 12 March 1947, p. 432.

93. Bartrop, *Australia and the Holocaust*, pp. 84–87.

94. Klaus Neumann, 2004, *Refuge Australia: Australia's Humanitarian Record*, Sydney, UNSW Press, p. 21.

95. Ann Beaglehole, 2013, *Refuge New Zealand: A Nation's Response to Refugees and Asylum Seekers*, Dunedin, Otago University Press, p. 35.

96. Abella & Troper, *None Is Too Many*, pp. x, 54–55.

97. Marrus, *The Unwanted*, p. 158.

98. Paul R. Bartrop, 1995, 'Canada, Australia and the Holocaust: Comparing the Refugee Record of the Two Largest Dominions', *Australian-Canadian Studies*, vol. 13, no. 1, p. 39.

99. See, for example, Human Rights Law Centre, 2014, 'Can't Flee, Can't Stay: Australia's Interception and Return of Sri Lankan Asylum Seekers', www.hrlc.org.au/wp-content/uploads/2014/03/HRLC_SriLanka_Report_11March2014.pdf; Amanda Hodge, 'Canberra, India "Water Down" UN Resolution on Sri Lankan Human Rights', *Australian*, 23 March 2013.

100. For example, F. Strahan to State Secretary [Victoria], Australian League for Peace and Democracy, 29 November 1938, NAA: A461, R420/1.

101. Skran, 'Profiles', pp. 292–293; James G. McDonald to Secretary-General of League of Nations, 27 December 1935, reproduced in 'Persecution in Germany', *Times* (London), 30 December 1935; '"Guest of Germany"' (editorial), *Times* (London), 30 December 1935.

102. Emery Barcs, 1980, *Backyard of Mars: Memoirs of the 'Reffo' Period in Australia*, Sydney, Wildcat Press, p. 44.

103. Kay Dreyfus, 2013, *Silences and Secrets: The Australian Experience of the Weintraubs Syncopators*, Clayton, Monash University Publishing.

104. 'Refugees. Professions' Attitudes', *Sydney Morning Herald*, 29 July 1938.

105. Barcs, *Backyard of Mars*, p. 46.

106. General Secretary, United Graziers' Association of Queensland, to Secretary, Prime Minister's Department, 9 January 1939, NAA: A461, Y349/3/5.

107. Rubinstein, *The Jews in Australia*, pp. 499–509.

108. Quoted in Suzanne D. Rutland, 2005, *The Jews in Australia*, Cambridge, Cambridge University Press, p. 52; see also Bartrop, *Australia and the Holocaust*, pp. 179–185.

109. Anne Andgel, 1988, *Fifty Years of Caring: The History of the Australian Jewish Welfare Society, 1936–1986*, Sydney, Australian Jewish Welfare Society and Australian Jewish Historical Society, p. 15.

110. Prime Minister's Department to High Commissioner's Office, 9 November 1938, NAA: A461, M349/3/5 PART 2.

111. 'Strathmore Brings Many Refugees', *Daily Mail* (Perth), 16 May 1939.

112. 'More Aliens Arrive', *Argus*, 23 May 1939.

113. 'Modern Germany Has Nationalised Beauty', *Daily Mail* (Perth), 18 May 1939.

114. 'On Board the Strathmore', *West Australian*, 17 May 1939; 'Strathmore's Passengers', *West Australian*, 17 May 1939.

115. 'Refugees' Conduct', *West Australian*, 25 May 1939.

116. Vera Mitchell, 'Refugees Defended' (letter to the editor), *Argus*, 29 May 1939; the letter responded to the article 'Severe Attack on Refugees', *Argus*, 25 May 1939.

117. 'In Free Land at Last', *Sun* (Sydney), 25 January 1939; the article portrayed Jan Erich Lossel, a refugee from Czechoslovakia.

118. For the following, see Louis Stein, 1979, *Beyond Death and Exile: The Spanish Republicans in France, 1939–1955*, Cambridge, Mass., Harvard University Press; Isabel de Palencia, 1946, *Smouldering Freedom: The Story of the Spanish Republicans in Exile*, London, Victor Gollancz; Marrus, *The Unwanted*, pp. 190–194.

119. Omar G. Encarnación, 2014, *Democracy Without Justice in Spain: The Politics of Forgetting*, Philadelphia, University of Pennsylvania Press, p. 165.

120. Robert Mason, 2009, 'Anarchism, Communism and Hispanidad: Australian Spanish Migrants and the Civil War', *Immigrants & Minorities*, vol. 27, no. 1, p. 35.

121. Nellie Quinlan to J. A. Lyons, 4 April 1939, NAA: A981, REF 14 PART 1.

122. Amirah Inglis, 1987, *Australians in the Spanish Civil War*, Sydney, Allen & Unwin, p. 198.

123. Extract from Cabinet minutes, 5 March 1938, NAA: A461, M420/1; Lyons to Australian High Commissioner London, 14 March 1938, NAA: A461, M420/1.

124. R. G. Menzies to John Curtin, 24 May 1939, NAA: A981, REF 14 PART 1.

125. A. R. Peters, 'Spanish Refugees', 24 April 1939, NAA: A433, 1939/2/174.

126. Arthur Calwell, *CPD*, Representatives, vol. 190, 12 March 1947, p. 578.

127. For the following, see Paul R. Bartrop, 1990, '"A Low Class of White People": The Garrett Report of 1939 and Plans for Jewish Immigration to Australia in the 1940s', *Menorah*, vol. 4, no. 1–2, pp. 28–39; Paul R. Bartrop, 2011, '"Almost Indescribable and Unbelievable": The Garrett Report and the Future of Jewish Refugee Immigration to Australia in 1939', *Journal of Ecumenical Studies*, vol. 46, no. 4, pp. 549–556.

128. T. H. Garrett to J. A. Carrodus, 24 August 1939, NAA: A659, 1947/1/2109.

129. T. H. Garrett, 'White Alien Immigration into Australia from Europe: Establishment of Organisation at Australia House', 28 June 1939, p. 5, NAA: A659, 1947/1/2109.

130. A. R. Peters, 'Question of Definition of Term "Refugee"', 12 January 1939, NAA: A433, 1943/2/46.

131. Garrett, 'White Alien Immigration into Australia from Europe', p. 6.

132. Bartrop, '"Almost Indescribable"', p. 556.

133. Garrett, 'White Alien Immigration into Australia from Europe', p. 4.

134. T. H. Garrett, 'Brief Notes of Tour of the Continent by the Assistant Secretary, Department of the Interior (Mr. T. H. Garrett), and the Chief Migration Officer (Major R. H. Wheeler) – 10th July 1939 to 1st August 1939', p. 13, NAA: A659, 1947/1/2109.

135. Rodney Gouttman, 'The Pilcher Conundrum', *Journal of the Australian Jewish Historical Society*, vol. 11, no. 1, pp. 79–81; Charlotte Carr-Gregg & Pam Maclean, '"A Mouse Nibbling at a Mountain': The Problem of Australian Refugee Policy and the Work of Camilla Wedgwood', *Australian Journal of Politics and History*, vol. 31, no. 1, pp. 49–60; Charlotte Carr-Gregg, 'The Work of the German Emergency Fellowship Committee, 1938–1941', in W. D. Rubinstein (ed.), *Jews in the Sixth Continent*, Sydney, Allen & Unwin, pp. 185–200.

136. See, for example, Alan Gill, 2004, *Interrupted Journeys: Young Refugees from Hitler's Reich*, East Roseville, Simon & Schuster, chapters 9–13.

137. Acting Official Secretary, Australia House to Secretary, Department of the Interior, 4 April 1939, with annotations by A. R. Peters, 10 May 1939, and H. S. Fall, 10 May 1939, NAA: A433, 1944/2/1703.

138. Glen Palmer, 1997, *Reluctant Refuge: Unaccompanied Refugee and Evacuee Children in Australia, 1933–1945*, East Roseville, Kangaroo Press, pp. 55–69, 200–201.

139. W. S. Matsdorf, 1994, *No Time to Grow: The Story of the Gross-Breeseners in Australia*, Sydney, University of Sydney, Mandelbaum Trust; Palmer, *Reluctant Refuge*, pp. 41–54, 200–202.

140. Palmer, *Reluctant Refuge*, pp. 41–54, 103–128.

141. www.britishpathe.com/video/lord-mayors-appeal-london.

142. H. Twyford to J. A. Lyons, 3 January 1939, NAA: A461, S349/3/5.

143. 'German Sudeten Non-Jewish Refugees', file note, 19 January 1939, NAA: A461, S349/3/5; Alfred Stirling to High Commissioner, 13 January 1939, NAA: A981, REF 8.

144. J. A. Carrodus to Secretary Prime Minister's Department, 21 December 1938, NAA: A461, S349/3/5.

145. Abella & Troper, *None Is Too Many*, pp. 48–49, 62.

146. The edited correspondence of Doris and Herbert Liffmann (later Liffman), along with Herbert Liffman's reminiscences, document the desperate attempts of one particular German Jewish couple, who arrived in Australia in 1938, to help bring out others: see Volker Elis Pilgrim, Doris Liffman & Herbert Liffman (eds), 1992, *Fremde Freiheit: Jüdische Emigration nach Australien: Briefe 1938–1940*, Reinbek, Rowohlt.

147. For example, 'Boy's Nine Day Trip from Germany to S.A.', *Mail* (Adelaide), 26 August 1939.

148. 'Boy's Long Flight', *Sydney Morning Herald*, 25 August 1939.

149. Rutland, *The Jews in Australia*, p. 62; Andgel, *Fifty Years of Caring*, p. 17.

150. Quoted in Rutland, *Edge of Diaspora*, p. 181.

151. Markus, 'Jewish Migration to Australia 1938–49', pp. 22–23; Rutland, *Edge of the Diaspora*, pp. 185–188; Blakeney, *Australia and the Jewish Refugees*, pp. 104–116, 149–155; Konrad Kwiet, 1987, 'Responses of Australian Jewry's Leadership to the Holocaust', translated by Jane Sydenham-Kwiet, in Rubenstein (ed.), *Jews in the Sixth Continent*, pp. 201–205; P. Y. Medding, 1968, *From Assimilation to Group Survival: A Political and Sociological Study of an Australian Jewish Community*, Melbourne, F. W. Cheshire, pp. 158–168.

152. Quoted in Rubinstein, *The Jews in Victoria*, p. 165; for a statement by Boas describing himself as a Jew only for two hours on Shabbat, see ibid., p. 166.

153. 'Jews' Advice to Refugees', *Sydney Morning Herald*, 13 May 1939.

154. J. Horgan, memorandum, 17 April 1939, NAA: A433, 1939/2/742.

155. McKinnon, memorandum, 14 April 1939, NAA: A433, 1939/2/742.

156. Magnus Brechtken, 1997, *Madagaskar für die Juden: antisemitische Idee und politische Praxis 1885-1945*, München, Oldenbourg; Hans Jansen, 1997, *Der Madagaskar Plan: die beabsichtigte Deportation der europäischen Juden nach Madagaskar*, translated by Markus Jung, Ulrike Vogl & Elisabeth Weissenböck, München, Herwig.

157. Marrus, *The Unwanted*, pp. 186–187.

158. Secretary, Newcastle District Assembly, Australian Labor Party, to Lyons, 17 October 1938, NAA: A461, MA349/3/5 PART 1.

159. Rubinstein, *The Jews in Australia*, pp. 121–130.

160. Israel Zangwill, quoted in 'One Million Jews', *Daily News* (Perth), 18 October 1910.

161. Blakeney, *Australia and the Jewish Refugees*, pp. 249–255; Wolf Simon Matsdorf, 1973–74, 'A New Jerusalem in Australia: The Kimberley Plan', *Wiener Library Bulletin*, vol. 27, no. 30–31, pp. 24–30.

162. I. N. Steinberg, 1948, *Australia – the Unpromised Land: In Search of a Home*, London, Victor Gollancz, pp. 146–153; I. N. Steinberg, n.d. (c. 1944), *A Jewish Settlement in Australia*, translated by Theodore H. Gaster, New York, Freeland League.

163. Blakeney, *Australia and the Jewish Refugees*, pp. 255–268.

164. Gerhard Fischer, 1989, *Enemy Aliens: Internment and the Homefront Experience in Australia, 1914–1920*, St Lucia, University of Queensland Press.

165. 'War Book of the Commonwealth of Australia', May 1939, chapter XII, p. 6, NAA: MP288/17, p. 1.

166. Klaus Neumann, 2006, *In the Interest of National Security: Civilian Internment in Australia During World War II*, Canberra, National Archives of Australia, pp. 10, 21–22.

167. 'Carlton Larrikin Attacks', *Herald* (Melbourne), 5 April 1939; 'Anti-Jewish Incidents', *Argus*, 6 April 1939.

168. Emery Barcs to Vica Barcs, 11 December 1941, Mitchell Library: MSS 5770, box 5, folder 'German Occupied Europe'.

169. Migrants' Consultative Council to H. S. Foll, 13 November 1940, NAA: A1608, N19/1/1 PART 2.

170. Walter Stolting to Intelligence Section Adelaide, 22 September 1939, NAA: D1915, SA4705.

171. Quoted in David Dutton, 2002, *One of Us? A Century of Australian Citizenship*, Sydney, UNSW Press, p. 98.

172. Archie Cameron, *CPD*, Representatives, vol. 166, 2 April 1941, p. 554.

173. Reproduced in Neumann, *In the Interest of National Security*, p. 20.

174. Konrad Kwiet, 1985, '"Be Patient and Reasonable!" The Internment of German-Jewish Refugees in Australia', *Australian Journal of Politics and History*, vol. 31, no. 1, p. 65.

175. Margaret Bevege, 1993, *Behind Barbed Wire: Internment in Australia During World War II*, St Lucia, University of Queensland Press, p. 116.

176. Aliens Tribunal No. 4 (Victoria), 'Walter Helmut Charles Ludwig Erwin Stolting', n.d. (June 1941), NAA: B741/5, V15423.

177. Walter Stolting to Marshall Lucas, 7 June 1941, NLA: MS 4965, series 1, folder 117, item 11389.

178. Gillard, Aliens Tribunal proceedings, Aliens Tribunal No. 4, 'In the matter of an objection by Walter Helmuth Carl Ludwig E. Stolting', 4 June 1941, p. 63, NAA: MP529/3, Tribunal 4/Stolting.

179. Intelligence Section attached to No 14D Internment Camp, 'Report on Internee S.3016', 7 May 1943, NAA: D1915, SA4705.

180. Jones to Camp Commandant, 14C-D Internment Camp, 21 February 1944, NAA: D1915, SA4705.

181. Gillard, 'In the matter of an objection by Walter Helmuth Carl Ludwig E. Stolting', p. 59.

182. 'Security Service Report for the South of South Australia, Fortnight ending 24th Sept. 43', report no. 101, emphasis added, NAA: D1915, SA4705.

183. Neumann, *In the Interest of National Security*, p. 15.

184. Yvonne Kapp & Margaret Mynatt, *British Policy and the Refugees, 1933–1941*, London: Frank Cass (1997), pp. 75–104.

185. On the *Dunera* internees, see Cyril Pearl, 1983, *The Dunera Scandal: Deported by Mistake*, London, Angus & Robertson.

186. Report on prisoner of war (Gerd Rafael Engel), 2 March 1942, NAA: M1103/2, N1605.

187. Quoted in Colin Golvan, 1990, *The Distant Exodus*, Crows Nest, ABC Enterprises, p. 19.

188. The experiences of some of them are well documented. Ludwig ('Lutz') Eichbaum arrived as a seventeen-year-old; see Sue Everett, 2010, *Not Welcome: A Dunera Boy's Escape from Nazi Oppression to Eventual Freedom in Australia*, Melbourne, Hybrid Publishers. Werner Pelz was eighteen when the *Dunera* arrived; see Roger Averill, 2012, *Exile: The Lives and Hopes of Werner Pelz*, Yarraville, Transit Lounge, and Werner Pelz, 1964, *Distant Strains of Triumph*, London, V. Gollancz.

189. Walter Kaufmann, 1954, 'Exile', *Meanjin*, vol. 13, no. 4, p. 540; Walter Kaufmann, 2013, *Schade, dass du Jude bist: Kaleidoskop eines Lebens: Autobiografische Erzählungen*, Münster, Prospero, p. 11.

190. Kaufmann to Commandant, 28 August 1941, NAA: A367, C58483.

191. Service and casualty form for Walter Kaufmann, NAA: MP1103/1, E39907; E. Hattam to Director, Commonwealth Investigation Branch, 13 November 1944, NAA: A367, C58483.

192. Paul R. Bartrop, 1993, 'Incompatible with Security: Enemy Alien Internees from Singapore in Australia', *Australian Jewish Historical Society Journal*, vol. 12, no. 1, pp. 149–169.

193. High Commissioner to Prime Minister, 20 November 1940, NAA: A2676, 642.

194. Geneviève Pitot, 1998, *The Mauritian Shekel: The Story of the Jewish Detainees in Mauritius, 1940–1945*, translated by Donna Edouard, Port Louis, Editions Vizavi.

195. War Cabinet minute, decision no. 642, 26 November 1940, NAA: A2676, 642; Menzies to High Commissioner, 6 December 1940, A2676, 642.

196. Paul Sauer, 1991, *The Holy Land Called: The Story of the Temple Society*, translated by Gunhild Henley, Melbourne, Temple Society Australia, pp. 235–246.

197. Bruce to Menzies, 23 December 1940, NAA: A1608, F19/1/1.

198. Department of the Interior to High Commissioner London, 30 January 1941, NAA: A1608, F19/1/1.

199. High Commissioner's Office to Department of the Interior, 15 May 1941, NAA: A1608, F19/1/1; Palmer, *Reluctant Refuge*, pp. 95–96; Pamela Rotner-Sakamoto, 1998, *Japanese Diplomats and Jewish Refugees: A World War II Dilemma*, Westport, Praeger, chapter 5.

200. Hillel Levine, 1996, *In Search of Sugihara: The Elusive Japanese Diplomat Who Risked His Life to Rescue 10,000 Jews from the Holocaust*, New York, Free Press.

201. War Cabinet minute, Agendum No. 130/1941, 9 April 1941, NAA: A5954, 370/10.

202. H. S. Foll, 'Admission of Polish refugees from Japan' (Cabinet submission), 8 April 1941, NAA: A5954, 370/10.

203. Neumann, *Refuge Australia*, pp. 55–56.

204. War Cabinet minute, Agendum No. 130/1941, 9 April 1941, NAA: A5954, 370/10.

205. The story of a German deserter is told in Neumann, *Refuge Australia*, pp. 54–55.

## CHAPTER 2: WARTIME REFUGEES AND NEW AUSTRALIANS

1. Diana Lary, 2001, 'Drowned Earth: The Strategic Breaching of the Yellow River Dyke, 1938', *War in History*, vol. 8, no. 2, pp. 191–207.

2. Irène Némirovsky, 2006, *Suite Francaise*, translated by Sandra Smith, London, Chatto & Windus.

3. Schechtman, *European Population Transfers*, pp. 388–389.

4. Jan Lingard, 2008, *Refugees and Rebels: Indonesian Exiles in Wartime Australia*, North Melbourne, Australian Scholarly Publishing, pp. 27–32; Jan Lingard, 2001, 'The First Asian Boat People', *Inside Indonesia*, vol. 68, www.insideindonesia.org/feature-editions/the-first-asian-boat-people; Esther Paterson, 1942, 'Sumatra in Port Melbourne – an Evacuee Colony', *Argus*, 23 May 1942; 'Javanese Find Accommodation', *Argus*, 16 April 1942.

5. Rupert Lockwood, 1970, 'The Indonesian Exiles in Australia, 1942–1947', *Indonesia*, vol. 10, pp. 37–56; Douglas Lockwood, 1982, *Black Armada: Australia & the Struggle for Indonesian Independence 1942–49*, Sydney, Hale & Iremonger, chapter 1; Margaret J. Kartomi, 2002, *The Gamelan Digul and the Prison Camp Musician Who Built It: An Australian Link with the Indonesian Revolution*, Rochester, University of Rochester Press, pp. 63–65.

6. 'War Book of the Commonwealth of Australia', May 1939, chapter XII, p. 6, NAA: MP288/17, 1.

7. *Gesetz über den Widerruf von Einbürgerungen und die Aberkennung der deutschen Staatsangehörigkeit* of 14 July 1933, www.documentarchiv.de/ns/1933/deutsche-staatsangehoerigkeit_ges.html.

8. Elfte Verordnung zum Reichsbürgergesetz, 25 October 1941, www.verfassungen.de/de/de33-45/reichsbuerger35-v11.htm.

9. Louise Burletson, 1993, 'The State, Internment and Public Criticism in the Second World War', in David Cesarani & Tony Kushner (eds), *The Internment of Aliens in Twentieth Century Britain*, London, Frank Cass, pp. 102–124; Kapp & Mynatt, *British Policy and the Refugees*, pp. 126–134.

10. François Lafitte, 1988, *The Internment of Aliens*, London, Libris, p. xxii.

11. Pearl, *The Dunera Scandal*, p. 147.

12. Ibid., p. 205.

13. Arthur Calwell, 1974, 'Foreword', in Noel W. Lamidey, *Aliens Control in Australia, 1939–46*, Sydney, N. Lamidey, p. 2.

14. Walter Stolting, 'Application for classification as "refugee alien"', 17 November 1943, NAA: D1915, SA4705.

15. Pearl, *The Dunera Scandal*, pp. 195–201; Klaus Loewald, 1985, 'The Eighth Australian Employment Company', *Australian Journal of Politics and History*, vol. 31, no. 1, pp. 78–89.

16. June Factor, n.d., 'Forgotten Soldiers: Aliens in the Australian Army's Employment Companies during World War II', www.yosselbirstein.org/pdf/eng/other/Forgotten_Soldiers.pdf.

17. Matsdorf, *No Time to Grow*, pp. 50–51.

18. William D. Rubinstein, 1997, *The Myth of Rescue: Why the Democracies Could Not Have Saved More Jews From the Nazis*, London, Routledge, pp. 94–95.

19. I. N. Steinberg to John Curtin, 18 September 1943, NAA: A433, 1944/2/50.

20. J. A. Carrodus, Chairman, Inter-Departmental Committee on Migration, 'Proposed Jewish settlement in the East Kimberleys', 22 March 1944, NAA: A445, 235/5/7.

21. F. M. Forde to I. N. Steinberg, 10 July 1945, NAA: A445, 235/5/7; J. B. Chifley to I. N. Steinberg, 16 July 1946, NAA: A445, 235/5/7.

22. I. N. Steinberg to Robert G. Menzies, 15 March 1950, NAA: A445, 235/5/7.

23. P. A. McBride for Prime Minister to I. N. Steinberg, 21 June 1950, NAA: A445, 235/5/7; H. E. Holt, 'The Freeland League for Jewish Territorial Colonization', Cabinet submission No. 99, 4 May 1950, NAA: A445, 235/5/7; A. S. Brown to H. E. Holt, 19 May 1950, NAA: A445, 235/5/7.

24. Catherine Dewhurst, 2014, 'The "Southern Question" in Australia: The 1925 Royal Commission's Racialisation of Southern Italians', *Queensland Historical Journal*, vol. 22, no. 4, pp. 316–332.

25. Caroline Kelly, 1943, 'The European Refugee in New South Wales 1938–1943', Canberra, Ministry for Post-War Reconstruction; Caroline Kelly, confidential notes, attachment to Caroline Kelly to A.R. Peters, 4 July 1945, NAA: A2998, 1952/105.

26. Kelly, 'The European Refugee in New South Wales', p. 20.

27. Pnhs Goldhar, 1939, *Dertseylungen fun Oystralye*, Melbourne, self-published; Herts Bergner, 1941, *Dos naye hoyz: novele*, Melbourne, Yidisher Natsionaler Bibliotek 'Kadimah'. In 1960 Bergner wrote another book about the lives of Jewish migrants in Australia: Herz Bergner, 1963, *Light and Shadow*, translated by Alec Braizblatt, New York, Thomas Yoseloff. See also Pam Maclean, 1995, 'The Australian-Yiddish Writer Pinchas Goldhar, 1901–1947', *Southerly*, vol. 55, no. 2, pp. 29–34; Pam Maclean, 1987, 'The Convergence of Cultural Worlds – Pinchas Goldhar: A Yiddish Writer in Australia', in W. D. Rubinstein (ed.), *Jews in the Sixth Continent*, Sydney, Allen & Unwin, pp. 127–150; M. J. Haddock, 1974, 'The Prose Fiction of Jewish Writers in Australia, 1945–1969: Part One', *Australian Jewish Historical Society Journal and Proceedings*, vol. 7, no. 7, pp. 495–512.

28. See Tadeusz Piotrowski (ed.), 2004, *The Polish Deportees of World War II: Recollections of Removal to the Soviet Union and Dispersal Throughout the World*, Jefferson, McFarland & Company.

29. Australian Legation Moscow to Department of External Affairs, 17 September 1943, NAA: A989, 1944/755/2 PART 1.

30. Krystyna Skwarko, 1974, *The Invited: The Story of 733 Polish Children Who Grew up in New Zealand*, Wellington, Millwood Press.

31. J. Horgan, 'Mr. and Mrs. Alexander Kerensky', 12 March 1945, NAA: A434, 1946/3/10191; see also Dusan Bojic, 'The Half-Hearted Revolutionary in Paradise', *ABC Lateline*, 22 September 2003, www.abc.net.au/lateline/content/2003/hc40.htm.

32. George Woodbridge (ed.), 1950, *UNRRA: The History of the United Nations Relief and Rehabilitation Administration*, New York, Columbia University Press, vol. 1, p. 147.

33. Woodbridge, *UNRRA*, vol. 1, p. 120; Woodbridge, *UNRRA*, vol. 3, p. 500.

34. Robert H. Johnson, 1951, 'International Politics and the Structure of International Organization: The Case of UNRRA', *World Politics*, vol. 3, no. 4, pp. 521, 531.

35. N. O. P. Pyke, 1949, 'Australia's UNRRA Contribution', *Australian Outlook*, vol. 3, no. 1, p. 79.

36. Quoted in David Day, 2001, *Chifley*, Pymble, HarperCollins, p. 275.

37. Colm Kiernan, 1978, *Calwell: A Personal and Political Biography*, West Melbourne, Nelson, pp. 54–55, 79–83.

38. Arthur Calwell, *CPD*, Representatives, vol. 169, 13 November 1941, p. 416.

39. Arthur Calwell, *CPD*, Representatives, vol. 172, 22 September 1942, p. 624.

40. Andrew Markus, 1984, 'Labour and Immigration: Policy Formation 1943–5', *Labour History*, no. 46, pp. 27–28.

41. 'Recommendations adopted by full Inter-departmental Committee on Migration', 5 October 1944, NAA: A461, A349/1/2 PART 5.

42. Arthur A. Calwell, 1972, *Be Just and Fear Not*, Hawthorn, Lloyd O'Neil, p. 99.

43. Harry Martin, 1989, *Angels and Arrogant Gods*, Canberra, Australian Government Publishing Service, pp. 1–2; George Kiddle, interviewed by Ann-Mari Jordens, 2008, transcript, pp. 18–20, NLA: ORAL TRC 5930/5.

44. Stephanie Peatling, 'Don't Hurtle Towards a Big Australia: PM', *Sydney Morning Herald*, 27 June 2010.

45. Statistics Section, Department of Immigration and Multicultural Affairs, 'Immigration: Federation to Century's End', Canberra: Department of Immigration and Multicultural Affairs (October 2001), p. 23, www.immi.gov.au/media/publications/statistics/federation/body.pdf.

46. Gwenda Tavan, 2012, 'Leadership: Arthur Calwell and the Post-war Immigration Program', *Australian Journal of Politics and History*, vol. 58, no. 2, pp. 203–220.

47. Arthur A. Calwell, 1945, *How Many Australians Tomorrow?*, Melbourne, Reed & Harris, p. 66.

48. Markus, 'Labour and Immigration: Policy Formation', p. 24.

49. Arthur Calwell, *CPD*, Representatives, vol. 185, 25 September 1945, p. 5859.

50. Ibid.

51. Ibid.

52. Leslie Haylen, 1969, *Twenty Years' Hard Labor*, South Melbourne, Macmillan, p. 98.

53. Commonwealth Immigration Advisory Committee, 'Report of the Commonwealth Immigration Advisory Committee', Canberra: Commonwealth Government Printer (1946).

54. Robert Menzies, *CPD*, Representatives, vol. 184, 29 August 1945, pp. 4979–4980.

55. Calwell, *Be Just and Fear Not*, pp. 101–102; Blakeney, *Australia and the Jewish Refugees*, p. 291.

56. For example, Katrina Stats, 2014, '"Characteristically generous"? Australian Responses to Refugees Prior to 1951', *Australian Journal of Politics and History*, vol. 60, no. 2, p. 185.

57. 'Calwell in Favour with Australian Jewry', *Smith's Weekly*, 19 January 1946.

58. Arthur Calwell, *CPD*, Representatives, vol. 186, 20 March 1946, pp. 420–421.

59. Rutland, *Edge of Diaspora*, p. 233.

60. Irene Eber, 2012, *Wartime Shanghai and the Jewish Refugees from Central Europe: Survival, Co-Existence, and Identity in a Multi-Cultural City*, Berlin, de Gruyter.

61. A. R. Peters to Secretary, Department of Information, 30 March 1942, NAA: SP112/1, 265/15/17.

62. Peter Vanlaw, n.d., 'Eva Baruch – Activist, Actress or Spy', http://forthelifeofme-film.com/2014/01/27/looking-eva-baruch/; Johannes Reichmayr, 2004, '"Anschluss" und Ausschluss: Die Vertreibung der Psychoanalytiker aus Wien', in Friedrich Stadler (ed.), *Vertriebene Vernunft I: Emigration und Exil österreichischer Wissenschaft*, Münster, Lit, pp. 171–178.

63. Suzanne D. Rutland, 1987, '"Waiting Room Shanghai": Australian Reactions to the Plight of the Jews in Shanghai after the Second World War', *Leo Baeck Institute Year Book*, vol. 32, p. 413.

64. '2500 Jews for Australia', *Newcastle Morning Herald*, 23 May 1946. Later that same year, the

Adelaide *News*, reporting the impending arrival of the *Hwa Lien* in Australia, reported that '2,000 or 3,000' Jewish migrants were waiting to come to Australia ('350 Jews for Australia', *News* [Adelaide], 31 December 1946).

65. 'Servicemen's Wives, Children, and Fiancées', *Argus*, 5 October 1946.

66. 'Record Batch of Fiancees', *News* (Adelaide), 15 October 1946.

67. 'Passengers Complain of Immigrants' Conduct', *Sydney Morning Herald*, 25 October 1946.

68. 'Aliens' Passage to Sydney', *Sydney Morning Herald*, 26 October 1946.

69. 'Wives from Britain', *Goulburn Evening Post*, 24 October 1946.

70. For example, Oscar Trebitsch, 'Immigrants from Europe' (letter to the editor), *Sydney Morning Herald*, 29 October 1946.

71. Arthur Calwell, *CPD*, Representatives, vol. 189, 7 November 1946, p. 39.

72. 'Protest on Migrants from Europe', *News* (Adelaide), 16 November 1946.

73. Henry Baynton Somer Gullett, *CPD*, Representatives, vol. 189, 27 November 1946, p. 661.

74. Ken Bolton in *Daily Telegraph* of 27 November 1946, quoted in Blakeney, *Australia and the Jewish Refugees*, p. 296.

75. 'R.S.L. President Defends Attitude on Alien Migrants', *Canberra Times*, 27 November 1946.

76. Arthur Calwell, *CPD*, Representatives, vol. 189, 28 November 1946, p. 749.

77. Doris Blackburn, *CPD*, Representatives, vol. 189, 28 November 1946, p. 748.

78. Arthur Calwell, *CPD*, Representatives, vol. 189, 28 November 1946, pp. 749, 751–752.

79. 'Most War Brides Reach Aust.', *Northern Star*, 9 October 1946.

80. For the following, see Antonia Finnane, 1999, *Far from Where? Jewish Journeys from Shanghai to Australia*, Carlton South, Melbourne University Press, pp. 185–189; Rutland, '"Waiting Room Shanghai"'; Rutland, 'Postwar Anti-Jewish Refugee Hysteria: A Case of Racial or Religious Bigotry?', *Journal of Australian Studies*, vol. 27, no. 77, pp. 69–79.

81. For example, 'Old Ferry to Bring 700 Refugees from Shanghai', *Townsville Daily Bulletin*, 16 December 1946.

82. 'New South Wales Jewish Board of Deputies: Welcome to Mrs. Van Tijn', *Hebrew Standard of Australia*, 6 February 1947.

83. Patrick Shaw to Department of External Affairs, 23 January 1947, NAA: A1067, IC46/25/16.

84. 'Refugees Acclaim Australia', *Argus*, 16 January 1947.

85. The *Sydney Morning Herald*, for example, told its readers that 'nearly 500' refugees had landed ('Refugees Arrive: 474 in Ship at Darwin', *Sydney Morning Herald*, 15 January 1947).

86. 'Darwin Besieged with Hwa Lien's 500 Passengers in Ship's Brief Stay in Port', *Northern Standard*, 17 January 1947; 'Refugees Arrive: 474 in Ship at Darwin', *Sydney Morning Herald*, 15 January 1947.

87. 'Refugee Migrants' (editorial), *Courier-Mail*, 16 January 1947.

88. Rutland, '"Waiting Room Shanghai"', p. 415; this was Brand's, rather than Calwell's, idea (Brand to Calwell, 12 January 1947, NAA: A433, 1947/2/574).

89. 'Refugee Racket Uncovered by Federal Police', *Sun* (Sydney), 21 January 1947.

90. 'Checking the Stranger at Our Gates' (editorial), *Sun* (Sydney), 22 January 1947.

91. 'Protest Over Jews', *News* (Adelaide), 22 January 1947.

92. 'Calwell Urges Tolerance, Welcome to Immigrants', *Sun* (Sydney), 28 January 1947.

93. 'A.N.A. Leader Attacks Selection of Immigrants', *Sun News-Pictorial* (Melbourne), 18 March 1947.

94. 'Most Australians Oppose Taking Homeless Jews', *Australian Gallup Polls*, nos 416–425,

March–April–May 1947.

95. Arthur Calwell, 1949, 'Foreword', in Ernest Platz, *New Australians: An Occupational Analysis of Jewish Migrants in Victoria*, Melbourne, Jewish Council to Combat Fascism and Anti-Semitism, p. 5.

96. 'Only 200 More Shanghai Refugees, Says Calwell', *Sydney Morning Herald*, 22 January 1947.

97. 'Calwell Urges Tolerance, Welcome to Immigrants', *Sun* (Sydney), 28 January 1947.

98. 'Fewer Landing Permits for Refugees', *Sydney Morning Herald*, 24 January 1947.

99. 'Calwell Urges Tolerance, Welcome to Immigrants', *Sun* (Sydney), 28 January 1947.

100. 'Only 200 More Shanghai Refugees, Says Calwell', *Sydney Morning Herald*, 22 January 1947; 'Fabulous Wealth from East in Refugee Ship', *Sun* (Sydney), 29 January 1947.

101. 'Jewish Refugees Have Huge Rolls of Money', *Canberra Times*, 29 January 1947.

102. 'Fabulous Wealth from East in Refugee Ship', *Sun* (Sydney), 29 January 1947.

103. 'Welcome the New Australian' (editorial), *Sun* (Sydney), 29 January 1947.

104. 'Javanese Stowaway in Amazing Adventure', *Northern Standard*, 9 August 1946.

105. 'Darwin Wants to Keep Game "Java Kid"', *Herald* (Melbourne), 10 August 1946.

106. McGuiness, file note, 14 October 1947, NAA: A446, 1958/61236.

107. 'NT Remembers Bas Wie's Great Escape', *7.30 Report*, ABC television, 7 July 2004, www.abc.net.au/7.30/content/2004/s1149010.htm; Jacqueline Bhabha & Mary Crock, 2007, *Seeking Asylum Alone: A Comparative Study: Unaccompanied and Separated Children and Refugee Protection in Australia*, Annandale, Themis Press, pp. 36, 48 n. 38.

108. Bondan to A. A. Calwell, 22 August 1946, NAA: A446, 1958/61236.

109. L. Liveris to Secretary, Department of Immigration, 20 July 1951, NAA: A446, 1958/61236.

110. Malcolm J. Proudfoot, 1957, *European Refugees: 1939–52: A Study in Forced Population Movement*, London, Faber and Faber, pp. 292–293.

111. Gil Loescher & John A. Scanlan, 1986, *Calculated Kindness: Refugees and America's Half-Open Door, 1945 to the Present*, New York, The Free Press, pp. 15–16.

112. Kim Salomon, 1991, *Refugees in the Cold War: Toward a New International Refugee Regime in the Early Postwar Era*, Lund, Lund University Press, pp. 170–177.

113. Proudfoot, *European Refugees*, p. 401; see also Gil Loescher, 2001, *The UNHCR and World Politics: A Perilous Path*, Oxford, Oxford University Press, pp. 37–39.

114. Constitution of the International Refugee Organization, Annex I, part I, section A, www.unhcr.org/3ae69ef14.html.

115. Egon F. Kunz, 1977, 'The Genesis of the Post-war Immigration Programme and the Evolution of the Tied-labour Displaced Persons Scheme', *Ethnic Studies*, vol. 1, no. 1, p. 36.

116. J. B. Chifley & H. V. Evatt, 'Australian Participation in the International Refugee Organisation and Post-UNRRA Relief', 10 May 1947, NAA: A2700, 695D.

117. Andrew Markus, 1984, 'Labour and Immigration 1946–9: The Displaced Persons Program', *Labour History*, no. 47, pp. 73–75, 78.

118. Noel W. Lamidey, 1970, *Partial Success: My Years as a Public Servant*, Hunters Hill, N. Lamidey, p. 72.

119. High Commissioner for the United Kingdom to Secretary for Dominion Affairs, 28 February 1947, NAA: A1068, IC47/46/1.

120. Calwell to Mackay, 26 May 1946, NAA: A1068, IC47/46/1; Calwell to Mackay, 27 May 1946, NAA: A1068, IC47/46/1; Department of Immigration to Australian High Commissioner New Delhi, 20 June 1946, NAA: A1068, IC47/46/1.

121. Arthur Calwell, *CPD*, Representatives, vol. 193, 15 October 1947, pp. 763–764.

122. '4000 Migrants Coming', *Daily News* (Perth), 5 June 1947.

123. 'Troopship Travel Frightens Migrants', *Argus*, 26 June 1947.

124. 'Film Star Send-off for Mr. Calwell: Leaves in Blaze of Publicity', *News* (Adelaide), 19 June 1947; Robert Edward Armstrong, diary, NLA: MS8953, folder 1.

125. 'New Move to Get Migrant Ships', *News* (Adelaide), 19 June 1947.

126. Australian High Commission to Department of Immigration, 23 June 1946, NAA: A1068, IC47/46/1.

127. On the Polish refugees in India, see Anuradha Bhattacharjee, 2012, *The Second Homeland: Polish Refugees in India*, New Delhi, Sage.

128. C. T. Moodie to Secretary, Department of External Affairs, 1 May 1947, NAA: A1068, IC47/3/191.

129. A. W. T. Webb to J. L. Allen, 10 April 1947, NAA, A1068, IC47/3/191.

130. J. L. Allen to Secretary, Department of External Affairs, 16 April 1947, NAA: A1068, IC47/3/191.

131. T. H. E. Heyes to Secretary, Department of External Affairs, 27 May 1947, NAA: A1068, IC47/3/191.

132. '3,000 Poles for Aust. This Year', *News* (Adelaide), 15 March 1947.

133. IRO press release, 21 July 1947, NAA: CP815/1, 021.114; 'Agreement between the Government of the Commonwealth of Australia and the Preparatory Commission of the International Refugee Organisation', 21 July 1947, NAA: A13307, 46/2.

134. Egon F. Kunz, 1988, *Displaced Persons: Calwell's New Australians*, Sydney, Australian National University Press, pp. 17–18.

135. John Hope Simpson, 1940, *The Refugee Question*, Oxford, Clarendon Press, p. 3.

136. Francesca Wilson, 1959, *They Came as Strangers: The Story of Refugees to Great Britain*, London, Hamish Hamilton, p. 237.

137. Emery Barcs, 'Migrants Are Not So Easy to Attract These Days', *News* (Adelaide), 6 February 1947.

138. Lamidey to Heyes, 8 July 1947, NAA: A445, 255/1/7.

139. Calwell to Australian High Commission New Delhi, 21 July 1947, NAA: A436, 1949/5/18.

140. Calwell to Australian High Commission New Delhi, 26 July 1947, NAA: A436, 1949/5/18.

141. Nutt to Lamidey, 21 July 1947, NAA: A445, 255/1/7.

142. Mackay to Peters, 30 July 1947, NAA: A445, 255/1/7.

143. Acting Commonwealth Migration Officer for W.A. to Secretary Immigration, 18 August 1947, NAA: A433, 1949/2/633.

144. 'Jobs Found Quickly for Polish Migrants', *Daily News* (Perth), 18 August 1947.

145. Calwell to Mackay, 27 May 1946, NAA: A1068, IC47/46/1; see also 'Wants Anglo-Indians Kept Out', *News* (Adelaide), 21 August 1947.

146. See, for example, Leslie Morgan's exhibition, 'Being Eurasian', at the Fremantle Arts Centre in 2013–2014 (Laetitia Wilson, 'Facing Up to Race, Identity', *West Australian*, 28 December 2013).

147. Play the Game by All, 'Jobs for migrants' (letter to the editor), *Daily News* (Perth), 25 August 1947.

148. T. W. White to F. Shedden, 25 August 1947, NAA: A816, 19/303/182.

149. Gerald Daniel Cohen, 2012, *In War's Wake: Europe's Displaced Persons in the Postwar Order*, New York, Oxford University Press, p. 108.

150. Greenhalgh to Heyes, 3 November 1947, NAA: A446, 1957/67774.

151. Heyes to Australian Migration Officer Berlin, 19 January 1948, NAA: A433, 1949/3/7658.

152. Greenhalgh to Heyes, 3 November 1947, NAA: A446, 1957/67774.

153. Arthur A. Calwell, 'To New Australians arriving on S.S. "Heintzelmann" [sic]', n.d. (November 1947), NAA: A446, 1957/67774.

154. Commonwealth Immigration Advisory Council, 3rd meeting, 7–8 May 1947, minute no. 45, Department of Immigration and Border Protection library.

155. 'Berlin July 17 and 18', record of meeting between Australian delegation and British Control Commission staff, n.d. (July 1947), NAA: A6980, S250104.

156. 'Displaced Persons Accepted as Migrants', *Canberra Times*, 17 July 1947.

157. 'Agreement between the Government of the Commonwealth of Australia and the Preparatory Commission of the International Refugee Organisation', 21 July 1947, NAA: A13307, 46/2; Noel W. Lamidey to Minister for Immigration, 8 September 1947, NAA: A6980, S250104.

158. Noel W. Lamidey to Minister for Immigration, 8 September 1947, NAA: A6980, 250104.

159. W. L. Brand to Heyes, 6 June 1949, NAA: A6980, S250296.

160. Heyes to N. St. C. Deschamps, 4 July 1950, NAA: A6980, S205296; see also Galleghan to Greenhalgh, 17 June 1949, NLA: MS8863/5.

161. Cohen, *In War's Wake*, p. 116.

162. A. J. Withers, 'Report on the Selection of Displaced Persons from Europe', n.d. (c. March 1948), NAA: A446, 1957/67774.

163. Greenhalgh to Secretary, Department of Immigration, 7 October 1947, NAA: A6980, 250104.

164. A. L. Nutt, 'Displaced Persons (nurses, waitresses and domestics) S.S. "General Heintzelman", Fremantle, 28.11.47', 1 December 1947, NAA: A446, 1957/67774.

165. H. B. M. Murphy, 1955, 'The Refugee Response in Australia', in H. B. M. Murphy (ed.), *Flight and Resettlement*, Paris, UNESCO, p. 126.

166. Martin, *Angels and Arrogant Gods*, pp. 16–17, 25.

167. A. L. Nutt, 'Particulars of typistes [sic] – Displaced Persons on board S.S. "General Stuart Heintzelman" arrived Fremantle, 28.11.1947', 29 November 1947, NAA: A446, 1957/67774.

168. Kathryn Hulme, 1954, *The Wild Place*, London, Shakespeare Head, p. 169.

169. T. W. White to Calwell, 24 July 1947, NAA: A816, 19/303/182.

170. For example, Stanislaw Gotowicz, 1998, *Bittersweet Bread*, London, Minerva Press, pp. 37–38.

171. Ruth Balint, 2014, 'Industry and Sunshine: Australia as Home in the Displaced Persons' Camps of Postwar Europe', *History Australia*, vol. 11, no. 1, pp. 112–127.

172. Department of Immigration to Galleghan, 7 April 1948, NAA: A436, 1948/5/506; A. L. Nutt to Immigration Publicity Officer, Department of Information, 9 February 1949, NAA: A436, 1948/5/506.

173. Minute paper, 'S.S. "General Stuart Heintzelman"', 4 December 1947, NAA: A446, 1957/67774; F. B. Cann to Collector of Customs, 28 November 1947, NAA: A433, 1949/3/7658; R. W. Gratwick to Commonwealth Immigration Officer Melbourne, 2 December 1947, NAA: A433, 1949/3/7658.

174. Arthur A. Calwell, 'Statement by the Minister for Immigration', 8 July 1948, NAA: A6980, S250105.

175. Diane Armstrong, 2001, *The Voyage of Their Life: The Story of the SS Derna and Its Passengers*, Pymble, Flamingo.

176. Kunz, *Displaced Persons*, p. 43.

177. R. H. Wheeler to Secretary, 10 March 1950, NAA: A6980, S250107.

178. Heyes to Galleghan, 26 July 1949, NAA: A434, 1949/3/16408.

179. Galleghan to Heyes, 3 August 1949, NAA: A434, 1949/3/16408.

180. For example, 'Girl Migrant as Central Figure at Ceremony', *West Australian*, 13 August 1949.

181. Statement by the Minister for Immigration, IM/101, 18 August 1949, NAA: A434, 1949/3/16408.

182. '£1000 for Calwell to Stage Kiss', *Sun* (Sydney), 18 August 1949; Eric John Harrison, *CPD*, Representatives, vol. 204, 7 September 1949, pp. 3–4; Eric John Harrison, *CPD*, Representatives, vol. 204, 30 September 1949, pp. 790–791.

183. Gay Breyley, 2005, 'Imagined Ancestral Communities of Displaced Australian Daughters: Evelyn Crawford's *Over My Tracks* and Lily Brett's *After the War* and *Unintended Consequences*', in Cynthia Huff (ed.), *Women's Life Writing and Imagined Communities*, New York, Routledge, p. 40.

184. Deschamps to Department of Immigration, 10 February 1950, NAA: A434, 1950/3/766.

185. Marginal note, 10 March 1950, on N. Deschamps to Secretary, Department of Immigration, 15 February 1950, NAA: A434, 1950/3/766.

186. Kunz, *Displaced Persons*, pp. 102–103.

187. Alan W. Joynes to Secretary, Department of Immigration, 23 December 1949, NAA: A445, 255/1/3.

188. The experience of Polish DPs from East Africa who were brought to Australia in 1950 is discussed in Maryon Allbrook & Helen Cattalini, 1995, *The General Langfitt Story: Polish Refugees Recount Their Experiences of Exile, Dispersal and Resettlement*, Canberra, Australian Government Publishing Service.

189. Jean I. Martin, 1965, *Refugee Settlers: A Study of Displaced Persons in Australia*, Canberra, Australian National University, p. 48.

190. Application for assistance of IRO for Ervin Viks, 3 May 1950, NAA: A12685, VIKS E.

191. Garfield Barwick, *CPD*, Representatives, vol. 30, 22 March 1961, p. 451.

192. K. Lemmik & E. Martinson, 1963, *12,000: Materials from the Trial of the Mass Murderers Juhan Jüriste, Karl Linnas and Ervin Viks, Held at Tartu on January 16–20 1962*, Tallinn, Estonian State Publishing House.

193. Mark Aarons, 2001, *War Criminals Welcome: Australia, a Sanctuary for Fugitive War Criminals Since 1945*, Melbourne, Black Inc., pp. 444–451.

194. Ruth Balint, 2012, 'The War Crimes Case of Károly Zentai and the Quest for Historical Justice', in Colin Tatz (ed.), *Genocide Perspectives IV: Essays on Holocaust and Genocide*, Sydney, UTS ePress, pp. 272–311.

195. *Minister for Home Affairs of the Commonwealth v Zentai* [2012] HCA 28 (15 August 2012), www.austlii.edu.au/au/cases/cth/HCA/2012/28.html.

196. 'Draft Lectures for Welfare and Information Officers on Displaced Persons Ships', lectures #7 and #11 (1948), NAA: A437, 1948/6/377.

197. Arthur A. Calwell, 1953, 'The Why and How of Post-war Immigration', in H. E. Holt et al., *Australia and the Migrant*, Sydney, Angus and Robertson, p. 10.

198. Glenda Sluga, 1988, *Bonegilla, a 'Place of No Hope'*, Parkville, History Department, University of Melbourne; Bruce Pennay, 2010, 'Selling Immigration: Bonegilla Reception and Training Centre, 1947–1971', *Victorian Historical Journal*, vol. 81, no. 1, pp. 113–130; Ann Tündern-Smith, 2007, *Bonegilla's Beginnings*, Wagga Wagga, Triple D Books.

199. Mills to Secretary, Department of Immigration, 13 November 1947, NAA: A445, 174/4/8.
200. Ibid.
201. Stolting to Education Office, 24 January 1948, NAA: A1361, 34/11/4 PART 701; Heyes to Director of Education, 21 April 1948, NAA: A1361, 34/11/4 PART 701.
202. Greenhalgh to Heyes, 3 November 1947, NAA: A446, 1957/67774.
203. Heyes to Minister for Immigration, 24 February 1950, NAA: A6980, S250240.
204. Harold Holt, *CPD*, Representatives, 14 June 1950, vol. 208, p. 4313.
205. Heyes to Minister for Immigration, 24 February 1950, attachment, NAA: A6980, S250240; Application for new certificate of registration, 5 April 1956, NAA: SP908/1, Yugoslavian/ Cindric Josef.
206. Heyes to Minister for Immigration, 8 November 1951, NAA: A6980, S250240; Nutt to Minister for Immigration, 10 March 1952, NAA: A6980, S250240.
207. 'Newspapers Ban Use of Term "DP"', *The New Australian*, no. 10 (October 1949), p. 2.
208. Frank Clune, 1950, *All Roads Lead to Rome: A Pilgrimage to the Eternal City, and a Look Around War-torn Europe*, Sydney, Invincible Press, p. 227.
209. James Jupp, 1966, *Arrivals and Departures*, Melbourne, Cheshire-Lansdowne, p. 116.
210. Henriette von Holleuffer, 2001, *Zwischen Fremde und Fremde: Displaced Persons in Australien, den USA und Kanada, 1946–1952*, Osnabrück, Universitätsverlag Rasch, 46. Estimates vary.
211. Schechtman, *European Population Transfers*, pp. 349, 452.
212. Ian Connor, 2007, *Refugees and Expellees in Post-War Germany*, Manchester, Manchester University Press, pp. 18–19.
213. Leo W. Schwarz, 1957, *Refugees in Germany Today*, New York, Twayne Publishers, p. 27.
214. Diana Kay & Robert Miles, 1988, 'Refugees or Migrant Workers? The Case of the European Volunteer Workers in Britain (1946–1951)', *Journal of Refugee Studies*, vol. 1, no. 3–4, pp. 214–236.
215. Johannes-Dieter Steinert & Inge Weber-Newth, 2008, 'German Migrants in Postwar Britain: Immigration Policy, Recruitment, and Reception', in Mathias Schulze et al. (eds), *German Diasporic Experiences: Identity, Migration, and Loss*, Waterloo, Wilfrid Laurier University Press, pp. 217–229.
216. For the story of Annie Maas O'Keefe, see London, *Non-White Immigration*; A. C. Palfreeman, 1967, *The Administration of the White Australia Policy*, Melbourne, Melbourne University Press; Nicholls, *Deported*, pp. 87–93; Sean Brawley, 1996, 'Da Heer Evatt: The O'Keefe Case and Dutch Perceptions of H. V. Evatt and Australian Foreign Policy', in David Day (ed.), *Brave New World: Dr H. V. Evatt and Australian Foreign Policy 1941–49*, St Lucia, University of Queensland Press, pp. 131–145; Sean Brawley, 2014, 'Finding Home in White Australia: The O'Keefe Deportation Case of 1949', *History Australia*, vol. 11, no. 1, pp. 128–148; Lynn Embrey & Colin Johnston, 2000, 'The 1948–49 Track and Field Season: Mrs. Blankers-Koen, Mrs. O'Keefe, Mr. Calwell; Lloyd LaBeach, Herb McKenley and Wally McArthur', *Sporting Traditions*, vol. 16, no. 2: pp. 55–70; Gwenda Tavan, 2005, *The Long, Slow Death of White Australia*, Melbourne, Scribe Publications, pp. 54–59.
217. *Daily Telegraph*, 15 February 1949.
218. Arthur Calwell, *CPD*, Representatives, vol. 201, 9 February 1949, p. 66.
219. *O'Keefe v Calwell* [1949] HCA (18 March 1949), www.austlii.edu.au/au/cases/cth/ HCA/1949/6.html.

220. *CPD*, Representatives, vol. 203, 30 June 1949, 1881–1884, 1893–1898, 1949–1950, 1952–1953.

221. *Koon Wing Lau v Calwell* [1949] HCA 65 (21 December 1949), www.austlii.edu.au/au/cases/cth/HCA/1949/65.html.

222. Arthur Calwell, quoted in John King, 2005, 'The Creation of a "Recalcitrant Minority": A Case Study of the Chinese New Guinea Wartime Refugees', *Journal of the Royal Australian Historical Society*, vol. 91, no. 1, pp. 48–57.

223. Pauline Hanson, *CPD*, Representatives, vol. 208, 10 September 1996, p. 3862.

224. Michael Kirby, 2009, 'Herbert Vere Evatt, the United Nations and the Universal Declaration of Human Rights after 60 Years', *University of Western Australia Law Review*, vol. 34, no. 2, pp. 245–255.

225. 'Court of Human Rights', file note for Alan Watt, n.d. (c. 17 February 1947), NAA: A1838, 856/13/2.

226. United Nations Economic and Social Council, 'Report of the Third Session of the Commission on Human Rights, Lake Success, 28 May to 18 June 1948', Annex A: 'Draft International Declaration of Human Rights', 28 June 1948, UN Doc. E/800.

227. Mary Ann Glendon, 2001, *A World Made New: Eleanor Roosevelt and the Universal Declaration of Human Rights*, New York, Random House, p. 92.

228. Peter Hempenstall, 1993, *The Meddlesome Priest: A Life of Ernest Burgman*, St Leonards, Allen & Unwin, pp. 281–285.

229. Alan Watt, 1972, *Australian Diplomat: Memoirs of Sir Alan Watt*, Sydney, Angus and Robertson in association with the Australian Institute of International Affairs, p. 137.

230. Minutes of the 121st meeting of the Third Committee, UN Doc. A/C.3/SR121; Annemarie Devereux, 2005, *Australia and the Birth of the International Bill of Human Rights 1946–1966*, Annandale, Federation Press, p. 70.

231. Jay Winter & Antoine Prost, 2013, *René Cassin and Human Rights: From the Great War to the Universal Declaration*, Cambridge, Cambridge University Press, p. 239.

232. H. Lauterpacht, 1950, *International Law and Human Rights*, London, Stevens & Sons, p. 422.

233. Ibid., p. 315.

234. Ibid., p. 346.

## Chapter 3: Defectors, Deserters and the 'Hard Core'

1. Kunz, 'The Genesis of the Post-war Immigration Programme'.

2. Deschamps to Heyes, 3 August 1950, NAA: A445, 194/2/3.

3. Greenhalgh to Secretary, Department of Immigration, 12 October 1950, NAA: A445, 194/2/3.

4. UNGA 86, A/RES/319(IV) of 3 December 1949, www.worldlii.org/int/other/UNGA/1949/86.pdf.

5. Heyes to Secretary, Department of External Affairs, 22 May 1950, NAA: A1838, 855/11/11 PART 2.

6. Glen Petersen, 2008, 'To Be or Not to Be a Refugee: The International Politics of the Hong Kong Refugee Crisis, 1949–55', *Journal of Imperial and Commonwealth History*, vol. 36, no. 2, pp. 171–172.

7. Gatrell, *The Making of the Modern Refugee*, chapter 5; Aristide R. Zolberg, Astri Suhrke & Sergio Aguayo, 1989, *Escape from Violence: Conflict and the Refugee Crisis in the Developing World*, New York, Oxford University Press, pp. 129–135.

8. Heyes to Secretary, Department of External Affairs, 23 April 1951, NAA: A1838, 855/11/11

PART 2. On the internal debates in Australia, see also David Palmer, 2009, 'The Quest for "Wriggle Room": Australia and the Refugee Convention, 1951–73', *Australian Journal of International Affairs*, vol. 63, no. 2, pp. 290–308.

9. F. H. Hawkins (for Premier of New South Wales) to Prime Minister, 16 August 1950, NAA: A461, O350/1/1.

10. United Nations Section, 'Draft Convention on the Status of Refugees and Stateless Persons', 23 May 1951, NAA: A1838, 855/11/11 PART 3.

11. [Patrick Shaw] to Department of External Affairs, 8 July 1951, NAA: A1838, 855/11/11 PART 3.

12. This and subsequent quotes are from United Nations High Commissioner for Refugees (ed.), n.d., 'The Refugee Convention, 1951: The Travaux Preparatoires Analysed and with a Commentary by Dr Paul Weis', Geneva: UNHCR, www.unhcr.org/4ca34be29.html. (The text is not paginated.)

13. Australian delegation Geneva to External Affairs, 17 July 1951, NAA: A1838, 855/11/11 PART 3.

14. 'Conference of plenipotentiaries on the status of refugees and stateless persons, Geneva 2nd July, 1951: brief for the Australian delegation', attached to A. H. Tange to Minister for External Affairs, 25 June 1951, NAA: A1838, 855/11/11 PART 3.

15. United Nations, 'Treaty Series: Treaties and International Agreements Registered or Filed and Recorded with the Secretariat of the United Nations', vol. 189, pp. 200–202, https://treaties.un.org/doc/publication/UNTS/Volume%20189/v189.pdf.

16. Intergovernmental Committee for European Migration, 1963, *ICEM: Behind the Scenes*, Geneva, ICEM.

17. Barry York, 2003, 'Australia and Refugees, 1901–2002: An Annotated Chronology Based on Official Sources', Canberra, Information and Research Services, Department of the Parliamentary Library, p. 134.

18. UN Security Council Resolution 16 of 10 January 1947, UN Doc. S/Res/16 (1947).

19. Allied and Associated Powers and Italy, Treaty of Peace, 10 February 1947, Article 21 (1), *American Journal of International Law*, vol. 42, no. 2 Supplement (1948), p. 56.

20. Carl J. Bon Tempo, 2008, *Americans at the Gate: The United States and Refugees During the Cold War*, Princeton, Princeton University Press, p. 37.

21. For a detailed description of Vladimir Petrov's and Evdokia Petrova's defections, see Robert Manne, 2004, *The Petrov Affair* (revised edition), Melbourne, Text Publishing; and David Horner, 2014, *The Spy Catchers: The Official History: 1949–1963*, Sydney, Allen & Unwin, pp. 317–348.

22. Robert Menzies, *CPD*, Representatives, vol. 3, 13 April 1954, pp. 325–326.

23. Karol Tököly to Secretary Department of External Affairs, 16 March 1948, NAA: A1067, IC46/15/15/2.

24. 'Czech Consul to Stay Here', *Canberra Times*, 27 March 1948.

25. Peter Hruby, 2010, *Dangerous Dreamers: The Australian Anti-Democratic Left and Czechoslovak Agents*, New York, iUniverse, pp. 179–182; Horner, *The Spy Catchers*, p. 291; 'Czech Consul General Seeks Asylum Here', *Canberra Times*, 5 April 1951; 'Political Asylum Sought by Czech Official', *West Australian*, 6 April 1951; 'Plea for Asylum by Mr. Felix', *Canberra Times*, 6 April 1951; 'Czech Official Given Asylum', *Canberra Times*, 27 April 1951; Josef Felix to Secretary Department of External Affairs, 2 April 1951, NAA: A1838, 1515/1/10/1.

26. Manne, *The Petrov Affair*, p. 117.

27. 'Czech Official Given Asylum', *Canberra Times*, 27 April 1951.

28. Harold Holt, marginal note on Heyes to Minister for Immigration, 9 August 1956, NAA: A6980, S250089.

29. Heyes to Minister for Immigration, 9 August 1956, NAA: A6980, S250089; W. K. Brown, 'Political asylum in Australia', 31 July 1956, NAA: A6980, S250089.

30. Cabinet minute, decision no. 487, 16 October 1956, NAA: A4926, 398.

31. J. C. G. Kevin to Secretary, Department of External Affairs, 19 November 1956, NAA: A1838, 1606/3.

32. For the relevant government records regarding Paranyuk's application to remain in Australia, see NAA: A1838, 1606/3; NAA: A1209, 1957/4351; and NAA: MP1139/1, 1957/4269.

33. 'Draft Lectures for Welfare and Information Officers on Displaced Persons ships', lecture #7 (1948), NAA: A437, 1948/6/377.

34. Anna Haebich, 2008, *Spinning the Dream: Assimilation in Australia 1950–1970*, Fremantle, Fremantle Press, pp. 121–137, 163–178; Jupp, *Arrivals and Departures*, pp. 142–151; Brian Murphy, 1993, *The Other Australia: Experiences of Migration*, Cambridge, Cambridge University Press in association with Ethnic Affairs Commission of New South Wales, chapter 6; Ann-Mari Jordens, 1997, *Alien to Citizen: Settling Migrants in Australia, 1945–75*, St Leonards, Allen & Unwin, pp. 147–150.

35. In Australia, Australian citizenship and British subjecthood coexisted until 1984; see John Chesterman, 2005, 'Natural-born Subjects? Race and British Subjecthood in Australia', *Australian Journal of Politics and History*, vol. 51, no. 1, pp. 30–39.

36. Jordens, *Alien to Citizen*, p. 173.

37. Empire Youth Movement in cooperation with the Commonwealth Department of Immigration, 1951, 'Pamphlet to Tell New Australians About the Royal Family', Melbourne, Empire Youth Council.

38. 'Erna Became a Cover Girl', *The New Australian*, no. 33 (September 1951), p. 1.

39. 'Youths May Become Citizens after Two Years in Australia', *The New Australian*, no. 35 (November 1951), p. 1.

40. Alistair Davidson, 1997, *From Subject to Citizen: Australian Citizenship in the Twentieth Century*, Cambridge, Cambridge University Press, pp. 91–94.

41. Andrew Riemer, 1992, *Inside Outside*, Pymble, Angus & Robertson, p. 12.

42. Loescher & Scanlan, *Calculated Kindness*, p. 51.

43. Louise W. Holborn, 1975, *Refugees: A Problem of Our Time: The Work of the United Nations High Commissioner for Refugees, 1951–1972*, London, Scarecrow Press, vol. 1, p. 403.

44. United Nations Section to Secretary External Affairs, 6 November 1956, NAA: A1838, 861/8/6 PART 1A.

45. Athol Townley, *CPD*, Representatives, vol. 13, 8 November 1956, p. 2142.

46. Hanan to Prime Minister, 9 November 1956, Archives New Zealand (hereafter 'ANZ'): EA W2619, 108/4/79/1 part 1.

47. Athol Townley, *CPD*, Representatives, vol. 13, 8 November 1956, p. 2142.

48. Arthur Calwell, *CPD*, Representatives, vol. 13, 8 November 1956, p. 2143.

49. Heyes to Jockel, 5 December 1956, NAA: A10034, 252/9/8-2.

50. E. L. Charles to G. C. Watson, 3 April 1957, NAA: A6980, S250229.

51. Heyes to Minister for Immigration, 9 May 1957, A6980, S250229.

52. C. C. F. Spry to Heyes, 8 May 1957, A6980, S250229.

53. Spry to Secretary, Department of Immigration, 9 April 1957, NAA: A6980, S250229.

54. Heyes, marginal note, 15 May 1957, and Townley, marginal note, 9 May 1957; both on Heyes to Minister, 9 May 1957, NAA: A6980, S250229.

55. G. M. Redshaw to Acting Secretary, Department of Immigration, 4 June 1957, NAA: A6980, S250229.

56. Hal Cook to Nutt, 19 July 1957, NAA: A6980, S250229.

57. Horner, *The Spy Catchers*, p. 516.

58. B. Campbell to W. M. Phillipps, 11 June 1957, NAA: A6980, S250230.

59. H. G. Brooks, 'Hungarian Refugees in Yugoslavia: Assessment of Operational Requirements', 18 June 1957, pp. 4–8, NAA: A6980, S250229.

60. Brooks to Acting Secretary, Department of Immigration, 8 August 1957, NAA: A6980, S250229.

61. Brooks to Secretary, Department of Immigration, 21 October 1957, NAA: A6980, S250229.

62. Martin, *Angels and Arrogant Gods*, p. 40.

63. Holborn, *Refugees*, vol. 1, p. 404.

64. Edward B. Marks, 1958, 'Mission Accomplished: How the Yugoslav Camps for Hungarian Refugees Were Closed', *Migration News*, vol. 7, no. 6, p. 20.

65. Louise W. Holborn, 1956, *The International Refugee Organization: A Specialized Agency of the United Nations: Its History and Work 1946–1952*, London, Oxford University Press, p. 483.

66. Peter Gatrell, 2011, *Free World? The Campaign to Save the World's Refugees, 1956–1963*, Cambridge, Cambridge University Press, p. 87.

67. Beaglehole, *Refuge New Zealand*, pp. 104–106.

68. B. M. Martyn, file note, 17 May 1960, NAA: A446, 1960/65417.

69. 'Press statement by the Minister for Immigration: 250,000th refugee arrives Wednesday', 18 June 1960, NAA: A446, 1960/65417.

70. 'Govt. Has Done Its Part; Now Public Must Help', '"Be Generous, Canberra"' and 'What Your Money Can Do', *Canberra Times*, 2 August 1960.

71. 'It's a Two-war [sic] Bargain', *Canberra Times*, 2 August 1960.

72. Stefanie Scherr, 2013, '"As Soon as We Got Here We Lost Everything": The Migration Memories and Religious Lives of the Old Believers in Australia', PhD thesis, Swinburne University of Technology.

73. Report of the United Nations High Commissioner for Refugees, 15 May 1953, UN Doc. A/2394.

74. Olga Bakich, 2000, 'Emigré Identity: The Case of Harbin', *South Atlantic Quarterly*, vol. 99, no. 1, pp. 51–76; Mara Moustafine, 2002, 'The Harbin Connection: Russians from China', in Shen Yuanfang & Penny Edwards (eds), *Beyond China: Migrating Identities*, Canberra, Centre for the Study of the Southern Chinese Diaspora, Australian National University, pp. 75–87; Mara Moustafine, 2002, *Secrets and Spies: The Harbin Files*, Milsons Point, Vintage, chapter 15.

75. O. C. W. Fuhrman to Department of External Affairs, 23 August 1948, NAA: A6980, S250253.

76. Department of Immigration, 'Refugees of European origin in the Far East', January 1963, NAA: C3939, N1963/75024; Holborn, *Refugees*, vol. 1, p. 623.

77. Heyes to Minister for Immigration, 7 February 1955, NAA: A6980, S250292; Heyes to Minister for Immigration, 30 May 1955, NAA: A6980, S250292.

78. Spry to Heyes, 2 March 1955, NAA: A6980, S250292.

79. Heyes, marginal note, 8 June 1954, on Nutt to Minister, 28 April 1954, NAA: A6980, S250276; W. K. Brown, 'Admission of non-British Europeans from China', 8 July 1955, NAA: A6980, S250292.

80. Nutt to Minister, 30 May 1957, NAA: A6980, S250292.

81. Spry to Heyes, 16 December 1957, NAA: A6980, S250292.

82. 'More Publicity Needed, Says Miss Australia', *Canberra Times*, 7 March 1962.

83. Vladimir Antonovich Verstak and dependents, visa application, 10 June 1952, NAA: A1630, 2015; see also Julie Ustinoff & Kay Saunders, 2004, 'Celebrity, Nation, and the New Australian Woman: Tania Verstak, Miss Australia 1961', *Journal of Australian Studies*, vol. 28, no. 83, pp. 66–73.

84. Application for naturalization of Tania Verstak, NAA: SP1122/1, N19057/63231.

85. Dorothy Drain, 'It Seems to Me', *Australian Women's Weekly*, 3 October 1962.

86. 'Miss Australia: The Gay Ambassador', *Australian Women's Weekly*, 14 March 1962.

87. 'Report of the Australian Delegation to the Sixth Session of the Executive Committee of the High Commissioner's Programme Held in Geneva from 6th to 10th November, 1961', November 1961, p. 14, NAA: A1838, 932/4/2 PART 3.

88. 'Asylum in Aust. for Polish Envoy' and 'Day of Drama at the Test', *Sun-Herald* (Sydney), 15 January 1961; 'Asylum Granted to Polish Family', *Times* (London), 16 January 1961.

89. Horner, *The Spy Catchers*, p. 463.

90. Spry to Prime Minister, 15 December 1960, NAA: A1838, TS1606/19.

91. 'Envoy Told of Alleged Money Loss', *Sydney Morning Herald*, 16 January 1961; 'Note to Govt. on Envoy's Defection', *Canberra Times*, 24 January 1961.

92. 'Family Out of Hiding', *Sydney Morning Herald*, 11 March 1961.

93. J. C. G. Kevin, 'Record of conversation with Mr. Weir', 18 March 1957, NAA: A1838, TS1606/2 PART 1; see also NAA: A1838, TS1606/6. The available archival records do not reveal whether or not the man was resettled in Australia.

94. Department of External Affairs to Australian embassy Washington, 7 July 1959, NAA: A1209, 1959/678.

95. Unless otherwise stated, the following draws on my 2005 article '"Stayputs" and Asylum Seekers in Darwin, 1961–1962, or How Three Portuguese Sailors Helped to Undermine the White Australia Policy' (*Journal of Northern Territory History*, vol. 16, pp. 1–15). The claim that Darwin residents had befriended the sailors on previous visits was made by the UNHCR representative in Australia (A. McIver to E. Jacobs, 28 February 1962, UNHCR Archives: 11,1 6/1/AUSL (I).)

96. Heydon to Minister for Immigration, 15 December 1961, NAA: A446, 1962/65208.

97. Garfield Barwick, 1995, *A Radical Tory: Garfield Barwick's Reflections and Recollections*, Annandale, Federation Press, p. 165.

98. Field officer to senior field officer, 23 June 1960, NAA: A6119, 3045.

99. H. G. Brooks, 'Report on Darwin operations relative to Malayan deportees Deraus bin Saris and Zainal bin Hashim', 11 October 1961, p. 1, NAA: A446, 1962/66082.

100. E. L. Charles, 'Notes of Discussions', 5 March 1962, NAA: A446, 1962/65620.

101. W. G. A. Landale, 'Record of conversation between the Portuguese Chargé d'Affaires and the Minister for External Affairs on 20 March 1962', NAA: A1838, 1525/3/248 PART 2.

102. P. R. Heydon, 'Note for Minister', 30 April 1962, NAA: A446, 1962/65620.

103. H[eydon] to Minister, n.d. (30 April 1962), NAA: A446, 1962/65620.

104. Beaglehole, *Refuge New Zealand*, pp. 122–124.

105. 'New Police Theory over Body', *Sydney Morning Herald*, 27 June 1959; 'Another Chinese Body Found in Harbour', *Sun-Herald* (Sydney), 28 June 1959.

106. F. M. Osborne to John McEwen, 6 July 1959, NAA: A1209, 1959/698.

107. The following draws on my 2011 article 'Asylum Seekers, Willy Wong, and the Use of History: From 2010 to 1962, and back' (*Australian Historical Studies*, vol. 42, no. 1, pp. 126–139).

108. Chi-Kwan Mark, 2007, 'The "Problem of People": British Colonials, Cold War Powers, and the Chinese Refugees in Hong Kong, 1949–62', *Modern Asian Studies*, vol. 41, no. 6, pp. 1145–1181.

109. For Wong's claims, see 'Attachment "A"', n.d. (1962); and W. J. Lee to Secretary, Department of Immigration, 9 February 1962, NAA: A6980, S203068.

110. Lee to Department of Immigration, 9 February 1962, NAA: A6980, S203068.

111. Nutt for Heydon to Minister, 20 February 1962, NAA: A6980, S203068.

112. A. R. Downer to Wilfrid Kent Hughes, 5 April 1962, NAA: A6980, S203068.

113. 'Press statement by the Minister for Immigration, the Hon. A. R. Downer, M.P. – April 14th, 1962', NAA: A1838, 1477/2/207.

114. Peter Heydon diaries, entry of 15 April 1962, NLA: MS 3155, Box 22, Folder 184.

115. Richard Hughes, 'Wong Did Go by Escort', *Herald* (Melbourne), 16 April 1962.

116. Far Easterner, 'The Fate of Willie Wong', *Sydney Morning Herald*, 18 April 1962.

117. Bert [Furler] to Ted [Charles], 25 April 1962, NAA: A6980, S203068.

118. Lee to Wilfred [sic] Kent Hughes, 26 February 1962, NAA: A6980, S203068.

119. A. J. P. Hall & Hall to Garfield Barwick, 18 May 1962, NAA: A1838, 1477/2/208.

120. See Klaus Neumann, 2004, 'Anxieties in Colonial Mauritius and the White Australia Policy', *Journal of Imperial and Commonwealth History*, vol. 32, no. 3, p. 10.

121. Martin, *Angels and Arrogant Gods*, p. 35.

122. Cabinet minute, decision no. 481, 15 September 1964, NAA: A446, 1970/95021.

123. Paul W. van der Veur, 'Political Awakening in West New Guinea', *Pacific Affairs*, vol. 36, no. 1, pp. 54–73; Peter Hastings, 1965, 'From Sabang to Merauke! Or, from Sorong to Samarai?', *New Guinea and Australia, the Pacific and South-East Asia*, vol. 1, no. 3, pp. 27–29; Nonie Sharp, 1977, *The Rule of the Sword: The Story of West Irian*, Malmsbury, Kibble Books, pp. 10–17; Ian Downs, 1980, *The Australian Trusteeship Papua New Guinea 1945–75*, Canberra, Australian Government Publishing Service, pp. 220–230.

124. Cabinet decision no. 375 of 6 August 1962, NAA: A5819, Volume 8/Agendum 330; Garfield Barwick, submission no. 330 of 19 July 1962, NAA: A5819, Volume 8/Agendum 330.

125. R. Rose to Secretary, Department of Territories, 27 June 1966, NAA: A1838, 932/5/14 PART 1.

126. 'Meeting Held in Department of External Affairs on 6th August, 1964', appendix, NAA: A1838, 3036/14/1/6 PART 1.

127. 'Papua and New Guinea – Trans-Border Movements', file note, n.d. (c. August 1963), NAA: A1838, 3036/14/1 PART 2.

128. R. Marsh, 'Policy Regarding Refugees from West New Guinea', 11 March 1964, NAA: A452, 1963/8261. According to Brian Toohey and William Pinwill, the Australian Secret Intelligence Service (ASIS) mounted anti-Indonesian operations in West Irian until 1967 or 1968; if it did, Barnes might not have been aware of them (see Brian Toohey and William Pinwill, 1989, *Oyster: The Story of the Australian Secret Intelligence Service*, Port Melbourne, William Heinemann, p. 95).

129. A. M. Bottrill to District Officer Wewak, 29 September 1964, NAA: A452, 1964/229.

130. Robert R. Cole to Secretary, Department of the Administrator, 1 October 1964, NAA: A452, 1964/229.

131. R. Aisbett, 'Benjamin Nikijuluw & family', 11 September 1964, NAA: A452, 1964/5800; G. A. Jockel to Minister of External Affairs, 30 September 1964, NAA: A1838, 3036/14/1/6 PART 1.

132. Barnes to Gorton, 9 December 1964, NAA: A1838, 3036/14/1/6 PART 1.

133. Spry to Secretary, Department of Territories, 19 January 1965, NAA: A452, 1964/5800.

134. Department of External Affairs to Australian embassy The Hague, 1 October 1964, NAA: A452, 1964/5800; C. R. Ashwin, 'Record of conversation with Mr. Djoko Joewono, Counsellor, Indonesian embassy, on 24th September 1965', NAA: A1838, 3036/14/1/6 PART 2; R. Marsh, 'Benjamin Nikijuluw, Indonesian applicant for political asylum in the Territory of Papua and New Guinea', 23 February 1966, NAA: A452, 1964/5800.

135. P. Weis, 1969, 'The United Nations Declaration on Territorial Asylum', *Canadian Yearbook of International Law*, vol. 7, pp. 95–97.

136. H. F. E. Whitlam, 'Additional paragraph to paper on asylum', 26 December 1958, NAA: A1838, 929/6/1 PART 1.

137. J. O. Clark to Lyons, 23 April 1958, NAA: A432, 1963/3273 PART 1.

138. This resolution was subsequently passed by the UN General Assembly: General Assembly Resolution 1400 (XIV), 4 March 1960, UN Doc. A/CN.4/128.

139. Heydon to Secretary, Department of External Affairs, 7 September 1966, NAA: A1838, 929/6/1 PART 3.

140. J. O. Ballard to Secretary, Department of External Affairs, 25 August 1967, NAA: A1838, 929/6/1 PART 3.

141. R. Throssell to Department of Immigration and Attorney General's Department, 28 October 1959, NAA: A1838, 929/6/1 PART 1.

142. E. J. Hook to Secretary, Department of External Affairs, 13 October 1965, NAA: A1838, 929/6/1 PART 3.

143. UN General Assembly, 'Declaration on Territorial Asylum', 14 December 1967, UN Doc. A/RES/2312(XXII).

144. For the following, see Maslyn Williams & Barrie Macdonald, 1985, *The Phosphateers: A History of the British Phosphate Commissioners and the Christmas Island Phosphate Commission*, Carlton, Melbourne University Press, pp. 464–477; Barrie Macdonald, 1988, *In Pursuit of Sacred Trust: Trusteeship and Independence in Nauru*, Wellington, New Zealand Institute of International Affairs, Victoria University, pp. 40–47; Gil Marvel Tabucanon & Brian Opeskin, 2011, 'The Resettlement of Nauruans in Australia', *Journal of Pacific History*, vol. 46, no. 3, pp. 337–356; Jane McAdam, 2012, *Climate Change, Forced Migration, and International Law*, Oxford, Oxford University Press, pp. 149–152.

145. Gil Marvel P. Tabucanon, 2012, 'The Banaban Resettlement: Implications for Pacific Environmental Migration', *Pacific Studies*, vol. 35, no. 3, pp. 343–370.

146. Department of Territories, n.d. (1952), 'The Trust Territory of Nauru', pp. 2–3, appended to J. Brack to Secretary, Department of Immigration, 25 June 1952, NAA: A6980, S250359.

147. 'Minutes of a special meeting of the Nauru Local Government Council with the Acting Administrator and D. McCarthy . . . on Monday, 5th December, 1960', p. 6, NAA: A452, 1961/3157 PART 1.

148. Ibid., p. 7.

149. Ibid., p. 18.

150. Ibid.

151. Ibid., p. 19.

152. 'Minutes of the adjourned special meeting of the Nauru Local Government Council with the Acting Administrator and D. McCarthy . . . on Tuesday, 13th December, 1960', p. 6, NAA: A452, 1961/3157 PART 1.

153. C. E. Barnes, Cabinet submission, 'Nauruan resettlement: purchase of Curtis Island', 7 January 1964, NAA: A452, 1963/6717.

154. 'What Does This *Do* to the White Australia Policy?', *Sunday Mail* (Brisbane), 29 September 1963.

155. Cabinet minute, decision no. 17, 16 January 1964, NAA: A452, 1963/6717; Cabinet minute, decision no. 136, 7 April 1964, NAA: A452, 1963/6717.

156. Bunting, notes of Cabinet meetings 16 January and 7 April 1964, NAA: A11099, 1/64.

157. Menzies to Nicklin, 22 January 1962, NAA: A452, 1961/3157 PART 1.

158. Quoted in Dutton, *One of Us?*, p. 151.

## CHAPTER 4: BORDER CROSSERS, EVACUEES AND POLITICAL REFUGEES

1. Tavan, *The Long, Slow Death of White Australia*, pp. 74–76; Klaus Neumann, 2006, 'Guarding the Flood Gates: The Removal of Non-Europeans, 1945–1949', in Martin Crotty & David Andrew Roberts (eds), *The Great Mistakes of Australian History*, Sydney, UNSW Press, p. 198.

2. Tavan, *The Long, Slow Death*, pp. 89–99.

3. Ibid., pp. 138–145.

4. Quoted in Tom Frame, 2005, *The Life and Death of Harold Holt*, Crows Nest, Allen & Unwin, p. 158.

5. Quoted in Tavan, *The Long, Slow Death*, p. 157.

6. Richards, *Destination Australia*, p. 257.

7. P. R. Heydon, 1965, 'Cooperative Administration in Immigration', *Public Administration*, vol. 24, no. 1, republished by Department of Immigration, www.immi.gov.au/about/anniversary/_pdf/cooperative-administration-in-immigration-heydon.pdf, p. 4.

8. United Nations High Commissioner for Refugees, 2000, *The State of the World's Refugees 2000: Fifty Years of Humanitarian Action*, Oxford, Oxford University Press, p. 53.

9. Denis Warner, 'Vietnam Refugees Look to Australia', *Herald* (Melbourne), 11 November 1964.

10. Heydon, 'Cooperative Administration', p. 4.

11. June Verrier, 1986, 'The Origin of the Border Problem and the Border Story to 1969', in Ron May (ed.), *Between Two Nations: The Indonesia–Papua New Guinea Border and West Papuan Nationalism*, Bathurst, Robert Brown and Associates, p. 41.

12. D. O. Hay to Secretary, Department of External Territories, 28 June 1968, NAA: A452, 1968/2812.

13. Loescher, *The UNHCR and World Politics*, pp. 98–100.

14. P. Brazil, 'Protocol Relating to the Status of Refugees', 28 November 1968, p. 8, NAA: A1838, 3036/10/2/3 PART 1; J. H. Greenwell to Administrator, n.d. (October 1973), p. 4, NAA: A1838, 3036/10/2/3 PART 2.

15. Loveday to Department of External Affairs, 5 June 1969, NAA: A10034, 225/6/18 PART 3.

16. Klaus Neumann, 2006, 'Hush-hushing the Whole Matter: The UNHCR, Australia and West Papuan Refugees', *Refuge*, vol. 23, no. 1, pp. 73–74.

17. Michael Joseph Cigler, 1986, 'The 1948 and 1968 Czech Refugee Settlers in Australia: A Comparison of the Settlement and Integration Processes among Two Waves of Settlers', PhD thesis, Deakin University, pp. 151–152; Michael Cigler, 1983, *The Czechs in Australia*, Melbourne, AE Press, pp. 111–112.

18. Billy Snedden, *CPD*, Representatives, vol. 60, 27 August 1968, p. 545.

19. Billy Snedden, *CPD*, Representatives, vol. 60, 28 August 1968, p. 646.

20. Billy Snedden, *CPD*, Representatives, vol. 60, 10 September 1968, p. 808.

21. Cigler, *The Czechs*, p. 116.

22. Bert James, *CPD*, Representatives, vol. 60, 11 September 1968, p. 932.

23. Bert James, *CPD*, Representatives, vol. 60, 24 September 1968, p. 1414.

24. Bert James, *CPD*, Representatives, vol. 60, 11 September 1968, p. 941.

25. Ian Kirkwood, 'Former Hunter MP Albert James a KGB Spy', *Newcastle Herald*, 11 August 2014.

26. J. S. Holloway, 'External Affairs Record of Inter-departmental Meeting on West Irian Refugees', 15 October 1968, NAA: A1838, 3036/14/1/6 PART 11.

27. Jack McCarthy, 'Refugee "Prisoners" Live Without Hope', *South-Pacific Post*, 21 May 1969.

28. R. S. Bell to Director, Department of District Administration, 30 May 1969, NAA: A452, 1969/2742.

29. D. N. Ashton to F. J. van Bruggen, 31 December 1971, NAA: A452, 1969/2742.

30. Ian Hancock, 2002, *John Gorton: He Did It His Way*, Sydney, Hodder, pp. 185, 213.

31. John Gorton, interviewed by Robert Moore for ABC Television, 25 January 1971, transcript, NAA: A1838, 581/1 PART 15.

32. Roland Cantley, notes, copied by D. J. O'Connor, 17 February 1969, NAA: A452, 1969/1177.

33. Sub-Collector of Customs Thursday Island to Commonwealth Director of Migration, 19 February 1969, NAA: A452, 1969/1177.

34. Quoted in First Assistant Secretary, Department of External Territories, minute, 21 February 1969, NAA: A452, 1969/1177.

35. For example, R. Rose to Secretary, Department of External Affairs, 27 June 1966, NAA: A1838, 932/5/14 PART 1.

36. Intelligence report Weam IR 11/69, 26 February 1969, p. 2, NAA: A452, 1969/21.

37. Charles, quoted in 'Summary Record of Interdepartmental Meeting Held at External Affairs – Friday, 21st February, 1969', NAA: A1838, 3036/14/1/6 part 12.

38. Rowland, quoted in 'Summary Record of Interdepartmental Meeting Held at External Affairs – Friday, 21st February, 1969', NAA: A1838, 3036/14/1/6 part 12.

39. P. J. Galvin, note for file, n.d. [21 February 1969], NAA: A452, 1969/1177.

40. Besley, quoted in 'Summary Record of Interdepartmental Meeting Held at External Affairs – Friday, 21st February, 1969', NAA: A1838, 3036/14/1/6 PART 12.

41. Ibid.

42. 'Eight Men in Raft Ordeal', *Sydney Morning Herald*, 18 February 1969; 'W. Irians Land After Six Weeks on Raft', *Canberra Times*, 18 February 1969; 'A Kon Tiki Voyage for 8 W. Irians', *Courier Mail*, 19 February 1969.

43. T. A. Byrnes to Commonwealth Director of Migration Brisbane, 28 February 1969, NAA: A1838, 3036/10/2/2/6.

44. Ibid.

45. R. Cantley, 'Flight by Frail Raft Across a Treacherous Sea', *Australian Women's Weekly*, 26 February 1969.

46. Gordon Freeth, *CPD*, Representatives, vol. 62, 6 March 1969, p. 462.

47. Quoted in '"Aggressive Tendencies" in Border Crossers', *Canberra Times*, 7 March 1969, and in 'Some Irian Border Crossers Sent Back', *Australian*, 7 March 1969.

48. Gordon Freeth, *CPD*, Representatives, vol. 62, 6 March 1969, p. 462; see Besley, file note, 7 March 1969, NAA: A452, 1969/1177.

49. D. O. Hay to Secretary, Department of External Territories, 17 April 1969, NAA: A452, 1969/1177.

50. Ibid.

51. A. Besley to Minister, 19 May 1969, NAA: A452, 1969/1177.

52. Klaus Neumann, 2002, 'Asylum Seekers and "Non-political Native Refugees" in Papua and New Guinea', *Australian Historical Studies*, vol. 33, no. 120, p. 369.

53. Hay to Secretary, Department of External Territories, 21 May 1969, NAA: A452, 1969/21.

54. R. P. Kekedo to District Commissioner Western District, 7 April 1970, NAA: A452, 1969/1177.

55. Report by Fernando Ortiz Sanz, 6 November 1969, paras 74–75, UN Doc. A/7723.

56. H. D. Anderson to Minister [of Foreign Affairs], 9 September 1971, NAA: A452, 1971/3122.

57. R. Woolcott to Deputy Secretary, 11 May 1967, NAA: A1838, 1500/1/20/47.

58. Intelligence report Vanimo, 3 August 1971, NAA: A1838, 3036/10/2/2/9 PART 1.

59. Anderson to Minister [of Foreign Affairs], 9 September 1971, NAA: A452, 1971/3122; Jack McCarthy, 'This Man Sacrificed Nearly All', *Post-Courier*, 11 August 1971; Ian Hicks, 'Former Diplomat Seeks NG Asylum', *Sydney Morning Herald*, 18 August 1971; Ian Hicks, 'Refugee Tells of Jailing' and 'Pleaders at the Border', *Sydney Morning Herald*, 20 August 1971.

60. M. G. M. Bourchier, file note, 4 August 1971, NAA: A1838, 3036/10/2/2/9 PART 1.

61. Mozes Weror to Minister for External Territories, 10 November 1971, NAA: A1838, 3036/10/2/2/9 PART 1.

62. Unless otherwise stated, the following draws on my 2006 article '"Our Own Interests Must Come First": Australia's Response to the Expulsion of Asians from Uganda', *History Australia*, vol. 3, no. 1, pp. 10.1–10.17.

63. B. A. Hepple, 1968, 'Commonwealth Immigrants Act 1968', *Modern Law Review*, vol. 31, no. 4, pp. 424–428; David Steel, 1969, *No Entry: The Background and Implications of the Commonwealth Immigrants Act, 1968*, London, C. Hurst; Randall Hansen, 1999, 'The Kenyan Asians, British Politics, and the Commonwealth Immigrants Act, 1968', *Historical Journal*, vol. 42, no. 3, pp. 809–834.

64. Jim Forbes, *CPD*, Representatives, vol. 79, 14 August 1972, p. 330.

65. Douglas-Home to British High Commission Canberra, 30 August 1972, TNA: FCO 31/1402.

66. David Aiers to Foreign and Commonwealth Office, 31 August 1972, TNA: FCO 31/1402.

67. J. K. Hickman to C. P. Scott, 24 August 1972, TNA: FCO 31/1382.

68. J. H. Paddick to High Commissioner, Australian High Commission Nairobi, 9 June 1970, NAA: A5758, 2/3-1.

69. J. H. Paddick, file note, n.d. (c. 4 October 1972), NAA: A5758, 201/4/9/IU PART 2.

70. Roger St. Vincent, 1993, *Seven Crested Cranes: Asian Exodus from Uganda: The Role of Canada's Mission to Kampala*, Ottawa, Canadian Immigration Historical Society.

71. J. H. Paddick, file note, 24 August 1973, NAA: A446, 1973/95106.

72. Foreign and Commonwealth Office, n.d. (24 August 1972), 'Ugandan Asians: "The Diplomatic Offensive"', TNA: FCO 31/1381.

73. Arthur Calwell, *CPD*, Representatives, vol. 81, 17 October 1972, p. 2742.

74. "'A Polyglot Nation'" (text of statement issued by Arthur Calwell on 2 May 1972), *Canberra Times*, 3 May 1972; 'Calwell Attacks Clergy: Colour Dispute', *Sydney Morning Herald*, 3 May 1972.

75. F. B. Cooper to Australian High Commissioner Nairobi, 13 September 1972, NAA: A5758, 201/4/9/IU PART 2.

76. Quoted in Gough Whitlam, 1985, *The Whitlam Government 1972–1975*, Ringwood, Penguin, p. 501.

77. Department of Immigration medical review, 2 May 1973, NAA: A446, 1973/95080.

78. 'Prime Minister's press conference 16/4/73', 16 April 1973, TNA: FCO 31/1618.

79. David Mortimer Taylor, quoted in 'Govt. Plans to Ease Restrictions on Entry of Ugandans', *Thames Star*, 11 January 1973; Beaglehole, *Refuge New Zealand*, pp. 67–72.

80. 'Record of Conversation', 30 March 1973, ANZ: ABKF 947 Acc W5182, Box 180 22/1/274 part 4.

81. Department of Immigration, selection assessment, 28 February 1973, NAA: A446, 1973/95080.

82. Robert Linford, interview with Al Grassby, 1984, NLA: ORAL TRC 4900/18.

83. Dutton, *One of Us?*, p. 82.

84. 'Monday conference', interview with William McMahon, 9 October 1972, quoted in Department of External Affairs to Australian High Commission Nairobi, 17 October 1972, NAA: A5758, 201/4/9/IU PART 2.

85. Gough Whitlam, 'Transcript of Prime Minister's Press Conference in London on 25 April 1973', p. 7, Whitlam Institute, University of Western Sydney: 000010382.

86. Eric Paulsen, 2006, 'The Citizenship Status of the Urdu-speakers / Biharis in Bangladesh', *Refugee Survey Quarterly*, vol. 25, no. 3, pp. 54–69.

87. Quoted in Hocking, *Gough Whitlam*, p. 282. As ambassador, Deschamps was highly critical of the Allende government and later apologetic when assessing the impact of the Pinochet regime (Deschamps to Moodie, 4 May 1972, NLA: MS Acc 05/106, box 11; Deschamps to Peacock, 12 August 1977, NLA: MS Acc 05/106, box 13).

88. Toohey and Pinwill, *Oyster*, pp. 140–141.

89. I. L. James to Secretary Foreign Affairs, Santiago memo no. 387, n.d. (c. October 1973), NAA: A1838, 4150/1/3.

90. James to Department of Foreign Affairs, 6 December 1973, NAA: A1838, 4150/1/3.

91. Australian embassy Bonn to Department of Foreign Affairs, 21 December 1973, NAA: A1838, 4150/1/3.

92. Loescher, *The UNHCR and World Politics*, p. 169.

93. United Nations High Commissioner for Refugees, *The State of the World's Refugees*, p. 127.

94. Caracas Convention on Diplomatic Asylum 1954, Article XII, www.oas.org/juridico/english/treaties/a-46.html.

95. Department of Foreign Affairs to Australian embassy Santiago, 9 December 1973, NAA: A1838, 4150/1/3.

96. United Nations Secretary-General, 'Question of Diplomatic Asylum', 2 September 1975, UN Doc. A/10139 (Part I).

97. Maarten den Heijer, 2013, 'Diplomatic Asylum and the Assange Case', *Leiden Journal of International Law*, vol. 26, no. 2, pp. 208–209; Paul Behrens, 2014, 'The Law of Diplomatic Asylum – A Contextual Approach', *Michigan Journal of International Law*, vol. 35, no. 2, p. 323.

98. Department of Foreign Affairs to Australian Permanent Mission United Nations Geneva, 8 February 1974, NAA: A446, 1974/95274.

99. D. R. Willesee to A. J. Grassby, 20 February 1974, NAA: A446, 1970/95133.

100. R. U. Metcalfe to Dempsey, 21 April 1969, NAA: A446, 1970/95133.

101. Department of Foreign Affairs to Australian embassy Santiago, 9 February 1974, NAA: A446, 1970/95133.

102. Australian embassy Santiago to Department of Foreign Affairs, 12 February 1974, NAA: A446, 1970/95133.

103. A. J. Grassby to E. G. Whitlam, 21 March 1974, NAA: A1209, 1975/220.

104. H. Neil Truscott to Secretary, Department of Prime Minister and Cabinet, 7 January 1974, NAA: A1209, 1975/220.

105. W. E. Bowler to Assistant Secretary Programme Control & Development Branch, 30 April 1975, NAA: A446, 1974/77554.

106. In an interview, David Taylor, the Department of Immigration's regional director responsible for South America, claimed that the department's selection officers classified some migrants as refugees to meet the Whitlam government's expectations (David Taylor, interviewed by Ann-Mari Jordens, 17 April 2008, NLA: ORAL TRC 5930/7).

107. P. McElligott to Prime Minister, 8 April 1975, NAA: A1209, 1975/220.

108. Department of Foreign Affairs to Australian embassy Santiago, 15 January 1975, NAA: A1209, 1975/220.

109. Grassby to Willesee, 12 March 1974, NAA: A446, 1974/95274.

110. James McClelland, *CPD*, Senate, 8 October 1975, vol. S.66, p. 968.

111. Whitlam, *The Whitlam Government*, p. 101.

112. Ibid., p. 178.

113. Ibid., p. 177.

114. H. Neil Truscott, administrative circular, 'Definition of "refugee"', 10 September 1974, NAA: A1838, 4150/1/3.

115. Clyde Cameron, *CPD*, Representatives, vol. 92, 5 December 1974, pp. 4797–4798.

116. Charles Price, 1990, 'Australia and Refugees 1921–1976', report for the National Population Council's Refugee Review, The Australian Immigration Research Centre, p. 48.

117. High Commission of the Republic of Cyprus in Canberra, n.d., 'Cypriot Community in Australia', www.mfa.gov.cy/mfa/highcom/highcomcanberra.nsf/community01_en/community01_en?OpenDocument

118. Jim McClelland, 1988, *Stirring the Possum: A Political Autobiography*, Ringwood, Viking, p. 159; Mark Lopez, 2000, *The Origins of Multiculturalism in Australian Politics 1945–1975*, Carlton South, Melbourne University Press, p. 373.

119. Senate Standing Committee on Foreign Affairs and Defence, 1977, 'Australia and the Refugee Problem', Parliamentary Paper No. 329/1976, Canberra, p. 20.

120. Nancy Viviani & Joanna Lawe-Davies, 1980, 'Australian Government Policy on the Entry of Vietnamese Refugees 1976 to 1978', Nathan, Griffith University, Centre for the Study of Australian-Asian Relations, p. 1; Nancy Viviani, 1980, *Australian Government Policy on the Entry of Vietnamese Refugees in 1975*, Nathan, Centre for the Study of Australian-Asian Relations, Griffith University, p. 15.

121. Clyde Cameron, 1980, *China, Communism and Coca-Cola*, Melbourne, Hill of Content, p. 229.

122. Dana Sachs, 2010, *The Life We Were Given: Operation Babylift, International Adoption, and the Children of War in Vietnam*, Boston, Beacon Press; Veronica Strong-Boag & Rupa Bagga, 2009, 'Saving, Kidnapping, or Something of Both? Canada and the Vietnam/

Cambodia Babylift, Spring 1975', *American Review of Canadian Studies*, vol. 39, no. 3, pp. 271–289.

123. For the following, see in particular Joshua Forkert, 2012, 'Refugees, Orphans and a Basket of Cats: The Politics of Operation Babylift', *Journal of Australian Studies*, vol. 36, no. 4, pp. 427–444.

124. T. L. Lewis to Whitlam, 4 April 1975, NAA: A1209, 1975/656.

125. Chronology of events, n.d. (c. 12 May 1975), NAA: A1838, 3014/10/15/4 PART 2.

126. Gough Whitlam, *CPD*, Representatives, vol. 94, 22 April 1975, p. 1948; E. G. Whitlam, marginal note, 14 June 1975, on K. H. Rogers to Acting Minister, 12 June, NAA: A1838, 1634/70/2 PART 3.

127. Malcolm Fraser, *CPD*, Representatives, vol. 94, 23 April 1975, p. 2018.

128. K. H. Rogers to Acting Secretary, 7 May 1975, NAA: A1838, 1634/70/2 PART 1.

129. Cameron, *China, Communism and Coca-Cola*, p. 230.

130. Department of Foreign Affairs to all posts, 6 May 1975, NAA: A1209, 1975/1144; K. H. Rogers to Acting Minister, 12 June 1975, p. 4, NAA: A1838, 1634/70/2 PART 3.

131. E. J. Norwood, Record of phone conversation with P. Heenan, 16 April 1975, NAA: A1838, 1634/70/2 PART 1.

132. Denis Ashton Warner, written submission, n.d. (c. 13 October 1975), in Senate Standing Committee on Foreign Affairs and Defence, 1976, 'South Vietnamese Refugees' (official Hansard report), vol. 1, Canberra, Senate, p. 244.

133. *New Zealand Parliamentary Debates* (hereafter 'NZPD'), vol. 396, 3 April 1974, p. 170; *NZPD*, vol. 396, 11 April 1975, p. 411. By 3 September 1975 New Zealand had admitted a mere ninety-nine Vietnamese (*NZPD*, vol. 401, 3 September 1975, p. 4091).

134. Roberto Rabel, 2005, *New Zealand and the Vietnam War: Politics and Diplomacy*, Auckland, Auckland University Press, chapter 13; Robin Gallienne, 1991, *The Whole Thing Was Orchestrated: New Zealand's Response to the Indo-Chinese Refugees Exodus 1975–1985*, Auckland, Centre for Asian Studies, University of Auckland, chapter 3.

135. Peter Terry, 'Fleeing South Vietnamese Ships May Risk Voyage to Australia: Federal Govt Takes Tough Stand on Uninvited Refugees', *Australian*, 6 May 1975.

136. 'Armada Heads for Australia', *Age*, 5 May 1975.

137. Nancy Viviani, *Australian Government Policy on the Entry of Vietnamese Refugees in 1975*, pp. 14, 21 n. 71.

138. Willesee to Prime Minister, 6 May 1975, NAA: A1209, 1975/1156.

139. 'Vietnamese refugees in Singapore', draft, n.d., attachment to K. H. Rogers to Gilchrist and others, 9 May 1975, NAA: A1838, 1634/70/2 PART 1.

140. D. O'Connor to Minister [of Police and Customs], 13 May 1975, NAA: A1209, 1975/988.

141. D. McElligott & R. Tynan to Prime Minister, 20 May 1975, NAA: A1209, 1975/1333.

142. 'Contingency planning: unauthorised arrival of Vietnamese', n.d. [20 May 1975], NAA: A1209, 1975/1333.

143. Ibid.

144. Quoted in K. H. Rogers to Feakes, 3 July 1975, NAA: A1838, 1634/70/2 PART 3.

145. Michael MacKellar, *CPD*, Representatives, vol. 96, 2 October 1975, p. 1668.

146. Gough Whitlam, 'Political activity by Vietnamese refugees', press statement no. 546, 21 August 1975, NAA: A1209, 1975/1689.

147. Cameron, *China, Communism and Coca-Cola*, p. 231.

148. 'Declaration signed by certain Vietnamese refugees', n.d. (1975), NAA: A1209, 1976/242 PART 1.
149. Michael MacKellar, *CPD*, Representatives, vol. 96, 21 August 1975, p. 379; Ian Sinclair, *CPD*, Representatives, vol. 96, 21 August 1975, p. 380; David Connolly, *CPD*, Representatives, vol. 96, 21 August 1975, pp. 389–391; Michael MacKellar, *CPD*, Representatives, vol. 96, 2 September 1975, pp. 828–831; Kevin Cairns, *CPD*, Representatives, vol. 96, 3 September 1975, pp. 914–915.
150. Gough Whitlam, press statement no. 517, 19 June 1975, Department of the Prime Minister and Cabinet: PM Transcripts, http://pmtranscripts.dpmc.gov.au/transcripts/00003786.pdf.
151. Alan Renouf to Minister, 13 May 1975, NAA: A1838, 3014/2/8 PART 5.
152. Wayne Julian Gibbons, transcript of evidence, 17 October 1975, Senate Standing Committee on Foreign Affairs and Defence, 1976, 'South Vietnamese Refugees', vol. 1, pp. 483–484.
153. E. J. Norwood to Rogers, 14 July 1975, NAA: A1838, 1634/70/2 PART 6.
154. Quoted in Nancy Viviani, 1976, 'Australians and the Timor Issue', *Australian Outlook*, vol. 30, no. 2, p. 199.
155. Marine Ops to Department of Prime Minister and Cabinet, 12 August 1975, NAA: A1209, 1975/1577.
156. J. D. Anderson to Prime Minister, 25 August 1975, NAA: A1209, 1975/1577.
157. J. D. Anderson to Prime Minister, 26 August 1975, NAA: A1209, 1975/1577.
158. File note, 'Evacuees from East Timor', n.d. (September 1976), NAA: A1838, 1634/69/2 PART 2.
159. L. E. W. Holt to Australian embassy Jakarta, n.d. (December 1975), NAA: A1838, 1634/69/2 PART 2.
160. J. A. D. Piper, record of conversation with L. Percival, Charge d'Affaires of the U.S. embassy, 19 August 1975, NAA: A1838, 1634/70/2/ PART 7.
161. K. H. Rogers, record of conversation with L. Percival, 28 August 1975, NAA: A1209, 1975/1502.
162. Alan Renouf to Rogers, 27 August 1975, NAA: A1838, 1634/70/2 PART 7.
163. R. J. Hamer to E. G. Whitlam, 21 August 1975, NAA: A1838, 1634/70/2 PART 7.
164. Whitlam to Hamer, 10 September 1975, NAA: A1838, 1634/70/2 PART 7.
165. G. Cotsell to Rogers, 24 October 1975, NAA: A1838, 1634/70/2 PART 8.
166. Rogers to Minister, 24 December 1975, NAA: A1838, 1634/70/2 PART 8.
167. Quoted in Dempsey to Minister, 2 April 1975, NAA: A446, 1974/77554.
168. John E. Mavor and others to C. R. Cameron, 31 July 1974, NAA: A446, 1974/95371.
169. Metcalfe to Minister, 4 July 1975, NAA: A446, 1974/77554.
170. Cameron, *China, Communism and Coca-Cola*, 230.
171. Nancy Viviani, 1984, *The Long Journey: Vietnamese Migration and Settlement in Australia*, Carlton, Melbourne University Press, p. 62.
172. Gough Whitlam & Gerard Henderson, 2003, 'The Whitlam Government and Indochinese Refugees', *Sydney Institute Quarterly*, vol. 7, no. 1, p. 14.
173. E. J. Norwood to Rogers, 14 July 1975, NAA: A1838, 1634/70/2 PART 6.
174. Quoted in Whitlam, *The Whitlam Government*, p. 498.
175. Price, *Australia and Refugees*, p. 34.
176. K. H. Rogers, 'Vietnamese refugees in Singapore', draft, 9 May 1975, NAA: A1838, 1634/70/2 PART 1.

CHAPTER 5: 'BOAT PEOPLE'

1. Malcolm Fraser & Margaret Simons, 2010, *Malcolm Fraser: The Political Memoirs*, Carlton, Miegunyah Press, p. 426.
2. Department of Immigration and Ethnic Affairs, 1976, 'Review of activities to 30 June 1976', Canberra: Australian Government Publishing Service, p. 35; Department of Immigration and Border Protection, 2014, 'Annual Report 2013–14', Belconnen, Department of Immigration and Border Protection, p. 267.
3. John Carrick, *CPD*, Senate, vol. S63, 23 April 1975, p. 1250.
4. Michael MacKellar, *CPD*, vol. 95, 21 May 1975, p. 2634.
5. Quoted in Fraser & Simons, *Malcolm Fraser*, p. 274.
6. Quoted ibid., p. 275.
7. Fraser to MacKellar, 23 January 1976, NAA: A1838, 1634/70/2 PART 9.
8. For the following, see Sheila Shaver, 2014, 'How a Study Lost its Funding: Jean Martin and Public Knowledge of the Refugee Experience', *Journal of Sociology*, published online 20 January 2014.
9. Fraser & Simons, *Malcolm Fraser*, p. 345.
10. Senate Standing Committee on Foreign Affairs and Defence, 'Australia and the Refugee Problem', pp. 65, 142–154.
11. Ibid., pp. 84, 98.
12. Ibid., pp. 35–36.
13. K. H. Rogers to Minister, 24 December 1975, with annotation by Andrew Peacock, 13 January 1976, NAA: A1838, 1634/70/2 PART 8.
14. Department of Immigration and Ethnic Affairs, 1977, 'Review of Activities to 30 June 1977', Canberra, Australian Government Publishing Service, p. 12.
15. Ibid., pp. 6, 22, 24.
16. Michael MacKellar, *CPD*, Representatives, vol. 102, 9 December 1976, p. 3695.
17. Ibid., pp. 3695–3696.
18. Ibid., p. 3695.
19. '60 Granted Residence', *Northern Territory News*, 27 April 1976.
20. Bruce Grant, 1979, *The Boat People: An 'Age' Investigation*. Harmondsworth, Penguin, pp. 7–8; see also pp. 14–15.
21. 'Vietnamese Refugees Can Stay', *Northern Territory News*, 28 April 1976.
22. Janet Phillips & Harriet Spinks, 'Boat Arrivals in Australia Since 1976', Parliamentary Library Research Paper, last updated 27 July 2013, p. 22; Viviani, *The Long Journey*, pp. 68–69.
23. Department of Immigration and Ethnic Affairs, 'Review of Activities to 30 June 1977', p. 15.
24. Ibid., p. 12.
25. Michael Humphrey, 2004, 'Lebanese Identities: Between Cities, Nations, and Trans-nations', *Arab Studies Quarterly*, vol. 26, no. 1, p. 40.
26. Michael Humphrey, 2001, 'Lebanese Since 1970', in Jupp (ed.), *The Australian People*, p. 561; Neil Truscott to Secretary, Department of Foreign Affairs, 28 January 1972, NAA: A1838, 1634/70/2 PART 9.
27. Metcalfe to all Australian overseas posts, 18 August 1971, NAA: A1838, 1634/131 PART 1.
28. Michael MacKellar, press release, IEA 42/76, 13 August 1976, NAA: A1838, 1634/131 PART 3.
29. Joint Committee on Foreign Affairs and Defence, 1976, 'The Lebanon Crisis: Humanitarian

Aspects', Parliamentary Paper No. 331/1976, p. 64.

30. Cabinet decision no. 1563 of 23 September 1976, NAA: A1838, 1634/131 PART 4.

31. A. D. Campbell to Greet, 12 November 1976, NAA: A1838, 1634/131 PART 4.

32. Campbell to Minister of Foreign Affairs, 19 November 1976, NAA: A1838, 1634/131 PART 4.

33. Michael Humphrey, 'Lebanese Since 1970', pp. 563, 565.

34. Michael MacKellar, *CPD*, Representatives, vol. 101, 13 October 1976, p. 1827.

35. D. Mentz to Minister of Foreign Affairs, 30 March 1977, NAA: A4250, 1977/1033.

36. G. J. Price to Acting Minister, 20 January 1977, NAA: A4250, 1977/1033.

37. Australian Embassy Bangkok to Department of Foreign Affairs, 9 December 1977, NAA: A4250, 1977/1033; G.J. Price to Acting Minister, 20 January 1977, NAA: A4250, 1977/1033.

38. Gavin Williams to D. Mentz, 21 March 1977, NAA: A4250, 1977/1033.

39. J. C. B. Jackson to Assistant Secretary ITEB, 8 September 1977, NAA: A4250, 1977/1033.

40. 'Draft Convention on Territorial Asylum' (1972), Addendum to the [1972] report of the United Nations High Commissioner for Refugees, UN Doc. A/9612/Add.3. For this and the following, see Atle Grahl-Madsen, 1980, *Territorial Asylum*, Stockholm, Almquist & Wiskell International.

41. Office of the United Nations High Commissioner for Refugees, 'Elaboration of a Draft Convention on Territorial Asylum: Report of the Secretary-General', 29 August 1975, UN Doc. A/10177.

42. 'Statement by Australian representative Ambassador O.L. Davis', appended to Jennifer Morison-Turnbull to Australian Permanent Mission to the United Nations, 27 October 1976, NAA: A1838, 938/43 PART 5.

43. 'Conference of Plenipotentiaries on territorial asylum, Geneva, 10 January – 4 February 1977' (brief for the Australian delegation), n.d. (1976), NAA: A1838, 938/43 PART 3.

44. Grahl-Madsen, *Territorial Asylum*, p. 61.

45. 'Report of the Australian delegation to the conference of Plenipotentiaries on Territorial Asylum, Geneva, 10 January – 4 February 1977', n.d. (31 March 1977), NAA: A1838, 838/43 PART 7.

46. G. J. L. Coles to W. H. Bray, 31 May 1977, NAA: A1838, 838/43 PART 8.

47. Senate Standing Committee on Foreign Affairs and Defence, 'Australia and the Refugee Problem', preface.

48. Peter Sim, in Senate Standing Committee on Foreign Affairs and Defence, 'South Vietnamese Refugees' (official Hansard report), vol. 2, p. 881.

49. Senate Standing Committee on Foreign Affairs and Defence, 'Australia and the Refugee Problem', p. 89.

50. Senate Standing Committee on Foreign Affairs and Defence, 1982, 'Indochinese Refugee Resettlement: Australia's Involvement', Parliamentary Paper No. 364/1981; Joint Standing Committee on Migration Regulations, 1992, 'Australia's Refugee and Humanitarian System: Achieving a Balance Between Refuge and Control', Parliamentary Paper No. 204/1992; Senate Legal and Constitutional References Committee, 2000, 'A Sanctuary Under Review: An Examination of Australia's Refugee and Humanitarian Determination Processes', Parliamentary Paper No. 133/2000; Senate Select Committee on a Certain Maritime Incident, 2002, 'Report', Parliamentary Paper No. 498/2002.

51. Joint Committee on Foreign Affairs and Defence, 'The Lebanon Crisis', p. 56.

52. Ibid., p. 66.

53. Australian Population and Immigration Council, 1977, 'Immigration Policies and Australia's Population: A Green Paper', Parliamentary Paper no. 41/1977, Canberra: Australian Government Publishing Service, chapter 6.

54. Michael MacKellar, *CPD*, Representatives, vol. 105, 24 May 1977, p. 1713; see also Cabinet minute, decision no. 2977, 23 May 1977, NAA: A12909, 1160.

55. M. J. R. MacKellar, 'The Liberal and National Country Parties: Immigration and Ethnic Affairs Policy', Canberra: Liberal Party Federal Secretariat (13 August 1975).

56. Michael MacKellar, *CPD*, Representatives, vol. 105, 24 May 1977, p. 1714.

57. Donald Lindsay Whitelum, in Senate Standing Committee on Foreign Affairs and Defence, 'South Vietnamese Refugees' (official Hansard report), vol. 1, p. 232.

58. Robert Thomas Henry, in Senate Standing Committee on Foreign Affairs and Defence, 'South Vietnamese Refugees' (official Hansard report), vol. 1, p. 310.

59. Michael MacKellar, *CPD*, Representatives, vol. 105, 24 May 1977, p. 1715.

60. Senate Standing Committee on Foreign Affairs and Defence, 'Australia and the Refugee Problem', p. 92.

61. Ted Innes, *CPD*, Representatives, vol. 105, 24 May 1977, p. 1717.

62. Ibid., p. 1718.

63. 'New Envoy', *Canberra Times*, 28 August 1972.

64. For this and the following, see Australian embassy Vientiane to Department of Foreign Affairs, 28 January 1977, NAA: A1838, 1634/64/2/1 PART 2; C.M. Sparke, record of conversation with Chansamone Vongsaphay, 19 July 1977, NAA: A1838, 3018/7/3 PART 5.

65. R. F. Osborn to Minister, 6 April 1977, NAA: A1838, 3018/7/3 PART 4.

66. J. A. Forsythe, record of conversation with Souban Srithirat, 29 April 1977, NAA: A1838, 1634/64/2/1 PART 2.

67. T. D. Wilson, summary of discussion between Department of Immigration and Department of Foreign Affairs, 6 July 1977, NAA: A1838, 3018/7/3 PART 5.

68. Andrew Peacock, Minister for Foreign Affairs, news release, 22 April 1980, NAA: A1838, 1606/200 PART 1.

69. Quoted in Viviani, *The Long Journey*, p. 70.

70. Department of Immigration and Ethnic Affairs, 'Review of Activities to 30 June 1977', p. 1.

71. Terry Butts, 'Eight Brave Sea to Achieve Dream', *Northern Territory News*, 26 September 1977.

72. David Trounce, 'Slow Start for Beer Can Boat', *Northern Territory News*, 5 September 1977.

73. Michael MacKellar, quoted in Conference of Ministers for Immigration, verbatim record, 18 October 1977, p. 56, Department of Immigration and Border Protection library.

74. Walter Jona, quoted in Conference of Ministers for Immigration, pp. 52–53.

75. Neil Batt, quoted in Conference of Ministers for Immigration, p. 49.

76. MacKellar, quoted in Conference of Ministers for Immigration, pp. 61–62.

77. Batt, quoted in Conference of Ministers for Immigration, pp. 57, 62.

78. Lyn Riddett, 1995, 'The Gateway and the Gatekeepers: An Examination of Darwin's Relationship with Asia and Asians, 1942–1993', *Journal of Australian Studies*, vol. 19, no. 46, pp. 65–67.

79. 'Viet Boat Slips In!', *Northern Territory News*, 3 November 1977.

80. Michael MacKellar, quoted in 'Refugees Confined to Boat', *Northern Territory News*, 16 November 1977; David Trounce, 'Health Checks for Refugees', *Northern Territory News*, 18 November 1977.

81. Fraser & Simons, *Malcolm Fraser*, p. 590.

82. Michael MacKellar, *CPD*, Representatives, vol. 109, 9 May 1978, pp. 2095–2096.

83. 'Refugees Arrive Undetected', *Sydney Morning Herald*, 22 November 1977.

84. *VNKG 1062* nominal roll, n.d., NAA: E37, NT 1979/10081.

85. Australian National Maritime Museum, n.d., 'Tự Do', http://anmm.gov.au/~/media/Files/Whats%20on/Tu_Do.pdf; Migration Heritage Centre New South Wales, n.d., '1975 *Tu Do* Refugee Boat', www.migrationheritage.nsw.gov.au/exhibition/objectsthroughtime/tudo.

86. 'Committee to Vet Future Refugees', *Australian*, 22 November 1977.

87. 'Refugees Arrive Undetected', *Sydney Morning Herald*, 22 November 1977.

88. Quoted in 'Eighth Vessel on Way', *Northern Territory News*, 23 November 1977.

89. 'Refugee Invasion Organised: Isaacs' and '317th Refugee Sails In!', *Northern Territory News*, 24 November 1977.

90. Ella Stack, quoted from transcript, ABC Radio *AM*, 23 November 1977, NAA: A1838, 3000/2/9/1 PART 4.

91. Grahame Morris & John Lisners, 'Viet Refugee Armada Ready', *Australian*, 25 November 1977.

92. 'Flight from Tyranny' (editorial), *Sydney Morning Herald*, 23 November 1977.

93. Viviani, *The Long Journey*, p. 77.

94. Quoted in O'Donohue to Humphries, 22 November 1977, NAA: A1838, 3000/2/9/1 PART 3.

95. Quoted in Morris & Lisners, 'Viet Refugee Armada Ready'.

96. 'Labor Might Send Boat Refugees Back', *Canberra Times*, 25 November 1977.

97. 'Australian Dockers Shout Abuse at Refugees', *Times* (London), 30 November 1977.

98. Mark Stanton, 'Refugee Voyages Being "Managed"', *Northern Territory News*, 25 November 1977.

99. Jon Isaacs, Northern Territory Legislative Assembly, Question Paper, question #98, 23 November 1977.

100. Paul Everingham, Northern Territory Legislative Assembly, Question Paper, answer to question #112, 24 November 1977.

101. Liberal Party Federal Secretariat, 'Speaker's Notes', Canberra: Liberal Party (November 1977), p. 34.

102. Michael MacKellar, press release, IEA 88/77, 22 November 1977, NAA: A1838, 1634/70/2 PART 17.

103. Philip Hudson, 'New PM Julia Gillard Vows to Address Issue of Asylum Seekers', *Herald Sun*, 3 July 2010; Heather Ewart, 'Gillard Walks Political Tightrope', *7.30 Report*, ABC television, 5 July 2010, www.abc.net.au/7.30/content/2010/s2945349.htm.

104. Quoted in 'Minister Gives Warning on Refugee Boats', *Sydney Morning Herald*, 23 November 1977.

105. 'Peacock Warns', Radio Australia, 24 November 1977, NAA: A1838, 3000/2/9/1 PART 4.

106. 'Fraser Warns Refugees', *Sydney Morning Herald*, 26 November 1977.

107. Rachel Stevens, 2012, 'Political Debates on Asylum Seekers during the Fraser Government, 1977–1982', *Australian Journal of Politics and History*, vol. 58, no. 4, p. 530.

108. 'Limit on Refugees Says P.M.', *Courier-Mail*, 26 November 1977; 'Fraser Warns Refugees', *Sydney Morning Herald*, 26 November 1977.

109. Secretary, Department of Immigration and Ethnic Affairs, to Minister for Immigration, 23 November 1977, NAA: A1838, 3000/2/9/1 PART 4.

110. M. L. Johnston, 'Ambassadorial tour of Northern Thailand: 13 to 17 December 1977', 9 January 1978, NAA: A1838, 3015/7/3 PART 10.

111. Joint statement by Michael MacKellar and Ralph Hunt, 'New refugee task-force for South-East Asia; increased coastal surveillance', IEA 90/77, NAA: A1838, 3000/2/9/1 PART 4.

112. A. D. Campbell to Minister of Foreign Affairs, 25 November 1977, NAA: A1838, 3000/2/9/1 PART 4.

113. 'Refugees Put Off Boat Trip', *Sydney Morning Herald*, 30 November 1977.

114. J. Blount, record of meeting D. Volker, A. Barclay, G. Humphries, A. D. Campbell, B. Hickey, K. Scott, J. Blount, 23 November 1977, NAA: A1838, 3000/2/9/1 PART 3.

115. 'Who Speaks for Pity?' (editorial), *Sydney Morning Herald*, 9 December 1977.

116. 'A Boat for Darwin' (editorial), *Courier-Mail*, 24 November 1977.

117. 'Dangers in the Flood of Viet Refugees' (editorial), *Australian*, 25 November 1977.

118. John Mayman, 'Lib Policies Blamed for Viet Influx', *Australian*, 26–27 November 1977.

119. Quoted ibid.

120. Quoted in 'Hawke: Return Bogus Refugees', *Australian*, 29 November 1977.

121. Katharine Gelber, 2003, 'A Fair Queue? Australian Public Discourse on Refugees and Immigration', *Journal of Australian Studies*, vol. 27, no. 77, pp. 23–30, 181–184; Michael Clyne, 2005, 'The Use of Exclusionary Language to Manipulate Opinion: John Howard, Asylum Seekers and the Reemergence of Political Incorrectness in Australia', *Journal of Language and Politics*, vol. 4, no. 2, pp. 173–196.

122. Mulvihill, quoted in Morris & Lisners, 'Viet Refugee Armada Ready'.

123. David Clune, 2010, 'Mulvihill, James Anthony (1917–2000)', in Ann Millar & Geoffrey Browne (eds), *The Biographical Dictionary of the Australian Senate. Volume 3: 1962–1983*, Sydney, University of New South Wales Press, p. 431.

124. Quoted in 'Pressure on Govt to Take In More Refugees', *Australian*, 5 December 1977.

125. Morris & Lisners, 'Viet Refugee Armada Ready'.

126. John Everingham, 'Facing Up to a Vietnam Refugee "Armada"', *Australian*, 25 November 1977.

127. Jeff Penberthy, 'Refugee Flood a Racket, Mayor Claims', *Sun-Herald*, 27 November 1977.

128. 'Viet "Armada" Denied', *Australian*, 28 November 1977.

129. 'Petition by Churchmen, Academics', *Canberra Times*, 28 November 1977.

130. 'Plea for Refugees', *Courier-Mail*, 29 November 1977.

131. 'Refugee Problem' (editorial), *Mercury* (Hobart), 28 November 1977.

132. 'Aid for Refugees' (editorial), *Sydney Morning Herald*, 28 November 1977.

133. Department of Foreign Affairs to Australian embassy Jakarta, 23 November 1977, NAA: A4359, 61/27 PART 3.

134. 'Navy Patrol will Escort Viet Ship', *Sydney Morning Herald*, 29 November 1977.

135. 'Vietnamese Soldiers Guarded', *Canberra Times*, 30 November 1977; Eric Beecher, 'Police Guard Viet Soldiers', *Age*, 30 November 1977.

136. Frank Cranston, 'Vietnam Rejected on Refugee Demand', *Canberra Times*, 2 December 1977; Don Greig, 'A Slight Case of Piracy?', *Canberra Times*, 8 December 1977.

137. Joint statement by Andrew Peacock and Michael MacKellar, 'Refugees', 29 November 1977, M95 / IEA 94/77, NAA: A1838, 3000/2/9/1 PART 4.

138. Jeff Foale, 'I.C.R.A. press release', Canberra, 29 November 1977, NAA: A1838, 1634/70/2 PART 17.

139. Quoted in Department of Foreign Affairs to Australian High Commission London, 1 December 1977, NAA: A1838, 1634/70/2 PART 18.
140. Joint statement by Andrew Peacock and Michael MacKellar, 'Refugees', 29 November 1977, M95 / IEA 94/77, NAA: A1838, 3000/2/9/1 PART 4; Jim Carey & Toni McCrae, 1982, *Peacock M.P.*, Adelaide, Rigby, pp. 139–144.
141. Michael Richardson, 'The Rising Tide of Refugees', *Sydney Morning Herald*, 29 November 1977.
142. Australian High Commission Singapore to Department of Foreign Affairs, 30 November 1977, NAA: A1838, 3000/2/9/1 PART 4.
143. Frank Cranston, 'Thai Envoy Links Mulvihill's View to Election', *Canberra Times*, 26 November 1977; Wichet Suthayakhom, 'Finding Homes for Refugees' (letter to the editor), *Canberra Times*, 26 November 1977.
144. Australian mission Geneva to Department of Foreign Affairs, 30 November 1977, NAA: A1838, 3000/2/9/1 PART 4.
145. Australian embassy Washington to Department of Foreign Affairs, 16 December 1977, NAA: A1838, 3015/7/3 PART 9.
146. Bernard Levin, 'What Happens to Humanity When There's Dirty Work Down Under', *Times* (London), 30 November 1977.
147. Gordon Freeth, 'Escaping to Australia', *Times* (London), 6 December 1977; Malcolm Mackay, 'Escaping to Australia', *Times* (London), 6 December 1977.
148. 'Liberals Take Election Lead', *Sydney Morning Herald*, 30 November 1977.
149. Penberthy, 'Refugee Flood a Racket, Mayor Claims'.
150. D. Volker, 'Meetings with Northern Territory leaders and officials', 6 December 1977, NAA: A1838, 3000/2/9/1 PART 5.
151. 'Hayden: It's Easy to Sail into Darwin', *Northern Territory News*, 6 December 1977.
152. '"No Right of Entry" – Hawke', *Courier-Mail*, 29 November 1977.
153. Quoted in '"Let Us In" Plea by 90,000 Refugees', *Australian*, 2 December 1977.
154. Quoted in 'Hawke: Return Bogus Refugees', *Australian*, 29 November 1977.
155. 'Landing Bar on Refugees', *Sydney Morning Herald*, 8 December 1977.
156. 'Refugee Boat Hard-line Denied', *Sydney Morning Herald*, 9 December 1977.
157. Australian mission Geneva to Department of Foreign Affairs, 7 December 1977, NAA: A1838, 3000/2/9/1 PART 5.
158. 'Jobless Key Concern', *Sydney Morning Herald*, 1 December 1977.
159. For example, C. J. Lloyd, 1979, 'A Lean Campaign for the Media', in Howard R. Penniman (ed.), *The Australian National Elections of 1977*, Washington, American Enterprise Institute for Policy Research, p. 246.
160. The suggestion that a tough line on asylum seekers is not necessarily a vote winner has been made persuasively by others: Peter Browne, 'Boats and Votes', *Inside Story*, 6 July 2010, http://insidestory.org.au/boats-and-votes; Peter Browne, 'Boats and Votes: More Evidence on the Opinion Gap', *Inside Story*, 16 July 2010, http://insidestory.org.au/boats-and-votes-more-evidence-on-the-opinion-gap; see also Tad Tietze, 'Why We Shouldn't Blame Voters for Our Appalling Asylum Policies', *New Matilda*, 15 July 2014, https://newmatilda.com/2014/07/15/why-we-shouldnt-blame-voters-our-appalling-asylum-policies.
161. Fraser & Simons, *Malcolm Fraser*, p. 421.
162. Moss Cass, 'Stop This Unjust Queue Jumping', *Australian*, 29 June 1978, www.safecom.org.au/pdfs/moss-cass_queue-jumpers.pdf.

163. Department of Immigration and Ethnic Affairs, 1978, 'Review of Activities to 30 June 1978', Canberra, Australian Government Publishing Service, p. 28.

164. Ibid., p. 26.

165. Michael MacKellar, *CPD*, Representatives, vol. 109, 9 May 1978, p. 2023.

166. Department of Immigration and Ethnic Affairs, 'Review of Activities to 30 June 1978', p. 28.

## Conclusion

1. Frank Crowley, 1986, *Tough Times: Australia in the Seventies*, Richmond, W. Heinemann, p. 241.

2. Michael MacKellar, 'Address . . . to the United Nations Association, Brisbane, 11 August 1979', NAA: A1838, 938/43 PART 9. In his address, MacKellar wondered whether Adam and Eve could be considered 'refugees, evacuees, displaced persons or emigrants'.

3. Barcs, *Backyard of Mars*, p. 5.

4. Andy Csorba, 2009, *Recollections of a Refo*, Melbourne, Nondescript Press, p. 23.

5. Cecile Kunrathy, 1963, *Impudent Foreigner*, Sydney, Edwards & Shaw, pp. 87–88.

6. David Martin, 1969, *Where a Man Belongs*, North Melbourne, Cassell Australia, p. 53.

7. United Nations High Commissioner for Refugees, Division of International Protection, Resettlement Service, 2015, 'UNHCR Global Resettlement Statistical Report 2013', Geneva, UNHCR, p. 62, www.unhcr.org/52693bd09.html.

8. 'Australia's contribution to the relief of the problem of refugees' (included in 'Brief for the Australian Delegation to the Working Party of the Executive Committee and the Third Session of the Executive Committee of the High Commissioner's Programme Commencing on the 4th and 6th April, 1960, at the Palais des Nations, Geneva', 29 March 1960), 1 March 1960, NAA: A1838, 932/4/2/ PART 2 ANNEX.

9. Chris Evans, 'Foreword', in Department of Immigration and Citizenship, 2009, *Refugee and Humanitarian Issues: Australia's Response*, Canberra, DIAC, p. 5.

10. Hope Simpson, 'Refugees', p. 188.

11. United Nations High Commissioner for Refugees, '2008 UNHCR Statistical Yearbook', p. 25, www.unhcr.org/4bcc59559.html.

12. York, 'Australia and Refugees, 1901–2002', pp. 24, 32, 88.

# INDEX

www.ingramcontent.com/pod-product-compliance
Lightning Source LLC
Chambersburg PA
CBHW031726280326
41926CB00098B/589